THE CONSTITUTIONS

OF

THE SOCIETY OF JESUS

AND THEIR

COMPLEMENTARY NORMS

THE CONSTITUTIONS

OF

THE SOCIETY OF JESUS

AND THEIR

COMPLEMENTARY NORMS

*A Complete English Translation
of the Official Latin Texts*

THE INSTITUTE OF JESUIT SOURCES
Saint Louis 1996

The Constitutions of the Society of Jesus and Their Complementary Norms:
A Complete English Translation of the Official Latin Texts
John W. Padberg, S.J., General Editor

Number 15 in Series I:
Jesuit Primary Sources in English Translation

An English translation of the original Latin text entitled
  Constitutiones Societatis Iesu et Normæ Complementariæ,
published in Rome in 1995 at the Curia of the Superior General
  of the Society of Jesus

First Edition
© 1996 by The Institute of Jesuit Sources
            3700 West Pine Boulevard
            St. Louis, MO 63108
   Tel: 314 977–7257
   Fax: 314 977–7263
   e-mail: ijs@sluvca.slu.edu

Library of Congress Catalogue Number 96-78469
   ISBN: cloth 1–880810–23–9
            paper 1–880810–24–7

CONTENTS

FOREWORD

This foreword is meant to explain to the reader certain distinctive features of this complete English translation of the Jesuit Constitutions and their complementary norms.

The annotated Constitutions and their norms are the expression of the revised legislation particular to the Society of Jesus as a religious order in the Church. In his preface to this volume, Very Reverend Peter-Hans Kolvenbach, superior general of the Society of Jesus, states the reasons for such a revision of the particular legislation of the Society of Jesus and the way in which it has been accomplished. At the conclusion of the work of revision mandated by the Thirty-fourth General Congregation, its results were published in an official Latin version. That volume, in accord with the decisions of the congregation, comprises two sections. First is presented the "original Ignatian text" of the Constitutions of the Society along with notes appended to it by authority of the congregation. Those notes indicate which parts of the Constitutions general Church law or decisions of general congregations of the Society have abrogated, modified, or clarified over the course of time. The second section of the Latin text contain the norms complementary to the Constitutions. They express both the spirit of the Constitutions and the appropriate way in which those Constitutions are to be lived out in the contemporary renewal of our life and our apostolates. By decision of the congregation, these two parts of our law were in the future to be published in one and the same volume, "so that," as Father Kolvenbach says, "the living internal unity that exists between these two parts of our law might shine forth more clearly."

As a help toward displaying that internal unity, this English translation places on facing pages the texts of the ten parts of the Constitutions and of the ten parts of the complementary norms corresponding to them. The brief table of contents, beginning on page v, will provide a first comprehensive glimpse of how that has been accomplished.

While the ten parts of the Constitutions and Norms take up the same subjects, they do so at different length and, at times within each part, in different order. As a result, once in a while either the Constitutions will occupy more pages than the Norms or vice versa. In order to retain the parallel structure of Constitutions and Norms, in order to obviate the need to leave pages blank now and then, in order to make clear which texts are Constitutions and which are Norms, and in order to keep this volume to a reasonable and handy size, certain conventions have been adopted. They are here described.

1. The Constitutions and Norms are regularly placed on facing pages.

2. The Constitutions and Norms are printed in different typefaces.

3. The text of the Constitutions is always bounded on both right and left sides of its page by thin vertical lines.

4. When the text of either Constitutions or Norms is notably longer than its companion text, the longer text is printed on both facing pages, always, however, in its own distinctive typeface and, for the Constitutions, always bounded by its vertical lines.

5. At the points where the text of either Constitutions or Norms stops in order to allow the more lengthy of the two to be printed on both facing pages, a shaded box clearly indicates where the temporarily interrupted facing pages resume. (See for example, page 163 or page 214.)

For ease of reference, the text of the Constitutions includes the customary sequential paragraph numbers included within brackets ([ ]). The text of the norms has its own such numbers, unbracketed, at the beginning of paragraphs. Within the text of the Constitutions there are two sets of superscript numbers. One such set of superscript numbers always *follows* a sentence or clause and refers to the footnotes at the bottom of that page. The other set of superscript numbers are "verse" numbers, placed at the *beginning* of sentences or at the *beginning* of major clauses within a sentence. Over the last several years these "verse" numbers have commonly been applied to similar sentences and clauses in new editions of the works of Saint Ignatius and to new vernacular translations. This allows the reader to refer to a particular place in any one of the works using reference numbers identical in almost all other editions or translations. Several examples of publications employing these new verse numbers are *Ecrits*, a French collection of works of Saint Ignatius; *The Spiritual Exercises of Saint Ignatius: A Translation and Commentary*, an American collection of such works; and *An Ignatian Concordance (Concordancia Ignatiana)*, published by the Spanish publishers Mensajero/Sal Terrae in cooperation with the Institute of Jesuit Sources. (See page 370 for examples of these two sets of numbers.)

The preparation of this English translation has been an example of generous and wholehearted Jesuit collaboration. In this it imitates the way in which the original documents came into being. The delegates to the Thirty-first and Thirty-second General Congregations renewed the Society's law in accord with Vatican II. Members of the Jesuit Curia in Rome labored long and hard over many years to provide, in several preliminary drafts of annotated Constitutions and Complementary Norms, a formal structure for this renovation. Consultations with experts from around the world were part of this process. Province congregations convened before the Thirty-fourth General Congregation examined such drafts in detail. The members themselves of the Thirty-fourth Congregation in special commissions and in general sessions throughout the time of the congregation carefully considered every portion of the texts and their implications. After the final comprehensive vote on March 18, 1995, that formally put these texts into place in the life of the Society, many members of the Curia once again labored with dedication over a period of many months to prepare the definitive and official Latin text.

So, too, with this English-language volume. The basis for the English text of the Constitutions is the translation by George E. Ganss, S.J., originally published in 1971. This has been corrected, revised, and updated in the last several years, with a view to publication in 1997 or 1998, along with his commentary and cross-references, in the Institute of Jesuit Sources' two volumes of collected writings of Saint Ignatius. A first-draft English translation of the Complementary Norms was prepared by Carl J. Moell, S.J., at that time resident in Rome serving as the assistant procurator general of the Society. George Ganss, John McCarthy, Martin O'Keefe, Martin Palmer, and Nicholas Pope, all members of the Society of Jesus associated with the Institute of Jesuit Sources, then entered into the lengthy and detailed preparation of this edition. They worked at everything from translating the comprehensive Latin index to scrutinizing and revising with editorial acumen each page of the translations of both Constitutions and Norms; from verifying footnotes to handcrafting virtually every page of the camera-ready copy; from proofreading the entire text to preparing for the world-wide distribution of copies of this volume. As director of the Institute of Jesuit Sources, I wish publicly to express to them my gratitude and, I am sure, the gratitude of whoever enjoys in this volume the results of their competence and generosity. It only remains now, as Pedro de Ribadeneira said in the preface of the first printed edition of the Constitutions, that all the members of the Society find in these texts "the bonds that fasten and weld this whole body together to be a dwelling for the heavenly Spirit and the grace of God, which is the real life of any religious order," so that "our name will be matched by our lives and our profession made manifest in deed."

John W. Padberg, S.J.

Director and General Editor
The Institute of Jesuit Sources

The date 1558, at the botton edge of the seal of the Society of Jesus used as an illustration on the cover of this book, marks the year in which the First General Congregation was held. It was this congregation that officially approved the Jesuit Constitutions.

PREFACE

of

VERY REVEREND PETER-HANS KOLVENBACH
Superior General of the Society of Jesus

1. General Congregation 33 (D. 6, II, 2) mandated that when our own law was being brought into conformity with the requirements of the new universal law of the Church regarding religious institutes (namely, the 1983 Code of Canon Law for the Latin Church and the 1993 Code of Canon Law of the Eastern Churches, should see to it that the preparations for the complete revision of our own law, to be put into final form by the next general congregation, should be made with appropriate studious effort. For the Society had for some time regarded such a revision of our law as desirable; and studies for getting it ready had already been undertaken some years prior to this at the urging and under the leadership of Reverend Father Pedro Arrupe, although he himself was not able to see these brought to a conclusion.

2. Such a true and substantial renovation of its own law, required by the decree *Perfectæ Caritatis* of Vatican Council II, and regulated by the *motu proprio Ecclesiæ Sanctæ* of Paul VI, the Society, for its part, had actually completed by means of General Congregations 31 (1965–66) and 32 (1974–75), which thoroughly adapted the Society's life and apostolate to the new needs of the times, while at the same time retaining a genuine fidelity to its proper character and original mission. None the less, the Society had not yet been able to give a formal, normative structure to the many decrees embodying this renovation and accommodation. And thus the pressing need to undertake such a task without delay.

3. After lengthy deliberation on the part of the Superior General with his consultors about the way for the Society to accom-

plish this revision most effectively, the following conclusions emerged:

a. First of all, it seemed good to make every effort to see that the Constitutions of St. Ignatius, an explicitation of the *Formula of the Institute of the Society of Jesus* as approved by the supreme pontiffs Paul III (1540) and Julius III (1550) and a privileged expression of the foundational spiritual and apostolic experience of the first companions, should occupy a central and real place in our law and, through that law, should serve to inspire and govern our entire present-day lives. Thus they had to be purged of elements that were obsolete or had been formally abrogated; and it had to be determined which points in them had in the course of time been modified or authentically interpreted. This was to be done, however, with the help of notes that a general congregation authoritatively appended to the original Ignatian text, without making any changes in the latter. Thus it was hoped that the Constitutions could recover their basic and fundamental inspirational and normative force for the life of the Society, without turning out to be a document that was purely spiritual and doctrinal, tied to ages past, and consequently out of tune with the times.

b. Those things that in the course of time had been decreed by subsequent general congregations and that seemed appropriate to retain in a modern renewal of our life and apostolate as a genuine and real expression of the spirit contained in the Constitutions should, once all unnecessary or obsolete elements had been removed, be reformulated and arranged according to the order of the Constitutions themselves, and should bear a permanent relationship to those Constitutions, as their "Complementary Norms," approved by a general congregation and alterable only by such a congregation.

c. Finally, so that the living internal unity that exists between these two parts of our law might shine forth more clearly and their ongoing spiritual identity might be more obvious, the two were, in future, to be published in one and the same volume.

The hope, surely, was that the Society could have available an instrument that would be at once legal and spiritual in character, authentically Ignatian, one that could help the Society "to proceed ever better in the path of the divine service, according to the nature of our Institute."

4. This manner of proceeding all the provincials discussed at their congregation held in September 1990 at Loyola and approved by general consent, since experts had already prepared a sort of first draft of the project.

5. Consultation was then undertaken with experts from the worldwide Society, nominated by the provincials, in regard to this first draft of the schema. Their discussions generated very many suggestions, which were made available to (and, indeed, provided considerable help to) those who were preparing the new draft. This latter, completed at the beginning of 1993, was sent to the provinces, so that their province congregations could examine it and could send to the general congregation postulata, as well as all manner of related suggestions about the project.

6. Nearly all the provinces scrutinized the schema in one way or other and made known their thinking about it in a very positive fashion. They called for the completion of a revision along the lines of the proposed schema (albeit appropriately revised), so that the general congregation could approve it. Many provinces, however, at the same time, sent along postulata and comments of great import and of great usefulness, which contributed to the fact that a "Final Proposal," written by a special commission and incorporating clear improvements, could be offered for the consideration of the general congregation.

7. The task of revising our own law deeply occupied General Congregation 34. For, on the one hand, it reserved certain points of the "Final Proposal" for its own discussion and decision, those that seemed of greater moment. On the other hand, each commission took on the part of the "Final Proposal" that it was to consider, along with the material related to it. Finally, a special commission was set up and made aware of all the suggestions that had occurred to everyone (commissions and individuals alike); it prepared the text to be voted upon, and over the space of an entire month proposed it to the congregation for a final vote piece by piece. On March 18 the congregation took a final comprehensive vote, with the greatest consensus and the greatest joy in the Spirit. It thus brought to a

happy conclusion work stretching out over several years, in which, in diverse fashion, virtually the entire Society had taken part.

8. Most gladly, then, my dearest brothers, do I now present to you our renewed Constitutions and their Complementary Norms, to be considered in your personal and communal prayer and to be observed in the spirit in which they have been written. Thus, with the help of God, may these, as Master Ignatius proposed, be "a certain path to him" in our enthusiastic following out of our mission in the Church, as "servants of the mission of Christ" under the leadership of the Roman Pontiff, for the greater praise and glory of Christ and for the good, the salvation, and the consolation of our fellow men and women, to whom we are sent in any region of the world whatsoever.

Peter-Hans Kolvenbach, S.J.
Superior General of the Society of Jesus

Rome, September 27, 1995

On the 455th anniversary of the papal approval of the Society of Jesus

PREFACE TO THE FIRST EDITION
OF THE CONSTITUTIONS

To the brethren of the Society of Jesus

Dearly beloved in Christ,

Here[1] at last, beloved brothers in Christ Jesus, is what we have all been so eagerly longing and praying for—our Society's Constitutions promulgated in their final form. Their appearance has been delayed longer than we had wished, but the reasons for this were both compelling and weighty; namely, that they might be drawn up with maturer deliberation and with greater devotion and care and, by being subjected to more prolonged trials, receive a form that would be more solid and enduring.

In the Apostolic See's letters establishing and confirming the Society, authorization had been granted to enact Constitutions on the understanding that once enacted and approved by the Society they would automatically be considered as approved and confirmed by the authority of the Apostolic See.[2] The Society was at that time scattered over the world and occupied with activities of great importance for faith and religion. Hence, it quite rightly entrusted its originator and founder, our Father Ignatius of holy memory, residing in Rome, with the task of writing and enacting the Constitutions.

---

[1] This preface, traditionally attributed to Father Pedro de Ribadeneira, appeared in the first edition of the Constitutions; but it was omitted after that, because, as Francesco Sacchini writes in his *History of the Society of Jesus* (Part 2, book 2, no. 50 [p. 48]), some considered that nothing should be added to the Constitutions except what Ignatius had written himself. But because a variety of introductory or additional material had to be appended in later editions of the Constitutions, there seems to be no objection now to restoring to its original place this outstanding document, approved by the first fathers. The text is taken from the 1863 Florentine edition of the Institute.

[2] Paul III, *Iniunctum Nobis,* March 14, 1544.

Carefully, wisely, and religiously did he undertake and carry out this task that had been laid upon him, to the extent that he made it his chief concern for a number of years. With many tears, ardent prayers, and repeated Sacrifices of the Mass, he implored from the Lord the anointing of the Holy Spirit, so that by the latter's inspiration and guidance he might accomplish through divine assistance what was impossible through human prudence. In this way, with immense toil he drew up the Constitutions with all their parts and brought them to completion.

But our Father was a man of remarkable prudence and modesty. He realized that customs differed throughout the world, and that not all things were right for all places. He knew that, if the Society was to have everywhere a single hue and form,[3] its Constitutions would have to be in the greatest possible agreement with all the practices of the provinces everywhere so as to enjoy permanent acceptance. Moreover, his estimation of himself was not so high that he was willing to rely in a matter of this magnitude exclusively upon his own way of proceeding or his own opinion and judgment.

Accordingly, during the Jubilee Year of 1550, he showed the Constitutions he had written to nearly all the surviving professed Fathers (who had come to Rome), and solicited their criticisms. Taking all these comments into account, along with various other points which had been turned up by day-to-day experience, he finally sent the Constitutions to Spain in 1553 for promulgation there. He also sent them to a limited number of other places, his intention being to test gradually how well the Constitutions meshed with the customs of all the provinces, and thus obtain the confirmation of experience for what had been originally established by reason.

All this would have been more than enough to ensure a reverent reception for the Constitutions. Nevertheless, in order to root them even more deeply in our spirits, a final hand was put to them by the general congregation last year, 1558, when the entire Society gathered in Rome to elect a superior general to succeed our departed Father Ignatius. After solemnization of the election, the Constitutions, which had been submitted for examination to the judgment of the entire general congregation, were received by it with great veneration and confirmed with unanimous enthusiasm.

The text of the Constitutions approved at that time was a copy of the autograph written by our Father Ignatius. Since this was

---

[3] See *Examen* chap. 2, no. 6 [30].

in Spanish, the congregation commissioned the newly elected Father General, along with several others judged competent for the task, to examine the Latin version which had been prepared.[4] They compared it carefully with the Spanish original. While not aiming at a word-for-word translation, their concern for an exact rendering of the ideas was such that they decided, especially in some passages, not to worry too much about idiomatic and elegant Latinity, but rather, following the ancient and approved practice of all the crafts, to try to express in our own special terminology the elements that are special to our order.

In addition, His Lordship Paul IV, by divine providence pope, submitted our Constitutions for examination to two most reverend cardinals, who returned them to us untouched, with not a word changed.[5] Later, His Holiness gave his apostolic blessing not just to the congregation there present but to the entire body of the Society throughout the world, reconfirming and establishing by his apostolic authority all the favors, privileges, and indults granted us by his predecessors.[6]

In view of all this, beloved brothers in Christ, we have no hesitation in presenting and publishing these Constitutions for your observance, backed as they are by such extensive deliberation and consensus. By authority of the most reverend vicar for Rome and of the master of the Sacred Palace, who have been placed in charge of the printing of books by the Supreme Pontiff, we present the Constitutions to you in printed form, thus obviating both the tiresome labor of making numerous copies by hand and the danger of errors creeping into such hand-copied texts. In this way we can

---

[4] See GC 2, dd. 78 and 79.

[5] These were Cardinals Giovanni Bernardinus Scotti, O.Theat., archbishop of Trani, and Joannes Suavius Reomanus (See MHSI, *Nadal* 2:14, 54, 58; Jerónimo Nadal, *Scholia,* 271). According to Sacchini, these were "said to be added": Cardinal Michele Ghislieri, O.P, who afterwards became Pope St. Pius V, and Clement Dolera. (See his *History of the Society of Jesus,* Part 2, book 1, no. 89).

[6] This refers to the approbation given *viva voce* by Paul IV on July 6, 1558, in the presence of the fathers of the First General Congregation; in an account dating back to that time, this approbation was expressed in these words: ". . . confirming moreover and approving by Our apostolic authority whatever graces and privileges, both spiritual and temporal, Our predecessors in the pontificate and We Ourselves granted to you and your Society" (MHSI, *Laínez* 8, 667).

ensure that the Constitutions reach you with greater ease and in a more correct form.

What need is there, brothers, for me to spur on and encourage men like yourselves—already running of your own accord at full speed—to the eager, perfect, and entire observance of these Constitutions? The grace of our vocation itself and our God-given decision to lead a holy life ought to be weighty motives—once we have grasped the character of our profession and embraced it with our whole hearts—for proceeding to bend every effort and exertion towards fulfilling what we have received and corresponding to the heavenly grace of our vocation.

This grace is set forth in the Formula of our Institute contained in the letters of the Apostolic See. There, however, our vocation and Institute are described in a global rather than detailed fashion. That is why it was deemed necessary to frame Constitutions that would give a fuller and more particularized treatment of various matters. These Constitutions contain our Society's sinews, our order's supporting walls, the bonds that fasten and weld this whole body together to be a dwelling for the heavenly Spirit and the grace of God, which is the real life of any religious order.

Here we shall find the pattern we are to imitate, the way we are to pursue, the light we are to follow, the perfection towards which we are to aspire. Here we shall find the mirror in which to inspect our own lives. Beholding in the Constitutions the finished portrait of all virtue and perfection, each of us should do his best to present a living expression of it in his own holy manner of life.

Here each of us should eagerly seek out whatever applies to his own formation and to the fulfillment of the duties of his particular state.

Here superiors ought to seek directives on how they should be an example to others; how they should govern those under them with conscientiousness and concern; how they should test the novices, educate the unlearned, strengthen the weak, and exercise the robust—in sum, how by their word and example they should lead all forward to perfection.

Here subjects should learn how to revere their superiors, loving them as fathers, respecting them as teachers, obeying them eagerly, trusting their advice, heeding their admonitions, and seeing in them Christ himself as the one who commands.

Here teachers should learn what disciplines to impart and what methods to use, and also what exercises to employ in strengthening their students' minds and forming them in virtue no less than in letters.

Here scholastics should learn to know the purpose of their studies, and how they should keep their work from overwhelming or cooling their fervor of spirit by learning how to couple prayer with study, piety with learning, heartfelt movement of the will with reflection in the mind.

What shall I say of our temporal coadjutors? Are they not also portrayed in the Constitutions—men of good conscience, peaceful, cooperative, lovers of perfection and given to devotion, happy with Martha's part?

The spiritual coadjutors, for their part, should be eager for all virtue as well as hardworking, steady, and afire with zeal for the salvation of souls.

The professed, who stand first in order and rank, should also excel by their example and heavenly manner of life. They should be like men marked out for death, ready, at the slightest bidding of the Supreme Pontiff and Vicar of Christ, to whom they have bound themselves by a special vow, to set off joyfully to preach Christ anywhere on earth, whether among pagans, Turks, or Indians, whether among believers or unbelievers. They should hold it a great privilege—as indeed it is—to pour out their blood, along with this momentary life, so that they might rejoice forever in immortality.

Finally, the Constitutions train us all for perfection, instructing us in the weapons to be used in combatting our three fierce and raging adversaries. They teach us how to counter the lust of the flesh with chastity, the lust of the eyes with poverty, and the pride of life with obedience. I shall say nothing of our observance of chastity (in which we should imitate the purity of the angels so far as our frailty allows), or of our observance of poverty (which is so strict that neither churches nor professed houses may acquire any rents, lands, or even perpetual endowments). As for obedience, however, by which we consecrate the chief and noblest part of ourselves to God, our Constitutions require of us that it be so prompt, eager, perfect, and integral that we do not swerve even a hairsbreadth from our superiors' commands. In matters falling under obedience, not only must our action be guided by the superior's command and our will by his will, but even—something much more difficult—our understanding by his understanding.

To sum up: men crucified to the world, and to whom the world itself is crucified[7] —such would our Constitutions have us to be; new men, I say, who have put off their affections to put on Christ;[8] dead to themselves to live to justice; who, with St. Paul in labors, in watchings, in fastings, in chastity, in knowledge, in long-suffering, in sweetness, in the Holy Spirit, in charity unfeigned, in the word of truth, show themselves ministers of God;[9] and by the armor of justice on the right hand and on the left, by honor and dishonor, by evil report and good report, by good success finally and ill success, press forward with great strides to their heavenly country. This is the sum and aim of our institute.

And so I beseech you, brothers in the Lord, that we may walk in a manner worthy of our vocation,[10] and, in order to know that vocation, may read and reread these Constitutions that have been bestowed upon us by the gift of God. Let us study them day and night. Let us vie with each other in learning them, pondering them, and keeping them. If we do so, our name will be matched by our lives and our profession made manifest in deed.

Farewell in Christ.

Rome, the house of the Society of Jesus, 1559

---

[7] See Gal. 6:14.

[8] See Eph. 4:24.

[9] See 2 Cor. 6:5–8.

[10] See Eph. 4:1.

DETAILED TABLE OF CONTENTS

PRINCIPAL ABBREVIATIONS

AAS: *Acta Apostolicæ Sedis*

ActRSJ: *Acta Romana Societatis Iesu*

c.:   Chapter of a part of the Constitutions

GC: General Congregation

CCEO: Code of Canons of the Eastern Churches

CIC: Code of Canon Law

CollDecr: *Collection of Decrees of General Congregations* (ed. 1977)

Const.:   *Constitutions of the Society of Jesus*

d.:   Decree of a general congregation

Examen: *General Examen of the Constitutions*

Form. of Cong.:   Formula of a congregation (general, of procurators, of province, and so forth)

FI: *Formula of the Institute* of Paul III or of Julius III

Inst.:   *Institute of the Society of Jesus* (Florence, 1892)

MI: Monumenta Ignatiana

MHSI: Monumenta Historica Societatis Iesu

CN: *Complementary Norms of the Constitutions of the Society of Jesus*

P.:   Part of the Constitutions

SpEx: *Spiritual Exercises of Saint Ignatius*

Apostolic letters and other pontifical documents are cited by the name of the pope and the first words of the document, with volume and page numbers added, if the document is found in *Inst., AAS,* or in *ActRSJ.*

I

FORMULAS OF THE INSTITUTE OF THE SOCIETY OF JESUS

Approved and Confirmed by

POPES PAUL III AND JULIUS III

I. FORMULAS OF THE INSTITUTE OF THE SOCIETY OF JESUS

Approved and Confirmed by
POPES PAUL III AND JULIUS III

<table>
<tr><td>

PAUL III

Taken from the apostolic letter Regimini militantis Ecclesiæ, *dated September 27, 1540. As expressed there, the* Formula *describing the Institute of Ignatius and his companions reads as follows:*

</td><td>

JULIUS III

Taken from the apostolic letter Exposcit debitum, *July 21, 1550:* ". . . A petition has been humbly submitted to us, begging us to confirm the formula which now contains the aforementioned Society's Institute, expressed more accurately and clearly than before, because of the lessons learned through experience and usage, but in the same spirit. The content of the formula follows, and it is this":*

</td></tr>
<tr><td>

1 ¹Whoever wishes to serve as a soldier of God beneath the banner of the cross in our Society, which we desire to be designated by the name of Jesus, and to serve the Lord alone and his vicar on earth, should keep in mind that once he has made a solemn vow of perpetual chastity he is a member of a community founded chiefly for this purpose: ²to strive especially for the progress of souls in Christian life

</td><td>

1 ¹Whoever desires to serve as a soldier of God beneath the banner of the cross in our Society, which we desire to be designated by the name of Jesus, and to serve the Lord alone and the Church, his spouse, under the Roman pontiff, the vicar of Christ on earth, should, after a solemn vow of perpetual chastity, poverty, and obedience, keep what follows in mind. He is a member of a Society founded chiefly for this

</td></tr>
</table>

and doctrine and for the propagation of the faith by the ministry of the word, by spiritual exercises and works of charity, and specifically by the education of children and unlettered persons in Christianity. [3]He should further take care to keep always before his eyes first God, and the nature of this Institute which is his pathway to God; and let him strive with all his effort to achieve this end set before him by God—[4]each one, however, according to the grace which the Holy Spirit has given to him and according to the particular grade of his own vocation, lest anyone should perhaps show zeal, but a zeal which is not according to knowledge.

purpose: [2]to strive especially for the defense and propagation of the faith and for the progress of souls in Christian life and doctrine, by means of public preaching, lectures, and any other ministration whatsoever of the word of God, and further by means of the Spiritual Exercises, the education of children and unlettered persons in Christianity, and the spiritual consolation of Christ's faithful through hearing confessions and administering the other sacraments. [3]Moreover, he should show himself ready to reconcile the estranged, compassionately assist and serve those who are in prisons or hospitals, and indeed to perform any other works of charity, according to what will seem expedient for the glory of God and the common good. Furthermore, he should carry out all these works *altogether free of charge and without accepting any salary for the labor expended in all the aforementioned activities.*[1] [4]Still further, let any such person take care, as long as he lives, first of all to keep before his eyes God and then the nature of this Institute which is, so to speak, a pathway to God; and then let him strive with all his effort to achieve this end set before him by God—[5]each one, however, according to the grace which the Holy Spirit has given to him and according to the particular grade of his own vocation.

¹ See [565], n. 17.

2 ⁵The selection of each one's grade as well as the entire distribution of employments shall be in the power of the superior or prelate who is to be elected by us, so that the proper order necessary in every well-organized community may be preserved. ⁶This superior, with the advice of his associates shall possess in the council, where the majority of votes always has the right to prevail, the authority to establish constitutions leading to the achievement of this end which we have set for ourselves. ⁷In matters that are more serious and lasting, the council should be understood to be the greater part of the whole Society which can conveniently be summoned by the superior; but in matters less important and more temporary it will be all those who happen to be present in the place where our superior will reside. ⁸All right to execute and command, however, will be in the power of the superior.

2 ⁶Consequently, lest anyone should perhaps show zeal, but a zeal which is not according to knowledge, the decision about each one's grade and the selection and entire distribution of employments will be in the power of the superior general or prelate who at any future time is to be elected by us, or in the power of those whom this superior general may appoint under himself with that authority, in order that the proper order necessary in every well-organized community may be preserved. ⁷This superior general, with the advice of his associates, shall possess the authority to establish constitutions leading to the achievement of this end which has been proposed to us, with the majority of votes always having the right to prevail. He shall also have the authority to explain officially doubts which may arise in connection with our Institute as comprised within this Formula. ⁸The council, which must necessarily be convoked to establish or change the Constitutions and for other matters of more than ordinary importance, **such as the alienation or dissolution of houses and colleges once erected,²** should be understood (according to the explanation in our

Constitutions) to be the greater part of the entire professed Society[3] which can be summoned without grave inconvenience by the superior general. [9]In other matters of lesser importance, the same general, aided by counsel from his brethren to the extent that he will deem fitting, will have the full right personally to order and command whatever he judges in the Lord to pertain to the glory of God and the common good, as will be explained in the Constitutions.

[2] Abrogated by CN 390, §3, with the approval of Pope John Paul II in a letter of June 10, 1995, sent by the Secretariat of State. (This faculty is now within the ordinary powers of the superior general, to be exercised after hearing the advice of his counsel and the major superior of the region in which the house and college are located; see CIC 616, §1).

[3] Abrogated by GC 34, d. 23 A, no. 2, 1°–2° (approved by Pope John Paul II in a letter dated June 10, 1995, and sent by the Secretariat of State).

3   [1]All the members should know not only when they first make their profession but daily, as long as they live, that this entire Society and each one individually are campaigning for God under faithful obedience to His Holiness [the pope] and the other Roman Pontiffs who will succeed him.

3   [1]All who make the profession in this Society should bear in mind, not only when they first make their profession but as long as they live, that this entire Society and the individual members who make their profession in it are campaigning for God under faithful obedience to His Holiness Pope

And although the Gospel teaches us, we know from orthodox faith, and we firmly profess that all the faithful in Christ are subject to the Roman Pontiff as to their head and the vicar of Jesus Christ, still, for the greater humility of our Society and the perfect mortification of each one of us and the abnegation of our own wills, we have judged that it is of the greatest profit to us to go beyond the ordinary obligations and bind ourselves by a special vow, so that whatever the present Roman Pontiff and others to come will wish to command us with regard to the progress of souls and the propagation of the faith, or wherever he may be pleased to send us to any regions whatsoever, we will obey at once, without subterfuge or excuse, as far as in us lies. We pledge to do this whether he sends us among the Turks or to other infidels, even to the land they call India, or to any heretics or schismatics, or to any of the faithful.

Paul III and his successors in the Roman pontificate. ²And although we are taught by the Gospel, and we know from the orthodox faith, and we firmly profess that all of Christ's faithful are subject to the Roman pontiff as their head and as the vicar of Jesus Christ, ³for the sake of greater devotion in obedience to the Apostolic See, of greater abnegation of our own wills, and of surer direction from the Holy Spirit, we have nevertheless judged it to be supremely profitable that each of us and any others who will make the same profession in the future should, in addition to that ordinary bond of the three vows, be bound by this special vow to carry out whatever the present and future Roman pontiffs may order which pertains to the progress of souls and the propagation of the faith; and to go at once, ⁴without subterfuge or excuse, as far as in us lies, to whatsoever provinces they may choose to send us—whether they decide to send us among the Turks or any other infidels, even those who live in the regions called the Indies, or among any heretics whatever, or schismatics, or any of the faithful.

4   ⁴Therefore, those who will come to us should, before they take this burden upon their shoulders, ponder long

4   ⁵Therefore those who will come to us should, before they take this burden upon their shoulders, ponder long

and seriously, as the Lord has counseled, whether they possess among their resources enough spiritual capital to complete this tower; ⁵that is, whether the Holy Spirit who moves them is offering them so much grace that with his aid they have hope of bearing the weight of this vocation. ⁶Then, after they have enlisted through the inspiration of the Lord in this militia of Christ, they ought to be prompt in carrying out this obligation which is so great, being clad for battle day and night.

5   ⁷However, to forestall among us any ambition for such missions or provinces, or any refusal of them, let each one promise never to carry on negotiations with the Roman pontiff about such missions directly or indirectly, but to leave all this care to God and to his vicar and to the superior of the Society. ⁸This superior, too, just like the rest, shall also promise not to approach the pontiff in one way or another about being sent on some mission, except with the advice of the Society.

6   ¹All should likewise vow that in all matters that concern the observance of this Rule they will obey the superior of the Society. ²The superior,

and seriously, as the Lord has counseled [Luke 14:30], whether they possess among their resources enough spiritual capital to complete this tower; ⁶that is, whether the Holy Spirit who moves them is offering them so much grace that with his aid they have hope of bearing the weight of this vocation. ⁷Then, after they have enlisted through the inspiration of the Lord in this militia of Christ, they ought to be prompt in carrying out this obligation which is so great, being clad for battle day and night [Eph. 6:14; 1 Peter 1:13].

5   ⁸However, to forestall among us any ambition of such missions or provinces, or any refusal of them, all our members should have this understanding: They should not either by themselves or through someone else carry on negotiations with the Roman pontiff about such missions, but leave all this care to God, and to the pope himself as his vicar, and to the superior general of the Society. ⁹Indeed, this general too, just like the rest, should not treat with the said pontiff about his being sent or not, unless after advice from the Society.

6   ¹⁰All should likewise vow that in all matters which pertain to the observance of this Rule they will be obedient to the one put in charge of the

however, should issue the commands which he knows to be opportune for achieving the end set before him by God and by the Society. In his superiorship he should be ever mindful of the kindness, meekness, and charity of Christ and of the pattern set by Peter and Paul, ³a norm which both he and the council should keep constantly in view. Particularly let them hold in esteem the instruction of children and the unlettered in the Christian doctrine of the Ten Commandments and other similar elementary principles, whatever will seem suitable to them in accordance with the circumstances of persons, places, and times. ⁴For it is very necessary that the superior and the council watch this ministry with diligent attention, since the edifice of faith cannot arise among our fellowmen without a foundation, and also since in our own members there is danger that as one becomes more learned he may tend to decline this occupation, less prestigious at first glance, ⁵although no other is in fact more fruitful either for the edification of the neighbor or for the exercise by our own members of activities that combine both humility and charity. Assuredly, too, both because of the great value of good order and for the sake of the constant practice of humility (never sufficiently praised), the subjects should always be

Society. (He should be the one best qualified for this office and will be elected by a majority of votes, as will be explained in the Constitutions.) ¹¹Moreover, he should possess all the authority and power over the Society which are useful for its good administration, correction, and government. He should issue the commands which he knows to be opportune for achieving the end set before him by God and the Society. In his superiorship he should be ever mindful of the kindness, meekness, and charity of Christ and of the pattern set by Peter and Paul, a norm which both he and the aforementioned council should keep constantly in view. ¹²Assuredly, too, because of the immense value of good order and for the sake of the constant practice of humility, never sufficiently praised, the individual subjects should not only be obliged to obey the general in all matters pertaining to the Society's Institute but also to recognize and properly venerate Christ as present in him.

obliged to obey the superior in all matters pertaining to the Society's Institute, and to recognize and properly venerate Christ as present in him.

7   ¹From experience we have learned that a life removed as far as possible from all contagion of avarice and as like as possible to evangelical poverty is more gratifying, more undefiled, and more suitable for the edification of our neighbors. We likewise know that our Lord Jesus Christ will supply to his servants who are seeking only the kingdom of God what is necessary for food and clothing. ²Therefore one and all should vow perpetual poverty, declaring that they cannot, either individually or in common, acquire any civil right to any stable goods or to any annually recurring produce or fixed income for the sustenance or use of the Society. Rather, let them be content with only the use of necessary things, when the owners permit it, and to receive money and the sale-price of things given them that they may buy what is necessary for themselves.

7   ¹From experience we have learned that a life removed as far as possible from all infection of avarice and as like as possible to evangelical poverty is more gratifying, more undefiled, and more suitable for the edification of our neighbors. We likewise know that our Lord Jesus Christ will supply to his servants who are seeking only the kingdom of God what is necessary for food and clothing. ²Therefore our members, one and all, should vow perpetual poverty in such a manner that *neither the professed,* either as individuals or *in common, nor any house or church of theirs can acquire any civil right to any annually recurring produce, fixed revenues, or possessions or to the retention of any stable goods*⁴ (except those which are proper for their own use and habitation); but they should instead be content with whatever is given them out of charity for the necessities of life.

⁴ See [555], nn. 9 and 10; [557], nn. 11 and 13; [561], n. 14; [562], n. 15.

8   ³They may, however, set up a college or colleges in universities capable of having

8   ³However, since the houses which the Lord will provide are to be dedicated to la-

fixed revenues, annuities, or possessions which are to be applied to the uses and needs of students. ⁷The general or the Society retains the full government or superintendency over the aforementioned colleges and students; ⁸and this pertains to the choice of the rectors or governors and of the scholastics; the admission, dismissal, reception, and exclusion of the same; the enactment of statutes; the arrangement, instruction, edification, and correction of the scholastics; the manner of supplying them with food, clothing, and all the other necessary materials; and every other kind of government, control, and care. ⁹All this should be managed in such a way that neither may the students be able to abuse the aforementioned goods nor may the professed Society be able to convert them to its own uses, but may use them to provide for the needs of the scholastics. ¹⁰At length, after their progress in spirit and learning has become manifest and after sufficient testing, they can be admitted into our Society. ¹All those who are in holy orders, even though they can acquire no right to benefices and fixed revenues, should nonetheless be obliged to recite the office according to the rite of the Church.

bor in his vineyard and not to the pursuit of scholastic studies; ⁴and since, on the other hand, it appears altogether proper that workers should be provided for that same vineyard from among the young men who are inclined to piety and capable of applying themselves to learning, in order that they may be a kind of seminary for the Society, including the professed Society; ⁵consequently, to provide facilities for studies, the professed Society should be capable of having colleges of scholastics wherever benefactors will be moved by their devotion to build and endow them. We now petition that as soon as these colleges will have been built and endowed (but not from resources which it pertains to the Holy See to apply), they may be established through authorization from the Holy See or considered to be so established. ⁶These colleges should be capable of having fixed revenues, annuities, or possessions which are to be applied to the uses and needs of the students. ⁷The general or the Society retains the full government or superintendency over the aforementioned colleges and students; ⁸and this pertains to the choice of the rectors or governors and of the scholastics; the admission, dismissal, reception, and exclusion of the same; the enactment of statutes; the arrangement, intruction, edification, and correction of the scholastics; the manner of supplying them with food, clothing, and all the other necessary materials; and every other kind of government, control, and care. [9]All this should be managed in such a way that neither may the students be able to abuse the aforementioned goods nor may the professed Society be able to convert them to its own uses, but may use them to provide for the needs of the scholastics. [10]These students, moreover, should have such intellectual ability and moral character as to give solid hope that they will be suitable for the Society's functions after their studies are completed, and that thus at length, after their progress in spirit and learning has become manifest and after sufficient testing, they can be admitted into our Society. [1]Since all the members should be priests, they should be obliged to recite the Divine Office according to the ordinary rite of the Church, but privately and not in common or in choir. [2]Also, in what pertains to food, clothing, and other external things, they will follow the common and approved usage of reputable priests, so that if anything is subtracted in this regard in accordance with each one's need or desire of spiritual progress, it may be offered, as will be fitting, out of devotion and not obligation, as a reasonable service of the body to God.

9   ¹These are the matters which we have been able to explain about our profession in a kind of sketch, which we are now doing that by this written document we may give succinct information, both to those who are asking us about our Rule of Life and also to those who will later on follow us if, God willing, we shall ever have imitators along this path. ²By experience we have learned that the path has many and great difficulties connected with it, so we have considered it appropriate to prescribe that no one should be received into this Society who has not been carefully tested and shown himself prudent in Christ and noteworthy for either his learning or the purity of his Christian life. Only in this case should he be admitted into the militia of Jesus Christ. May Christ deign to be favorable to these our tender beginnings, to the glory of God the Father, to whom alone be glory and honor forever. Amen.

9   ³These are the matters which we were able to explain about our profession in a kind of sketch, through the good pleasure of our previously mentioned sovereign pontiff Paul and of the Apostolic See. We have now done this, that we may give succinct information, both to those who ask us about our plan of life and also to those who will later follow us if, God willing, we shall ever have imitators along this path. ⁴By experience we have learned that the path has many and great difficulties connected with it. Consequently we have judged it opportune to decree that no one should be permitted to pronounce his profession in this Society unless his life and doctrine have been probed by long and exacting tests (as will be explained in the Constitutions). ⁵For in all truth this Institute requires men who are thoroughly humble and prudent in Christ as well as conspicuous in the integrity of Christian life and learning. ⁶Moreover, some persons will be admitted to become coadjutors either for spiritual or temporal concerns or to become scholastics. After sufficient probations and the time specified in the Constitutions, these too should, for their greater devotion and merit, pronounce their vows. But

their vows will not be solemn ([7]except in the case of some who with permission from the superior general will be able to make three solemn vows of this kind because of their devotion and personal worth). [8]Instead, they will be vows by which these persons are bound as long as the superior general thinks that they should be retained in the Society, as will be explained more fully in the Constitutions. But these coadjutors and scholastics too should be admitted into this militia of Jesus Christ only after they have been diligently examined and found suitable for that same end of the Society. [9]And may Christ deign to be favorable to these our tender beginnings, to the glory of God the Father, to whom alone be glory and honor forever. Amen.

Faculty to Establish Constitutions and the Approbations of the Institute in General and of the Constitutions in Particular

1. Paul III, in the apostolic letter *Regimini militantis Ecclesiæ* of September 27, 1540 (first approval of the Institute with the number of persons restricted to sixty):

> . . . granting to them nevertheless freely and licitly to establish Constitutions which they agree among themselves to be in accord with the purpose of this Society and for the glory of our Lord Jesus Christ and the good of the neighbor.

2. Paul III, in the apostolic letter *Iniunctum Nobis* of March 14, (1543) 1544 (faculty of admitting into the Society of Jesus any suitable persons without restriction in number and of establishing Constitutions):

> And We grant by a special favor of the Apostolic Authority the permission to establish whatever particular Constitutions they judge to be in accord with the purpose of this Society and for the glory of our Lord Jesus Christ and the good of the neighbor; to change or modify both those Constitutions already established and those to be established in the future, according to the changed circumstances of time and place; or completely to abandon them and to establish new ones, which after they have been changed and modified or completely established anew are by that fact to be considered confirmed by Apostolic Authority.

3. Paul III, in the apostolic letter *Exponi Nobis* of June 5, 1546 (faculty of admitting coadjutors who can also be promoted to sacred orders, and so forth)

4. Julius III, in the apostolic letter *Exposcit debitum* of July 21, 1550 (another confirmation of the Institute and declaration of indults)

5. Gregory XIII, in the apostolic letter *Quanto fructuosius* of February 1, (1582) 1583 (The Society of Jesus, its Institute, privileges, and Constitutions are confirmed, and those who after the novitiate pronounce three vows, even though simple, are declared to be truly and properly religious.)

6. Gregory XIII, in the apostolic letter *Ascendente Domino* of May 25, 1584 (a new confirmation of the Institute of the Society of Jesus):

> By a similar act and from our certain knowledge, and with the fullness of the apostolic power, by this letter We approve and confirm the praiseworthy Institute of the Society . . . and also the Constitutions, statutes, and decrees of whatever type, considering them as explicitly stated as if they were inserted literally into the present document.

7. Paul V, in the apostolic letter *Quantum religio* of September 4, 1606 (confirmation of the Institute and privileges, and of the approval of the Constitutions granted by Gregory XIII and Gregory XIV, along with a new concession)

8. Clement XIII, in the apostolic letter *Apostolicum pascendi* of January 7, (1764) 1765 (constitution by which the Institute of the Society of Jesus is once again confirmed)

9. Pius VII, in the apostolic letter *Sollicitudo omnium Ecclesiarum* of August 7, 1814 (The Society of Jesus is restored throughout the entire world.)

10. Leo XIII, in the apostolic letter *Dolemus inter alia* of July 13, 1886 (a new confirmation of the Institute and privileges of the Society of Jesus)

11. Pius XI, in the apostolic letter *Paterna caritas* of March 12, 1933 (a new confirmation of the Institute and privileges of the Society of Jesus, even after the new Code of Canon Law)

> From certain knowledge and with a will favorable to the Society of Jesus, We once again in virtue of our Apostolic Authority sanction the confirmation of our predecessor Leo XIII of the privileges and particular law of the same Society, insofar as it is necessary; and We declare that the confirmation remains in full force even after the new Code of Canon Law, with the exception of those privileges that have been expressly revoked by the same Code and have not subsequently been restored in any way by Us.

II

Saint Ignatius of Loyola

THE CONSTITUTIONS
OF THE SOCIETY OF JESUS

PRELIMINARY REMARKS CONCERNING THE NOTES ADDED TO THE CONSTITUTIONS

1. Two kinds of notes are added to the text of the Constitutions: some approved by the general congregation and others prepared by the editors of this edition. The first kind is printed in bold black type and so is clearly distinguished from all else; the other kind is printed in ordinary type. Hence, it is apparent that only texts of the first kind are backed by the authority of the general congregation and have a particular effect on the text of the Constitutions. But notes of the second kind have been added after due consideration only for the sake of clarity and convenience.

2. In the notes possessing the authority of the general congregation, the following terms are used:

Declaratum (clarified or explained) means that a particular place or point of the Constitutions has later been authoritatively interpreted by a general congregation and this interpretation must be regarded as authoritative.

Obrogatum (modified or changed) means that a particular place or point of the Constitutions has been modified by some disposition either of the universal law of the Church or of some general congregation.

Abrogatum (abolished or abrogated) means that a particular place or point of the Constitutions has lost its binding force because of some contrary disposition or determination either of the universal law of the Church or of some general congregation.

3. The text itself of the Constitutions is preserved unchanged. However, as indicated above, those passages that have subsequently been authoritatively clarified, modified, or abrogated are printed in **boldface type;** moreover, passages that have been abrogated are enclosed in braces *({ })* as well.

II-A

THE FIRST AND GENERAL EXAMEN

[1]THE FIRST AND GENERAL EXAMEN WHICH SHOULD BE PROPOSED [A] TO ALL WHO ASK FOR ADMISSION INTO THE SOCIETY OF JESUS

CHAPTER 1

[2]THE INSTITUTE OF THE SOCIETY OF JESUS AND THE DIVERSITY OF ITS MEMBERS

[1]   [3]This least congregation, which at its earliest foundation was named the Society of Jesus by the Holy See, [4]was first approved by Pope Paul III, of happy memory, in the year 1540. Later it was confirmed by the same Holy Father in 1543 and by his successor Julius III in 1550. [5]On other occasions too it is mentioned in different briefs and apostolic letters granting it various favors, after highly approving and confirming it.

[2]   *A. [2]This Examen is usually proposed to all[1] after they enter the house of the first probation. [3]Nevertheless, if in a particular case discre-*

The Examen is a document of an informative character, offering information on the Society to its candidates. Hence, most of what is contained in the Examen is later proposed as norms in the Constitutions, but is recorded here merely as information. But it does contain some points that are truly normative and are not found later in the Constitutions.

Therefore, by decree of General Congregation 34 notes are added to the Examen that for the most part simply refer to the corresponding place in the Constitutions or the Complementary Norms, and as such these "editorial notes" are not approved by the general congregation. But there are other notes, fewer in number, added to normative points, that are not repeated in the Constitutions; these have been expressly approved by General Congregation 34 and as such are added here. As is the case elsewhere in this book, these points are distinguished by **boldface type.** *But what is proposed in the Constitutions as abolished is here enclosed in braces ({}) in the text of the Examen. (ED.)*

[1] (See *CN* 26, 31.)

tion should suggest that another and more summary examen be proposed, or that the present text be handed out to be read without asking for replies about its contents, or if the knowledge possessed about some candidate is already sufficient, it would not be necessary to examine him by means of this present text. ⁴The examiner, however, ought to discuss this with the superior and follow his opinion. ⁵In most instances, it is before the candidates enter the house that they will be examined about certain essential matters, especially those which bar admission.

[3]   2. ¹The end of this Society is to devote itself with God's grace not only to the salvation and perfection of the members' own souls, ²but also with that same grace to labor strenuously in giving aid toward the salvation and perfection of the souls of their neighbors.

[4]   3. ¹To achieve this end more effectively, the three vows of obedience, poverty, and chastity are taken in the Society. ²Poverty is understood to mean that the Society neither wishes **nor is able to possess any fixed revenues for its living expenses**² **or for any other purpose.**³ **This holds true** not only for the individual members but also **for the churches or houses of the professed Society.**⁴ ³Neither may the members accept any stipend or alms for Masses, sermons, lectures, the administration of any of the sacraments, or for any other pious function among those which the Society may exercise in accordance with its institute (even though such acceptance would be permissible for others). ⁴**Such stipends or alms** are customarily given in recompense for the ministries mentioned; ⁵but the Society's members **may not accept them** from anyone other than God our Lord; and it is purely for his service that they ought to do all things.⁵

[5]   4. ¹Furthermore, although the Society owns colleges and houses of probation *[B]* which have fixed revenues for the living expenses of the scholastics before they enter into the professed Society or its houses, ²nevertheless, in conformity with the bull which is explained in the Constitutions, these revenues may not be used for another purpose. Neither the houses of the professed **nor**

---

² (See note 10 to [555].)

³ (See *CN* 199, for apostolic institutes; 204, for the Society; 205, for provinces and regions.)

⁴ (See note 9 to [555].)

⁵ (See note 17 to [565].)

anyone of the professed or their coadjutors may use these reve-nues for themselves.[6]

[6]   B. ¹These houses of probation are like branches of the colleges where those who will later be placed in the colleges are received and tested for a time.

[7]   5. ¹In addition to the three vows mentioned, the professed Society also makes an explicit vow to the present or future sover-eign pontiff as the vicar of Christ our Lord. This is a vow to go anywhere His Holiness will order, whether among the faithful or the infidels, ²without pleading an excuse and without requesting any expenses for the journey, for the sake of matters pertaining to the worship of God and the good of the Christian religion.

[8]   6. ¹In other respects, for sound reasons and with attention always paid to the greater service of God, in regard to what is exterior the manner of living is ordinary. It does not have any regular penances or austerities which are to be practiced through obligation. ²But those may be taken up which each one, with the superior's approval, thinks likely to be more helpful for his spiritual progress, as well as those which the superiors have authority to impose upon the members for the same purpose.

[9]   C. ¹This decision will be left within the superior's power; and he may delegate his authority to the confessor or other persons when he thinks this expedient.

[10]   7. ¹**The persons who are received into this Society of Jesus, considered as a whole, are of four classes** [D],[7] in view of the end which the Society pursues. But on the side of those who enter, all ought to be men of the fourth class which will be described below.

[11]   D. ¹In addition to these four classes of members, *some are ac-cepted for solemn profession of three vows, in conformity with the bull of Julius III.*[8]

[12]   8. ¹First, some are received **to make the profession** in the Society with four solemn vows (as has been stated), **after they have undergone the required experiences and probations.**[9] ²These members should possess sufficient learning, as is explained later on

---

⁶ (See CN 197; 205, 1°.)

⁷ (See *CN* 6.)

⁸ (See note 17 to [520]; *CN* 6, §1, 3°.)

⁹ (No one is now admitted to make profession immediately after he has undergone the probations of the novitiate: see *CN* 6, §2; 119.)

in the Constitutions [518, 519], and they should be tested at length in their life and habits, in conformity with what such a vocation requires. ³Also, all of them must be priests before their profession.

[13]   9. ¹The second class consists of those who are **received to become coadjutors**¹⁰ in the service of God and to aid the Society in either spiritual or temporal matters. ²After their experiments and probations these are to take three simple vows of obedience, poverty, and chastity, without taking the fourth vow of obedience to the pope or any other solemn vow. ³They should be content with their grade, knowing that in the eyes of our Creator and Lord those gain greater merit who with greater charity give help and service to all persons through love of his Divine Majesty, whether they serve in matters of greater moment or in others more lowly and humble.

[14]   10. ¹The third class consists of those **who are received to become scholastics,**¹¹ since they seem to have the ability and other qualifications suitable for studies. They are received so that after being educated they may be able to enter the Society either as professed or as coadjutors, as will be judged expedient. ²To become approved as scholastics of the Society, these too must undergo their experiments and probations and then pronounce the same three simple vows of poverty, chastity, and obedience, ³along **with a promise that they will enter the Society**¹² in one of the two manners just mentioned (as will be seen later in the Constitutions [537–41]), for the greater glory of God.

[15]   11. ¹The fourth class consists of those who are **received indeterminately for whatever they will in time be found fit.**¹³ The Society does not yet determine for which of the aforementioned grades their talent is best suited. ²They in turn should enter as still indifferent with respect to whichever of the previously mentioned grades the superior will think best. In fact all, as far as they themselves are concerned, ought to enter with a disposition of this kind, as has been said.

---

¹⁰ (No one is now admitted to take the vows of formed coadjutors immediately after he has undergone the probations of the novitiate: see CN 6, §2, 119.

¹¹ (Approved brothers are considered in the same way as approved scholastics: see *CN* 6, §1, 2°.)

¹² (See note 28 to [541]; *CN* 131, §2.)

¹³ (See *CN* 6, §1, 1°.)

[16]   12. ¹Furthermore, before anyone is admitted to profession or is required according to our Institute to take the previously mentioned simple vows of a coadjutor or of a scholastic, **he will have two complete years of probation** *[E]*.¹⁴ ²Further still, to be admitted into either of the first two grades, the professed or the formed coadjutors, **the scholastics will have an additional year after the completion of their studies.**¹⁵ This time may be prolonged when the superior thinks it advisable.

[17]   *E. ¹Although they have an appointed period of two years, those who desire to take their vows before the two years expire are not deprived of the freedom, devotion, spiritual profit, and merit which are found in binding oneself to Christ our Lord. However, it is good that they not take these vows without the superior's permission. ²Nor will they through taking them be admitted before the ordinary time either as professed, or as formed coadjutors, or as approved scholastics.*

[18]   13. ¹During this two-year period (in which no special habit of the Society is received *[F]*), and before the time when they ought to bind themselves by vows in the Society, ²each one ought on several occasions to see and ponder the bulls of the Institute of the Society, and the Constitutions and rules which he must observe in it *[G]*. ³The first time is **when he is in the house of the first probation,**¹⁶ where those desiring to enter the Society are customarily received as guests for twelve or fifteen days so that they may reflect more carefully upon their whole situation, before they enter a house or college of the Society to live and associate with the others *[H]*. ⁴The second time is upon completing their six months of experiments and probations. ⁵The third is after another six months, {and similarly afterwards until the one who is to become a professed at the end of his studies makes his profession, and the one who is to become a coadjutor takes his three vows},¹⁷ and the one who is to be an approved scholastic pronounces his three vows with his promise. ⁶This is done so that both sides may proceed with greater clarity and knowledge in our Lord, and also that the more the subjects' constancy has been tested, the more stable and firm

---

¹⁴ (Moreover one who is to take final vows must have spent at least ten complete years in the Society: see *CN* 119.)

¹⁵ (See note 8 to [514].)

¹⁶ (See *CN* 31.)

¹⁷ **Abolished by GC 34, as regards the reading of the bulls;** this obligation now applies only to the time of novitiate and of tertianship.

they may be in the divine service and in their original vocation, for the glory and honor of his Divine Majesty.

[19]   F. ¹Although there is no specified habit, it will be left to the discretion of the one in charge of the house to decide whether he will allow the novices to go about in the same clothes which they brought from the world or have them wear others; ²or again, when the garments become worn, whether he will give to the novices others more suitable for their own needs and for their service of the house.

[20]   G. ¹It will not be necessary for the novices to see all of the Constitutions, but only an extract showing what they need to observe, ²unless for special reasons the superior may think that some person should be shown all of them.

[21]   H. The phrase "to live and associate with the others" is used because at their first entrance the candidates are kept apart from the rest for twelve or fifteen days, or even as long as twenty, in the house of the first probation, as will be seen in Part I of the Constitutions.

CHAPTER 2

¹SOME CASES ABOUT WHICH A CANDIDATE
TO THE SOCIETY SHOULD BE QUESTIONED [A]

[22]   1. ²Among the cases about which all candidates ought for good reasons to be questioned, **the first is this: Has the candidate separated himself from the bosom of the Holy Church by denying the faith, or by falling into errors against it ³in such a way that he has been condemned for some heretical proposition or declared suspect of one by public verdict [B], ⁴or by being excommunicated in infamy as a schismatic after he has spurned the authority and guidance of our holy mother the Church?**[18]

[23]   A. ¹Although the cases which follow **are impediments that exclude one from the Society,**[19] it is not wise to propose them as such before the truth about them has been brought to light; for someone desiring to enter might conceal the truth if he knew that these are impediments, and so forth. ²Nevertheless, it is good to inform the confessor so as to alert his conscience should he not have replied truthfully.

[24]   B. ¹It is evident that one who has been suspected of an erroneous opinion in a matter concerning the Catholic faith should not be admitted while such a suspicion lasts.

---

[18] (See note 8 to [165]; CN 27, 28, 1°.)

[19] (See note 7 to [164]; CN 27, 28.)

[25]   2. ¹The second case is **that of ever having committed homi-cide**²⁰ **or of having been publicly infamous because of enormous sins** *[C].*²¹

[26]   *C.* ¹*This infamy bars admission in the place where it exists.* ²*But when one fell into the infamy in very distant places and has completely brought himself back to the divine service, the infamy will not exclude him from the Society. It should, however, make the Society more cautious during the probation of such a candidate.*

[27]   3. ¹The third case is **that of having taken the habit of a religious institute** of friars or clerics, by living under obedience with them for a time, whether profession was made or not; **or the case of having been a hermit**²² in monastic garb.

[28]   4. ¹{**The fourth case is that of being under the bond of consummated matrimony**²³ **or of legal servitude}.**²⁴

[29]   5. ¹The fifth case is that of **suffering from an illness from which the judgment may become obscured and unsound, or that of having a notable disposition to fall into such an illness.**²⁵

[30]   6. ¹These cases mentioned above are impediments of such a kind that **no person with any one of them may be received into the Society.**²⁶ ²For, in addition to other reasons, it appears to us in our Lord that, because of the ordinary and common weakness of many persons, those who hope to enter the Society in order to be good and faithful sowers in the Lord's field and to preach his divine word will be instruments the more apt for this purpose, the less they are marked by the first and second defects.

³Similarly, candidates with the third defect are not received. For it appears to us in our Lord that every good Christian ought to be stable in his first vocation, above all when it is so holy, one in which he has abandoned all the world and dedicated himself completely to the greater service and glory of his Creator and Lord.

⁴Finally, we are convinced in his Divine Majesty that, in addition to the greater edification of our neighbors, the more all

---

²⁰ (See note 9 to [168]; *CN* 28, 2°.)

²¹ (See note 10 to [168]; *CN* 28, 3°.)

²² (See note 11 to [171]; *CN* 28, 4°.)

²³ (See note 12 to [173].)

²⁴ (See note 13 to [173].)

²⁵ (See note 14 to [175]; *CN* 30.)

²⁶ (See notes 19 to [23] and 7 to [164]; *CN* 27, 28.)

the professed, coadjutors, and scholastics are free from these impediments and the more they are all of one color or likeness, so much the more will they be able to be preserved in the Lord with the help of his divine grace.

⁵Neither is anyone received with the last two impediments. For the fourth would be detrimental to the neighbor, unless the consent of the wife or master is given and the other circumstances required by law are observed. ⁶The fifth, too, would be a notable detriment to the Society itself.

[31]   7. ¹If one of these impediments is discovered in a candidate, he should be interrogated no further and left as consoled in our Lord as is possible *[D]*. ²If no such impediment is discovered, he should be examined further *[E]* in the following manner.

[32]   D. ¹*However, if some outstanding qualities are noticed in him, the examiner should inform the superior before sending him away.*

[33]   E. ¹*The order used in the examination is: first, to go through what is asked of all the candidates;* ²*second, what is asked especially of those who are learned; third, what is asked especially of those who are received to become coadjutors;* ³*fourth, what is asked of those who are received to become scholastics;* ⁴*finally, what is asked of those who are still indifferent. Moreover, what pertains to the persons is taken up first, and then what they must observe.*

CHAPTER 3

¹SOME QUESTIONS TOWARD GAINING A BETTER KNOWLEDGE OF THE CANDIDATE

[34]   1. ²Certain things ought to be asked in order to know the candidates better; and in reply to these questions they ought with sincerity to tell the whole truth *[A]*. ³If some of the matters require secrecy, it will be kept to the extent that reason demands and the one questioned requests. ⁴Thus, beginning with his name, he should be asked what he is called, how old he is, and where he was born.

[35]   A. ¹*The obligation to tell the truth in this examination should bind under sin,* {*a sin reserved to the same person to whom the candidate was obliged to reveal what he concealed, or to another who holds his place*},²⁷ ²*in order to avoid the deception*²⁸ *which could arise from the*

---

²⁷ **Abolished.** (Regarding reservation of sins; in the present law, whether universal or proper to the Society, no sins are reserved.)

²⁸ (See note 8 to [212].)

candidate's failure to open his mind sincerely to his superior. Such deception could also be the source of inconveniences and notable harm for the entire religious institute.

[36]   2. ¹Was the candidate born of a legitimate marriage or not? and if not, what were the circumstances?

²Has he come from a family long Christian or one recently converted?

³Has any of his ancestors been accused or censured for errors against our Christian religion? In what manner?

⁴Are his mother and father still alive? What are their names? ⁵In what circumstances are they? What is their occupation and manner of living? Are they in temporal need *[B]* or are they well enough off? In what manner?

[37]   B. *¹If the parents are in present and extreme need of the candidate's aid, it is evident that such a one should not be admitted. Rarely, however, do such necessities occur.*

[38]   3. ¹If at some time a difficulty or doubt should arise in his mind either **about any debts**²⁹ or as to whether he is obliged to help his parents or relatives in some spiritual or corporal necessity or in another temporal need of whatsoever kind by visiting them or helping in some other manner, ²is he willing to relinquish his personal judgment and opinion and leave the matter to the conscience or judgment of the Society or of his superior to decide upon what he thinks to be just? And is the candidate willing to abide by that decision?

[39]   4. ¹How many brothers and sisters has he, married and single? ²What is their occupation and manner of living?

[40]   5. ¹Has he at any time given a promise of marriage, and in what manner *[C]*? Has he had or does he have any child?

[41]   C. *¹{If he gave the promise by words immediately effective, by consummating the marriage},*³⁰ *or by some equivalent procedure, ²he would be considered to have the fourth impediment. This forbids acceptance into the Society for the one who has it, unless the conditions are present which are required for a married man to become a religious.*

[42]   6. ¹Has he **any debts**³¹ or civil obligations? ²If so, how great are they and of what kind?

---

²⁹ (See note 17 to [185].)

³⁰ (See notes 23 to [28] and 12 to [173].)

³¹ (See notes 29 to [38] and 17 to [185].)

[43]   7. ¹Has he learned any manual trade? **Does he know how to read and write? If he does, he should be tested as to how he writes and reads, if this is not already known.**³²

[44]   8. ¹Has he had or does he have any illnesses, concealed or manifest, and what is their nature? ²Especially, he should be asked whether he has any stomach trouble or headaches or trouble from any other congenital impediment or defect in some part of his body. This should be not only asked but subjected to examination so far as possible.

[45]   9. ¹**Has he received any sacred orders?**³³ Is he under obligation from vows to make a pilgrimage or to do something else?

[46]   10. ¹What has been his manner or inclination, from his early years up to the present, in matters regarding the welfare of his conscience? ²First, in regard to prayer, how often has he been accustomed to pray during the day and the night, at what hour, with what bodily posture, what prayers, and with what devotion or spiritual experience?

        ³How has he conducted himself in regard to attendance at Mass, other divine services and sermons? ⁴In regard to good reading and good conversations? ⁵In regard to the meditation or pondering of spiritual things?

[47]   11. ¹He should be asked whether he has held or holds any opinions or ideas different from those which are commonly held in the Church and among the teachers whom she has approved; ²and whether he is willing, if at some time he should hold any, to defer to what may be determined in the Society as to what ought to be held about such matters.

[48]   12. ¹He should be asked whether in regard to any scruples or spiritual difficulties whatsoever, or in regard to whatsoever other difficulties which he has or in time may have, he will let his case be judged by others in the Society who are learned and virtuous persons *[D]*, and whether he will follow their opinion.

[49]   D. ¹*The choice of these persons to whom the one in such difficulties should entrust himself will belong to the superior, when the subject is content with that choice. Or the subject himself may choose them with the superior's approval. ²If in a given case and for a good reason the superior*

---

³² (As a matter of fact, a higher degree of education is now required even for brothers; for scholastics see also *CN* 86.)

³³ (See CIC 644: "Superiors are not to admit to the novitiate secular clerics if their proper ordinary has not been consulted . . ."; CCEO 452, §1.)

should think that God our Lord will be better served and the one with the difficulties more helped by having one or several of those who are to judge the difficulties come from outside the Society, this can be permitted. ³But the choice of such persons, or at least their approval, should be left to the superior, as has been said.

⁴If the difficulties touch on the superior's own person, the choice or aforementioned approval will belong to the consultors. ⁵However, no one below the general or the provincial, even though he is a rector of a college or a superior of some house, may without permission from one of these place such difficulties concerning his person, or allow them to be placed, within the arbitration of others from outside the Society.

[50]   13. ¹Is he determined to abandon the world and to follow the counsels of Christ our Lord?

²How much time has elapsed since he made this general decision to abandon the world?

³After making this decision, has he wavered in it, and to what extent? ⁴About how much time has elapsed since his desires to leave the world and follow the counsels of Christ our Lord began to come? What were the signs or motives through which they came?

[51]   14. ¹Does he have a deliberate determination in the Lord to live and die with and in this Society of Jesus our Creator and Lord? And since when? ²Where and through whom was he first moved to this?

³If he says that he was not moved by any member of the Society, the examiner should proceed. ⁴If the candidate says that he was so moved (and it is granted that one could licitly and meritoriously move him thus), it would seem to be more conducive to his spiritual progress to give him a period of some time, in order that, by reflecting on the matter, he may commend himself completely to his Creator and Lord as if no member of the Society had moved him, ⁵so that he may be able to proceed with greater spiritual energies for the greater service and glory of the Divine Majesty.

[52]   15. ¹If, after thus reflecting about the matter, he feels and judges that it is highly expedient for him to enter this Society for the greater praise and glory of God our Lord, and the better saving and perfecting of his own soul by helping his neighbors's souls as well, ²and if he requests to be admitted in our Lord into this Society with us, then the examination may be carried forward.

CHAPTER 4

¹SOME OBSERVANCES WITHIN THE SOCIETY WHICH ARE MORE IMPORTANT FOR THE CANDIDATES TO KNOW

[53]　1. ²They should be told that the intention of the first men who joined themselves together in this Society was that those received into it should be persons already detached from the world and determined to serve God totally, whether in one religious institute or another. ³Accordingly, all those who seek admission into the Society **ought, before they begin to live under obedience in any house or college belonging to it, to distribute all the temporal goods they might have and renounce**³⁴ and dispose of those they might expect to receive. ⁴This should be done first of all in regard to matters of debt and obligation if there are any (and in that case provision should be made as soon as possible); if there are none, they should make the distribution in favor of pious and holy causes, according to the words, "He scatters abroad, he gives to the poor" [Ps. 111:9; 2 Cor. 9:9], ⁵and according to those of Christ, "If you wish to be perfect, go, sell what you have, and give to the poor; . . . then come, follow me" [Matt. 19:21]—⁶thus making the distribution according to their own devotion and removing from themselves all hope of ever possessing those goods at any time.

[54]　2. ¹If for some good reasons a candidate does not abandon those goods immediately, **he will promise to give them all up, as was stated, with promptitude after one year from his entrance has elapsed at whatsoever time during the remainder of the period of probation the superior will give him the order.**³⁵ ²When this period has passed, the professed before their profession, and the coadjutors before their three public vows, must relinquish them in fact and distribute them to the poor, as was stated. ³This is done to follow more perfectly the evangelical counsel, which does not say "give to your relatives," but "to the poor"; ⁴and also to give to all a better example of divesting oneself of disordered love of relatives, to avoid the disadvantage of a disordered distribution which proceeds from the aforementioned love, ⁵and, by closing the door on recourse to parents and relatives and profitless remembrance of them, to help them persevere in their vocation with greater firmness and stability.

---

³⁴ (See note 5 to [254]; *CN* 32.)

³⁵ (See preceding note.)

[55]   3. ¹However, if there should be doubt whether it would be more perfect to make the gift or renunciation of these goods in favor of the relatives rather than others, because of their equal or greater need and other just considerations, ²even so, since there is danger that flesh and blood may draw candidates to err in such a judgment, they must be content to leave this matter in the hands of one, two, or three persons of exemplary life and learning (such as each one may choose with the superior's approval [A]), ³and to acquiesce in what these persons decide to be more perfect and conducive to the greater glory of Christ our Lord.

⁴Consequently, the candidate should be asked if he is willing to dispose of his goods immediately (in the manner which has been stated), or if he is content to be ready to make that distribution when the superior will order it after the first year has passed.

[56]   A. ¹*This should be interpreted to mean persons inside the Society, unless the superior for a just reason thinks that some of them should be externs.*

[57]   4. ¹The candidates should be informed that no one after entering the house may keep money in his own possession or in that of a friend outside the house in the same region, ²but rather that they should distribute this money for pious works or give it for keeping to the one in the house who has this charge. This person will note down all that each one brings, in case it may be necessary on some occasion to have this knowledge [B].

³Accordingly, the candidates should be asked whether, if they have any money, they will be content to dispose of it in the manner just stated.

[58]   B. ¹*If it happens that a candidate is dismissed and he has given something to the Society, it ought to be returned to him, in conformity with the declaration in Part II, Chapter 3 [224].*

[59]   5. ¹If the candidates are ecclesiastics, they should likewise be informed that, once they have been incorporated into the Society as professed or as coadjutors, they **may not retain any benefices;**[36] ²also, that during the time of probation, after its first year, as was stated above, they must dispose of them according to their own devotion whenever it shall seem good to the superior, ³resigning them to the one who conferred them, or giving them to pious works to worthy persons for whom they will be instruments in the

---

[36] (See *CN* 32, §4. There are in the Church hardly any benefices properly so called since the enactment of CIC 1272.)

service of God. ⁴If the person should think that he ought to give them to relatives, this should not be done unless one, two, or three persons, as was stated above, judge this to be more expedient and a greater service to God our Lord.

[60]   6. ¹Since communications from friends or relatives, whether oral or written, generally tend to disturb rather than help those who attend to the spiritual life, especially in the beginning, ²the candidates should be asked whether they will be content **not to converse with such persons**³⁷ {**and not to receive or write letters, unless on some occasions** the superior judges otherwise; ³also whether during the whole time they stay in the house they will be willing **to have all their letters seen**},³⁸ both those written to them and those which they send, leaving to the one charged with this matter the care of delivering or not delivering them as he will judge to be more expedient in our Lord.

[61]   7. ¹Everyone who enters the Society, following the counsel of Christ that "everyone who has given up father" and so forth [Matt. 19:29], must make up his mind to leave his father, mother, brothers, sisters, and whatever he had in the world. ²Even more, he should take as made to himself the statement "If anyone comes to me without hating his father, mother, and even his own life, he cannot be my disciple" [Luke 14:26].

³Consequently he should take care to put aside all merely natural affection for his relatives and convert it into spiritual [C], by loving them only with that love which rightly ordered charity requires. He should be as one who is dead to the world and to self-love and who lives only for Christ our Lord, while having him in place of parents, brothers, and all things.

[62]   C. ¹*So that the manner of speaking may assist that of thinking, it is a holy counsel to adopt the practice {of saying **not that they have but that they did have parents or brothers and sisters**},³⁹ and so forth, thus indicating that they do not have what they forsook in order to have Christ in place of all things.* ²*However, this ought to be observed more by those who are in greater danger of some disorder in natural love, as novices might often be.*

---

³⁷ (See note 1 to [244].)

³⁸ (See note 3 to [246].)

³⁹ **Abolished by GC 34.** (According to the letter of the law, because this way of speaking is completely obsolete; but the underlying spirit is very important.)

[63]   8. ¹For the sake of his greater progress in his spiritual life, and especially for his greater lowliness and humility, he should be asked whether he will be willing to have all his errors and defects, and anything else which will be noticed or known about him, manifested to his superiors by anyone who knows them outside of confession; ²and further, whether he along with all the others **will be willing to aid in correcting and being corrected, and to manifest one another with due love and charity, in order to help one another more in the spiritual life, especially when this will be requested of him by the superior who has charge of them for the greater glory of God.**⁴⁰

[64]   9. ¹Furthermore, before he enters the house or college, or after his entrance, **six principal testing experiences**⁴¹ are required, in addition to many others which will be treated in part later. ²When the superior approves, these experiences may be advanced, postponed, adapted, and in some case replaced by others, according to persons, times, and places, with their contingencies.

[65]   10. ¹The first experience consists **in making the Spiritual Exercises for one month,**⁴² a little more or less; that is to say, in the person's examining his conscience, thinking over his whole past life and making a general confession, ²meditating upon his sins, contemplating the events and mysteries of the life, death, resurrection, and ascension of Christ our Lord, ³exercising himself in praying vocally and mentally, according to the capacity of the persons, as he will be instructed in our Lord, and so on.

[66]   11. ¹The second experience is to serve for another month in hospitals or one of them. The candidates take their meals and sleep in it or in them, or serve for one or several hours during the day, according to the times, places, and persons. ²They should help and serve all, the sick and the well, in conformity with the directions they receive, in order to lower and humble themselves more, ³thus giving clear proof of themselves to the effect that they are completely giving up the world with its pomps and vanities, so that in everything they may serve their Creator and Lord, crucified for them.

[67]   12. ¹The third experience is to spend another month in making a pilgrimage without money, but begging from door to door

---

⁴⁰ **Clarified by an authentic interpretation in** *CN* **235.**

⁴¹ **Clarified by** *CN* **46.**

⁴² (See *CN* 46, §2.)

at times, for the love of God our Lord, in order to grow accustomed to discomfort in food and lodging. 2Thus too the candidate, through abandoning all the reliance which he could have in money or other created things, may with genuine faith and intense love place his reliance entirely in his Creator and Lord. 3Or both of these months may be spent in one or more hospitals, or both in making a pilgrimage, as may seem better to the candidate's superior.

[68]   13. 1The fourth experience consists in the candidate's employing himself, after entrance into the house, with all diligence and care in various low and humble offices, while giving a good example of himself in all of them.

[69]   14. 1The fifth experience is that of explaining the Christian doctrine or a part of it in public to boys and other simple persons, or of teaching it to individuals, as opportunity offers and what seems in our Lord more profitable and suitable to the persons.

[70]   15. 1In a sixth experience the candidate, who now has been tested and found edifying, will proceed farther by preaching or hearing confessions, or in both together, in accordance with the times, places, and capacity of each.

[71]   16. 1Before they enter the second year of their probation, **which is made in the houses or colleges,**43 all must spend six months in undergoing the six experiences just mentioned and six additional months in different ones. 2These experiences may be gone through in whole or in part throughout the entire previously stated time of a candidate's probation; the sequence may vary in accordance with what is found expedient in our Lord.

3**In the case of the scholastics, the experiences may be undergone during their studies or after their completion,**44 according to persons, places, and times. 4But this must be observed in its entirety: Before the professed make their profession, and before the formed coadjutors take their three public though not solemn vows, two years of experiences and probations must be completed. 5**In the case of the scholastics,** when their studies have been finished, in addition to the time of probation required to become an approved scholastic, before one of them makes profession or is admitted as a formed coadjutor, **a further third year must be**

---

43 **Modified by CIC 647–48 and CCEO 456, §1.** (In regard to the house where the canonical novitiate must be made and in regard to the time of living in it for the canonical validity of the same; see also *CN* 42.)

44 (See *CN* 46, §1.)

spent[45] [6]in passing through various probations, especially those tests mentioned above [64] if he did not make them previously, and through some of them even if he did make them, for the greater glory of God.

[72]   17. [1]**During the time of these experiences and probations, no one ought to say that he is a member of the Society.**[46] [2]Rather, when occasion arises, one who on the side of the Society has been examined to become a professed (even though on his own side he entered as a candidate still indifferent) ought to say that he is undergoing the probationary experiences while desiring to be admitted into the Society in whatsoever manner it may desire to make use of him for God's glory. [3]If he has been examined to become a coadjutor, he should say that he is going through the testing experiences while desiring to be received into the Society as a coadjutor. [4]The same method of replying is meant for the scholastics and the others who have been examined as candidates still indifferent, in conformity with the particular examen which each of them undergoes.

[73]   18. [1]In regard to these probationary experiences, what follows should be diligently observed. [2]That is to say, when someone has completed the first experience, the Exercises, the one who gave them should inform the superior of what he thinks of the exercitant in regard to the end which the Society seeks.

[74]   19. [1]When he has finished the second experience, that of serving in hospitals, he should bring back the testimony of the directors or of the one who has charge of those who serve in that hospital, about the good example he gave.

[75]   20. [1]When he has completed the third experience, the pilgrimage, he should bring from the farthest place he reached, or somewhere near it, testimony from one or several dependable persons that he arrived there while pursuing his devotion and without a complaint from anyone.

[76]   21. [1]After the fourth experience, that of his doing humble chores in the house, his testimony will be the edification which he gave to all those in that house.

[77]   22. [1]After the fifth experience, his teaching Christian doctrine, and the sixth, that of preaching or hearing confessions, his

---

[45] (See note 15 to [16].)

[46] (But see *Examen* c. 1, no. 7 [10], P. V, c. 1, A [511] and *CN* 6.)

testimony about both, if he lives in the house will be that coming from its members and the edification received by the people where the house is. ²If his preaching and hearing of confessions was in other places outside that town and house, he should bring testimony from those places where he stayed for some time or from public persons (with much account made of all those who are ordinaries) ³who can establish full assurance that he has sown God's word and performed the office of confessor while employing sound doctrine and good practices and without offending anyone.

[78]   23. ¹In addition to these testimonials, the Society can also, as far as it deems expedient, gather other reports for its greater satisfaction, to the glory of God our Lord.

[79]   24. ¹When such testimonials about the experiences are not brought, the reason ought to be investigated with great diligence, ²by effort to learn the truth about the entire matter, so that better provision may be made in regard to everything that is helpful to serve his Divine Goodness better, through the help of his divine grace.

[80]   25. ¹Likewise, after anyone is in the house he should not go out of it without permission. ²**One who is not a priest should confess and receive the most Holy Sacrament every eighth day,** unless the confessor thinks he has an impediment to Communion. ³One who is a priest **will confess at least every eighth day and will celebrate Mass more frequently.**⁴⁷ He will also observe any other ordinances or constitutions of the house, according to what will be indicated to him in its rules.

    ⁴**All the members of the house should apply themselves to learning Christian doctrine.**⁴⁸ Those whom the superior thinks should preach should do so; ⁵but among these there should be no one of those who were admitted to become temporal coadjutors.

[81]   26. ¹If he is pleased to remain in the Society, his food, drink, clothing, shoes, and lodging will be what is characteristic of the poor; ²and he should persuade himself that it will be what is worst in the house, for his greater abnegation and spiritual progress and to arrive at a certain equality and common norm among all. ³For where the Society's first members have passed through these necessities and greater bodily wants, the others who come to it

---

⁴⁷ (See notes 6 to [261], 5 to [342], 7 to [343], 22 to [584].)

⁴⁸ (See *CN* 48, §1.)

should endeavor, as far as they can, to reach the same point as the earlier ones, or to go farther in our Lord.

[82]   27. ¹Likewise, in addition to the other pilgrimages and probations explained above, the professed before making their profession, the coadjutors before taking their vows, ²and (when the superior thinks it wise) the scholastics before becoming approved and pronouncing their vows with the promise mentioned above, ³**should engage in door-to-door begging for the love of God our Lord**¹⁹ for a period of three days at the times assigned to them, thus imitating the Society's earliest members. ⁴The purpose is that, going against the common manner of human thinking, they may be able in God's service and praise to humble themselves more and make greater spiritual progress, giving glory to his Divine Majesty. ⁵Another purpose is to enable them to be more disposed to practice begging when they are so commanded, or find it expedient or necessary ⁶when they are traveling through various parts of the world, according to what the supreme vicar of Christ our Lord may order or assign to them; or, in his place, the one who happens to be superior of the Society. ⁷For our profession requires that we be prepared and very much ready for whatever is enjoined upon us in our Lord and at whatsoever time, ⁸without asking for or expecting any reward in this present and transitory life, but hoping always for that life which lasts for all eternity, through God's supreme mercy.

[83]   28. ¹But to come down to details, during the tests of humility and abnegation of oneself through the performance of lowly and humble tasks, such as working in the kitchen, cleaning the house, and all the rest of these services, ²one should take on more promptly those that offend his sensibiities more, if he has been ordered to do them.

[84]   29. ¹When someone goes to the kitchen to do the cooking or to help him who is doing it, with great humility he must obey the cook in all things pertaining to his office, by showing him always complete obedience. For if he should not do this, neither, it seems, would he show obedience to any other superior, ²since genuine obedience considers, not the person to whom it is offered, but Him for whose sake it is offered; and if it is exercised for the sake of our Creator and Lord alone, then it is the very Lord of everyone who is obeyed. ³In no manner, therefore, ought one to consider whether it is the cook of the house who gives the order or

---

¹⁹ **Modified by** *CN* **128, 5°**. (They are to spend some time in ministries among the poor and marginalized.)

its superior, or one person rather than another. ⁴For, to consider the matter with sound understanding, obedience is not shown either to these persons or for their sake, but to God alone and only for the sake of God our Creator and Lord.

[85]   30. ¹Therefore it is better that the cook should not request his helper to do this or that, but that he should modestly command him by saying, "Do this" or "Do that" *[D]*. ²For if he requests him, he will seem to be speaking rather as man to man; and it does not seem right and proper for a lay cook to request a priest to clean the pots and do other similar tasks. ³But by commanding him or saying, "Do this" or "Do that," he will show more clearly that he is speaking as Christ to man, since he is commanding in His place. ⁴Thus the person who obeys ought to consider and heed the order which comes from the cook, or from another who is his superior, as if it were coming from Christ our Lord, so that he may be entirely pleasing to his Divine Majesty.

[86]   *D. ¹To request and to command, each is good. Nevertheless, at the beginning one is aided more by being commanded than by being requested.*

[87]   31. ¹This same attitude applies to the other lowly duties when someone is helping in them, ²and likewise in the same manner to the subordinate officials *[E]* who, receiving their authority from the superior, govern the house.

[88]   *E. ¹Such, customarily, are the minister, the subminister, or other equivalent officials in colleges.*

[89]   32. ¹In time of illness one ought to observe obedience with great integrity not only toward his spiritual superiors that they may direct his soul, but also and with equal humility toward the physicians and infirmarians that they may care for his body; ²for the former work for his complete spiritual welfare and the latter for that which is corporal. ³Furthermore, the one who is sick should, by showing his great humility and patience, try to give no less edification in time of illness to those who visit him and converse and deal with him than he does in time of full health, for the greater glory of God.

[90]   33. ¹For the surer achievement of everything hitherto stated and for the candidate's own greater spiritual progress, he should be asked whether he is willing to be entirely obedient in everything which has been stated and explained here, ²and to perform and fulfill all the penances which will be imposed on him for his errors and negligences, or for one thing or another.

[91]   34. ¹After pondering the matter in our Lord, we consider it to be of great and even extraordinary importance in his Divine Majesty that the superiors should have a complete understanding of the subjects, ²that by means of this knowledge they may be able to direct and govern them better, and while caring for them guide them better into the paths of the Lord.

[92]   35. ¹Likewise, the more thoroughly they are aware of the interior and exterior affairs of their subjects, with so much greater diligence, love, and care will they be able to help the subjects and to guard their souls from the various difficulties and dangers which might occur later on. ²Later, in conformity with our profession and manner of proceeding, we must always be ready to travel about in various parts of the world, on all occasions when the supreme pontiff or our immediate superior orders us. ³Therefore, to proceed without error in such missions, or in sending some persons and not others, or some for one task and others for different ones, ⁴it is not only highly but even supremely important that the superior have complete knowledge of the inclinations and motions of those who are in his charge, and to what defects or sins they have been or are more moved and inclined; ⁵so that thus he may direct them better, without placing them beyond the measure of their capacity in dangers or labors greater than they could in our Lord endure with a spirit of love; ⁶and also so that the superior, while keeping to himself what he learns in secret, may be better able to organize and arrange what is expedient for the whole body of the Society.

[93]   36. ¹Wherefore, whoever wishes to follow this Society in our Lord or to remain in it for his greater glory must be obliged to the following. Before he enters the first probation or after entering it, before his going through the general examination or some months later (if postponement should seem wise to the superior), ²in {confession}⁵⁰ or in secret or in another manner which may be more pleasing or spiritually consoling to him, **he must manifest his conscience with great humility, transparency, and charity,**⁵¹ without concealing anything which is offensive to the Lord of all men. ³He must give an account of his whole past life, or at least of the more essential matters, to him who is the superior of the Society, or to the one whom he assigns to the candidate from among the superiors or subjects, according to what he thinks best, ⁴so that

---

⁵⁰ (In regard to making the manifestation of conscience in confession: see note 4 to [551].)

⁵¹ (See *CN* 155.)

everything may be provided for better in our Lord, to the greater spiritual help of each one with the more copious grace of God for the greater glory of his divine Goodness.

[94]   37. ¹The candidates, proceeding thus with an increase of grace and spirit and with wholehearted desires to enter this Society and persevere in it for their entire lives, will do the same thing on various other occasions, ²until those who are to be professed make their profession and those who hope to be formed coadjutors take their vows, in the following manner.

[95]   38. ¹After one of the candidates has for the first time given an entire account of his life to the superior of the house, he should begin from that same day and, without repeating the past manifestation which he then made, give a second account of his life for the following six months or a little more or less, to the same superior or to another whom he has appointed. ²Afterwards, beginning with this second and proceeding in the same manner, every half year he will give a similar account. ³The last one will be given thirty days or a little more or less before those who are to be professed make their profession and the coadjutors take their vows.

[96]   39. ¹The scholastics will proceed in the same manner except that in the first account which they will give after completing their studies, they will begin from the last which they gave in the house from which they were sent to their studies. ²Or, if for some reason they have never given the account of their whole life, they will do so.

[97]   40. ¹Thus also it seems that the formed coadjutors and professed, when they find themselves in a place where they are under obedience to a superior of the Society, should give him an account of their conscience every year, or more often if the superior thinks they ought to, in the manner stated and commencing from the last which they gave, and so forth.

[98]   41. ¹A candidate who thinks that God our Lord gives him courage and strength in regard to all that has been said, and who judges his incorporation into this Society to be conducive to the greater divine glory and more salutary for his own conscience, ²ought to see the bulls and Constitutions and all the rest which pertain to the Society's Institute, in the beginning and afterwards every six months, as was stated above [18]. ³In addition to this, he ought to make a general confession of his whole past life to a

priest {whom the superior appoints for him,}⁵² because of the many benefits which this entails.

⁴But if he has made such a general confession to someone of the Society on another occasion, for example, while making the Exercises or even without making them, it will suffice for him to begin the general confession from the other one and proceed to the point where he is; ⁵and afterwards he should receive the most holy body of Christ our Lord. ⁶In this same way, he will continue to make a general confession in the manner stated, every six months beginning from the last, ⁷thus procuring a continuous increase of integrity and virtues and intense desires in our Lord to give great service in this Society to his Divine Majesty.

⁸When he has completed the two years of probation, and shown himself always obedient and edifying in his association with others and in various tests, ⁹and has with great humility performed the penances which will be imposed on him for his errors and negligences or defects; ¹⁰and when he and the Society or the superior of the house are content, he may be incorporated into the Society. ¹¹He should previously consider the bulls and Constitutions and make the general confession, as was stated above, ¹²recollecting himself for a period of one week in order to make the confession better and to confirm himself in his first determination; during this week he should make some Exercises, either his previous ones or others. ¹³Afterwards **he will make** his oblation and vows, **either the solemn vows in the case of the professed or the simple vows in that of the coadjutors and scholastics,**⁵³ in the manner which will be explained later in the Constitutions [524–46], for the greater divine glory and greater profit of his own soul.

[99]   42. ¹They should be advised that after they have taken the aforementioned vows, **according to the content of the bulls they may not transfer to other religious institutes unless the superior of the Society grants permission.**⁵⁴

[100]   43. ¹However, when the time of the probation has elapsed, if the candidate is content and desires **to be admitted thus as a**

---

⁵² **Abolished by CIC 630, §1.** ("Superiors are to recognize the due freedom of their members concerning the sacrament of penance . . ."; and CCEO 473, §2, 3°, and 474, §2.)

⁵³ **Modified by CN 6, §2; 119.** (At the end of the novitiate all take the first vows. For final vows at least ten complete years must have been spent in the Society.)

⁵⁴ (See CIC 684; CCEO 487–88.)

professed or a coadjutor[55] or a scholastic, but if there is doubt on the part of the Society about his talent or conduct, [2]it will be safer to have him wait another year, or whatever time will seem wise later on, until both parties are content and satisfied in our Lord.

[101]   44.   [1]It is likewise very important to bring to the attention of those who are being examined, emphasizing it and giving it great weight in the sight of our Creator and Lord, to how great a degree it helps and profits in the spiritual life to abhor in its totality and not in part whatever the world loves and embraces, and to accept and desire with all possible energy whatever Christ our Lord has loved and embraced. [2]Just as the men of the world who follow the world love and seek with such great diligence honors, fame, and esteem for a great name on earth, as the world teaches them, [3]so those who proceed spiritually and truly follow Christ our Lord love and intensely desire everything opposite. That is to say, they desire to clothe themselves with the same garb and uniform of their Lord because of the love and reverence owed to him, [4]to such an extent that where there would be no offense to his Divine Majesty and no imputation of sin to the neighbor, they desire to suffer injuries, false accusations, and affronts, and to be held and esteemed as fools (but without their giving any occasion for this), [5]because of their desire to resemble and imitate in some manner our Creator and Lord Jesus Christ, by putting on his garb and uniform, since it was for our spiritual profit that he clothed himself as he did. [6]For he gave us an example that in all things possible to us we might seek, with the aid of his grace, to imitate and follow him, since he is the way which leads men to life. [7]Therefore the candidate should be asked whether he finds himself with such desires, which are so salutary and fruitful for the perfection of his soul.

[102]   45.   [1]Where through human weakness and personal misery the candidate does not experience in himself such ardent desires in our Lord, he should be asked whether he has any desires to experience them. [2]If he answers affirmatively that he does wish to have such holy desires, then, so that he may the better reach them in fact, [3]he should be questioned further: Is he determined and ready to accept and suffer with patience, with the help of God's grace, any such injuries, mockeries, and affronts entailed by the wearing of this uniform of Christ our Lord, and any other affronts offered him, [4]whether by someone inside the house or the Society (where he desires to obey, abase himself, and gain eternal life) or outside it by

---

[55] (See note 53 to [98].)

any persons whatsoever on earth, returning them not evil for evil but good for evil?

[103] 46. ¹The better to arrive at this degree of perfection which is so precious in the spiritual life, ²his chief and most earnest endeavor should be to seek in our Lord his greater abnegation and continual mortification in all things possible; ³and our endeavor should be to help him in those things to the extent that our Lord gives us his grace, for his greater praise and glory.

CHAPTER 5

¹ANOTHER EXAMEN, SOMEWHAT MORE PARTICULARIZED, FOR THE EDUCATED, SPIRITUAL COADJUTORS, AND SCHOLASTICS

[104] 1. ²So that better knowledge and understanding of these candidates may be gained, these questions should be put to each one. Where did he study? In which faculty? What authors and what doctrine? How long? In his own opinion, how has he progressed? And especially, what facility has he in the Latin language?

[105] 2. ¹Has he received a degree in the liberal arts, or in theology, or canon law, or another faculty?

[106] 3. ¹Does he think he has a memory to grasp and retain what he studies?

²Does he think that his intellect enables him to penetrate quickly and well what he studies?

³Does he find in himself a natural or voluntary inclination to studies?

[107] 4. ¹Does he think that the study was injurious to his bodily health?

²Does he feel that he has the spiritual and bodily strength to bear the labors required in the Society, whether it be in studies during their time or in the Lord's vineyard when the time comes to work in it?

[108] 5. ¹If he is a priest, has he had experience in hearing confessions, or preaching, or other means of helping his neighbor?

[109] 6. ¹To fulfill the function of sowing and dispensing the divine word and of attending to the spiritual aid of the neighbors, it is expedient to possess a sufficiency of sound learning; ²and for the students too to give a proof of their progress in what they have studied. Therefore **all will be examined through their delivering a**

lecture about each branch of learning which they have studied;[56] [3]and afterwards before leaving the first probation, and later upon entrance into the second if so ordered, each one will deliver an exhortation, as will be seen later.

[110] 7. [1]Likewise, when a candidate is a priest, or when he becomes one, he should be advised **that he should not hear confessions inside or outside the house,**[57] or administer any sacraments, [2]without his undergoing special trial, rendering edification, and being given permission from his superior, during all the time of his probation. [3]Neither ought he to celebrate in public before he has done so privately before one or several members of the house. [4]{He **should also be told to conform his manner of saying Mass to that of the Society's members among whom he is living}**[58] and to the edification of those who are to hear him.

[111] 8. [1]For a greater humility and perfection of the educated, the spiritual coadjutors, and the scholastics, [2]if there should be a doubt as to whether one of those who will enter the Society is suitable to make profession or to become a spiritual coadjutor or a scholastic in it, the following should be done. [3]On the premise that it is much better and more perfect that he let himself be judged and governed by the Society, since the Society will know no less than he what is required to live in it; [4]and also that greater humility and perfection will be imputed to him and he will show a greater love and confidence toward those who are to govern him, [5]he ought to be asked whether he will leave his own opinion and judgment in the hands of the Society or its superior, [6]in order to do that which the superior will tell him, [7]that is, become **either a member of the Society which is thus professed** and bound to the vicar of Christ our Lord, or a coadjutor in it, **or a scholastic carrying on his studies in it.**[59]

[8]He should be interrogated further as follows. If the superior should wish to keep him perpetually only as a coadjutor in the external affairs of the Society (as one occupied with the salvation of his own soul), is he ready to be employed in low and humble offices [9]and to spend all the days of his life for the benefit and aid of the Society, believing that by serving it he is serving his Creator

---

[56] (See note 22 to [198].)

[57] (See *CN* 90.)

[58] **Abolished by GC 34.** (The manner of celebrating Mass in the Society does not differ from that of other priests; see note 23 to [401].)

[59] (See note 53 to [98].)

and Lord and doing all things for the love and reverence due to him?

CHAPTER 6

¹ANOTHER EXAMEN, FOR COADJUTORS ALONE

[112] 1. ²To give a better understanding to each one of these coadjutors, what was touched on earlier should be further explained, namely, that both spiritual coadjutors and temporal coadjutors are received into this Society. ³**The spiritual coadjutors are priests**⁶⁰ and possess a sufficiency of learning to help in spiritual matters. ⁴**The temporal coadjutors do not receive sacred orders**⁶¹ **and, whether they possess learning or not,**⁶² **can help in the necessary exterior matters.**⁶³

[113] 2. ¹It is more characteristic of the spiritual coadjutors to aid the Society by hearing confessions, giving exhortations, and teaching Christian doctrine or other branches of study. The same favors may be given to them as to the professed for the aid of souls.

[114] 3. ¹It is more characteristic of the temporal coadjutors to exercise themselves in all the low and humble services which are enjoined upon them, although they may be employed in more important matters in accordance with the talent God may have given them. ²They should believe that by helping the Society in order that it may the better attend to the salvation of souls, they are serving the same Lord of all, since they are doing this out of love and reverence for him. ³They ought therefore to be prompt in carrying out the tasks given to them thoroughly and with all possible humility and charity. ⁴By this they both obtain their own full share and partake in all the good works which God our Lord deigns to accomplish through the entire Society for his greater service and praise, as also in the indulgences and privileges granted by the Apostolic See to the professed for the good of their souls.

[115] 4. ¹Even so, in their spiritual conversations they should strive to obtain the greater interior progress of their neighbor, ²to show

---

⁶⁰ (Scholastics who are ordained permanent deacons by way of exception may be admitted to the grade of spiritual coadjutor; see *CN* 124.)

⁶¹ (There may be temporal coadjutors who are promoted to the permanent diaconate; see *CN* 124.)

⁶² (See *CN* 81, §3; 83, §3; 98; 243, §2.)

⁶³ (See *CN* 6.)

what they know, and to stimulate those whom they can to do good, inasmuch as our Lord has given care of his neighbor to everyone [Ecclus. 17:12].

[116] 5. ¹If someone has been instructed and examined to become a spiritual coadjutor (devoting himself to the spiritual matters which are appropriate and suitable to his first vocation), ²**he ought not to seek,** directly or indirectly, through himself or someone else, to urge or attempt any **change** from his first vocation to another, namely, from that of a spiritual coadjutor **to that of a** professed or **scholastic**[64] or temporal coadjutor. ³Instead, with all humility and obedience, he should continue traveling along the same path which had been shown to him by the One who knows no change and in whom no change is possible.

[117] 6. ¹In the same manner, if someone has been examined and trained to become a temporal coadjutor (devoting himself in everything to the things which are appropriate and suitable to his first vocation), ²he ought not to seek in one way or another to pass from the grade of temporal coadjutor to that of a spiritual coadjutor or a scholastic or a professed. {**Neither ought he,** even if he does remain in the same grade, **to seek more learning than he had when he entered**}.[65] ³But he ought with much humility to persevere in giving service in everything to his Creator and Lord in his first vocation and to endeavor to grow in the abnegation of himself and in the pursuit of genuine virtues.

[118] 7. ¹Such coadjutors should also be asked whether, as something characteristic of their vocation, they will be content and at peace to serve their Creator and Lord in low and humble offices and ministries, of whatever kind they may be, for the benefit of the house and the Society; and whether they will be ready to spend all the days of their lives in those occupations, ²believing that in this they are serving and praising their Creator and Lord, by doing all things for his divine love and reverence.

[119] 8. ¹All the coadjutors, spiritual as well as temporal, **after passing through two years** of experiences and probations, and one year more **if they have been scholastics**[66] (as was explained before [16, 71]), if they wish to remain in the Society and the Society or its

---

[64] (See *CN* 6, §2: no one is now admitted as a spiritual coadjutor who has not previously been an approved scholastic.)

[65] **Abolished by** *CN* 81, §3; 83, §3; 98; 243, §2.

[66] (See note 8 to [514].)

superior is satisfied, ²**must, in conformity with the bull of Julius III, make their oblation of three vows**⁶⁷ (public though not solemn) of obedience, poverty, and chastity, as was said in the beginning. ³From then on they remain as formed coadjutors, either spiritual or temporal, ⁴in such a way that on their side they are perpetually obliged to live and die in our Lord in and with this Society, for the greater glory of the Divine Majesty and for their own greater merit and stability [A]. ⁵Nevertheless the Society or its superior (who ought to care for the common good) may, when it is evident that no help is obtained from them for the greater service of God, but rather the opposite, **dismiss them and remove them from its community,**⁶⁸ ⁶the persons remaining from that time free in every respect and without the obligation of any vow.

[120] *A.* ¹*Their being bound on their own side is good, since their stability is what is being sought;* ²*and (as appears in the apostolic bull) it is not unjust for the Society to be free to dismiss them when their remaining in it is not expedient.* ³*For in that case they remain free;* ⁴*and an individual can more readily fail to do what he ought than the Society or its general, who alone will be able to dismiss;* ⁵*and he ought not to do it without quite abundant grounds, as will be seen in Part II of the Constitutions.*

CHAPTER 7

¹ANOTHER EXAMEN FOR SCHOLASTICS: FIRST, BEFORE THEIR ADMISSION TO STUDIES [A]

[121] 1. ²When the scholastics have passed through the aforementioned experiences and probations, if they judge it good to study in the colleges or houses of the Society, so as to be maintained in them in the Lord of all men, and if the Society or its superior is likewise satisfied with them, ³for their greater merit and stability they must, either before they go to their studies or when they are in them, pronounce the simple vows of poverty, chastity, and obedience, ⁴along with the promise to God our Lord that upon completing their studies they will enter the Society, understanding by entrance making profession or becoming formed coadjutors in it should it be willing to admit them. ⁵From that time on they will be considered approved scholastics of the Society. ⁶The said Society remains free and does not oblige itself to admit them either to

---

⁶⁷ (See note 53 to [98].)

⁶⁸ (See note 6 to [208].)

profession or as formed coadjutors if they have made a poor show-ing during their studies and if its superior should judge that their admission would not be a service to God our Lord. 7In such a case they are freed from their vows.

[122] A. 1This examen, as well as the one above, is given not only to those who are sent to their studies for the first time, but also to those who are continuing them, when they come to the house to transfer elsewhere.69

[123] 2. 1If at some time during the studies those who have shown greater inclination toward studies than for any other ministry in the Society give a proof or clear indication in regard to themselves, 2whereby the Society or its superior judges that, **through lack of ability, experience of ill health, or other deficiencies,**70 they are not suited to succeed in studies, 3they should be asked whether they will accept with patience being dismissed, with freedom from all past promises.

[124] 3. 1One who is found sufficiently capable for the studies should be asked whether he will allow himself to be directed in regard to what he should study, and how, and how long, according to what will seem best to the Society, or its superior, or to the superior of the college where he will study.

[125] 4. 1Will he be content to live in the same manner as the others, without seeking any more superiority or advantage than the least of those living in the college, and leaving the concern for his well-being entirely to its superior?

[126] 5. 1Is he determined, when his studies and probations are completed, to enter the Society in order to live and die in it for the greater glory of God?

[127] 6. 1When he has been thus examined and instructed, he may begin to get himself ready to go to his studies or to continue them. Likewise, he should prepare himself to undergo various other experiences and probations during the studies. 2{If for some legiti-mate reasons and in view of some good purposes **he has not gone through these experiences** before he went to his studies, **after**

---

69 **Modified by** CN 26, 31. (The examen is now given before entrance and during the first probation.)

70 (See notes 9 to [212] and 10 to [216].)

completing them he must undergo all the experiences and probations explained above}.[71]

¹FOR THOSE WHO HAVE COMPLETED
THEIR STUDIES

[128] 7. ²The scholastics who have completed their studies, before
they enter the Society or any of its houses to be admitted into it
for total obedience and complete common living in our Lord,
should be asked in general ³whether they remain firm in their
determination, vows, and promise which they made to God our
Lord before they went to their studies, or during the studies if they
had been received in the colleges.

[129] 8. ¹Likewise, they should be questioned and examined in
detail by means of the same questions and examen first used
before they went to their studies.[72] ²The purpose is that the superiors may have a fresher memory and knowledge of the scholastics,
and also better and more completely know their firmness and
constancy, or any change if one occurred in the matters which were
first asked and affirmed.

CHAPTER 8

¹ANOTHER EXAMEN, FOR THOSE STILL INDIFFERENT

[130] 1. ²For a better understanding of a candidate who is to be
examined as one still indifferent, so that both sides may proceed
with greater knowledge and clarity in our Lord, ³he will receive this
instruction and advice. At no time and in no way may he or should
he seek or try to obtain, directly or indirectly, one grade rather
than another in the Society [A], that of a professed or a spiritual
coadjutor rather than a temporal coadjutor or a scholastic. ⁴But
yielding to complete humility and obedience, he ought to leave all
the concern about himself, and about the office or grade for which
he should be chosen, to his Creator and Lord and, in his name and
for his divine love and reverence, to the same Society and its
superior.

---

[71] **Abolished by** *CN* **46.** (See note 44 to [71]: The probations and experiments now take place in the novitiate.)

[72] (See *CN* 26, 31: the examen now takes place before entrance and
during first probation.)

[131] A. ¹*However, when something occurs constantly to these candidates as being conducive to the greater glory of God our Lord, they may, after prayer, propose the matter simply to the superior and leave it entirely to his judgment, without seeking anything more thereafter.*

[132] 2. ¹After he has been thus advised, he will be asked whether he finds himself entirely indifferent, content, and ready to serve his Creator and Lord in whatever office or ministry to which the Society or its superior will assign him.

²Likewise this question should be put to him. If the Society or its superior desires to keep him always only for low and humble offices (in which he devotes himself to the salvation of his own soul), ³is he ready to spend all the days of his life in such low and humble offices, for the benefit and service of the Society, ⁴in the conviction that by this he is serving and praising his Creator and Lord and doing all things for his divine love and reverence?

[133] 3. ¹If he is thus entirely satisfied in our Lord with all that has been said, he can be instructed and examined about the remaining matters, by means of some or all of the aforementioned examens, as may be found more expedient. ²The aim is that both sides may be content and satisfied while proceeding with greater clarity in everything, while all things are being directed and ordered toward greater service and praise of God our Lord.

II-B

THE CONSTITUTIONS
OF THE SOCIETY OF JESUS,
WITH THEIR DECLARATIONS

III

COMPLEMENTARY NORMS
TO THE CONSTITUTIONS
OF THE SOCIETY OF JESUS

II-B: THE CONSTITUTIONS OF THE SOCIETY OF JESUS AND THEIR DECLARATIONS

¹PREAMBLE TO THE CONSTITUTIONS

[134]   1. ²Although God our Creator and Lord is the one who in his Supreme Wisdom and Goodness must preserve, direct, and carry forward in his divine service this least Society of Jesus, just as he deigned to begin it; ³and although on our own part what helps most toward this end must be, more than any exterior constitution, the interior law of charity and love which the Holy Spirit writes and imprints upon hearts; ⁴nevertheless, since the gentle disposition of Divine Providence requires cooperation from his creatures, and since too the vicar of Christ our Lord has ordered this, and since the examples given by the saints and reason itself teach us so in our Lord, ⁵we think it necessary that constitutions should be written to aid us to proceed better, in conformity with our Institute, along the path of divine service on which we have entered.

[135]   2. ¹Moreover, while the consideration which comes first and has more weight in the order of our intention regards the body of the Society as a whole, whose unity, good government, and preservation in well-being for the greater divine glory are primarily in view, ²nevertheless, inasmuch as this body is made up of its members, and what occurs first in the order of execution pertains to the individual members, in regard to their admission, progress, and distribution into the vineyard of Christ our Lord, ³it is from this consideration that we shall begin, with the help which the Eternal Light will deign to communicate to us for his own honor and praise.

For the structural and typographical arrangement of the Constitutions and Norms, see pages viii and 19.

INTRODUCTORY DECREE
TO THE COMPLEMENTARY NORMS

1° That an ever more perfect observance of our Constitutions and our Institute[1] may be fostered and promoted, General Congregation 34 by its own proper authority approves and promulgates this collection, *Complementary Norms of the Constitutions of the Society of Jesus,* drawn up for the most part from decrees of previous general congregations—in particular GCs 31, 32, 33, and 34.

2° Decees of previous general congregations, insofar as they are not derogated from or changed either by later decrees or by these Complementary Norms, have their own proper declarative, directive, or inspirational force, along with the decrees of this General Congregation 34, and provide the context for better understanding the Norms and interpreting them correctly.

3° The Complementary Norms can be changed and derogated from only by a general congregation.

4° The Complementary Norms are always to be published along with the Formula of the Institute and the Constitutions of the Society of Jesus, as annotated by this General Congregation 34, in one and the same volume.

5° Abrogated is the *Collection of Decrees of General Congregations,* drawn up by General Congregation 27 (1923) and from time to time revised by later general congregations; the latest edition was published in 1977.[2]

---

[1] See P. VI, c. 1, no. 1 [547].

[2] See *ActRSJ* 17:90–105.

¹PREAMBLE TO THE DECLARATIONS AND OBSERVATIONS ABOUT THE CONSTITUTIONS

[136]   ²*The purpose of the Constitutions is to aid the body of the Society as a whole and its individual members toward their preservation and increase for the divine glory and the good of the universal Church;* ³*they ought therefore, besides being singly and as a whole conducive to the purpose just stated, to possess three characteristics:*

⁴*First, they should be complete, to provide for all cases as far as possible.*

⁵*Second, they should be clear, to give less occasion for scruples.*

⁶*Third, they should be brief, as far as the completeness and clarity allow, to make it possible to retain them in the memory.*

⁷*For the better realization of these three characteristics, the more universal and summary Constitutions will be presented in a handier form, so that they may be observed inside and shown to externs when that is expedient.* ⁸*But in addition to them, we have thought it wise in our Lord to compose also these Declarations and observations. They possess the same binding force as the other Constitutions, and can give more detailed instruction to those who have charge of the other members about some matters which the brevity and universality of the other Constitutions left less clear.* ⁹*The Constitutions and the Declarations both treat of matters which are unchangeable and ought to be observed universally; but they must be supplemented by other ordinances which can be adapted to the times, places, and persons in different houses, colleges, and employments of the Society, although uniformity ought to be retained among all the members as far as possible.* ¹⁰*These ordinances or rules will not be treated here, except by remarking that everyone ought to observe them when in a place where they are observed, according to the will of whoever may be his superior.*

¹¹*To return now to the subject matter treated here, the order of these Declarations will correspond to that of the Constitutions, part for part and chapter for chapter, whenever something in a chapter needs to be explained.* ¹²*This will be indicated by a letter in the margin of the Constitutions, and corresponding to this will be the same letter in the text of the Declarations. Thus we shall proceed in an orderly fashion, with the help of him who as the Most Perfect and Infinite Wisdom is the beginning of all order.*

PREAMBLE
THE MISSION AND IDENTITY
OF THE SOCIETY AND ITS INSTITUTE

SECTION 1: THESE COMPLEMENTARY NORMS OF THE CONSTITUTIONS OF THE SOCIETY OF JESUS AS AN EXPRESSION OF ITS CHARACTER AND CHARISM

1   The Society of Jesus intends always to take a very close look at its own nature and mission, in order that, faithful to its own vocation, it can renew itself and adapt its life and its activities to the exigencies of the Church and the needs of the men and women of our times, according to its proper character and charism.[1]

2   §1. The character and charism of the Society of Jesus arise from the Spiritual Exercises which our holy father Ignatius and his companions went through. Led by this experience, they formed an apostolic group rooted in charity, in which, after they had taken the vows of chastity and poverty and had been raised to the priesthood, they offered themselves as a holocaust to God,[2] so that serving as soldiers of God beneath the banner of the cross and serving the Lord alone and the Church his spouse under the Roman Pontiff, the vicar of Christ on earth,[3] they would be sent into the entire world[4] for "the defense and propagation of the faith and for the progress of souls in Christian life and doctrine."[5]

§2. The distinguishing mark of our Society, then, is that it is at one and the same time a companionship that is reli-

---

[1] GC 31, d. 1, no. 2.

[2] See "Deliberation of the First Fathers" (a. 1539), MHSI, Mon. Ign., *Const.*, I, 2.

[3] See *FI* no. 1.

[4] GC 31, d. 1, no. 2.

[5] *FI* no.1.

¹Declarations on the Preamble

[137] A. ²It is usually good, especially in the order of practice, to proceed from the less to the more perfect; for what is first in the order of execution is last in the order of consideration, since such planning first considers the end and then descends to the means to attain it. ³Accordingly, we shall organize all the following Constitutions under ten principal parts:

⁴Part I.   The admission to probation for those who desire to follow our Institute.

⁵Part II.   The dismissal of those who do not seem suitable for it.

⁶Part III.   The care of those who remain and the fostering of their progress in the spiritual life and in the virtues.

⁷Part IV.   The instruction in learning and other means of helping the neighbor for those who have made progress in the spiritual life and virtue.

⁸Part V.   The incorporation into the Society of those who have been thus instructed.

⁹Part VI.   What those who have been incorporated must observe in regard to themselves.

¹⁰Part VII.   What should be observed in regard to our neighbors, when the workers are distributed and employed in the vineyard of Christ our Lord.

¹¹Part VIII.   What pertains to keeping those thus distributed united with one another and with their head.

¹²Part IX.   What pertains to the head and to the government which descends from him to the body.

¹³Part X.   What pertains in general to the preservation and increase of the entire body of this Society in its well-being.

¹⁴This is the order which we shall follow in the Constitutions and the Declarations, looking to the end which we all seek, the glory and praise of God our Creator and Lord. ∎

gious, apostolic, sacerdotal,[6] and bound to the Roman Pontiff by a special bond of love and service.[7]

3   These original and substantial elements of the identity and mission of the Society are contained in the Formulas of the Institute and declared in the Constitutions of the Society of Jesus.[8]

4   §1. According to these documents, explained by later general congregations, the mission of the Society consists in this, that as servants of Christ's universal mission in the Church and in the world of today,[9] we may procure that integral salvation in Jesus Christ which is begun in this life and will be brought to its fulfillment in the life to come.[10] Therefore the mission of the Society today is defined as the service of faith, of which the promotion of justice is an absolute requirement.[11]

§2. The service of faith and the promotion of justice constitute one and the same mission of the Society. They cannot, therefore, be separated one from the other in our purpose, our action, our life;[12] nor can they be considered simply as one ministry among others, but rather as that ministry whereby all our ministries are brought together in a unified whole.[13]

§3. This mission also includes, as integral dimensions of evangelization, the inculturated proclamation of the Gospel and dialogue with members of other religions.[14] Hence, in our mission, the faith that seeks justice is a faith that inseparably engages other traditions in dialogue and evangelizes cultures.[15]

5   §1. These Complementary Norms of the Constitutions of the Society of Jesus, for the most part taken principally from decrees of general congregations, try to gather together the principal fruits of today's renewal as a present-day expression of the

---

[6] See GC 34, d. 6, especially no. 8.

[7] See GC 32, d. 2, no. 24; see Paul VI, "Allocution to the Fathers of CG 32," December 3, 1974.

[8] *FI* nos. 2, 9; see *CollDecr* d. 12 (GC 31, d. 4, no. 3).

[9] GC 34, d. 1, no. 8.

[10] GC 33, d. 1, no. 34.

[11] GC 32, d. 4, no. 2; d. 2, no. 2.

[12] GC 32, d. 2, no. 8; see GC 33, d. 1, no. 38.

[13] GC 32, d. 2, no. 9; see GC 33, d. 1, no. 38; GC 34, d. 2, no. 14.

[14] GC 34, d. 2, nos. 15, 20.

[15] GC 34, d. 2, no. 21.

genuine image of the Society and as a necessary help in applying its Constitutions according to their deeper requirements.

§2. But if this genuine image of the Society cannot be perfectly converted into normative expressions, these Norms must always be referred back to this image as expressed in the Formula of the Institute and in the Constitutions. For this image is the primary pattern, whose outline the present Norms ought to express by their very nature,[16] and in whose light they must be interpreted.

SECTION 2: THE PERSONS WHO COMPOSE THE SOCIETY

6 §1. The Society of Jesus, in which all members, each according to the proper mode of his vocation, participate in the same vocation and mission, understood in their broadest as well as their most precise senses,[17] consists of the following members:

1° Novices, whether destined to become priests or brothers.[18] Some can also be admitted as "indifferents," either on their part or on the part of the Society;[19] but before the end of the novitiate, they must move out of the state of indifference.[20]

2° Those who at the end of the novitiate and after profession of first vows prepare themselves for or exercise the priesthood or other activities for the assistance of the Society, and after the time required by the particular law governing each one pronounce final vows in one of the two ways indicated below in 3° or 4°. (In the Formula of the Institute[21] these are called "scholastics" or "coadjutors," but in the Constitutions "approved scholastics" or "temporal coadjutors."[22]

---

[16] See John Paul II, Const. apost. "Sacræ disciplinæ leges," *AAS* (1983), p. xi.

[17] See P. V, c. 1, A [511]; *Examen*, c. 1, nos. 7–11 [10–15]; *FI* passim.

[18] See P. V, c. 1, A [511]; *Examen*, c. 1, no. 12 [16]; c. 4, no. 17 [72].

[19] See *Examen*, c. 1, no. 11 [15]; c. 8, nos. 1–3 [130–33].

[20] *CollDecr* d. 17 (see GC 4, d. 52).

[21] *FI* no. 9.

[22] *Const.*, passim.

3° Priests and brothers who pronounce final simple vows, of whom some, albeit rarely, can take solemn vows.[23] (In the Formula of the Institute and in the Constitutions, they are called respectively "spiritual coadjutors" or "temporal coadjutors").[24]

4° Priests professed of four solemn vows.[25]

§2. All candidates are now first admitted as novices, so that after probations and studies and the time required by law have been completed, they may be definitively received into the Society.[26]

SECTION 3: THE INSTITUTE OF THE SOCIETY

CHAPTER 1

THE INSTITUTE OF THE SOCIETY AND ITS PARTS

7   The term "Institute of the Society" means both our way of living and working[27] and the written documents in which this way is authoritatively and legitimately proposed. Among these documents some are laws properly so called; others, however, are documents which inspire or illustrate our spirituality or our way of proceeding or which set forth the legitimate traditions of the Society.[28]

8   To maintain faithfully the grace of our vocation as described in the Institute, the *Spiritual Exercises* of our holy founder stands in first place, both as a perennial source of those interior gifts upon which depends our effectiveness in reaching the goal

---

[23] See *FI* of Julius III, no. 9; *Examen,* c. 1, D [11]; P. V, c. 3, no. 3 [520].

[24] See *FI* of Julius III, no. 9; *Examen,* c. 1, no. 9 [13]; c. 6, no. 8, A [119, 120]; P. V, c. 4, no. 1 [533]; no. 3 [537].

[25] See *FI* of Julius III, no. 3; *Examen,* c. 1, no. 8 [12].

[26] See *CN* 119; P. V, c. 1, no. 1 [510].

[27] See Paul III, *Regimini militantis* (1540); Julius III, *Exposcit debitum* (1550); *FI* of Paul III, nos. 1, 9; *FI* of Julius III, nos. 1, 2, 9; *Pream.,* no. 1 [134]; P. I, c. 2, no. 4 [152]; c. 3, I [186]; P. IV, c. 7, no. 3 [398]; P. VI, c. 1, no. 1 [547]; c. 3, no. 4 [586]; c. 5 [602]; P. VII, c. 1, no. 1 [603]; etc.

[28] *CollDecr* d. 1, a (GC 31, d. 4, no. 2).

set before us[29] and as the living expression of the Ignatian spirit that must temper and interpret all our laws.[30]

9 §1. The Formula of the Institute or fundamental "Rule" of the Society has primacy of dignity and authority in the Institute. It was set down first by Paul III (1540), then more exactly and in greater detail by Julius III (1550); it was approved in specific form by many of his successors and has obtained in a special way the status of pontifical law.

§2. There are also other laws of the Institute that have obtained the status of pontifical law, but not all have been approved by the Holy See in the same way; hence they enjoy varying degrees of dignity and authority.

§3. Apostolic letters, rescripts, and indults issued for the Society also pertain to the pontifical law specific to the Society.[31]

10 The following are also parts of the Institute:

1° The Constitutions and the General Examen, with their respective declarations, which our holy Father Ignatius composed by virtue of an apostolic faculty granted to the Society;[32] they were reviewed and approved by General Congregation 1.

2° Laws enacted by general congregations and rules approved by them or by their authority.[33]

3° General rules, rules of particular offices, ordinations and instructions, whether for a limited territory or for the whole Society, enacted by the superiors general within their competence.[34]

11 §1. The Constitutions, General Examen, and their respective Declarations are of equal authority among themselves[35] and retain their full authority[36] unless, in the case of individual deter-

---

[29] See P. X, no. 2 [813].

[30] *CollDecr* d. 1, a (GC 31, d. 4, no. 2).

[31] *CollDecr* d. 1, a (GC 31, d. 4, no. 2).

[32] Paul III, *Regimini militantis;* Id., *Iniunctum Nobis;* Julius III, *Exposcit debitum.*

[33] See *CollDecr* d. 3, §2; *FI* of Paul III (1540) and Julius III (1550), no. 2.

[34] See *CollDecr* d. 4, §1 (GC 1, d. 143; GC 7, d. 76).

[35] *Pream.* to Decl. on *Const.* [136]; P. VI, c. 1, A [548].

[36] See *CollDecr* d. 2, §1.

minations when these have been legitimately changed or abrogated by prescriptions of the universal law or by decrees of general congregations, or if the circumstances have so changed that they can no longer be applied; in this case the matter should be declared by a general congregation or, for the exercise of good governance, by the superior general.

§2. The Latin version of these documents approved by the Fourth General Congregation is to be considered authoritative and can be changed only by a general congregation.[37]

§3. The Spanish autograph version, approved by the First and the Fifth General Congregations, is to be preserved with veneration and can serve as an aid to a congregation and to the superior general in explaining that version.[38]

12 §1. Whatever is decreed by a general congregation is presumed to be a law established by it, unless something else is evidently the case according to the nature of the question or because of a positive declaration. Such laws are

1° The canons and decrees of congregations that contain norms and determinations

2° The formulas of congregations, that is, of a general congregation, of a province congregation, of a congregation of procurators, of a congregation to elect a temporary vicar

3° Rules that have been approved by the authority of a general congregation, that is, the Rules of Modesty, composed by St. Ignatius, [rules for] the office of the Vicar General, the rules for assistants, and the rules for the admonitor of the general

§2. Unless a general congregation declares otherwise, the following do not have the force of law:

1° Decrees passed prior to the election of a general but not subsequently confirmed

2° Decrees passed subsequent to the election but, by the desire of the congregation, not promulgated

§3. For the promulgation of decrees, unless a congregation itself has determined otherwise, it is both necessary and sufficient that they are sent to the provinces by the superior general in the

---

[37] *CollDecr* d. 2, §2 (GC 4, d. 50; GC 5, d. 76; GC 23, d. 27; GC 24, d. 27).

[38] GC 27, *CollDecr* d. 2, §3 (GC 1, dd. 15, 78; GC 3, d. 26; GC 5, d. 61).

name of the congregation, with the purpose of making them known in the houses.[39]

13   §1. All rules and ordinances established by the superiors general, unless some other provision is explicitly made, are presumed to be in force as long as they are not revoked by them or by a general congregation.

  §2. Whatever additions or changes a superior general, acting on a mandate from a general congregation, makes in rules established by his own authority, in ordinances, or in instructions have the same authority as if they had been made by the superior general acting purely on his own initiative.[40]

  §3. Instructions, as understood in our law and practice,[41] even those issued for the worldwide Society, have only advisory force, unless the contrary is indicated.[42]

14   What the universal law determines should be inserted in "the fundamental code" of institutes of consecrated life[43] are contained in the Formula of the Institute and are declared in the respective places of the Constitutions and the decrees of general congregations that declare or modify them on the topics mentioned above.[44]

CHAPTER 2

APPLICATION AND INTERPRETATION OF THE INSTITUTE AND DISPENSATION FROM IT

15   Our Institute, according to the spirit of the Constitutions,[45] with great care and without deviation in anything,[46] but at the same time always out of love and desire of all perfection,[47] by

---

[39] *CollDecr* d. 3, §§2–4 (GC 1, d. 115; GC 2, d. 31; GC 3, dd. 4, 33; GC 4, dd. 2, 43, 44, 48, 50; GC 20, dd. 17, 18; GC 22, d. 44, no. 7; GC 31, d. 19, no. 15); see P. VIII, c. 7, C [718].

[40] *CollDecr* d. 4, §§2–3 (GC 1, d. 143; GC 7, d. 76; GC 7, d. 72; see GC 4, d. 3).

[41] See CIC 34.

[42] *CollDecr* d. 5 (see GC 7, d. 81).

[43] See CIC 587; §1, 578; CCEO 426.

[44] *FI* nos. 2, 9.

[45] *Pream.*, no. 1 [134].

[46] P. VI, c. 5 [602]; see P. IV, c. 10, no. 5 [424]; P. VI, c. 1, no. 1 [547]; P. IX, c. 3, no. 8 [746]; c. 6, A [790]; P. X, no. 13 [826].

[47] P. VI, c. 5 [602].

means of discreet charity,[48] under the direction of superiors,[49] is to be applied by taking into account persons, places, and times, and other circumstances.[50] We must always keep in mind the purpose, "which is no other than the greater divine service and the good of those who live in this institute."[51]

16   Should any doubts perchance arise in the Formula of the Institute, the general congregation has the authority to declare them.[52]

17   Only a general congregation can authoritatively interpret the Constitutions and laws passed by general congregations; however, it is within the power of the superior general to declare the meaning of these documents, as well as of the Formula itself, as regards their practical application to good governance; and his interpretations constitute a preceptive norm.[53]

18   §1. The replies of the generals interpreting the Institute, even if given to individual provinces, nevertheless have obligatory force for all provinces as declarative interpretations of law, provided that the general has proposed them as such for the whole Society.

§2. Other replies, even though sent to the whole Society as matters of information, oblige only those provinces to which they are given; for the others, however, they constitute an advisory norm only.[54]

19   §1. In particular cases the general can validly dispense from the Constitutions and from laws passed by a general congregation, that is, for individual persons, houses, or provinces, unless in a given matter his power has been limited; he does not licitly dispense, however, unless it is according to the mind of the legis-

---

48 See P. II, c. 2, no. 1 [201]; no. 5 [217]; c. 3, A [219]; c. 4, B [237]; P. III, c. 1, no. 15 [269]; no. 25 [287]; P. IV, c. 13, no. 5 [462]; P. VI, c. 3, no. 1 [582]; P. IX, c. 3, no. 11 [754].

49 See P. IV, c. 10 [424]; P. IX, c. 3, no. 8 [746]; c. 6, A [790].

50 See *Pream.* to Decl. on *Const.* [136]; P. II, c. 2, A [211]; P. III, c. 2, C [297]; P. IV, c. 4, B [343]; c. 5, no. 1 [351]; c. 7, no. 2 [395]; c. 13, A [455]; C [458]; no. 5 [462]; P. VI, c. 2, N [581]; P. VII, c. 2, no. 1 [618]; P. VIII, c. 1, no. 8 [671]; P. IX, c. 3, no. 8 [746]; c. 3, no. 11 [754].

51 P. IX, c. 3, no. 8 [746].

52 See *FI* of Julius III, no. 2.

53 *CollDecr* d. 9 (GC 3, d. 33; GC 4, d. 19).

54 GC 27, *CollDecr* d. 10.

lator.[55] But for rules and ordinations enacted by himself or by his predecessors, he has full power of dispensation from them.

§2. Other superiors have the power of dispensing from these laws to the extent that it has been communicated to them.[56]

CHAPTER 3
THE PRESERVATION AND RENEWAL OF THE INSTITUTE

20   §1. The substantials or fundamentals of our Institute are, most especially, the matters contained in the Formula of Julius III (1550). For the Formula exhibits "the nature, purpose, spirit, and character"[57] and the fundamental structure of the Society, based, with the help of grace, on the principles of the Gospel and the experience and wisdom of our holy father Ignatius and his companions.

§2. Also among the substantials are included those matters without which the substantials of the Formula can be preserved either not at all or barely. General congregations have the power to state what these substantials are, as they have done at times;[58] moreover the superior general has the same power, to be exercised on a temporary basis and for the sake of practical application.[59]

21   §1. A general congregation can indeed declare substantials contained in the Formula of the Institute, but cannot change them on its own authority. Moreover, a definitive change in them should not be requested of the Holy See without the clearest of reasons and, if the case warrants it, without previous experimentation.[60]

§2. Substantials outside the Formula of the Institute continue to have stable force unless it should happen that a general congregation judges that the connection of any of them with the substantials in the Formula has been lost or notably weakened. But if there is a question of changing them, a general congrega-

---

[55] See P. IX, c. 3, no. 8, D [746, 747]; *CollDecr* d. 11.

[56] See P. IV, c. 10, B [425]; P. IX, c. 3, D [747].

[57] CIC 578.

[58] See GC 27, *CollDecr* d. 13.

[59] *CollDecr* d. 12 (GC 31, d. 4, no. 3).

[60] See *CollDecr* d. 14, §§2–3 (GC 1, d. 16; GC 31, d. 4, no. 3).

tion is first to state whether the proposed item to be changed should be considered a substantial outside the Formula of the Institute, according to no. 20, §2, and whether a truly serious reason exists for changing it.

§3. In regard to those matters that are not substantials in our Institute, the Constitutions can be changed by a general congregation if a truly reasonable cause recommends it, according to the norms laid down in its Formula.

§4. Decrees and rules of general congregations, as well as rules and ordinations drawn up by superiors general, not only may be changed by the aforesaid authorities in accordance with the competence of each, but also should be changed by those authorities to provide for the continual adaptation of them to the needs of the times.[61]

22 §1. It is permitted to provincial congregations to treat of the substantials of the Institute, provided there are serious reasons, and in accordance with the norms laid down in the Formula of the Province Congregation.

§2. When sending postulata to the general or province congregation, all should bear in mind what is said in nos. 20–21; and each, with due love of the patrimony of the Society and with due regard for his own responsibility, should propose what he desires for the renewal and adaptation of the Institute, realizing, moreover, that the light necessary for making such postulata will be obtained not only from dialogue but most of all from prayer.[62]

23 Every adaptation of the Institute should aim at always establishing whatever seems to contribute most, all things considered, to the knowledge, love, praise, and service of God and to the salvation of souls. For our holy Father Ignatius laid these down as the foundation or first criterion of all our laws.[63]

---

[61] *CollDecr* d. 14, §§1–4 (GC 7, d. 76; GC 31, d. 4, no. 3).

[62] *CollDecr* d. 15 (GC 31, d. 4, no. 3).

[63] *CollDecr* d. 14, §5 (GC 31, d. 4, no. 3).

PART I

¹THE ADMISSION TO PROBATION

CHAPTER 1

²THE PERSON WHO ADMITS

[138] 1. ³**The authority to admit to probation**¹ will belong to those whom the superior general of the Society thinks fit, and to the extent he thinks good. In communicating this authority he will look to what is conducive to the greater service to God our Lord.

[139] 2. ¹When someone who seems suitable for our Institute offers himself to a person who lacks such authority to admit him, he may send this applicant to one who has it *[A]*, or write to him and inform him about the applicant's qualifications ²and then act as directed by him in our Lord, should the latter be able to settle the matter from a distance *[B]*.

[140] A. *²If a good applicant of this kind cannot easily be sent to the one who has the authority, anyone may, while the one possessing authority is being informed, receive the applicant provisionally as a guest in his house if he judges this to be necessary or highly opportune, until he receives a reply to the report which he sent. ³Then he will act according to the order which will be given him.*

[141] B. *¹Those who can admit while absent are: ordinarily, the provincial superiors; extraordinarily, any commissaries of the general or the same provincial. ²But the more ordinary practice will be to communicate to the rectors of colleges and the local superiors* **authority to receive into their house or college**² *those present whom they judge suitable.*

[142] 3. ¹It is highly important for the divine service to make a proper selection of those who are admitted and to take care to know their abilities and vocation well. ²Therefore if the one who

---

¹ **Clarified by** *CN* **24.** (There it is stated who can admit.)

² **Modified by** *CN* **40.** (Admission is in the novitiate house itself.)

PART I
ADMISSION TO PROBATION

CHAPTER 1
THE FACULTY OF ADMITTING TO PROBATION

24 §1. Provincials have the faculty of admitting to probation that the general habitually communicates to them.

§2. Others have only the faculty of admitting that the general or the provincial has communicated to them.[1]

§3. Only the general, by privilege, can validly admit to the novitiate candidates who have not completed their seventeenth year of age.[2]

> **The text of the Norms resumes on page 75.**

---

[1] See P. I, c. 1, B [141].

[2] See P. I, c. 2, no. 12 [160]; c. 3, K [187]; Benedict XIV, *Exponi Nobis*; Leo XII, Rescript of March 2, 1827; CIC 643, §1, 1°; CCEO 450, 4°.

has the aforementioned authority does not do all that himself, he should have, among those who reside more permanently in the same place as himself, someone to aid him in getting to know, conversing with, and examining those who come. ³This helper should possess discretion and skill in dealing with persons so different in temperament and disposition, so that things may be carried out with greater clarity and satisfaction on both sides for the divine glory.

[143]   4. ¹Both the one who has the authority to admit and his helper ought to know the Society well and be zealous for its good functioning, so that no other consideration will be able to deter him from what he judges in our Lord to be more suitable for his divine service in this Society. ²Therefore he should be very moderate in his desire to admit [C]. Furthermore, ³so that he may be more free from disordered affection where occasion for it might exist (as in the case of relatives or friends), anyone in whom this danger is in any way feared ought not to perform the function of examiner.

[144]   C. ¹Just as care should be taken to cooperate with the divine motion and vocation, endeavoring to secure in the Society an increase of workers for the holy vineyard of Christ our Lord, ²so also much thought should be given so as to admit only those who possess the qualifications required for this Institute, for the divine glory.

[145]   5. ¹Whoever has this charge ought to keep in writing whatever pertains to it *[D]* so that he may better and more precisely carry out what is sought in this matter for the divine service.

[146]   D.   ¹*In every place where someone has the authority to admit, there ought to be a complete text of the Examen in the languages which are ordinarily found necessary, such as the vernacular of the place of residence and Latin.* ²*The Examen is proposed to the one who seeks admission before he enters the house to live in common with the others. The impediments which necessarily bar admission are proposed even before entrance into the first probation.*

³*There will likewise be in writing another Examen containing the matter which is to be proposed every six months during the two years of probation;* ⁴*also another, very short, which those can use who deal with applicants, so that both sides may know what should be known before reception into the first probation.* ⁵*They should likewise have the office of the examiner in writing and see that its prescriptions are carried out.*

CHAPTER 2
¹THE CANDIDATES WHO SHOULD BE ADMITTED

[147] 1. ²To speak in general of those who should be admitted, the greater the number of natural and infused gifts someone has from God our Lord which are useful for what the Society aims at in his divine service, ³and the more assurance the Society has about these gifts, the more suitable will the candidate be to be admitted.

[148] 2. ¹To speak in particular of those who are admitted to become coadjutors **in temporal or external matters³** (under the presupposition that they should not be more numerous than is necessary to aid the Society in occupations which the other members could not fulfill without detriment to the greater service of God *[A]*), ²they ought to be men of good conscience, peaceful, docile, lovers of virtue and perfection, inclined to devotion, ³edifying for those inside and outside the house, content with the lot of Martha in the Society, well-disposed towards its Institute, and eager to help it for the glory of God our Lord *[B]*.

[149] A. ¹*Such are ordinarily, in large houses, the occupations of a cook, steward, buyer, doorkeeper, infirmarian, launderer, gardener, and alms gatherer (in a place where the members live on alms); and there could be others of this kind. ²But depending on the more or fewer members in the houses or colleges and the greater or lesser distraction entailed in the tasks, it might or might not be necessary to assign persons to them full-time. ³Consequently this matter should be left to the discretion of the one in charge of the others. ⁴But he should be told to keep in mind the purpose for which such members are accepted into this Society, that is, the need to relieve those who are laboring in the Lord's vineyard, or who are studying to labor in it later, so that they may apply themselves to pursuits which bring greater service to God our Lord.*

[150] B. ¹*If an applicant is perceived to have such a disposition that he is unlikely in the long run to remain satisfied while serving in external matters,* **because an inclination for study** *or the priesthood* **can be observed in him,** ²**it would not be wise to admit him to become a temporal coadjutor**⁴ *if he does not appear to have the ability to advance as far as would be necessary.*

---

³ (See *CN* 6.)

⁴ **Clarified by** *CN* 81, §3; 83, §3; 98; 243, §2. (In regard to studies of the brothers.)

CHAPTER 2
THOSE ADMITTED TO PROBATION

25   §1. In order to attain the goals of probation, sufficient human maturity and suitable preparation are requirements for candidates.

§2. For this purpose, candidates can in different ways be recommended to certain selected fathers and brothers who will help them towards obtaining maturity in their vocation while they prepare for entrance into the novitiate by means of studies and apostolic experiments.[3]

§3. Where it is deemed necessary, special programs are to be established to help candidates who will become brothers and who lack adequate preparation.[4]

§4. Sufficient information about the Society should be given to them at this time, both by direct conversation and from a study of its history, as also from its principal documents, both older ones (such as the Formula of the Institute, the General Examen, and the Constitutions or excerpts from them) and more recent ones.[5]

26   §1. A personal examination should be accurately made of candidates' lives, endowments, and aptitude for the Society, their right intention, their defects of both soul and body, as well as of any impediments or hindrances that may happen to exist, paying special attention to and adapting to our own times the instructions found in the Examen, and the Constitutions.[6]

§2. Other appropriate means should also be used so that the Society knows them fully; therefore, unless the candidates are already well known, information should be sought concerning their health, virtues, education, practice of the Christian life, temperament, talents, studies completed and with what success, the condition of their family and its social circumstances;[7] and,

---

[3] See GC 31, d. 8, no. 13.

[4] GC 34, d. 7, no. 14.

[5] This norm is useful for planning the prenovitiate.

[6] See *Examen*, passim, and P. I, cc. 2–3 [147–89]; GC 31, d. 8, no. 13.

[7] See P. I, c. 4, D [196].

[151]   3. ¹In regard to their exterior these candidates ought to have a good appearance, health, and age as well as the strength for the bodily tasks which occur in the Society. ²They should also have or give hope of having some good ability to help the Society.

[152]   4. ¹In view of the end of our Institute and our manner of proceeding, we are convinced in our Lord that to admit persons who are very difficult or unserviceable to the congregation is not conducive to his greater service and praise, even though their admission would be useful to themselves.

[153]   5. ¹Those who are admitted to serve in spiritual matters should have the following qualifications, because of what a ministry of this kind requires for the help of souls.

[154]   6. ¹In regard to the intellect, they should have sound doctrine, or ability to acquire it, and in respect to practical matters, discretion or evidence of the good judgment which is necessary to acquire it.

[155]   7. ¹In regard to the memory, they should have aptitude to learn and faithfully retain what has been learned.

[156]   8. ¹In regard to the will, they should be desirous of all virtue and spiritual perfection, peaceful, constant, and resolute in whatever enterprise of the divine service they undertake, and zealous for the salvation of souls. ²For that reason they should also have an affection toward our Institute, which is directly ordered to help and dispose souls to gain their ultimate end from the hand of God our Creator and Lord.

[157]   9. ¹In regard to the exterior, a pleasing manner of speech, so necessary for communications with one's fellowmen, is desirable.

[158]   10. ¹They should have a good appearance, by which those with whom they deal are usually more edified.

[159]   11. ¹They should have the health and strength by which they can sustain the labors of our Institute.

[160]   12. ¹**They should be of an age**⁵ **suitable for what has been stated, that is, more than fourteen years for admission to**

---

⁵ **Clarified by** *CN* **24, 3.** (From universal law, one who enters the novitiate must have completed seventeen years of age—CIC 643, 1°; CCEO 450, 4°—or eighteen years of age—CCEO 450, 4°; but by privilege the Society can admit him before that age; this faculty however is reserved to the general.)

when necessary for a fuller knowledge of them, a recommendation should be sought from those skilled in psychology. The
secrecy of consultation, the candidate's freedom, and norms
established by the Church are, however, to be strictly safeguarded.[8]

§3. For the same purpose candidates may be invited to live
for a time in one of our communities that is suitable for this.

---

[8] GC 31, d. 8, no. 13; see CIC 642, 220.

probation and more than twenty-five years for profession.[6]

[161] 13. ¹The extrinsic gifts of nobility, wealth, reputation, and the like, just as they do not suffice if those others are lacking, so they are not necessary when the others are present. ²But to the extent that they aid toward edification, they render more fit to be admitted those who would be fit without them because they have the other qualifications mentioned above. ³The more an applicant is distinguished for those qualifications, the more suitable will he be for this Society unto the glory of God our Lord, ⁴and the less he is distinguished by them, the less suitable [C]. ⁵But the measure to be observed in all things will be taught by holy unction of the Divine Wisdom [1 John 2:20, 27] to those who are charged with this matter, undertaken for his greater service and praise.

[162] C. ¹To be completely suitable for the Society an applicant ought to have everything that has been mentioned. However, if someone lacks one or another of those qualifications, such as bodily strength, or the age for the profession, or something similar, ²and if it is judged in the Lord that this lack is compensated for by his other qualities and that, when everything is taken into account, his admission would be a service to God our Lord and conducive to the end of the Society, ³a dispensation may be granted him by the superior general or by the other superiors to the extent that he has communicated his authority to them.

CHAPTER 3
¹THE IMPEDIMENTS TO ADMISSION

[163] 1. ²Although the charity and zeal for souls practiced by this Society in accord with the end of its Institute embraces persons of every kind to serve them and help them in the Lord of all to attain to beatitude, ³nevertheless, when there is a question of incorporating persons into the same Society, that charity and zeal ought to embrace only those who are judged useful for the end it seeks (as has been said [143, 144]).

[164] 2. ¹Among the impediments to admission, some **exclude it completely**,[7] for compelling reasons which move us in our Lord.

---

⁶ **Modified by** *CN* 119. (No longer is a certain age required, but after entering the novitiate, one must spend ten years in the Society before pronouncing his last vows.)

⁷ **Modified by** *CN* 27, 28. (Impediments that are invalidating in the Constitutions are now prohibitions to admission without permission of the general.)

Chapter 3
Impediments to Admission

27   Besides what is established by universal law,[9] the Society retains no proper impediment rendering admission invalid.

28   The following are admitted illicitly without permission of the general:

1° One who, after completion of his sixteenth year of age,[10] has publicly withdrawn from the Catholic Church by denying the faith in any way whatsoever;[11]

---

[9] See CIC 643, §1; CCEO 450.

[10] See CIC 1323, 1°.

[11] See *Examen*, c. 2, no. 1, B [22, 24]; P. I, c. 3, no. 3, A, B [165–67]; GC 27, *CollDecr* d. 23.

[165] 3. ¹Such impediments are: to have separated oneself for a time from the bosom of the Holy Church, by denying the faith in the midst of infidels, or by falling into errors against the faith and having been condemned because of them by a public sentence *[A]*, or by withdrawing as a schismatic from the unity of the Church *[B]*.⁸

[166]   A. ¹*Even though one has not been condemned by a public sentence, if his error has been public and he has been highly suspect and there is fear that proceedings may be instituted against him, he ought not to be admitted. But this judgment will be left to the superior general.*

[167]   B. ¹*With respect to schism, if someone was born in a schismatical region, so that the schism was not simply an individual sin committed by the person himself but a general sin, he would not be understood to be excluded from the Society for this cause (and the same holds true of one born in a heretical region). ²Rather, what is envisaged is a person who is under infamy and excommunication after having contemned the authority and vigilance of our holy mother the Church, so that the heresy or schism is the person's individual sin, not the general sin of the nation or country.*

[168] 4. ¹Another impediment is: to have been a homicide *[C]*⁹ or infamous *[D]* because of enormous sins.¹⁰

[169]   C. ¹*In regard to a homicide no declaration is added, just as none is given about the remaining impediments. ²But when there is doubt as to whether he is a homicide or not, the decision will be left to the judgment of the generals, who in such doubts will not be lenient. ³If someone has deliberately ordered the committing of homicide and the effect followed, he too would be regarded as a homicide, even though he did not perpetrate the deed by his own hand.*

[170]   D. ¹*Infamy because of enormous sins is understood to be an impediment in the place where the sinner was declared infamous. ²If he should, when far from that place, give such signs of repentance that they reestablish confidence in him, he could be admitted in our Lord. ³Which sins of this kind are enormous and which are not will be left to the judgment of the superior general.*

---

⁸ **Modified by** *CN* 27, 28, 1°. (In regard to the character of the impediment and in regard to its tenor.)

⁹ **Modified by** *CN* 27, 28, 2°. (In regard to the character of the impediment and in regard to its tenor.)

¹⁰ **Modified by** *CN* 27, 28, 3°. (In regard to the character of the impediment and in regard to its tenor.)

2° One who has publicly committed voluntary homicide or has effectively brought about an abortion, and all who have positively cooperated;[12]

3° One who, because of some crime committed or because of depraved morals, has lost his good reputation, in the region where this occurred;[13]

4° One who has made temporary profession in another religious institute;[14] or has made first incorporation in a secular institute or society of apostolic life or common life in the manner of religious;[15] or who as a hermit has professed the three evangelical counsels into the hands of the diocesan bishop and confirmed them by a vow or other sacred bond, and has observed his own plan of life under the direction of that same bishop;[16]

5° One who, after completion of his fourteenth year of age, has been converted to the Catholic faith; this applies for three full years after his conversion;[17]

6° One who has completed fifty years of age.[18]

§2. The superior general should be very strict in granting permission in the first three cases.[19]

29   Prohibitions arising from the law of the Society do not bind in cases of a doubt of law; in cases of a doubt of fact, however, provincials can dispense from them, except in the case of voluntary homicide, which is reserved to the general.[20]

---

[12] See *Examen*, c. 2, no. 2 [25]; P. I, c. 3, no. 4, C [168, 169]; CC 27, *CollDecr* d. 24; CIC 1041, 4°.

[13] See *Examen*, c. 2, no. 2, C [25, 26]; P. I, c. 3, no. 4, D [168, 170].

[14] See CIC 655–56; CCEO 526–27.

[15] See CIC 723, 735; CCEO 554.

[16] See CIC 603, §2.

[17] GC 27, *CollDecr* d. 26; see CIC 1042, 3°; CCEO 762, §1, 8°.

[18] See P. I, c. 3, no. 15, K [185, 187].

[19] See *Examen*, c. 2, no. 6 [30]; P. I, c. 3, no. 2 [164].

[20] See GC 27, *CollDecr* d. 29; P. I, c. 3, C [169]; CIC 14.

[171]   5. ¹Another impediment is: **to have received the habit** *[E]* **of a religious institute, or to have been a hermit with the garb of a monk.**¹¹

[172]   *E.* ¹*Not only if he has made profession, but even if he has worn the habit a single day, such a one cannot be admitted, for the reasons touched on in the Examen [30]. However, this should be understood of taking the habit with the intention of becoming a religious, not through any other accidental reason.*

[173]   6. ¹{**Another impediment is to be bound by the bond of matrimony**¹² **or of legal servitude}** *[F].*¹³

[174]   *F.* ¹*In case this bond should be dissolved by the consent of the master or the wife, with observance of the other circumstances which are customarily observed in accord with the sound teaching and practice of the Holy Church, this impediment would cease to exist.*

[175]   7. ¹Another impediment is **to be mentally ill, with the result that the judgment becomes obscured and unsound, or to have a notable disposition toward such illness,**¹⁴ as is treated more at length in the Examen [29] *[G].*

[176]   *G.* ¹*In regard to all these impediments it is expedient that neither the superior general nor the whole Society should be able to dispense, since it is universally good that no dispensation be granted from them.* ²*However, should one of these impediments be found in a person who has such other qualifications as to give certitude that the Society could be much helped by him in the service of God our Lord,* ³*and should the* **person himself petition the supreme pontiff or his nuncio or chief penitentiary**¹⁵ *for permission, notwithstanding the Constitutions, to be received into the Society, its superior general not being opposed,* ⁴*then the superior general may give his consent, so long as the door would not*

---

¹¹ **Modified by** *CN* **27, 28, 4°.** (In regard to the character of the impediment.) **Clarified by** *CN* **28, 4°.** (In regard to its tenor.)

¹² **Abolished.** (As an impediment established by the proper law of the Society; for according to universal law—CIC 643, §1, 3°; CCEO 450, 6°—a married man is invalidly admitted to the novitiate during a marriage.)

¹³ **Abolished.** (Legitimate slavery, that is, one sanctioned by positive law, no longer exists.)

¹⁴ **Modified by** *CN* **30.** (As a strict impediment; it remains as an "impediment" rendering a candidate unsuitable or less suitable, according to P. I, c. 3, no. 8, H [177–78] and 16 [185].)

¹⁵ **Modified by** *CN* **28.** (In the case of prohibitions to admission, the permission of the general is required.)

30   Those who have the faculty of admitting should use great caution in admitting a candidate about whom, because of mental illness[21] or particular personality problems, there is doubt whether he is suitable for a personal, communitarian, and apostolic life in the Society or whether he will persevere in it.[22]

The text of the Norms resumes on page 87.

---

[21] See *CollDecr* d. 25, §2 (GC 30, d. 60); *Examen,* c. 2, no. 5 [29]; P. I, c. 3, no. 7 [175].

[22] See *CollDecr* d. 27 (GC 29, d. 39; see GC 5, dd. 52, 53; GC 6, d. 28).

be opened to large numbers or to anyone, as has been stated, without exceptional qualities.

[177] 8. ¹There are other impediments, none of which by itself [H] bars admission to the Society, but which nevertheless render the applicant less suitable; and the defect could be so serious that God would not be served by receiving one who has it.

[178] H. ¹Each of the impediments of this second category could of itself suffice to bar admission. ²But since there might be other compensating excellent qualities such that it would appear in our Lord that one of these defects ought to be tolerated, ³the discernment of this case is left to the discretion of the one who has the authority to admit. It will also belong to him to make a dispensation in such cases, subject to the judgment of the superior, who ought to be informed of any difficulty that might arise and whose opinion should be followed.

[179] 9. ¹These impediments are of the following kind. In regard to the interior, passions which seem uncontrollable, or sinful habits of which there is no hope of much emendation.

[180] 10. ¹An intention that is not as right as it ought to be for entrance into a religious institute but is mixed with human designs.

[181] 11. ¹Inconstancy or notable listlessness, so that the applicant seems unlikely to amount to much.

[182] 12. ¹Indiscreet devotions which lead some to fall into illusions and errors of importance.

[183] 13. ¹A lack of learning or of intellectual ability or of memory to acquire it, or of facility in speech to explain it, in candidates who manifest an intention or desire to progress farther than temporal coadjutors customarily do.

[184] 14. ¹A lack of judgment or a notable obstinacy in one's personal opinions, which is very troublesome in any congregation.

[185] 15. ¹In regard to the exterior, a lack of bodily integrity, illnesses and weakness, or notable ugliness [I].

Age too tender, or **too advanced** [K].[16]

Debts[17] or civil obligations [L].

---

[16] **Modified by CN 28, 6°.** (The age of more than fifty years is a cause of illicit admission.)

[17] (Note CIC 644: "Superiors are not to admit to the novitiate . . . those who, burdened by debts, cannot repay them"; and for other prescriptions, see CCEO 452.)

[186] I. ¹It is to be noticed that persons who have notable disfigurements or defects such as humpbacks and other deformities, whether they be natural or accidental, such as those from wounds and the like, are not suitable for this Society. ²**For these defects are hindrances for the priesthood**¹⁸ and do not help toward the edification of the neighbors with whom, according to our Institute, it is necessary to deal. ³An exception may be made where, as was stated above [162, 178], there are outstanding virtues and gifts of God such that bodily defects of this kind would be expected to increase rather than decrease edification.

[187] K. ¹**As to the age requirement** of fourteen years **for admission to** probation and twenty-five **for profession,**¹⁹ in particular cases where for special reasons it is judged conducive to the intended end of God's greater service that this age be anticipated, the superior general will be able to dispense after thought and consideration. ²Similarly, in cases of excessive age he will consider whether bearing with this detriment is expedient for the common good or not.

[188] L. ¹In regard to debts, great care should be taken that there be no occasion of scandal or disquiet; even more so in civil obligations where the law intervenes, over and above considerations of edification.

[189] 16. ¹The more one suffers from any these defects, the less suited he is to serve God our Lord in this Society for the aid of souls. ²Furthermore, the one charged with admissions should be vigilant that charity for an individual does not impair the charity for all, which should always be preferred as being of greater moment for the glory and honor of Christ the Lord.

---

¹⁸ (An irregularity because of bodily deformity that prevents one from properly carrying out his ministry at the altar—see 1917 CIC 984, 2°—no longer exists: CIC 1041.)

¹⁹ **Modified by** *CN* 119. (See note 6 to [160].)

Chapter 4

[1]The Manner of Dealing with Those Admitted

[190] 1. [2]We are strongly convinced in our Lord that it is of great importance for the service of his Divine and Supreme Majesty through this least Society that those received in it not only be tested for a long time before incorporation into it [3]but also be well known before they are admitted to the probation which is made by living in common with those of the house. [4]Hence, it is good that next to where we live in common there be quarters [A] where those being admitted may stay as guests for twelve to twenty days, or longer if it seems good to the superior, [5]so that during this time **they may be more fully informed about the Society and the Society may become better acquainted with them in our Lord.**[20]

[191] A. [1]*Where there cannot be a different house of first probation next to our own, some separation should be procured within the house [2]so that those being received will have less occasion to converse with persons other than those appointed by the superior.*

[192] 2. [1]Admission to this house, called the house of the first probation, may be given more quickly to applicants who clearly appear to be fit to serve God our Lord in this Society. [2]On the other hand, those who are clearly seen to be unsuitable may, with the assistance of advice and whatever other means charity may dictate so that they may serve God our Lord elsewhere, be dismissed right away.

[193] 3. [1]Sometimes the clarity needed on the Society's side may still be lacking even after the candidate has expressed his desire, been tactfully questioned about the first category of impediments, and had the substance of our Institute and the trials and difficulties entailed in it explained to him. [2]If this should happen, even though the applicant manifests an efficacious determination to enter the Society to live and die in it (and in general no one lacking such a determination should be admitted to the first probation [B]), the final reply and decision should be put off for a time [C], [3]during which the case can be considered and commended to God our Lord and appropriate means can be employed to get to know the applicant and also to test his steadfastness [D]. [4]But the extent of this postponement and investigation should be left to the prudent

---

[20] **Clarified by** *CN* **31.** (In regard to the way of doing first probation.)

CHAPTER 4
THE METHOD OF ADMITTING TO PROBATION

31   Those who seem suitable for the Society should spend some days of first probation, as seems necessary or suitable for each, inside or outside the community of the novices; they should consider in their own minds and before God their vocation, having before their eyes, if it seems appropriate, the different vocations that are possible—namely, that of a brother and that of a priest[23]—and also their intention, so as to be confirmed therein. They should also get to know better and to meditate on the documents, both the older ones and the recent ones, that describe the Society's purpose, spirit, and characteristics. At the same time the examination should be completed, if necessary, and any deficiencies that occurred in it prior to admission should be supplied. Toward the end of the first probation, they should make the Spiritual Exercises for at least three days.[24]

32   §1. One who enters the novitiate, if he has personal property, is to promise that he will renounce it whenever after the completion of the first year of probation superiors will mandate it.[25]

§2. This promise, which is neither a vow nor a mere intention, is made under this condition: "if he will have persevered and the superior will have ordered him."[26]

§3. The renunciation of property, however, should be made a short time before final vows and, unless the general decrees otherwise, should have no effect prior to the taking of these vows.[27]

§4. However, the resignation from ecclesiastical benefices, insofar as they still exist, should occur immediately after first vows and be made known to legitimate ecclesiastical authority as soon as possible; it will take effect, however, when its acceptance is communicated to the one making the resignation.[28]   ∎

---

[23] See GC 34, d. 7, no. 15.

[24] See *CollDecr* d. 30 (see GC 4, d. 67); P. I, c. 4, no. 1, A [190, 191]; no. 5 [198].

[25] See *CollDecr* d. 176, §1 (GC 3, d. 19); *Examen*, c. 4, no. 2 [54]; P. III, c. 1, nos. 7, 25, F [254–55, 287]; P. VI, c. 2, H [571]; contrary to CCEO 460, 467, §1, toward the end.

[26] *CollDecr* d. 176, §1 (GC 3, d. 19).

[27] CollDecr d. 176, §2 (see GC 7, d. 17, nos. 4–7; GC 15, d. 8); see CIC 668, §4; CCEO 467, §1.

[28] *CollDecr* d. 176, §3 (see GC 1, d. 140; GC 5, d. 19), see CIC 1272.

consideration of the one having authority to admit; and he should always keep in view the greater service of God.

[194]   B.   ¹If for valid reasons a candidate not yet entirely resolved to serve God our Lord in this Society is admitted into the house, he should be received as a guest and not for the first or the second probation. ²But the one in charge should not easily permit this for more than three days, nor without permission from the superior general or at least from the provincial. ³This permission should be granted less readily where there are novices present than where there are not.

[195]   C.   ¹This temporary postponement of the final reply and decision, and the investigation in order to know the applicant better, should ordinarily be observed. ²But in particular cases (for example, when unusual qualifications are present and also a danger that such persons would be turned away or much disturbed by the postponement), the appropriate investigations could be made more summarily ³and the applicants admitted into the house of the first probation or, after being examined, sent to other places of the Society.

[196]   D.   ¹The means which can be used to come to know the applicant are the summary examen which inquires about impediments of the first category, as well as the second category treated in chapter 3, such as lack of health or bodily integrity and civil obligations or debts.

²It will be similarly helpful if, besides the examiner, some additional persons from among those designated by the superior deal and associate with the applicant. ³Further, when his name and those who know him have been learned, information about him can be gathered from outside the house, if no one inside it knows him sufficiently.

⁴It will also help to have him **go to confession in our church for some time**²¹ before he enters the house. ⁵When the doubt persists, to have him make spiritual exercises will aid not a little toward gaining the clarity needed in his regard for the glory of God our Lord.

[197]   4.   ¹After the decision has been made in our Lord that it is proper to admit such an applicant to probation, he may enter, dressed as he customarily was or in the manner in which each one finds more devotion, unless the superior thinks otherwise. He should be placed as a guest in the aforementioned house or separate quarters, ²and on the second day he should be told how he should conduct himself in that place, and especially that (unless the

---

²¹ (Note by analogy CIC 630, §1: "Superiors are to recognize the due freedom of their members concerning the sacrament of penance"; see also CCEO 473, §2, 2°; 474, §2.)

superior for urgent reasons thinks otherwise) he should not deal either by word of mouth or by writing with others from outside or inside the house, except for certain persons who will be assigned to him by the superior. ³The purpose is that he may with greater freedom deliberate with himself and with God our Lord about his vocation and intention to serve his Divine and Supreme Majesty in this Society.

[198] 5. ¹When two or three days have passed after he entered the probation, he will begin to be examined more in detail according to the method explained amid the functions of the examiner. ²The text of the Examen should be left with him that he may consider it more slowly in private. ³Subsequently he will carefully read the bulls, Constitutions, and rules which must be observed in the Society and the house he enters *[E]*. **⁴Those who have studied should deliver a lecture on each branch of learning they have studied, in the presence of persons appointed by the superior, so as to give an idea of their capacities as to learning and manner of presentation.²²**

[199] E. ¹*For those who do not understand the bulls in Latin, an explanation of their substance would suffice, and likewise of the substance of the Constitutions and rules. ²That is, each candidate should be shown those of them which he himself needs to observe. ³A summary of them can be made and left (as also the Examen) with each candidate for him to consider more slowly in private.*

[200] 6. ¹During this time of the first probation the candidates will also manifest their consciences to the superior or the one he assigns, unless this is postponed through the superior's decision. ²They will make a general confession (if they have not done this previously) **{to the one appointed for them}.²³** ³In a book provided for this purpose, they write down and sign with their own hand what they have brought to the house *[F]*, and also their agreement to observe everything that has been proposed to them. ⁴Then, having concluded their reconciliation and received the most holy Sacrament, they will enter the house of common living and association where the second probation is made during a longer time.

[201] F. ¹*If they do not know how to write, someone else will write in their presence and in their name.*

---

²² **Modified by** *CN* 26, §2; 91. (Today the same purpose can be achieved in other ways.)

²³ **Abolished by** CIC 630, §1; CCEO 473, §2, 2°; 474, §2.

[202] 7. ¹What has been said about those newly entering will be observed in large part also with regard to those who come from studies or from other places of the Society, {who have not been admitted to profession or as formed coadjutors},²¹ and who have not been thoroughly examined elsewhere *[G]*. ²In this way, the greater the clarity employed in each instance, the more stable each candidate will be in his vocation ³and the better the Society will be able to discern whether it is expedient for him to remain in it for the greater glory and praise of God our Lord.

[203] *G.* ¹*Except for postponing admission to the first probation, which cannot be done with those who have already been in other houses of the Society, almost everything else holds true also of them.* ²*However, the better known and the more settled they are, the less necessary are the measures for knowing and assuring those admitted to probation.*

---

²¹ **Abolished.** (This norm cannot be applied, since all scholastics pronounce their first public vows before being admitted to studies; see *CN* 6, §1, 2°.)

PART II

¹THE DISMISSAL OF THOSE WHO WERE ADMITTED BUT DID NOT PROVE THEMSELVES FIT

CHAPTER 1

²WHO CAN BE DISMISSED, AND BY WHOM

[204] 1. ³Just as it is useful for the end sought in this Society, namely, the service of God our Lord by helping souls, to preserve and multiply the workers who are found fit and useful for carrying this work forward, ⁴so is it also expedient to dismiss those who are found unsuitable, and who as time passes make it evident that this is not their vocation or that their remaining in the Society does not serve the universal good. ⁵However, just as there should not be excessive readiness in admitting candidates, so should there be even less to dismiss them; instead, one should proceed with much consideration and pondering in our Lord. ⁶And although the more fully one has been incorporated into the Society the more serious ought the reasons to be, ⁷nevertheless, no matter how advanced the incorporation may be, there may be situations when a given person can and ought to be separated from the Society *[A]*, as will be seen in chapter 2.

[205] A. ²*Although all may be dismissed, as is stated in the Constitutions, there will be less difficulty in the case of some than of others. ³If those admitted to the house of the first probation should show, during those days before they live in common with the others, that they are not fit for the Society, they could be dismissed with greater facility than others.*

⁴*The second degree of difficulty is of those who are in the second probation in houses or colleges and have not bound themselves by any vow, when it is judged by experience that their remaining in the Society is not conducive to greater service to God.*

⁵{*The third degree is of those who on their own side have bound themselves by vows **but who have not yet been accepted among the***

PART II
DISMISSAL FROM THE SOCIETY

CHAPTER 1
THE FACULTY TO DISMISS

33   §1. The provincial, by a faculty habitually communicated by the general, can dismiss novices of his own province.

§2. The provincial can dismiss all members with simple vows, according to the faculty that the superior general, in individual cases, will have communicated to him.

§3. Only the general can dismiss the professed of solemn vows, according to the norms of universal law or our own law.[1]

> **The text of the Norms resumes on page 97.**

---

[1] See P. II, c. 1, no. 2, C [206, 208]; CIC 699, §1; CCEO 553.

*approved scholastics or formed coadjutors of the Society upon comple-
tion of the time given them for probation}.*[1]

[6]The fourth degree, requiring greater reflection and cause, **is
that of the approved scholastics.**[2]

[7]*The fifth degree, entailing still greater difficulty, is that of the
formed coadjutors whether spiritual or temporal, if it is judged necessary
to dismiss them after their taking their public though not solemn vows.*

[8]*In some cases even the professed, no matter what their rank and
dignity in the Society, could be dismissed, if it is judged that to retain
them would be harmful to the Society and a disservice to God our Lord.*

[9]*Beyond what has been stated, the more obligations there are
toward a person because of his good service, or the more qualities he has
for helping the Society in the service of God our Lord, the greater should
the difficulty be in dismissing him.* [10]*Similarly, on the contrary, the fact
that the Society has no obligation, and that the person is poorly suited to
help it toward its purpose in the divine service, will make his dismissal
easier.*

[206] 2. [1]The authority to dismiss will be vested primarily in the
Society as a whole when it is assembled in a general congregation.
[2]The superior general will have the same authority in all other cases
except one involving himself. [3]**As for the remaining members of the
Society, each one shares in this authority in the measure that it is
communicated to him by the head.**[3] [4]It is good, however, that it be
communicated amply to the provincial superiors *[B]* and, with
proper proportion, to the local superiors or rectors for whom its
sharing seems good *[C]*, [5]so that the subordination of holy obedience may be the better preserved in the whole body of the Society,
the better the members understand that they depend on their
immediate superiors and that it is very profitable and necessary for
them to be subject to these superiors in all things for Christ our
Lord.

[207] B. [1]*{Even if the superior general communicates very ample
authority in the letters patent which he sends to the subordinate
superiors in order that the subjects may have greater respect and be the*

---

[1] Abolished by *CN* 6, §1, 2°. (This third degree does not now exist; at
the completion of two years' probation, all either take public vows—and
thus are admitted among the approved scholastics or coadjutors—or, if
they are not suitable for the Society, they are dismissed.)

[2] (The same applies to approved brothers: see *CN* 6, §1, 2°.)

[3] Clarified by *CN* 33.

more humble and obedient toward them, ²*this authority may neverthe-*
less be restricted and limited by means of private letters, according to
*what seems expedient}.*⁴

[208] C. ¹*In regard to those who are in the first probation and in the*
second before taking their vows, whoever has the authority to admit them
may also dismiss them, unless special circumstances intervene. ²*Such*
would be the case if they have been sent to the house or college where
they are by the superior general or the provincial, or directed there by
someone to whom respect is due, or if they have deserved so well of the
Society that special respect is due to them. ³*For in these and similar cases*
a person of this kind ought not to be sent away by just any superior,
unless the reasons are so urgent and serious that beyond any doubt his
dismissal would be the will of his superiors.

⁴*In regard to those in the houses or colleges who are bound by*
vows **and the scholastics**⁵ *already approved after the two years of proba-*
tion, if it should become necessary to dismiss them, the local superior
should not do this without informing the provincial. ⁵*The provincial, in*
accordance with the authority given him by the general, will be able to
dismiss them or not without informing the general.

⁶**The formed coadjutors, whether spiritual or temporal, ought**
not to be dismissed without the knowledge and consent of the gener-
al⁶—⁷*unless in some very remote regions (such as the Indies) it should be*
necessary to communicate this authority to the provincial, or unless by
way of exception and for important reasons the general has communi-
cated this authority to someone in whom he had as much confidence as in
himself.

⁸**In regard to the professed, even less ought such authority be**
communicated to the lower superiors,⁷ *unless the general has been*
informed and the matter carefully weighed ⁹*so that it seems that to*
dismiss such a one helps for the service of God and the common good of
the Society. This is the case if he is contumacious or incorrigible and the like.

---

⁴ **Abolished.** (This way of acting, if it was ever in use, is now outdated
and contrary to the modern mentality.)

⁵ (The same applies to approved brothers: see *CN* 6, §1, 2°.)

⁶ **Clarified by** *CN* 35.

⁷ **Modified by** *CN* 33, §3; 35, §2; see CIC 695–702; CCEO 500–503. (Only
the general can dismiss the professed, with the confirmation of the Holy
See, according to the norms of universal law.)

CHAPTER 2

1THE CAUSES FOR DISMISSAL

[209] 1. 2The discreet charity of the superior who has the authority to dismiss ought to ponder before God our Lord the causes which suffice for dismissal. But to speak in general, they seem to be of four kinds.

[210] 2. 1The first cause is present if it is perceived in our Lord that someone's remaining in this Society would be contrary to the honor and glory of God, because this person is judged to be incorrigible in some passions or vices which offend his Divine Majesty. 2The more serious and culpable these are, the less ought they to be tolerated, even if they might not scandalize others because they are occult [A].

[211] A. 2How far toleration should be shown for certain of the defects which are said to be contrary to the divine honor, and those which are contrary to the good of the Society 3depends on many particular circumstances of persons, times, and places. Consequently this must be left to the discreet zeal of those who have charge of the matter. 4The more difficulty and doubt they have, the more will they commend the matter to God our Lord and the more will they discuss it with others who can be helpful toward perceiving the divine will in the matter.

[212] 3. 1The second cause is present if it is perceived in the Lord that to retain someone would be contrary to the good of the Society. Since this is a universal good, it ought to be preferred to the good of a single individual by one who is sincerely seeking the divine service. 2This would be the case if in the course of the probation **impediments or notable defects should be discovered which the applicant failed to mention earlier during the examination** [B],8 3or if experience should show that he would be quite useless and a hindrance rather than a help to the Society **because of his notable incompetency for any task whatever** [C];9 4much more so if it is judged that he would be harmful by the bad example of his life, especially if he shows himself unruly or scandalous in

---

8 (In regard to impediments that may be detected, see CIC 643 and CCEO 450. In regard to impediments and prohibitions to admission—CN 28—and other defects that were truly concealed, care should be taken to ascertain whether there may have been deceit in the admission, in which case it may have been invalid: see CIC 643, §1, 4°, and CCEO 450, 5°.)

9 **Clarified by** CN 34. (In regard to dismissal because of grave lack of aptitude.)

CHAPTER 2

CAUSES FOR DISMISSAL

34   Places in the Constitutions[2] that treat of dismissal because of a lack of health or aptitude are to be understood in this way:

1° If during the time of the novitiate, an illness or a weakness should be discovered of such a nature that the man does not seem to be able to carry on our work, he can be dismissed, while observing the law of charity;

2° However, after first vows and before final vows, no one can be dismissed against his will for causes for which he is not culpable, except only for outstanding ineptitude; nor can anyone be dismissed for poor health, whether physical or psychological, if his infirmity was contracted because of the Society's negligence or through work performed in it. Apart from this, however, poor health which is other than insanity can constitute a cause for even unwilling dismissal if in the judgment of experts it renders a man unsuited for leading his life in the Society, or if it is clear that before vows it was fraudulently concealed or disguised.[3]

> **The text of the Norms resumes on page 101.**

---

[2] See *Examen*, c. 7, no. 2 [123]; P. II, c. 2, nos. 3, 4, B [212, 213, 216].

[3] See GC 27, *CollDecr* d. 31; CIC 689, §§2–3; CCEO 547, §§2–3.

words or deeds [D]. ⁵To tolerate this would be attributable not to charity but to its very opposite on the part of one who is obliged to preserve the peace and well-being of the Society which is in his charge.

[213]   B. ¹In the case of someone who at the time of his entrance revealed an illness or a predisposition to one and was admitted on trial of his health, ²should it be seen he does not improve and it appears that he will be unable to perform the labors of the Society in the future, it will be permissible to dismiss him, rendering him such aid outside the house as true charity requires.

³If he entered without any condition, having manifested his illness but in hopes that he would prove more fit than is found by experience to be the case, then—even though he could be likewise dismissed in view of his lack of the health which would be necessary for our Institute—more reflection ought to be devoted to his case; ⁴and still more if he entered healthy and became ill in the service of the Society. ⁵For in that case, if he himself is unwilling, it would be wrong to send him out of the Society for that reason alone.

⁶If someone at his entrance concealed an infirmity, when this infirmity is discovered he can without doubt be more freely and justly dismissed. ⁷But whether he ought in fact to be sent away or not, by reason of other qualities of value for the divine service, will be left to the superior's discretion. ⁸This same reasoning holds if it is discovered that in some other matter he failed to tell the truth in his examination. ⁹But if he dissimulated one of the five impediments, in that case it is not just that he should remain in the Society, in conformity with what was said in Part I [164, 176].

[214]   C. ¹If he does not bring back a good report from the probationary experiences outside and inside the house, and if the remedies which charity requires before dismissal do not suffice, ²it is better to dismiss him than to incorporate into the Society persons who are seen to be unsuitable for its Institute.

[215]   D. ¹One is a scandal to others when he is occasion of their sinning by his example, more so if he entices them by persuasive words to some evil, particularly to instability in their vocation or to discord, or if he attempts something against the superiors or the common good of the Society. ²For in matters of this sort it is wrong that anyone who falls into them should remain in the Society.

³If it has been necessary to send someone away not so much because of the kind or number of his sins as to undo the scandal he has given to others, ⁴and if he should be a good subject except for this,

prudence will consider whether it is expedient to give him permission to go to some far-distant region of the Society, without leaving the Society.

[216] 4. ¹The third cause is present if someone's remaining is seen to be simultaneously against the good of the Society and of the individual. ²For example, this could arise from the body, if during the probation **such illnesses and weakness are observed in a person that it seems in our Lord that he would be unable to carry on the labor which is required in our manner of proceeding in order to serve God our Lord in that way.**¹⁰ ³It could also arise from the temper of his mind, if the one who was admitted to probation is unable to bring himself to live under obedience and to adapt himself to the Society's manner of proceeding, because he is unable or unwilling to submit his own judgment, or because he has other hindrances arising from nature or habits.

[217] 5. ¹The fourth cause is present if his remaining is seen to be contrary to the good of others outside the Society. ²This could arise from disclosure of **the bond of marriage**¹¹ or {**legal servitude**},¹² or of significant **debts**,¹³ when he had **concealed the truth**¹⁴ about the matter in the examination.

³Should any of these four causes exist, it seems that God our Lord will be better served by giving the person a decent dismissal than by employing indiscreet charity in retaining him in whom the causes are found.

---

¹⁰ **Clarified by** *CN* **34.** (In regard to dismissal because of lack of sufficient health for the exercise of our ministries.)

¹¹ (In the case of marriage the admission was invalid by reason of CIC 643, §1, 2°.)

¹² **Abolished.** (See note 13 to [173].)

¹³ (See note 17 to [185].)

¹⁴ (Perhaps the admission could have been invalid from deceit: see CIC 643, §1, 4°, and CCEO 450, 5°.)

CHAPTER 3

¹THE MANNER OF DISMISSING

[218] 1. ²With those who must be dismissed, that manner ought to be employed which before God our Lord is likely to give greater satisfaction to the one who dismisses as well as to the one dismissed and to the others within and without the house *[A]*. ³For the satisfaction of the one who dismisses, for the causes mentioned above, three points should be observed.

[219] A. *²It is to be noted that the Constitutions treat of the manner of dismissing persons when this is done publicly and for public reasons. ³Besides these, however, certain persons **might be dismissed occultly**¹⁵ in cases where the reasons are occult (and these can be many, some of them without sin) and perturbation among the others is feared if they are not disclosed. ⁴In such cases it is better to send those dismissed away from the house on some pretext such as their going through experiences, rather than to make public their dismissal.*

⁵To dismiss such persons in this way, it will suffice that the superior who has authority for this, commending himself to God our Lord and hearing the opinion of one or several others (if he judges in the Lord that he ought to discuss the matter with them), should make his decision and put it into effect.

⁶It is also to be noted that what has been stated about the manner of dismissing is more applicable to those who are in probations and less to those who have been incorporated into the Society as approved scholastics and formed coadjutors; ⁷and much less to the professed, in whose case the charity and discretion of the Holy Spirit will indicate the manner which ought to be used in the dismissal, should God our Lord permit this to become necessary.

[220] 2. ¹The first point to be observed is that he should pray and order prayers in the house for this intention (although the person's identity remains unknown), that God our Lord may make his holy will known in this case.

[221] 3. ¹The next point is that he should confer with one or more persons in the house who seem more suitable and hear their opinions.

---

¹⁵ (Dismissal of itself is a public fact at least by law; therefore it can only be occult insofar as it can be carried out discreetly.)

CHAPTER 3

THE MANNER OF DISMISSAL

35   §1. As to the manner of dismissing formed members with simple vows, besides automatic dismissal provided in universal law,[4] the Society retains its proper right flowing from the very nature of their vows, observing, however, the principles of natural and canonical equity and the right of the one being dismissed to have suspensive recourse to the Holy See.[5]

§2. In the manner of dismissing the professed of solemn vows, the universal law must be observed.[6]

The text of the Norms resumes on page 105.

---

[4] See CIC 694; CCEO 497.

[5] See *FI* no. 9; *Examen,* c. 6, no. 8, A [119, 120]; P. V, c. 4, B [536]; Resp. of Commis. for Interp. CIC, June 29, 1918 (*ActRSJ* 2:608); see also *ActRSJ* 13:574–75. Hence there must be grave causes for a dismissal, truly proved, that are known to the superior, and these must be revealed to the member, giving him the opportunity to reply. If recourse is had to the Holy See, the dismissal does not have effect until an answer has been given.

[6] See CIC 694–96; CCEO 500–503.

[222]   4. ¹The third point is that, ridding himself of all affection and keeping before his eyes the greater divine glory and the common good, and the good of the individual as far as possible, he should weigh the reasons on both sides and make his decision to dismiss or not.

[223]   5. ¹For the satisfaction of the one dismissed, three further points ought to be observed. One, pertaining to the exterior, is that as far as possible he should leave the house without shame or dishonor and take with him whatever belongs to him *[B]*.

[224]   *B.* ¹*In regard to what is found to belong to him, there is no difficulty in deciding that he should take it.* ²*But with respect to what he may have spent or given to the Society, or in case he stayed in one of its houses or colleges fraudulently,* ***it will be left to the discretion of the one who dismisses him, taking into account the demands of equity and edification, to decide whether or not he ought to be given anything beyond what is found to belong to him, and if so, how much.***¹⁶

[225]   6. ¹The second point, pertaining to the interior, is to try to send him away with as much love and charity for the house and as much consoled in our Lord as is possible.

[226]   7. ¹The last, pertaining to his personal condition, is to try to guide him in taking up some other good means of serving God, in religious life or outside it as may seem more conformable to his divine will, ²assisting him with advice and prayers and whatever in charity may seem best.

---

¹⁶ Clarified by *CN* 36.

[227]   8. ¹Likewise, for the satisfaction of the others inside and outside the house, three things ought to be observed. ²One is that everything possible should be done to ensure that no one is left troubled in spirit by the dismissal; satisfactory grounds for it can be given to whoever needs it *[C]*, ³touching as little as possible upon faults in the person which are not public (even if he has them).

[228]   *C. ¹To withhold or to give, in public or in private, an explanation of the causes for the dismissal will be more expedient or less in proportion to the greater or less esteem and love in which the person was held within and without the house.*

[229]   9. ¹A second is that they should not be left disaffected or with a bad opinion in his regard, as far as this is possible. ²Rather, they should have compassion for him and love him in Christ and recommend him in their prayers to the Divine Majesty, that God may deign to guide him and have mercy on him.

[230]   10. ¹A third is to take steps so that those in the house who are not acting with as much edification as they ought may profit by this example and may fear the same thing if they refuse to do so; ²and also that persons outside the house who have learned of the matter may be edified at seeing that nothing is tolerated in the house that ought not to be, for the greater glory of God our Lord.

CHAPTER 4

¹THE SOCIETY'S WAY OF DEALING WITH THOSE WHO LEAVE OF THEMSELVES OR ARE DISMISSED

[231] 1. ²It seems to us in our Lord that, when persons are sent away or depart of their own accord from one place, they should not be received in another **unless the person who dismissed them, or the superior of the place from which they left, or the superior general, or whoever acts for him has been informed and given his consent,**¹⁷ ³lest lack of knowledge and information occasion any mistake, to the disservice of God our Lord [A].

[232] *A. ²It is said in general that one who departed of his own accord or was dismissed should not be received into another house without informing and getting word from the superior of the house or college where the person had been. ³Nevertheless, it will be left to the discretion of the superior of the house where the person goes, to consider whether or not to receive him unofficially until he receives a reply from the superior whose order he must follow.*

[233] 2. ¹The privileges which were granted to such persons as members of the Society are understood to cease from the time they cease to be members.

[234] 3. ¹**Those who are dismissed should be advised that they remain free from the simple vows if they took them according to the formula which the Society uses and which will be seen in Part V; and that consequently they do not need a dispensation to be freed from them.**¹⁸

[235] 4. ¹In the case of those who leave without permission, if they were previously regarded as unsuitable for the Society no effort need be made to bring them back; ²instead, they should be directed to another institute where they may serve God our Lord, and their vows dispensed so that they will not be left with scruples.

[236] 5. ¹If they are persons such that it seems a service to God our Lord not to let them go in this way, especially if it is clear that they left through some strong temptation or when misled by others, ²steps may be taken to bring them back **{and the privileges granted by the Apostolic See concerning this matter can be em-**

---

¹⁷ **Clarified by** *CN* **38.**

¹⁸ (See CIC 701 and CCEO 502, according to which "vows, rights, and obligations derived from profession cease ipso facto by legitimate dismissal.")

CHAPTER 4

THE MANNER OF PROCEEDING WITH THOSE
WHO ARE DISMISSED

36   The Society is bound by no juridical obligation toward those who are dismissed, in the form of compensation for any work they performed in the Society; nevertheless, superiors should see that equity and charity are fulfilled, by giving them a subsidy insofar as it is needed and the resources of the house or province permit.[7]

37   Someone who has been dismissed unwillingly, without fault on his part and for no legitimate reason, in such a way that his dismissal is invalid, should be restored to his prior state without having to repeat the novitiate.[8]

38   One who has been lawfully dismissed from the Society at his own request after completing the novitiate or after first vows, unless the reasons for which he was dismissed still continue,[9] can be readmitted by the superior general, after hearing the opinion of his council, without the obligation to repeat the novitiate. It is the role of the superior general to determine an appropriate probation prior to pronouncement of the vows of the biennium and the length of time to be spent before final vows.[10]   ■

---

[7] See *CollDecr* d. 33 (see GC 7, d. 3); P. II, c. 3, B [224]; CIC 702; CCEO 503.

[8] *CollDecr* d. 32 (GC 8, d. 58).

[9] See P. II, c. 4, no. 7 [241].

[10] See CIC 690, §1; contrary to CCEO 493, §2.

ployed, to the extent the superior thinks good in the Lord} *[B]*.[19] ³When a subject thus won back returns, it will be left to the discretion of the one in charge to consider whether he ought to make some satisfaction and how great it ought to be [C], ⁴or whether it is better to proceed altogether in a spirit of gentleness, taking into account the good of the subject won back and the edification of the members of the house.

[237] *B.* ¹*In the case of persons who abandon the Society, even if they are judged fit for it, and then enter and take the habit in another religious institute, it does not seem that the Society should attempt or take legal measures to bring them back.*[20] ²*Prior to their taking the religious habit, such measures as well-ordered and discreet charity dictates may be taken to win them back to the place where it is judged in our Lord that they should serve him.*

[238] *C.* ¹*In regard to the satisfaction to be made by those who return of their own accord and are received, or by those who return after being won back, its purpose is the edification of the others and the help of the person who returned.* ²*Therefore determination should be made in the light of circumstances of persons, times, and places whether or not such satisfaction should be made; and, if it should, how much.* ³*This entire matter must be referred to the discretion of the superior in whose house or college the person enters.*

[239] 6. ¹If someone returns of his own accord to the house or college which he left without permission, and if he is judged suitable in other respects to serve God our Lord there, it should be seen whether he comes with a genuine intention to persevere *[D]* and to undergo satisfaction or trials of whatever sort. ²If not, it would seem to be a sign that he does not come with genuine repentance or deserve to be accepted.

---

[19] **Abolished.** (The privileges referred to here, with a change in the universal law, are no longer applicable, because such apostates do not exist; but superiors should make diligent efforts to seek after members unlawfully absent from the religious house with the intention of withdrawing from the control of their superiors and aid them to return and persevere in their vocation: see CIC 665, §2.)

[20] (In the present law, this can only refer to those who have not yet pronounced vows after the two-year novitiate, since from CIC 643, §1, 3°, "one who is presently held by a sacred bond with any institute of consecrated life is invalidly admitted to the novitiate"; see also CCEO 450, 7°.)

[240] D. ¹*When there is doubt about the constancy of those who return of their own accord, they could be placed in a hospital or in other experiences where, by serving Christ's poor out of love to him for some time, they may show their stability and constancy, ²and in part do penance for their earlier fickleness.*

[241] 7. ¹If someone who has been dismissed returns to the same house from which he was justly sent away and is ready to make all satisfaction, and if the same causes for which he was dismissed still persist, it is certain that he ought not to be admitted. ²If they do not persist and the one who dismissed him judges that God our Lord would be served through his being received back into that or another house, he should inform the general or the provincial superior and follow the directive which will be given him.

[242] 8. ¹Whether the person returning had left of his own accord or had been dismissed, if he is readmitted he should be examined over again; upon entering the house he should make his general confession, from the last which he made, ²and undergo the other probations or experiences as the superior judges proper, looking always to general and individual edification, for the glory of God our Lord.

PART III
¹THE PRESERVATION AND PROGRESS OF THOSE WHO REMAIN IN PROBATION

CHAPTER 1
²THE PRESERVATION PERTAINING TO THE SOUL AND TO PROGRESS IN VIRTUES

[243] 1. ³Just as with regard to the admission of those whom God our Lord calls to our Institute by giving them suitable ability for it, and the dismissal of those who through lack of such ability reveal that they have not been called by his Divine Wisdom, there is need of the considerations expounded so far, ⁴so also due consideration and provident care must be employed toward preserving in their vocation those who are being retained and tested in the houses or colleges, and toward enabling them to make progress both in spirit and in virtues along the path of the divine service, ⁵in such a manner that care is also taken of the health and bodily strength necessary to labor in the Lord's vineyard. ⁶Consequently what pertains to the soul will be treated first [243–91] and then what pertains to the body [292–306].

[244] 2. ¹In regard to the soul, it is of great importance to keep those who are in probation away from all imperfections and from whatever can impede their greater spiritual progress. ²For this purpose it is highly expedient that they should cease from all communication by conversation and letters with persons who may dampen their resolves [A]; ³further, that while they advance along the path of the spirit, **they should deal only with persons and about matters which help them toward what they were seeking when they entered the Society for the service of God our Lord** [B].¹

[245] A. ²If in some place a person is bothered or disquieted by persons who are not walking in the path of the spirit, the superior should consider whether it will be expedient to have him move to another place where he can apply himself better in the divine service. ³In that case his

---

¹ **Clarified by** *CN* 53. (In regard to healthy relations with others.)

PART III
SPIRITUAL FORMATION OF NOVICES

CHAPTER 1

THE NOVITIATE IN GENERAL

39   §1. If it can be done, a novitiate house should be established in each province.[1]

§2. The novitiate house should, as far as possible, be located in a place where the novices' probation can be conducted according to the manner of life and mission proper to the Society.[2]

40   The novitiate begins on the day when the candidate, by the authority of the provincial or some other authorized person, is admitted into the novitiate house to begin probation, even first probation.[3]

41   The novitiate is to continue for two complete years,[4] nor can the general licitly dispense from this except for reasons of serious moment and after observing the prescriptions of universal law.[5]

42   Except for the time required by universal law, the novitiate can validly be undergone in any house of the Society.[6]

43   §1. Ordinarily the novitiate should be common for all candidates.[7] The only differences in method introduced are those

---

[1] GC 27, *CollDecr* d. 35; see CIC 647; CCEO 522.

[2] See GC 31, d. 8, no. 22.

[3] See GC 27, *CollDecr* d. 37.

[4] See Gregory XIII, *Ascendente Domino; Examen,* c. 1, no. 12 [16]; c. 4, nos. 16, 41 [71, 98]; P. IV, c. 3, no. 3 [336].

[5] GC 27, *CollDecr* d. 36, §1; P. V, c. 1, C [515]; see CIC 648; CCEO 523.

[6] See *CollDecr* d. 36, §2 (GC 7, d. 98); CIC 647–49; CCEO 522.

[7] See GC 32, d. 6, no. 12.

future superior ought to be given such information about the man as will enable him the better to assist him and the others in his charge.

[246]   B. ¹*If it seems on some occasion that someone should be permitted to speak to relatives or friends whom he had in the world, this ought to be done in the presence of someone designated by the superior and briefly, unless for special reasons he who holds the principal charge orders otherwise.*² ²{*Likewise, if anyone in the house should write to any place or person, it should be done with permission, and he should show the letter to the one appointed by the superior.* ³*If anyone writes to him, the letters should likewise go first to the one who was appointed by the superior, and he will see them and give them or not to the one to whom they are addressed, according as he thinks expedient for his greater good, to the divine glory*}.³

[247]   3. ¹For the same reason they should not leave the house except at the time and with the companion the superior decides upon *[C]*; and within the house they should not converse with one another according to their own choice but with those whom the superior designates, ²so that they may be edified and helped by the others in our Lord through their good example and spiritual conversation, and not the opposite *[D]*.

[248]   C. ¹*The superior will consider whether certain persons of whom he has assurance may be sent out alone; and also whether or not he should grant some a single permission for many occasions, or whether they must ask permission each time they go out.*

[249]   D. ¹*Ordinarily it is good for the novices not to converse with one another but to keep silence among themselves except for the occasions when speech is necessary, dealing rather with mature and discreet persons whom the superior will indicate for each one.* ²*Likewise, where two have their beds in the same room, one of them should be a person of whom there is no doubt that the other will be improved by him. For the same reason, too, it is good to have some of the older men between the rooms of the younger ones who are alone.*

³*Ordinarily, no one should enter another's room without permission of the superior; and if he has permission to enter, the door should stay open as long as he is in the room with the other, so that the superior and the other officials appointed for the purpose may enter whenever it is proper.*

---

² **Clarified by** *CN* 53. (In regard to healthy relations with them.)

³ **Abolished by GC 34.**

required by the different modes of one and the same service to which all are called.[8]

§2. In this spirit, from the beginning a suitable sharing of life and work should be fostered among all the novices, whereby they can be thoroughly known to one another and helped to esteem and realize each one's own vocation. In external matters such as food, clothing, and lodging, there should be complete equality.[9]

CHAPTER 2

THE FORMATION OF THE NOVICES

44   §1. The novitiate is a time at once of formation and of probation, during which the grace of vocation should be cultivated and during which it should already manifest its fruitfulness.[10]

§2. But for those who entered as indifferents, it is also an opportune time to discern their future vocation to brotherhood or priesthood.[11]

45   §1. The apostolic purpose is to be considered the principle that regulates the entire formation of our members.[12] Therefore, the whole formation of our members from the novitiate on must be understood and promoted as a process of integration into the apostolic body of the Society, as a formation in mission.[13]

§2. What is later set down in Part IV about the formation of our members after the novitiate in general and about their spiritual formation and community life is also to be applied appropriately to the novices.

46   §1. A vocation is to be tested by various experiments that, in St. Ignatius's view, constitute the specific characteristic of the novitiate; these must place the novices in those circumstances wherein they can give evidence of what they really are and show

---

[8] GC 31, d. 8, II, toward the beginning.

[9] GC 31, d. 8, no. 18.

[10] GC 31, d. 8, II, toward the beginning; see CIC 646.

[11] See GC 34, d. 7, no. 15.

[12] GC 31, d. 8, no. 4.

[13] See GC 32, d. 6, no. 7; see nos. 12–13.

[250] 4. ¹All should take special care to guard with great diligence the gates of their senses (especially the eyes, ears, and tongue) from all disorder, ²to preserve themselves in peace and true humility of their souls, and to show this by their silence when it should be kept and, when they must speak, by the discretion and edification of their words, ³the modesty of their countenance, the maturity of their walk, and all their movements, without giving any sign of impatience or pride. ⁴In all things they should try and desire to give the advantage to the others, esteeming them all in their hearts as if they were their superiors [Phil. 2:3] and showing outwardly, in an unassuming and simple religious manner, the respect and reverence appropriate to each one's state, ⁵so that by consideration of one another they may thus grow in devotion and praise God our Lord, whom each one should strive to recognize in the other as in his image.

[251] 5. ¹While eating they should be careful to observe temperance, decorum, and propriety both interior and exterior in everything. ²A blessing should precede the meal, and it should be followed by a thanksgiving which all should recite with proper devotion and reverence. ³**While the meal is being eaten, food should be given also to the soul, through the reading of a book**⁴ which is devotional rather than difficult so that all can understand it and draw profit from it, or through having someone preach during that time according to what the superiors may order, or through doing something similar for the glory of God our Lord *[E]*.

[252] *E. ¹Similar things might be the reading of edifying letters or some other exercise that might on occasion be deemed appropriate.*

[253] 6. ¹Generally, all those who are in good health should be busy with spiritual or exterior occupations. ²Furthermore, just as those who perform duties should be given alleviation if they need it, so if they have time left over they should occupy themselves with other things, ³so that idleness, the source of all evils, may have no place in the house as far as this is possible.

[254] 7. ¹So that they may begin to experience the virtue of holy poverty, all should be taught that they must not have the use of anything as their own. ²**However, it is not necessary for them to dispossess themselves of their property *[F]* during the probation, except where the superior should order this, after expiration of**

---

⁴ **Clarified** (GC 31, d. 20, no. 1, entrusted to the superior general prudently to provide what should be done about reading at table in each province or region.)

how they have made their own the spiritual attitudes proper to our vocation. New experiments, of the sort that would fulfill this purpose today, ought to be prudently and boldly pursued.

§2. Primacy in the novices' formation should be given to the Spiritual Exercises, since of all the experiments they are the chief and fundamental one. Let them, therefore, be well prepared for, made at the most advantageous time, and presented in all their force and spiritual vigor.[14]

47 §1. Education towards familiarity with God in prayer should be carried out in the apostolic atmosphere of the Exercises. The daily exercises of piety should tend to arouse personal love for Christ and teach the seeking of familiar communion with God in all things. Care should also be taken that the novices clearly understand how the different means presented in the Constitutions themselves (examination of conscience, prayer, meditation, reading, and so forth) serve to complement one another.[15]

§2. Besides the time of prayer prescribed for all in probation (see no. 67, §2), novices should give themselves to prayer for another half hour daily. The length of this time of prayer can be discreetly prolonged or lessened for each one according to the judgment of the director.[16]

48 §1. All the novices during the time of the novitiate should receive both a deeper initiation into the mystery of Christ and a fuller knowledge of the sources of the Society's spiritual doctrine and manner of life, chiefly to be drawn from the Society's history and the examples of the saints.

§2. Hence all should be instructed from the outset concerning the religious and apostolic character of our common vocation, and of the different ways of sharing in it, according to the proper identity of a priest and a brother in the one mission of the Society.

§3. Instruction should be given from the outset to the scholastic novices concerning the priestly character of their vocation,[17]

---

[14] See GC 31, d. 8, nos. 14–15; see *Examen,* c. 4, nos. 9–10 [64–65]; no. 16 [71]; c. 7, no. 6 [127]; P. IX, c. 3 no. 8, E [746, 748].

[15] GC 31, d. 8, no. 16.

[16] *CollDecr* d. 41 (GC 1, d. 97; GC 4, d. 59; GC 31, d. 56, no. 1).

[17] See GC 34, d. 6, no. 23.

the first year,[5] because he judges that for some person such property is an occasion of temptation and of making less progress in spirit because of his placing some disordered love and confidence in it. ³In that case the disposition should be made in conformity with the counsels of Christ our Lord [G]. ⁴However, it is left to the devotion of each one to apply his property, or a part of it, to one pious work rather than to another, according to what God our Lord will give him to perceive as being more conducive to his divine service, as was stated in the Examen [53–59].

[255]   F. ¹*The dispossession applies both to a person's own property presently held, either in his own power or in that of others, and to his right or claim in court to any property he expects, whether of secular or ecclesiastical goods. ²The time when this should be done will be left to the arrangement of the superior general or the one to whom he delegates the matter.*

[256]   G. ¹*Before entering, each one may do what he pleases with his property;* ²*but after his entrance he ought to dispose of it, whether it be ecclesiastical or secular, as befits a man leading the spiritual life. ³Consequently, if he deems that he ought to dispose of it by giving it to relatives, he ought to have recourse to and abide by the judgment of one, two, or three persons of learning and goodness, so as to do what they judge to be more perfect and pleasing to God our Lord, ⁴after consideration of all the circumstances, as is stated at greater length in the Examen [53–59].*

[257]   8. ¹Likewise they should understand that they may not lend, borrow, or dispose of anything in the house unless the superior knows it and consents.

[258]   9. ¹If someone at entrance or after he has entered under obedience should find it to his devotion to dispose of his temporal goods, or a part of them, in favor of the Society, ²it is beyond any doubt a matter of greater perfection, detachment, and abnegation of all self-love not to single out particular places with fond affection, or through that affection to apply his goods to one place rather than to another [H]. ³Rather, he does better if, while desiring the greater and more universal good of the Society (which is directed to greater divine service and greater universal good and spiritual progress of souls), ⁴he leaves to him who has charge of the whole Society this judgment as to whether the goods ought to be applied to one place rather than to another of that same province.

---

⁵ **Clarified by** *CN* **32.** (How this renunciation is to be understood and practiced.)

and to the brothers concerning the meaning and value of their works and activities for promoting the objective of the Society.[18]

49   Let self-denial be primarily exercised humbly and simply in the everyday demands of our vocation. Particular mortifications should, however, be undertaken, under the guidance of obedience, as indicated by the individual's requirements, the Church's call, and the world's needs. Moreover, let the novices learn, in theory and by practice, to shape their life by austerity and sobriety.[19]

50   The practice of community life should both develop the brotherhood of our members and benefit the affective maturity of the novices.[20]

51   Human virtues are to be fostered, because they make the apostolate more fruitful and religious life happier; among these virtues are goodness of heart, sincerity, strength of mind and constancy, diligent care for justice, openness of mind and respect for differing beliefs of others, politeness, and other similar qualities.[21]

52   The novices are to be stimulated to assume responsibilities with prudent and discerning charity, so that they may more successfully acquire spiritual maturity and more freely adhere to their vocation.[22]

53   Although entrance into the novitiate should entail a real separation from the life previously led in the world, superiors should nevertheless provide that the novices, while consistently maintaining a spirit of recollection, should have sufficient social contact with their contemporaries (both within and outside the Society). Likewise the necessary separation from parents and friends should take place in such a way that genuine progress in affective balance and supernatural love is not impeded.[23]

54   §1. Education towards a discerning charity by means of spiritual direction and obedience presupposes complete trust and freedom between Father Master and the novices.[24]

---

[18] See GC 31, d. 8, no. 21.

[19] GC 31, d. 8, no. 20.

[20] GC 31, d. 8, no. 18.

[21] See GC 31, d. 8, no. 10.

[22] See GC 31, d. 8, no. 23.

[23] GC 31, d. 8, no. 22; see P. III, c. 1, no. 2, A, B; no. 3, C [244–48].

[24] GC 31, d. 8, no. 19.

⁵For the general is better able than another to know what is expedient and what pressing needs are present throughout the whole Society. Furthermore, he can take account of the kings, princes, and lords, seeing to it that no cause of offense may be given to them ⁶and that the matter may lead to the greater edification of all, and to greater spiritual progress of souls and glory of God our Lord.

[259] H. ¹*In this matter as in all others, the rectors, local superiors, or provincials, and any other persons who deal with the one desiring to make such a disposition ought to represent to him that which is more perfect and in which he will gain greater merit before God our Lord. ²Nevertheless, if they should observe in him a preference for one place more than another (which is something imperfect), even though he does give up his own judgment, they could inform the superior general, or the one who holds his place, as to whether it seems that some imperfection ought to be tolerated ³in the hope that it will one day cease and that God our Lord will supply what is lacking to the person for the greater divine glory and his own greater perfection.*

[260] 10. ¹They should be taught how to guard themselves from the illusions of the devil in their devotions and how to defend themselves from all temptations. They should know the means which may exist for overcoming these and applying themselves to the pursuit of the true and solid virtues, ²whether with many spiritual visitations or with fewer, by endeavoring always to go forward in the path of the divine service.

[261] 11. ¹They should practice the daily examination of their consciences and **confess and receive Communion at least every eight days,**⁶ **unless the superior for some reason orders otherwise.** ²**{There should be one confessor for all, assigned by him who has charge of the others}.**⁷ ³Or if this is impossible *[I]*, everyone should at least have his own regular confessor to whom he should keep his conscience completely open, **{and who should be informed about the cases which the superior reserves to himself. ⁴These cases will be those where it appears necessary or highly expedient for the superior to have knowledge, so that he may the better provide**

---

⁶ **Modified by** CIC 663, §2, and CCEO 473; 474, §1. (With regard to frequenting the sacraments.)

⁷ **Abolished by** CIC 630, §1, and CCEO 473, §2, 2°; 474, §2. ("Superiors are to recognize the due freedom of their members concerning the sacrament of penance. . . .")

§2. It will benefit the spiritual, apostolic, intellectual, and affective formation of the novices if they are associated with some other selected men besides the director, who at certain times can assist him in his work, in order to provide the novices with a richer and fuller image of the Ignatian vocation.[25]

55   §1. Except for the time prescribed by universal law for the validity of the novitiate, the provincial can permit the novices, but not beyond one semester, the type of study, especially theological and philosophical, needed for obtaining a diploma or for completing that sort of formation by which one is prepared to take up duties. But if study of this sort is to be prolonged beyond a semester, the matter is to be referred to the general. Let this permission be given only to those to whom it can be granted without spiritual harm, taking into consideration persons and places, as will be judged in the Lord.[26]

§2. After fulfilling the canonical time required by universal law, no one who is not a priest is to be sent to colleges of extern students to act as a teacher there or a prefect of boys; nor should he be occupied in other services outside the novitiate unless these are undertaken as experiments.[27]

56   When the time of the noviceship is ended, if some of the novices, well endowed with the qualities requisite for this vocation, still have not shown sufficient maturity and there is hope that within a reasonable period of time they will have attained it, major superiors, using our privilege,[28] may postpone the taking of first vows or even extend the novitiate for a time by introducing some longer experiment; but without permission of the general this should not be prolonged beyond a semester.[29]

---

[25] GC 31, d. 8, no. 25; see CIC 651, §§2–3; CCEO 524, §2.

[26] See *CollDecr* d. 38, §1 (GC 2, d. 14; GC 20, d. 12, 2°).

[27] See *CollDecr* d. 38, §2 (GC 20, d. 12, 3°).

[28] Council of Trent, sess. 25, Concerning Regulars, c. 16 (Dec. 3, 1563).

[29] See GC 31, d. 8, no. 24. See *Examen,* c. 4, no. 43 [100]; P. V, c. 1, no. 3 [514].

remedies and protect those whom he has in his charge from any harm}.[8]

[262] 1. ¹This might not be conveniently possible because of the large numbers, or because some individual would seem to be helped more by another confessor than by the ordinary one, for reasons that might arise. The superior will consider these and provide as he judges in our Lord to be expedient.

[263] 12. ¹It will be beneficial to have a faithful and competent person to instruct and teach the novices how to conduct themselves inwardly and outwardly, to encourage them to this, to remind them of it, and to give them loving admonition [K]; ²a person whom all those who are in probation may love and to whom they may have recourse in their temptations and open themselves with confidence, hoping to receive from him in our Lord counsel and aid in everything. ³They should be advised, too, that they ought not to keep secret any temptation which they do not tell to him or to their confessor or to the superior, being happy to have their entire soul completely open to him. ⁴Moreover, they will tell him not only their defects but also their penances or mortifications, or their devotions and all their virtues, with a pure desire to be directed if in anything they have gone astray, ⁵and not wishing to be guided by their own judgment unless it is in agreement with the opinion of him whom they have in place of Christ our Lord.

[264] K. ¹This person will be the master of novices or whomever the superior appoints as being fittest for this charge.

[265] 13. ¹Temptations ought to be guarded against by their opposites, for example, if someone is seen to be inclined to pride, by exercising him in lowly matters deemed helpful for humbling him; and similarly of other evil inclinations.

[266] 14. ¹Furthermore, for the sake of decorum and propriety, **it is expedient that women should not enter the houses or colleges but only the churches** [L];[9] ²and that arms should not be kept in the house, nor instruments for vain purposes [M], but only such instruments which are helpful toward the end which the Society seeks, the divine service and praise.

[267] L. ¹The custom that women should not enter houses or colleges of the Society ought generally to be observed. ²However, if they are per-

---

[8] **Abolished.** (In present law, universal or proper to the Society, there are no reserved [cases] sins.)

[9] **Clarified by** CN 147, §3; 327, §§2–3.

CHAPTER 3

OTHER THINGS REFERRING TO NOVICES

57   §1. As far as concerns all goods that they actually possess, novices should, from the time they first enter and for the duration of the novitiate,

1° Yield the administration of these goods to whomever they choose; only the general can dispense them from this obligation;

2° Make disposition of both the use and the usufruct of these goods; this can be used for paying debts, if there are any, or otherwise for the benefit of the poor or other pious causes (unless just reasons suggest some other course), inside the Society or outside it, as the one making the disposition shall wish, but with the consent of the provincial. Those making the disposition may, to be sure, decide that the gain will accrue to the principal; but they may not use these goods in any other way for their own advantage.

§2. Before first vows they should, for the entire period before renunciation

1° Yield the administration of these same goods to whomever they wish;

2° Dispose of the use and the usufruct as in §1, 2°; but they may not decide that after the novitiate the gain should accrue to the principal beyond the amount necessary to ensure that the purchasing power of the capital remains undiminished.

§3. If they wish, they may by means of a single act of disposition at the beginning of the novitiate satisfy the requirements of both §1 and §2.[30]

58   Any private vows that novices may have pronounced prior to their entrance are suspended for as long as they remain in the Society.[31]   ■

---

[30] *CollDecr* d. 40 (see GC 7, d. 17, nos. 1, 2, 3, 6; GC 10, d. 2; GC 11, d. 15; GC 12, d. 36; GC 17, d. 11); see interpretation of Fr. General for the practical conduct of good governance, March 8, 1984 (*ActRSJ* 19:184); see CIC 668, §§1–2; CCEO 525, §2.

[31] *CollDecr* d. 39 (GC 1, d. 132); see CIC 1198 and CCEO 894, concerning private vows taken before profession.

sons of great charity, or of high rank as well as charity, the superior in his discretion may for just reasons give a dispensation for them to come in and look about if they so wish.

[268] M. ¹Such are **instruments for games and for music,**¹⁰ *profane books, and similar objects.*

[269] 15. ¹The procedure to be followed in corrections and penances will be left to the discreet charity of the superior and of those whom he may delegate in his place, ²who will measure them in accord with the disposition of persons and with general and individual edification, for the divine glory [N]. ³Each one ought to accept them in a good spirit with a genuine desire of his emendation and spiritual profit, even if they are not given for a defect that is blameworthy.

[270] N. ¹In giving corrections it should be noted that, while discretion may change this order in a particular case, those who fall into a fault ought to be admonished the first time with love and with gentleness, ²the second time with love and in such a way that they feel abashed and ashamed, ³the third time with love and the instilling of fear. ⁴However, the penance for public faults must be public, disclosing only what will most conduce to the edification of all.

[271] 16. ¹**In the house there should be a syndic**¹¹ whose duty is to look out for all details regarding matters of decorum and exterior propriety. ²He should go through the church and the house, note what is unbecoming, and inform the superior or, if he has received such authority, the person at fault, so as to be of greater help in our Lord.

[272] 17. ¹In their illnesses all should try to draw fruit from them, not only for themselves but for the edification of others, by not being impatient or difficult to please, ²but instead having and showing great patience and obedience toward the physician and infirmarian, and employing good and edifying words which show that they accept the sickness as a gift from the hand of our Creator and Lord, since it is a gift no less than is health.

[273] 18. ¹As far as possible, we should all think alike and speak alike, in conformity with the Apostle's teaching [Phil. 2:2]; ²and **differing doctrines ought not to be permitted,**¹² either orally in

---

¹⁰ **Abolished by GC 34.** (This norm should be considered obsolete.)

¹¹ (The duty of the syndic is usually given to the minister, who in larger houses is assisted by a subminister.)

¹² (Concerning doctrine to be held in the Society, see *CN* 99–105.)

sermons or public lectures, or in books *[O]*; ³(and it will not be permissible to publish books without the approval and permission of the superior general, who will entrust the examination of them to at least three persons of sound doctrine and clear judgment about the field in question).¹³ ⁴Even in judgment about practical matters, diversity, which is commonly the mother of discord and the enemy of union of wills, should be avoided as far as possible. ⁵This union and agreement among them all ought to be sought most earnestly, *[P]* and the opposite ought not to be permitted, ⁶so that, united among themselves by the bond of fraternal charity, they may be able better and more efficaciously to apply themselves in the service of God and the aid of their fellowmen.

[274] O. ¹*Novel doctrines must not be admitted; and in the case of opinions divergent from what is commonly held by the Church and its teachers, they should submit to what is laid down in the Society, as was explained in the Examen [47].* ²*Furthermore, on matters where Catholic teachers hold different or opposed opinions, an effort should likewise be made to obtain uniformity in the Society.*

[275] P. ¹*Passion or any anger of some in the house toward others should not be permitted.* ²*If anything of the sort arises, the parties should be made to reconcile immediately, with appropriate satisfaction.*

[276] 19. ¹Since progress in virtue is much aided by the good example of the older members encouraging the rest to imitate them, ²the superior (unless for special reasons he judges something else expedient), and all the other priests for whom he thinks it wise, will on occasion during the year perform for a time the duty or duties of those who serve, ³so that the practice of such duties may be more pleasing to the others who are assigned to them for the greater service and glory of God our Lord.

[277] 20. ¹On some days each week instruction should be given in Christian doctrine, the manner of making a good and fruitful confession *[Q]*, receiving Communion, assisting at Mass and serving it, praying, meditating, and reading, in accordance with each one's capacity.¹⁴ ²Likewise, care should be taken both that they learn what is proper and not let it be forgotten, and that they put what they have learned into practice, all of them devoting time to spiritual things and striving to acquire devotion to the extent that divine grace imparts it to them. ³Toward this purpose, it will be

---

¹³ **Modified by *CN* 296.** (In regard to approval and consent of the general.)

¹⁴ **Clarified by *CN* 48, §1.**

helpful to give all or some of the Spiritual Exercises to those who have not made them, as may be judged expedient for them in our Lord *[R]*.

[278] Q. ¹*In addition to the manner of confessing well, {a time to confess will be assigned to them; and if they miss it, they should not be given food for the body until they have taken their spiritual nourishment}*.¹⁵ ²*Moreover, one who confesses to another than to his ordinary confessor ought*¹⁶ *later to open his whole conscience to his own confessor, as far as he remembers, so that he, being ignorant of nothing which pertains to it, may the better aid him in our Lord.*

[279] R. ¹*Those who are proficient and doing well on their own in spiritual exercises and have a method for proceeding in them, or who have other occupations,* ²*may be dispensed by the superior in whole or in part from the common rules in this matter.*

³*Some are capable of making the spiritual exercises but lack experience in them. It is sometimes good to aid these by coming down with them to detailed considerations which incite them to the fear and love of God and to the virtues and their practice, as discretion will show to be expedient.*

⁴*If anyone is seen to be unfit for exercises of this kind (as might be the case with a temporal coadjutor), he should be given exercises suited to his capacity with which to aid himself and serve God our Lord.*

[280] 21. ¹It is good that all (unless the superior has exempted someone) practice preaching inside the house *[S]*. The purpose, in addition to making good use of some of the time after meals on this, is so that they may take courage and get practice in using the voice, method, and the like; ²show the talent which God our Lord gives them in this field; and express their good ideas for their own edification and that of their neighbors. ³They should speak often of what pertains to abnegation of themselves, the virtues, and all perfection, and should exhort one another to these things, particularly to union and fraternal charity.

[281] S. ¹*Those who preach in the house should not reprimand any of their brethren of the house or of the Society. The preachers in the churches should also beware of giving such a reprimand, unless the superior has*

---

¹⁵ **Abolished.** (By virtue of CIC 630, §1: "Superiors are to recognize the due freedom of their members concerning the sacrament of penance . . ."); see also CCEO 473, §2, 2°; 474, §2.)

¹⁶ (See *CN* 227, §3: "Each one should have his regular confessor to whom he ordinarily confesses.")

been informed about the matter. ²*However, a preacher may both encourage himself and his brethren to go forward in greater service to God. But this is more suitable in sermons within the house than in the church.*

[282] 22. ¹It will be very specially helpful to perform with all possible devotion the tasks in which humility and charity are practiced more; ²and, to speak in general, the more one binds himself to God our Lord and shows himself more generous toward his Divine Majesty *[T],* the more will he find God more generous toward himself and the more disposed will he be to receive daily greater graces and spiritual gifts.

[283] T. ¹*To bind oneself more to God our Lord and to show oneself generous toward him is to consecrate oneself completely and irrevocably to his service, as those do who dedicate themselves to him by vow.* ²*But although this is a great help toward receiving more abundant grace, no one ought to be commanded or in any way constrained to do it within the first two years.*

³*But if some through their own devotion are spontaneously impelled to anticipate the vow, it should not be received into anyone's hands nor should there be any solemnity; rather, the individual should offer the vow to God our Lord in the secret of his own soul.* ⁴*When any do this, it is good that they ask for the ordinary form of the simple vows and, as an aid to memory, retain in writing what they have promised to God our Lord.*

[284] 23. ¹It is very helpful for making progress and highly necessary that all devote themselves to complete obedience, recognizing the superior, whoever he is, as being in the place of Christ our Lord and maintaining interior reverence and love for him. ²They should obey entirely and promptly, not only by exterior execution of what the superior commands, with due fortitude and humility and without excuses or complaints, even though things are commanded which are difficult and repugnant to sensitive nature *[V],* ³but also by striving interiorly to have genuine resignation and abnegation of their own wills and judgments, bringing their wills and judgments wholly into conformity with what the superior wills and judges in all things **in which no sin is seen,**¹⁷ ⁴and regarding the superior's will and judgment as the rule of their own, so as to conform themselves more completely to the first and supreme rule of all good will and judgment, which is the Eternal Goodness and Wisdom.

---

¹⁷ **Clarified by** *CN* **154.** (For cases of a conflict of conscience.)

[285] V. ¹It will be helpful that superiors see to it that those who are in probation should sometimes experience their obedience and poverty, by testing them for their greater spiritual progress in the manner in which God tested Abraham [Gen. 22], and that they may give evidence of their virtue and grow in it. ²But in this the superiors should as far as possible observe the measure and proportion of what each one can bear, as discretion will dictate.

[286] 24. ¹For their greater exercise in obedience, it is good and indeed quite necessary that they obey not only the superior of the Society or house but also the subordinate officials holding authority from him, in all matters for which they were given such authority over them. ²They should accustom themselves to consider, not who the person is whom they obey, but rather who he is for whose sake they obey and whom they obey in all, who is Christ our Lord.

[287] 25. ¹All should love poverty as a mother, and according to the measure of holy discretion all should, when occasions arise, feel some of its effects. ²Further, as is stated in the Examen [53–59], they should be ready **after the first year to dispose of their temporal goods whenever the superior may command it,**¹⁸ in the manner which was proposed to them in the aforementioned Examen.

[288] 26. ¹All should strive to keep their intention right, not only in regard to their state of life but also in all particular details, ²in which they should aim always at serving and pleasing the Divine Goodness for its own sake and because of the incomparable love and benefits with which he has anticipated us rather than for fear of punishments or hope of rewards, although they ought to draw help from these also. ³They should often be exhorted to seek God our Lord in all things, removing from themselves as far as possible love of all creatures in order to place it in the Creator of them, loving him in all creatures and all creatures in him, in conformity with his holy and divine will.

[289] 27. ¹The study which those who are in probation will have in the houses of the Society should, it seems, be about what will help them toward what has been said on the abnegation of themselves and toward further growth in virtue and devotion. ²**Generally speaking, there will be no literary studies in the house (unless it appears that for special reasons an exception ought to be made for some members) [X].**¹⁹ ³For the colleges are for acquiring learn-

---

¹⁸ Clarified by *CN* 32.

¹⁹ Clarified by *CN* 55, §1. (Concerning the possibility of pursuing studies

ing, the houses so that those who have acquired it may put it into practice or so that those yet to acquire it may lay a foundation of humility and virtue for it.

[290]   X.   ¹*Although in general literary studies are not pursued in the houses of the Society, all those who attend to preaching and confessing may study what is helpful toward their purpose.*²⁰ ²*If it is expedient for some individual to study other matters also, it will be left to the superior's discretion to determine this and to grant a dispensation for it.*

[291]   28.   ¹There should be someone to give the novices these or similar reminders every week or at least every fifteen days, or else they should be required to read them, lest they be forgotten through the condition of our frail human nature and so cease to be practiced. ²Furthermore, several times a year all should ask the superior to order that penances be given them for their negligence in keeping the rules, so that this care may show that which they have for progressing in the service of God.

CHAPTER 2
¹THE PRESERVATION OF THE BODY

[292]   1.   ²Just as an excessive preoccupation with the needs of the body is blameworthy, so too a proper concern for the preservation of one's health and bodily strength for the divine service is praiseworthy and should be exercised by all. ³Consequently, when they perceive that something is harmful to them or that something else is necessary in regard to their diet, clothing, living quarters, office, or occupation, and similarly of other matters, all ought to give notice of this to the superior or to the one whom he appoints. ⁴But here they should observe two things. First, before informing him they should recollect themselves to pray, and after this, if they feel that they ought to represent the matter to him who is in charge, they should do so. ⁵Second, once they have represented it by word of mouth or by a short note so that he will not forget, they should leave the whole care of the matter to him ⁶and regard what he ordains as better, without arguing or insisting upon it either themselves or through another, whether he grants the request or not [A]. ⁷For the subject must persuade himself that what the superior

in the novitiate.)

²⁰ (See *CN* 240–43: concerning ongoing formation.)

decides after being informed is more suitable for the divine service and the subject's own greater good in our Lord.

[293] A. ¹*Even though the subject who represents his need ought not on his part to argue or urge the matter,* ²*nevertheless if the superior is insufficiently informed and wishes further explanation, the subject will give it.* ³*Should the superior happen to forget to make provision after he has indicated his intention of doing so, it is not out of order to remind him or to represent it anew, with due modesty.*

[294] 2. ¹There should be a regular order, as far as possible, for the time of eating, sleeping, and rising, and it should ordinarily be observed by all *[B]*.

[295] B. ¹*The order of times for eating and sleeping should ordinarily be observed by all.* ²*However, if for special reasons something else is expedient for an individual, the superior will consider whether or not he should be dispensed.*

[296] 3. ¹In regard to food, clothing *[C]*, living quarters, and other bodily needs, care should be taken with the divine aid that, while there is occasion for testing their virtue and self-abnegation, nothing be lacking that is needed to sustain and preserve nature for God's service and praise, ²due account being taken of individual persons in our Lord.

[297] C. ¹*In regard to clothing, its purpose should be kept in view, which is to keep off cold and preserve decorum.* ²*Beyond this, it is good for those who are in probation to take advantage of their garments as means to the mortification and abnegation of themselves and to trample on the world and its vanities.* ³*This should be done to the extent that the nature, usage, office, and other circumstances of the persons permit.*

⁴*In the case of the approved scholastics and those attending to study, it seems that in respect to clothing more attention could be paid to exterior propriety and convenience, in view of the labors of study and the fact that the colleges have a fixed income, although all superfluity should be ever avoided.* ⁵*In the cases of particular persons, one could well act as is fitting for each one.*

[298] 4. ¹Just as it is unwise to assign so much physical labor that the spirit should be oppressed and the body be harmed *[D]*, ²so too some bodily exercise to help both the body and the spirit is ordinarily expedient for all, even for those who must apply themselves to mental labors. ³These too ought to be interrupted by exterior activities and not prolonged or undertaken beyond the measure of discretion.

[299]   D. ¹*For an hour or two after taking a meal, especially during the summer, strenuous exertions of body or mind ought as far as possible not to be allowed (measuring each need with all possible charity), although other light activities may be pursued during this time. ²Outside these hours also it is not good to continue to work for a long time without some proper relaxation or recreation.*

[300]   5. ¹The chastisement of the body ought not to be immoderate or indiscreet in abstinences, vigils [E], and other external penances and labors [F] which cause harm and prevent greater goods. ²Hence each one should keep his confessor informed of what he does in this matter. If the latter thinks that there is excess or has a doubt, he should refer the matter to the superior. ³All this is in order to proceed with greater light and so that God our Lord may be more glorified through our souls and bodies.

[301]   E. ¹*It seems that the time for sleeping ought to be, in general, between six and seven hours, and that they ought not to sleep without nightclothes, unless it be because of some necessity which the superior recognizes. ²But since no precise rule is possible in such great diversity of persons and constitutions, the shortening or prolonging of this time will be left to the discretion of the superior, ³who will take care that each one retains what his constitution requires.*

[302]   F. ¹*Each one ought to be ready to undertake whatever employment may be assigned to him. ²Nevertheless, in the case of those which require stronger and more vigorous men, such as those in the sacristy, porter's lodge, or infirmary, care should be taken to assign to them persons who have the physical constitution required for the offices, as far as will be possible.*

[303]   6. ¹It is good that there be a person in the house to superintend what pertains to the preservation of health in those who possess it (particularly those who are weaker because of age or other causes) and its restoration in those who are sick, ²and to whom any who feel themselves more than ordinarily indisposed should be obliged to make it known so that a suitable remedy may be provided as charity requires [G].

[304]   G. ¹*Great care should be taken of the sick. As soon as their illness is reported to the infirmarian, if he judges it to be serious he should inform the superior ²and a physician should be called. Ordinarily there will be only one physician, unless the superior thinks otherwise in particular cases, ³and his directions should be followed, as far as possible, in regard to the regimen and medicines. The sick man should not involve himself otherwise than by exercising his patience and obedience, leaving the care*

of everything else to the superior and his ministers, through whom Divine Providence directs him.

⁴Moreover, although our vocation is to travel through the world and to live in any part of it where there is hope of greater service to God and of help of souls, ⁵nevertheless, if experience shows that a person cannot stand the climate of a particular region and continues in bad health there, it will be up to the superior to consider whether the subject ought to be transferred to another place where, in better bodily health, he may be able to employ himself better in the service of God our Lord. ⁶But to request such a change or to show oneself inclined to it will not be the part of any of those sick, who should leave this concern to the superior.

[305]   7. ¹In what pertains to the conservation of the temporal goods, all should have the concern to which charity and reason oblige them. But beyond that, it will be good to have someone who is charged more particularly with caring for these goods as the property and possession of Christ our Lord. ²In regard to other necessary matters also, efforts should be made to have a sufficiency of officials, especially for things that are more appropriately done inside the house than outside it *[H];* ³and it is good that the temporal coadjutors should learn these offices if they do not know them, everything being always directed to the greater glory of God our Creator and Lord.

[306]   *H. ¹The officials for things more appropriately done inside than outside the house would be the launderer, barber, and the like, whom it is good to have in a house if possible.*

PART IV

¹THE LEARNING AND OTHER MEANS OF HELPING THEIR NEIGHBOR THAT ARE TO BE IMPARTED TO THOSE WHO ARE RETAINED IN THE SOCIETY

PREAMBLE

[307]   1. ²The end steadfastly pursued by the Society is to aid its own members and their neighbors in attaining the ultimate end for which they were created. ³For this, in addition to the example of one's life, learning and skill in expounding it are required. Hence, once the proper foundation of abnegation of themselves and the needed progress in virtues is seen to be present in the new members, ⁴it will be necessary to provide for the edifice of learning, and of skill in employing it so as to help make God our Creator and Lord better known and served.

⁵For this, the Society undertakes colleges as well as some universities, where those who prove themselves worthy in the houses but have entered the Society unequipped with the necessary learning may be instructed therein and in the other means of helping souls. ⁶Hence, with the favor of the Divine and Eternal Wisdom and for his greater glory and praise, we shall treat first of what pertains to the colleges and then of the universities.

[308]   A. ¹The aim and end of this Society is, by traveling through the various parts of the world at the order of the supreme vicar of Christ our Lord or of the superior of the Society itself, to preach, hear confessions, and use all the other means it can with the grace of God to help souls. ²Consequently it has seemed to us necessary, or at least highly expedient, that those who will enter the Society be persons of good life and sufficient learning for the aforementioned work. ³However, those who are both good and learned are relatively few; and even among these few, most are already seeking rest from their labors. ⁴We have thus found it a quite difficult matter to increase the numbers of this Society with such good and learned men, in view of the great labors and the great abnegation of self which are required in the Society.

⁵Therefore all of us, desiring to preserve and increase the Society for the greater glory and service of God our Lord, have thought it wise to

PART IV
FORMATION OF OUR MEMBERS
AFTER THE NOVITIATE

CHAPTER 1
GENERAL NORMS

59 §1. Since the formation of all our members is directed toward the apostolic objective of the Society, namely, that they may be able[1] "with the help of God to benefit both their own souls and those of their neighbors,"[2] this objective is to be considered the principle which regulates the entire formation of our members.[3]

§2. The choice made by General Congregation 32 concerning the mission of the Society in today's world as the service of faith, of which the promotion of justice is an absolute requirement,[4] must give new vigor to our formation, so that it may respond to the requirements of evangelization in a world that is often infected by atheism and injustices,[5] and may equip our members for entering into dialogue with people and meeting the cultural problems of our times.[6]

60 We should conceive and plan for the total formation of our members as a process of progressive integration of the spiritual and community life, of the apostolate, and of studies, in such a way that the richness of the spiritual life should be the source of the apostolate, and the apostolate in turn the motive for study and for a deeper spiritual life.[7]

---

[1] GC 31, d. 9, no. 1.

[2] P. IV, c. 5, no. 1 [351].

[3] GC 31, d. 8, no. 4.

[4] GC 32, d. 4, no. 2; d. 2, no. 2.

[5] See GC 32, d. 4, nos. 24–30.

[6] See GC 32, d. 4, passim; GC 34, d. 4, no. 5.

[7] GC 32, d. 6, no. 11; GC 31, d. 9, no. 2.

take another path, ⁶that of admitting young men whose good habits of life and talent give hope that they will become both virtuous and learned in order to labor in the vineyard of Christ our Lord. ⁷We shall likewise accept colleges under the conditions stated in the apostolic bull, whether these colleges are within universities or outside of them; and, if they are within universities, whether these universities are governed by the Society or not. ⁸For we are convinced in our Lord that in this way greater service will be given to his Divine Majesty, with those who will be employed in that service being multiplied in number and making progress in learning and virtues.

⁹Consequently, we shall treat first of what pertains to the colleges and then of what concerns the universities. ¹⁰With regard to the colleges, we shall discuss first what pertains to the founders [in chapter 1]; ¹¹second, what pertains to the colleges founded, in regard to their material or temporal aspects [chapter 2]; ¹²third, what pertains to the scholastics who will study in them, in regard to their admission [chapter 3], preservation [chapter 4], progress in learning [chapters 5, 6, 7] and in other means of helping their fellowmen [chapter 8], and their removal from study [chapter 9]; ¹³fourth, what pertains to the government of the colleges [chapter 10].

61   §1. The provincial is responsible for all aspects of the formation of those who belong to his province. He is responsible for both the persons and the institutions of the Society charged with formation. However, it is appropriate that there be a delegate who should have immediate care for the various aspects of formation of each young man in the province (or in the larger region, where circumstances so dictate).

§2. There should be provincial and interprovincial commissions to advise superiors in the direction of formation in accord with local conditions.

§3. These commissions should be made up of those who are in charge of formation, and also of some who are working in various apostolic ministries and some who are in formation. They should evaluate the status of formation in the province or region on a regular basis.[8]

62   In institutions where those in formation are taught by our own members, these professors should remember that the mission that they have received from the provincial extends also to the formation of these men. Therefore, a team of professors should be chosen which has the aptitude for carrying on scholarly work, for teaching, and for cooperating in the integral formation of our members. With regard to this point, professors should be conscious of their responsibility toward the Society, even though the provincial has entrusted a special responsibility for formation to certain members.[9]

63   Where the faculty or institution is directed by the Society but the academic direction is separate from the religious direction [of the community], superiors should promote mutual cooperation in order to achieve the integral formation of our members.[10]

The text of the Norms resumes on page 141.

---

[8] GC 32, d. 6, no. 31; see GC 31, d. 9, no. 16.

[9] See GC 32, d. 6, no. 48; ibid., no. 30.

[10] GC 32, d. 6, no. 49, b.

CHAPTER 1

¹THE REMEMBRANCE OF THE FOUNDERS AND BENEFACTORS OF THE COLLEGES¹

[309] 1. ²It is highly proper for us to do something on our part in return for the devotion and generosity shown toward the Society by those whom the Divine Goodness employs as his ministers to found and endow its colleges. ³First of all, therefore, in every college let a Mass be said in perpetuity each week for its founder and benefactors, living and dead.

[310] 2. ¹Likewise, at the beginning of each month all the priests in the college should be obliged, in perpetuity, to celebrate one Mass for these same persons.

²Each year, too, on the anniversary of the day when the possession of the college was handed over, let a solemn Mass [A] be celebrated in it for the founder and benefactors. All the other priests dwelling there are to celebrate Mass for the same intention.

[311] A. ¹*The solemnity is understood to be according to the manner employed in the Society and in the place where the Mass is celebrated.*

[312] 3. ¹On that day a wax candle is to be presented to the founder, or to one of his closer relatives [B], or in whatever way the founder may stipulate. The candle should contain his coat of arms or emblems of his devotions, as a sign of the gratitude due in our Lord [C].

[313] B. ¹*If there is, after a time, no descendant of the founder in the place where the college was founded, the candle can be sent to wherever one of his descendants may be found, ²or it can be placed on the altar on which the divine sacrifice is offered, in the name and place of the founder.*

[314] C. ¹*This candle signifies the gratitude due to the founders, not any right of patronage or any claim belonging to them or their successors against the college or its temporal goods, for none such will exist.*

[315] 4. ¹As soon as a college is handed over to the Society, the superior general should notify the entire Society, in order that each priest may celebrate three Masses for the living founder and the benefactors, that God our Lord may sustain them by his own hand and cause them to advance in his service. ²When the general learns

---

¹ This entire chapter 1 [309–319] is modified as regards concrete determinations, but the spirit of the gratitude of the Society toward founders and benefactors is retained: *CN* 413.

that God has taken them from this life to the other *[D]*, he should instruct the priests to celebrate three more Masses for their souls.

³Whenever it is stated that Masses must be celebrated by the priests, all the rest who dwell in the colleges and are not priests ought to pray for the same intention for which the priests are celebrating. For the same obligation of showing gratitude is incumbent in the Lord on them as well as on the priests.

[316] D. ¹*In the case of communities, which have continuous existence, these Masses will be celebrated for their deceased members, particularly for those to whom we are more indebted in our Lord.*

[317] 5. ¹The founders and benefactors of such colleges become in a special way sharers in all the good works of those colleges and of the whole Society.

[318] 6. ¹In general, the Society should deem itself especially obligated to them *[E]* and to their dear ones, both during their lifetime and after their death. It is bound, by an obligation of charity and love, to show them whatever service it can according to our humble profession, for the divine glory.

[319] E. ¹*What has been stated ought to be observed in its entirety in the case of those who found complete colleges.* ²*The superior general will decide in the Lord which part of it to carry out for those who only give an initial foundation.*

CHAPTER 2
¹THE MATERIAL ASPECTS OF THE COLLEGES

[320] 1. ²In regard to accepting colleges which are freely offered to the Society that it may administer them in all respects according to its Constitutions, the superior general will have the full authority in the name of the whole Society.

[321] 2. ¹When a founder desires to attach conditions which are not fully in conformity with the order and manner of proceeding customarily employed by the Society, ²it will be left to the same general to consider (after hearing the opinion of the others whom he will judge to have better understanding in these matters), whether or not, when everything is taken into account, the acceptance of the college is helpful to the Society toward the end it is seeking, the service of God. ³But if in the course of time the Society should find itself burdened, it can bring the matter up in a general congregation and decree that the college should be abandoned, or that the burden should be lightened, or that

additional means should be found to bear it, ⁴in case the general has not made provision for the matter before the congregation assembles, as is expedient in our Lord.

[322] 3. ¹**The authority to abandon or alienate colleges or houses once accepted will belong jointly to the general and the Society** *[A]*.² ²{Since this is like severing a member from the Society's body and is a lasting and important matter, **it is better that the whole Society should be consulted about it**}.³

[323] *A.* ²*The superior general and the Society will decide jointly whether colleges or houses once accepted ought to be abandoned or not.* ³{***But this can be done in a general congregation, or without it through votes sent in by those who have the right***}.⁴ ⁴*In such a case neither the Society nor its general may give away to persons outside the Society what is thus abandoned, or any part of it.* ⁵*But when the Society relinquishes the charge it held, the parties who in the foundation may on their side have reserved this authority to themselves, will be able to apply what is thus abandoned to something else, according to their own devotion.* ⁶*If there is no reservation of this kind, the Society may proceed according to its Institute in whatever way it judges to be more conducive to the glory of God.*

[324] 4. ¹In colleges of the Society, no curacies of souls, obligations to celebrate Masses, or similar duties should be accepted which greatly distract from study and impede the aim which is pursued in the colleges for the divine service. ²Similarly, such duties should not be undertaken in the houses or churches of the Professed Society, which as far as possible ought to be left free to accept the missions from the Apostolic See and other works for the service of God and the help of souls *[B]*.

[325] *B.* ¹*With regard to not accepting obligations and so on, what is meant is a prohibition against accepting obligations of saying Masses or of similar duties which correspond to the fixed revenue which is given.* ²*However, in the presence of sufficient reasons there is less difficulty in accepting one of easy or slight obligation (it must not be a curacy of souls), especially if it causes little or no distraction or loss of time.* ³*But such obligations are not possible for the houses of the professed, since these houses do not have fixed incomes nor the professed themselves sufficiently stable residence.* ⁴*Other obligations pertaining to lectures or*

---

² **Clarified by** *CN* **402, §3.** (This is now an ordinary faculty of the general, to be used after hearing his council.)

³ **Abolished by** *CN* **402, §3.**

⁴ (See the two preceding notes.)

lecturers are not under discussion here. However, these too will be accepted in the colleges and universities only after much consideration, and not beyond the limit which the superior general will judge to be conducive to the common good and that of the Society for the glory of God our Lord.

[326]   5. ¹The Society will take possession of the colleges with the temporal goods which pertain to them *[C]*, appointing as rector one whose talents are more suited for this. ²He will take charge of maintaining and administering their temporal goods, ³providing for the necessities both of the material building and of the scholastics who are dwelling in the colleges or of those who are preparing themselves to go to them *[D]*, and also of those who are carrying on the affairs of the colleges outside of them *[E]*. The rector should keep account of everything so that he can render it when and to whomever the general may order him. ⁴The general, inasmuch as he may not apply the temporal goods of the colleges to his own use or that of his relatives or of the Professed Society *[F]*, will proceed with all the more rectitude in his superintendence of these goods, for the greater glory and service of God our Lord.

[327]   *C. ¹As the bulls state, for the use of its scholastics the Society will carry on the administration of the fixed revenue through the superior general or the provincial or someone else to whom the general will entrust the matter, ²in order to guard and preserve the possessions and the fixed revenues of the colleges even in court if this should be expedient or necessary. ³The same general or someone to whom he entrusts the work will also have the care of receiving whatever else is given to such colleges for their maintenance and growth in regard to their temporalities.*

[328]   *D. ¹Those who are preparing themselves to go to the colleges are those who are living in the houses of probation, and those who are being sent to their studies from the houses of the professed Society or from the houses of probation.*

[329]   *E. ¹Those who are carrying on the affairs of the colleges outside of them are understood to be chiefly the procurators, who take care of the affairs of the Society in the curia of the supreme pontiff or of other rulers. ²But in regard to what must be contributed for these and other necessary expenditures, the general, observing due proportion, will issue the order by himself or through another.*

[330]   *F. ¹When it is stated that the Society or its general may not avail themselves of the fixed revenues of the colleges, this should be understood, in conformity with the statements in the bull, as meaning that they may not divert these fixed revenues to their own private uses. ²However, they*

may make expenditures in favor of all those who work for the benefit of these colleges, as, for example, any administrators, preachers, lecturers, confessors, visitors, and other professed or similar persons who contribute to the spiritual or temporal benefit of those colleges. ³Likewise even without such a reason, a small sum may be spent upon any member whatever of the Society, in giving him food for a day or a little traveling money or the like when he passes through the college en route to one place or another. ⁴For such small amounts are counted as nothing, ⁵and scruples are eliminated about acting either inhumanely on the one hand or against the intention of the Apostolic See on the other.

[331] 6. ¹In colleges⁵ which from their own fixed revenue can support twelve scholastics in addition to their teachers, neither alms nor other gifts should be begged or accepted, for the greater edification of the people [G]. ²When colleges are not that well endowed, some alms may be accepted but may not be begged unless the college happens to be so poor that it is also necessary to beg them, at least from some persons. ³For in such a case, with a view always kept on the greater service of God and the universal good, it will be permissible to beg alms, and even for a time from door to door in any necessity which might require it.

[332] G. ¹*However, if there are benefactors who wish to give an estate or fixed revenue, it could be accepted so as to support that many more scholastics and teachers for greater service to God.*

CHAPTER 3

¹THE SCHOLASTICS WHO ARE TO BE STATIONED IN THE COLLEGES

[333] 1. ¹In regard to the scholastics for whose instruction the colleges are accepted, the first point to be considered in our Lord is what qualifications they should have to be sent or admitted to the colleges.

[334] 2. ¹First of all, no one with any of the five impediments stated in Part I [164–76] will have a place as a scholastic in any college of the Society [A]. ²Apart from the coadjutors who are necessary for the service and help of the college, the rest ought to be such subjects as give reasonable hope of turning out to be fit laborers in the vineyard of Christ our Lord through their example and learning. ³The more capable they are, the better their habits of

---

⁵ (These norms [331–32] are now to be understood rather in a general sense, namely, of not seeking alms not necessary for colleges of our men.)

conduct, and the healthier they are to endure the labor of study, the more suitable are they and the sooner can they be sent to the colleges and admitted into them.

[335] A. ²*When someone has been declared suitable by the Vicar of Christ to live in a house of the Society, he is also understood to be suitable to live in the colleges.*

[336] 3. ¹However, only those are admitted as approved scholastics who have undergone their probation in the houses or in the colleges themselves ²and who, after two years of experiences and probation and after pronouncing their vows along with the promise to enter the Society, are received to live and die in it, for the glory of God our Lord.

[337] 4. ¹Besides those just mentioned, others too are admitted to study, namely, those who before the end of the two-year period and its aforementioned probations are sent from the houses to the colleges because this seems expedient, or those who are received in the colleges. ²But these are not considered to be approved scholastics until they have completed the two years and pronounced their vows with the promise and are then admitted as such *[B]*.

[338] B. ¹*Where the Society's colleges⁶ do not have a sufficient number of scholastics with the promise or intention of serving God our Lord in the Society, it will not be contrary to our Institute, with permission from the general and for the time which seems good to him, to admit other poor students who do not have such an intention, ²provided that the impediments mentioned in Part I [164–76] are not found in them and they are subjects of such fitness as to give hope that they will turn out to be good workers in the vineyard of Christ our Lord, because of their ability or basic knowledge of letters, good habits of conduct, suitable age, ³and other qualities which are seen in them for the divine service, which alone is sought in the case of both members of the Society and externs.*

⁴*Students of this kind ought to conform themselves to the scholastics of the Society in the matter of confessions, studies, and manner of living. But their dress should be different and their living quarters separate within the same college, ⁵in such a way that the scholastics of the Society are apart by themselves without being mingled among the externs, although they may have dealings with the externs as far as the*

---

⁶ (These remarks have practically no application in present circumstances.)

superior judges this suitable for greater edification and service to God our Lord.

⁶*Even if there should be a sufficient number of our own scholastics, it is not contrary to our Institute to admit into the college someone who has no intention of becoming a member of the Society where the agreement made with the founders so requires* ⁷*and it is seen that to accept the college under such a condition is of value for the end which the Society seeks, or on account of other exceptional and important reasons.* ⁸*However, students of this kind ought to live apart and, with the superior's permission, to associate only with certain members of the Society.*

⁹*The poverty of these extern students will be determined by the superior general or by someone to whom he communicates this authority.* ¹⁰*Moreover, to admit on occasion and for good reasons the sons of rich or noble persons, who pay their own expenses, does not seem excluded.*

¹¹*The suitable age seems to be from fourteen to twenty-three years, unless the students are persons who possess a basic knowledge of letters.* ¹²*Generally speaking, the more qualities they possess of those desired in the Society, the more suitable will they be for admission.* ¹³*Nevertheless, care should be taken to be strict rather than easy in accepting such students.* ¹⁴*Furthermore, a careful choice should be made of those who are to be admitted, by subjecting them to an individual examination before admission.*

¹⁵*Some persons, although rather rarely, could be admitted among our own members for particular reasons considered cogent by the superior.*

CHAPTER 4
¹THE CARE AND WELFARE OF THE SCHOLASTICS IN THE COLLEGES

[339] 1. ²For the care and welfare of those who live in the colleges, in regard to the body and external matters, what was stated in Part III [292–306] will suffice. That is, special attention should be given to their abstaining from studies at times inopportune for bodily health, to their taking sufficient sleep, ³and to their observance of moderation in mental labors so as to be able to keep at them longer both during their studies and later on when using what they have studied for the glory of God our Lord.

[340] 2. ¹In regard to spiritual matters, the same procedure as is used with those received in the houses will be used with those

Chapter 2

Spiritual Formation

64   §1. During the time of studies the formation of our members should be such that they learn to place great value on their own vocation and, motivated by the internal law of love, will more and more embrace our way of proceeding, just as they were taught in the novitiate.[11]

§2. The vocation, tested and strengthened during the novitiate, should continue its growth throughout the whole time of formation. Accordingly, it is necessary to provide an appropri-

---

[11] *CollDecr* d. 80 (GC 18, d. 22 no. 9).

received in the colleges as long as they are still going through probations. ²However, once they have satisfactorily completed them and are devoting themselves to studies, while care must be taken that they do not through fervor in study grow cool in their love of true virtues and of religious life, ³still they will not at that time have much place for mortifications or for long prayers and meditations [A]. ⁴For their devoting themselves to learning, which they acquire with a pure intention of serving God and which in a certain way requires the whole person, will be not less but rather more pleasing to God our Lord during this time of study.

[341] *A. ¹If the rector because of special reasons judges some prolongation expedient in a particular case, there will always be place for discretion.*

[342] 3. ¹Consequently, in addition to confession and Communion every eight days [B]⁷ and daily Mass, **they will have one hour, during which they will recite the Hours of Our Lady,** ²examine **their consciences twice each day, and add other prayers according to each one's devotion to fill out the rest of the aforesaid hour.**⁸ ³They will do all this according to the order and judgment of their superiors, whom they oblige themselves to obey in place of Christ our Lord.

[343] *B. ¹To go more often than every eight days should not be allowed except for special reasons, taking more account of need than of devotion. ²But neither should reception be deferred beyond eight days unless there are special reasons.⁹ For such reasons, Mass could also be omitted on some day, and for some persons the period of prayer could be lengthened or shortened. ³This will remain wholly within the discretionary power of the superior.*

The specified hour will be taken, somewhat more or less, for the recitation of the Hours of Our Lady. ⁴Nevertheless in the case of the scholastics who are not obliged to recite the Divine Office, the hour can more easily be changed at times to meditations and other spiritual exercises by which the hour is filled out, ⁵especially with some who do not advance spiritually by one method, so that with God's grace they may be helped more by another. This is to be done with the permission or through the order of their

---

⁷ **Modified by CIC 663, §2; 664, and CCEO 473, §1; 474, §1.** (With regard to frequenting the sacraments.)

⁸ **Modified by CN 67, §2.** (In regard to time given to prayer and Mass.)

⁹ **Modified.** (See note 7.)

ate transition and continuity between the novitiate and subsequent formation, and between various stages of the latter.[12]

§3. Special care should be given to those who are in formation, especially for two years after their first vows.[13]

65   The process of apostolic formation must favor the personal assimilation of Christian experience, an experience that is spiritual, personal, vital, rooted in faith, nourished by daily prayer and the Eucharist; an experience that makes us capable of cooperating with God for the spiritual growth of believers and of communicating the gift of faith to nonbelievers.[14]

66   §1. There should be an organic unity in the entire formation, so that from the beginning of the novitiate and throughout the entire course of studies, spiritual formation, the work of study, and apostolic activity should be closely integrated. All who have charge of the training of our members, either in government or in teaching, should diligently and harmoniously work together for this integration.[15]

§2. In a special way spiritual directors should help towards this. Wise and competent spiritual directors are to be prepared and chosen, who can offer fraternal help in the Lord to our members during their time of formation, helping them achieve a true discernment of spirits.[16]

§3. Those in formation should frequently go to a spiritual director; the superior should approve the spiritual director whom each one chooses from among those designated for this office.

67   §1. Our members during the entire time of their formation should be carefully helped to grow in prayer and a sense of spiritual responsibility towards a mature interior life, in which they will know how to apply the rule of discerning love that St. Ignatius prescribed for members after the period of their formation.[17]

---

[12] GC 31, d. 8, no. 31.

[13] *CollDecr* d. 83 (GC 18, d. 22, no. 6); GC 31, d. 8, no. 29; Fr. Peter-Hans Kolvenbach, "On Formation from the End of Novitiate to the Beginning of Regency," *ActRSJ* 20:80–106.

[14] See GC 32, d. 6, no. 9, a, b.

[15] GC 31, d. 9, no. 2; see ibid., d. 8, nos. 5, 33; GC 32, d. 6, no. 14.

[16] GC 32, d. 8, nos. 29, 33.

[17] GC 31, d. 14, no. 12, 1°; see P. VI, c. 3, no. 1 [582].

superiors, ⁶whose duty it will always be to consider whether, for certain reasons with particular persons, something different is more expedient, in order to carry it out while keeping in view the genuine devotion of the subjects or of the founder, and also the circumstances of persons, times, and places.

⁷For those who do not have experience in spiritual things and desire to be helped in them, some points for meditation and prayer could be proposed to them in the way that seems best for persons of this kind.

⁸{Whether, during that time of the Mass when the priest is not speaking aloud to be understood by the people, the scholastics may use some of their assigned hour to recite a part of the Hours will belong to the elders or superiors to decide. ⁹These superiors should provide for this according to the persons, places, conditions, and times, in the way that seems best to them for the greater divine glory}.¹⁰

[344] 4. ¹Others (for example, some of the temporal coadjutors who do not know how to read) will have in addition to the Mass their hour, during which they will recite the rosary or crown of our Lady *[C]*, ²and they will likewise examine their consciences twice a day, or engage in some other prayers according to their devotion, as was said about the scholastics.

[345] C. ¹*In regard to the recitation of the rosary, they should be instructed how to think or meditate about the mysteries which it contains, so that they may carry out this exercise with greater attention and devotion.* ²*Moreover, if those who know how to read should find more profit in it than in the recitation of the Hours, they could be changed for what will be more helpful, as was already stated.*

[346] 5. ¹For greater devotion, and to refresh the memory of the obligation they are under and confirm themselves more solidly in their vocation, **it will be good for the scholastics twice each year, at Easter and Christmas** *[D]*, **to renew their simple vows** *[E]*,¹¹ which will be discussed in Part V [chapter 4]. ²Anyone who has not taken these vows will pronounce them when the two years of probation have passed, as the Examen states.

[347] D. ¹*If the rector, with authorization from the superior, should think that it would be more convenient to hold this renewal on some other principal feasts in particular cases, this too could be done.* ²*Likewise,*

---

¹⁰ **Abolished.** (As being contrary to existing liturgical norms.)

¹¹ **Clarified by** *CN* 75.

§2. To foster this growth, the Society retains the practice of an hour and a half as the time for prayer, Mass, and thanksgiving. Each one should be guided by his spiritual director as he seeks that form of prayer in which he can best advance in the Lord. The judgment of superiors is normative for each.[18]

§3. Each one should determine with his superior what time he gives to prayer and preparation for it.

68   The methodical reading of Holy Scripture should proceed by a gradual initiation, leading to a deeper knowledge of the Mystery of Christ. Likewise, throughout the whole course of training they should learn to take an active part in the Liturgy and come to understand it more deeply.[19]

69   §1. Those who are in charge of formation should take care that our members, especially in the period immediately after the novitiate, become familiar with the sources of the spirituality of the Church and the Society, with its history and traditions, and that they study them with a view toward their own progress and the progress of others.[20]

§2. It is important that we strengthen in our formation the mystical dimension of Christian faith and of our spirituality, so that we can encounter the spiritual traditions of others. A closer acquaintance with the beliefs and practices of other religions must be given through special courses and actual involvement in a pluralistic religious milieu.[21]

70   Those in charge of formation should take care that our members in formation are progressively formed to a sense of the Church, in the spirit of the rules of St. Ignatius,[22] and to a mature love for the Church, according to the requirements of our vocation.[23]

71   Today's conditions demand that a member of the Society during the whole course of formation should practice spiritual

---

[18] GC 31, d. 14, no. 12, 2°; see d. 8, no. 35.

[19] GC 31, d. 9, no. 20; see ibid., d. 8, nos. 29, 37.

[20] GC 32, d. 6, no. 33.

[21] See GC 34, d. 5, no. 9.3.

[22] See *SpEx* [352–70].

[23] See *FI* no. 1.

by the feasts of Easter and Christmas is meant either their octaves or the eight days preceding the feasts.

[348] E. ¹What a scholastic in the Society promises is to be incorporated into it so as right away to observe actual chastity, poverty, and obedience as practiced in the Society, and this whether he is admitted to become a professed or a formed coadjutor after his studies. ²{Consequently, the superior can admit him right away as a scholastic},¹² but only under probation as to his eventually becoming a professed or a coadjutor. ³Because of this arrangement, even with a vow of poverty he can retain possession of his temporal goods up to a certain time during his probation which the superior will decide.¹³

[349] 6. ¹When they must go to schools open to the public (for they will not go to other places without requesting permission), they should go and return {in pairs} [F],¹⁴ and with the interior and exterior decorum which is proper for the edification of themselves and of others. ²Their conversation with students from outside the Society should be only about matters pertaining to learning or spirituality, so that thereby they may find help in everything to the greater divine glory.¹⁵

[350] F. ¹The rector will designate those who are to accompany each other, and these will be those who derive most benefit from being together.

> The text of the Constitutions resumes on page 150.

---

¹² **Abolished by** *CN* 6, §1, 2°. (By pronouncing vows at the end of the novitiate, approved scholastics and brothers are by that very fact admitted as such.)

¹³ **Clarified by** *CN* 32.

¹⁴ **Abolished.** (As a strict norm it is obsolete.)

¹⁵ **Clarified by** *CN* 111.

discernment about the concrete choices which, stage by stage, the service of Christ and the Church require of him.[24]

72   §1. Provision should be made in each stage of the training for personal maturity, especially of the emotions (the advice of trained psychologists should be used when it is necessary).[25] In this way, the balanced development of the spiritual, intellectual, and affective life will be secured, and the true maturity of the whole person will be achieved.[26]

§2. Our members in formation should be given frequent occasions for exercising responsibility in leading the spiritual and intellectual life more actively and spontaneously, in doing some work in the house, and in vigorously carrying on various apostolic experiments as well.[27]

73   Great care should be taken to direct each one according to his own gifts, both natural and supernatural. At the same time a sense of solidarity and collaboration should be fostered and every trace of egoism removed.[28]

74   Throughout their entire formation the scholastics should keep in view the priestly character of our vocation, so that study, prayer, and all other activities may be imbued with a desire of serving God and the Church with priestly love for people. Especially before they come to theology and during the time of theology, they should be provided with opportunity to secure a deeper understanding of their priestly calling.[29]

75   "For greater devotion and to refresh the memory of the obligation to God they are under, . . . twice each year"[30] those who have not yet taken final vows should renew their first vows,[31] after a suitable preparation by means of the annual Exercises or the customary triduum or, if more briefly, by intensified time for recollection and prayer.

---

[24] GC 32, d. 6, no. 12.

[25] See CIC 642, 220.

[26] GC 31, d. 9, no. 5.

[27] GC 31, d. 9, no. 6; see d. 8, no. 36.

[28] GC 31, d. 9, no. 7.

[29] GC 31, d. 8, no. 34; GC 34, d. 6, especially no. 24.

[30] See P. IV, c. 4, no. 5 [346]; P. V, c. 4, no. 6, H [544, 546].

[31] See *CollDecr* d. 154, §1 (GC 8, d. 35).

CHAPTER 3

COMMUNITY LIFE DURING FORMATION

76   In houses of formation the community that the young constitute among themselves and with other members of the Society should foster participation in the life of the Society as an apostolic body. In it there is real communication and a sharing of life, even on the spiritual level, as well as cooperation and mutual responsibility in studies and also in apostolic works.[32]

77   §1. In arranging the community life of our houses of formation, the community life proposed as proper to those living in the apostolate must be kept in view as the model for which our younger members are to be prepared. But the pedagogical nature of the years of formation, the nature of the studies or activities in these houses, and the number of members make some suitable adaptations of community life necessary.

§2. In these houses there should be more room for common participation in some forms of prayer, especially for active and varied participation in a community celebration of the Eucharist, and for some short common prayer every day.

§3. Each one's sense of community, as a necessary prerequisite for the apostolic life of the Society, should be seriously tested and formed during these years.

§4. Attention must be paid to education for dialogue among themselves and with superiors, for cooperation and obedience, and for fraternal correction, all of which tend to form men who are capable of making the best possible choices, with the help of supernatural illumination and sufficient advice from others.[33]

78   The number of members in houses of formation should be such that mutual relations may be spiritual and fraternal, the discipline familial, and the government truly paternal.[34]

79   If, indeed, our members in formation live at times in apostolic communities, care must be taken that the communities are such as can willingly assume the responsibility of formation,

---

[32] GC 32, d. 6, no. 15.

[33] See GC 31, d. 19, no. 8, a, b, c, d; see d. 9, nos. 8, 10; GC 32, d. 6, no. 10.

[34] GC 31, d. 9, no. 9; see ibid., no. 32.

along with those who have special charge of formation in the province. The provincial is to designate someone to be responsible for helping them to pursue serious studies and to carry on their apostolic work while still maintaining close ties with their companions.[35]

80   In due proportion and under direction, relationships between younger members of different nations should be fostered, either for the sake of higher studies or for learning modern languages, or for apostolic experiments. This will greatly increase future understanding and unity in the Society.[36]

---

[35] See GC 32, d. 6, no. 15; see GC 31, d. 8, no. 41.

[36] GC 31, d. 19, no. 8, g.

CHAPTER 5

¹WHAT THE SCHOLASTICS OF THE SOCIETY SHOULD STUDY¹⁶

[351]   1. ²Since the end of the learning which is acquired in this Society is with God's favor to help the souls of its own members and those of their neighbors, it is by this norm that the decision will be made, both in general and in the case of individual persons, as to what subjects ours ought to learn and how far they ought to advance in them. ³And since, generally speaking, help is derived from the humane letters of different languages *[A]*, logic, natural and moral philosophy, metaphysics, scholastic and positive theology *[B]*, and Sacred Scripture, these are the subjects which those who are sent to the colleges should study *[C]*. ⁴They will devote themselves with greater diligence to the parts which are more helpful for the end mentioned above, taking into account circumstances of times, places, persons, and other such factors, as seems expedient in our Lord to him who holds the principal charge.

[352]   A. ¹*In addition to grammar,* ²*rhetoric is understood to be under the classification of humane letters.*

[353]   B. ¹*If there should not be enough time in the colleges to read the councils, decrees, holy doctors, and other moral subjects, each one could, with the approval of his superiors, read these privately after leaving studies, especially if he is well grounded in the scholastic doctrine.*

[354]   C. ¹*According to the age, ability, inclination, and basic knowledge which a particular person has, or in accordance with the common good which is hoped for, he could be applied to all these subjects or to one or several of them.* ²*For whoever cannot distinguish himself in all of them should strive to do so in at least one.*

[355]   2. ¹What particular studies each individual scholastic should make will likewise be left to the discretion of the superiors *[D]*. ²Nevertheless, when someone has aptitude, the better he is grounded in the aforementioned subjects the better will it be.

[356]   D. ¹*Some could be sent to the colleges not in hope of their coming out with the learning previously described but rather to lighten the burden of others; for example, a priest to hear confessions and so on.* ²*For these, and for others who because of age or other reasons cannot be expected to obtain a good grounding in all the subjects mentioned, it would be good, following the superior's directions, to study what they can* ³*and try to make progress in the languages and cases of conscience and,*

---

¹⁶ Clarified by *CN* 81–105.

CHAPTER 4

FORMATION IN STUDIES

81   §1. Since the purpose of studies in the Society is apostolic, through their studies our members should acquire that breadth and excellence in learning that are required to achieve this end.[37]

§2. The Society confirms its proper option for a profound academic formation of its future priests—theological as well as philosophical, humane, and scientific, persuaded that, presupposing the testimony of one's own life, there is no more apt way to exercise our mission.[38]

§3. Inasmuch as brothers participate in the apostolic activity of the Society according to the gifts received from God, they should receive appropriate theological instruction and adequate formation in what concerns their work.[39]

§4. For this reason, our members in formation should be reminded that their special mission and apostolate during the time of study is to study.[40]

82   Our studies should foster and stimulate those very qualities that today are often choked off by our contemporary style of living and thinking: a spirit of reflection and an awareness of deeper, transcendent values.[41]

83   §1. Studies in the Society, both ordinary and special, are governed by the common laws of the Church, by the norms found in this chapter, and by the General Norms of Studies promulgated by the superior general, which are to be continually revised and adapted to new needs.[42]

§2. In the different provinces or regions embracing several provinces, the provincial or group of provincials must draw up and regularly revise a Provincial or Regional Order of Studies, which, with the approval of the general, will adapt and

---

[37] GC 31, d. 9, no. 13; see GC 32, d. 6, no. 21.

[38] GC 32, d. 6, no. 22; see GC 34, d. 6, no. 21; P. IV, *Pream.*, no. 1 [307].

[39] See GC 32, d. 6, no. 23; see GC 31, d. 7, no. 7.

[40] GC 32, d. 6, no. 22.

[41] GC 32, d. 6, no. 22.

[42] GC 32, d. 6, no. 37.

in sum, in whatever can be of greatest use to them for the common good of souls.

[357] 3. ¹The rector will consider and decide by means of a suitable examination how much time should be given to each subject, and when the scholastics should pass on to another.

[358] 4. ¹**The doctrine** which they ought to follow in each subject should be that which is safest and **most approved**, as also the authors who teach it. ²The rectors will take care in this regard, conforming themselves to what is decided in the Society as a whole for the greater glory of God *[E].*¹⁷

[359] E. ¹*In books of humane letters by pagan authors, nothing immoral should be lectured on; what remains can be put to use by the Society like the spoils of Egypt. ²In the case of Christian authors, even though a work may be good it should not be lectured on when the author is bad, lest attachment to him be acquired. ³Furthermore, it is good to determine in detail the books which should be lectured on and those which should not, both in the humanities and in the other faculties.*

CHAPTER 6
¹MEANS FOR THEIR LEARNING WELL
THE AFOREMENTIONED SUBJECTS

[360] 1. ²In order to make good progress in these subjects, the scholastics should strive first of all to keep their souls pure and their intention in studying right, by seeking in their studies nothing except the glory of God and the good of souls. ³Moreover, they should frequently beg in prayer for grace to make progress in learning for the sake of this end.

[361] 2. ¹Next, they should have a firm resolution to be genuine and earnest students, persuading themselves that while they are in the colleges they cannot do anything more pleasing to God our Lord than to study with the intention mentioned above; ²likewise, that even if they never have occasion to employ the matter studied, the very toil of study, duly undertaken because of charity and obedience, is itself a very meritorious work in the sight of the Divine and Supreme Majesty.

[362] 3. ¹The impediments which distract from study should also be removed, both those arising from excessive or improperly or-

---

¹⁷ **Clarified by** *CN* 99–105. (In regard to the teaching to be imparted to our members.)

fill out the General Norms, considering the special circumstances of each place.[43]

§3. In these Orders of Studies provision is to be made for the formation in studies of the brothers, according to the norm of no. 98.

84   In provinces where scholastics study in faculties or institutions which do not belong to the Society, superiors should see to it that the formation proper to the Society is provided with all necessary means, for example, by rounding out the curriculum with special courses.[44]

85   Although the curriculum of studies for the scholastics may be arranged in a number of ways, such unity ought to be observed in the regional programs as to make it possible for them, without extreme difficulty, to take part of their training in another province or region.[45]

86   Before they begin philosophy and theology, scholastics should have completed that training in letters and sciences which in each nation is required before higher studies are begun. This training, if it has not been completed before entrance into the Society, is to be completed in the novitiate and, if necessary, later. Where it is possible, they should acquire knowledge of Latin and Greek, or at least sufficient preparation and knowledge that they can understand and use with ease the sources of so many sacred sciences and the documents of the Church.[46]

87   Scholastics are to devote at least two years to the study of philosophy. But when these studies are combined with other subjects or with the study of theology, they must be pursued in such a way that the equivalent of two years is devoted to them.[47]

88   In faculties or institutions where the curriculum in philosophy and theology allows for several variations, the superior of the scholastics or the prefect of studies, according to the determination of the provincial, is responsible for arranging the curric-

---

[43] GC 31, d. 9, no. 16; GC 32, d. 6, no. 50.

[44] GC 32, d. 6, no. 49, a.

[45] GC 32, d. 6, no. 46.

[46] See GC 31, d. 9, no. 17.

[47] GC 32, d. 6, no. 41; see also nos. 24–25; GC 31, d. 9, no. 22.

dered devotions and mortifications *[A]* and those springing from external cares and occupations, whether in duties inside the house *[B]* ²or outside it in conversations, confessions, and other activities with one's fellowmen, to the extent that these may be avoided in our Lord *[C]*. ³For in order that the scholastics may be able to help their neighbors better later on by what they have learned, it is wise to postpone exercises such as these, pious though they are, until after the years of study, since there will be others to attend to them in the meantime. ⁴All this should be done with a greater intention of service and the divine glory.

[363] A. ²*This is the general practice. But if an individual finds it necessary to apply himself to devotion and mortification, it will be left to the discretion of the one who holds the principal charge to consider how far he should go in these matters.*

[364] B. ¹*To give aid at some hour to those who hold these burdensome duties is not improper;* ²*but to assume them permanently is more properly the work of the coadjutors, and these can be provided to lighten this burden for those who are studying.*

[365] C. ¹*Consequently, to avoid such hindrances those not yet in holy orders would do well to put off ordination until they complete their studies.* ²*However, because of needs that may arise it is at times necessary to dispense from this.*

³*Moreover, this work of helping the neighbors could be supplied by some who have finished their studies or who are sent to the colleges specially for this purpose.* ⁴*Likewise, for the more demanding domestic offices inside the college, it will be good to have persons who are not primarily intent upon studies, such as temporal coadjutors or persons who are there for purposes of probation rather than study.*

[366] 4. ¹An order should be observed in pursuing the branches of knowledge. The scholastics should acquire a good grounding in Latin before they attend lectures on the arts; and in the arts before they pass on to scholastic theology; and in it before they study positive theology. ²Scripture may be studied either concomitantly or later on.[18]

[367] 5. ¹The languages too in which Scripture was written or into which it was translated may be studied either previously or

---

[18] The program of studies [366–83] has been modified by *CN* 81–88 insofar as they were concrete determinations; but many of the criteria included here are valid and useful even today.

ulum of each scholastic according to his ability and his future apostolic work.[48]

89   All who are preparing for the priesthood in the Society must devote to theological studies at least the four-year period prescribed by the Church.[49] But where the regular course of theology is completed in three years, a fourth year is to be added, which should be dedicated either to preparation for a degree in theology or, in an appropriate program, to the integration of theological studies into one's formation, especially one's pastoral formation.[50]

90   Members of the Society should not be allowed to hear confessions unless they have been found qualified for this ministry by a special examination on their pastoral competence and moral theology. Those who are already priests when they are admitted may be exempted from this examination if their qualifications are already clearly established in some other way.[51]

91   Those who, prior to their entrance into the Society, have completed some of their philosophy or theology courses should be examined on their progress in them unless their attainments are evident from some other source; and then they should complete these studies insofar as necessary.[52]

92   Provincials should see to it that in general all scholastics acquire the licentiate in either theology or philosophy and that those who manifest greater interest and talent should continue further studies in order to acquire higher degrees.[53]

93   §1. To determine whether those who have not acquired a higher academic degree, at least a licentiate, have attained the level of learning in sacred sciences required for profession of four vows, they must undergo a comprehensive examination in theology before three examiners approved by the appropriate major superior.[54]

---

[48] GC 32, d. 6, no. 39.

[49] CIC 250; CCEO 348, §1.

[50] GC 32, d. 6, no. 42; see also no. 24; GC 31, d. 9, no. 23; P. IV, c. 9, no. 3 [418]; P. V, c. 2, no. 2 [518].

[51] See *CollDecr* d. 127, §2 (GC 30, d. 66; see GC 13, d. 16, no. 2; GC 20, d. 25, no. 1); 128, §2 (see GC 13, d. 16, no. 4).

[52] *CollDecr* d. 128, §1 (GC 7, d. 33, no. 1; GC 11, d. 24, no. 4).

[53] GC 32, d. 6, no. 38; see GC 31, d. 9, no. 21.

[54] See GC 32, d. 6, no. 51 (modified by GC 34).

later on, according to what seems best to the superior in accordance with the various cases and the diversity of the persons. This too will remain within his discretion *[D]*. ²But if the languages are studied, one of the ends pursued should be to defend the version which the Church holds as approved.

[368] *D. ¹It would be good for them to have their degrees in theology or at least to be fairly well versed in it, so that they know the interpretations of the holy Doctors and the decisions of the Church, in order that the study of languages may be profitable rather than harmful. ²However, if some are seen to be so humble and firm in their faith that in their cases nothing harmful is to be feared from the study of languages, the superior may grant an exemption to them that they may devote themselves to these languages when this would be conducive to the common good or that of the individual.*

[369] 6. ¹All the students should attend the lectures of the public professors designated for them by the rector *[E]*. ²It is to be desired that these professors should be learned, diligent, and assiduous; and that, whether they be members of the Society *[F]* or from outside it, they should strive to further the students' progress both in the lectures and in the academic exercises.

[370] *E. ¹If something else is expedient for an individual, the superior will consider the matter with prudence and may grant an exemption. ²What has been said about public lectures does not exclude private lectures within the college or outside it when these may be necessary or profitable.*

[371] *F. ¹No member of the Society will give lectures publicly without the approbation and permission of the provincial superior (except in the lower classes or for a time because of some necessity). ²But those who have the talent, especially those who have finished their studies, can be employed in lecturing if matters of greater importance do not require something else.*

[372] 7. ¹There should be a general library in the colleges, ²if possible, and those who in the judgment of the rector ought to have a key should have one. ³Furthermore, each one should have the books that he requires *[G]*.

[373] *G. ¹However, they ought not to write annotations in these books; and the one in charge of the books should keep an account of them.*

[374] 8. ¹The scholastics should be regular in attending the lectures, diligent in preparing for them beforehand, in repeating them afterwards *[H]*, in asking about points they do not understand,

§2. Particulars of this examination in regard to its length, program, method of giving grades, and so on are to be determined in the Provincial or Regional Order of Studies to be approved by the general.[55]

94   Special studies, understood in view of their apostolic character, should be earnestly fostered by superiors. Those who undertake such studies, especially in secular universities, should be assisted to understand and personally to assimilate the interrelationship between these studies and their philosophy and theology. They should have special spiritual assistance and should be integrated into the life of a community of the Society.[56]

95   A solid education should be fostered in literature, in the arts, in sciences, also in social sciences, the better to understand reality and to undertake the analysis of it;[57] and also in history and in various aspects of the culture of the region where the apostolate will be carried on, as well as in modern means of social communication.[58]

96   §1. Throughout the entire course of studies, scholastics should practice those means of expression that are suited to the people of our age. Skilled in the arts of writing and speaking, they can become better preachers of the Gospel of Christ. Suitable opportunities should be provided for access to the audiovisual media and for instruction on how they can be used successfully in the apostolate.[59]

§2. To secure this during both early and ongoing formation, we must provide well-organized communication curricula for all. These will show how to subject to critical evaluation the ways of self-expression that this new culture has, how to judge its aesthetic dimension, and how to use the communications media in group effort.[60]

97   In order to facilitate communication with other cultures and throughout the universal Society, all our members in formation, scholastics and brothers, are to learn one or other modern

---

[55] GC 32, d. 6, no. 51.

[56] GC 32, d. 6, no. 43; see GC 31, no. 9, nos. 33–40; "Document of Fr. General on Special Studies," *ActRSJ* 20:737–45.

[57] See GC 32, d. 4, no. 44; ibid., no. 35.

[58] GC 32, d. 6, no. 44; see GC 31, d. 9, no. 18.

[59] GC 31, d. 9, nos. 18, 19; see GC 32, d. 6, no. 27.

[60] See GC 34, d. 15 no. 9.

and in noting down what may be useful to assist the memory later on [I].

[375] *H. ¹The rector should take care that these repetitions take place at a fixed time in the schools or in the house. One student should repeat the matter and the others should listen. They should propose to one another the difficulties which occur and have recourse to the professor in matters which they cannot solve satisfactorily among themselves. ²The rector will also attend to the disputations and other scholastic exercises that are judged expedient in accordance with the subjects which are being treated.*

[376] *I. ¹Superiors will determine whether it will be helpful for those beginning their studies to have notebooks for writing down the lectures, and noting above and along the margin whatever seems useful. ²Those who are more advanced in the humanities and the other faculties should carry sheets of paper on which to note down the lectures or whatever strikes them as noteworthy; afterwards they should set down in notebooks, with better arrangement and order, what they desire to keep for the future.*

[377] 9. ¹The rector of the college should also take care to see how all, the teachers as well as the students, are fulfilling their duty in our Lord.

[378] 10. ¹Because of the utility there is in the practice of disputation (especially for those who are studying arts and scholastic theology), the scholastics should participate in the disputations or ordinary circles of the schools which they attend, even if not of the Society; and they should endeavor to distinguish themselves by learning joined with modesty. ²Within the college too, after dinner on Sunday or some other day of the week (unless a special reason impedes the exercise), it is good to have someone from each class of the students of arts and theology, whom the rector will designate, defend some theses. ³During the preceding afternoon these theses will be posted in writing on the door of the schools, so that those who wish may come to dispute or to listen. ⁴After these defendants have briefly proved their theses, those from within and without the house who wish to object may do so. ⁵Someone will preside to direct the disputants, resolve and clarify the doctrine under discussion for the benefit of the hearers, and give the signal for the disputants to stop, dividing the time so that everyone will have an opportunity for disputation.

[379] 11. ¹In addition to the two kinds of disputations mentioned, an hour ought also to be designated each day for holding

language besides their own. All should be familiar with English; those whose mother tongue is English should learn another modern language, chosen from among those that are more commonly used.[61]

98 §1. The studies of brothers should be in accord with the needs of the province and the Society as well as their future apostolic work.[62] In the years immediately following the novitiate, a theological program should be offered to all as either the only discipline or at least the principal one. Nor, among other disciplines offered them, should instruction "concerning behavior-patterns, emotional attitudes, and thought processes of contemporary social life"[63] be omitted. They should also pursue cultural and technical studies during the time of formation. This training of the brothers in studies should also be confirmed with suitable degrees.[64]

§2. The better to achieve this, brothers in formation should, if possible, live in communities of scholastics[65] or in other communities in which they are helped in pursuing their studies; they should not be burdened with other occupations, so that they will have time to devote to studies.

CHAPTER 5

THE TEACHING TO BE IMPARTED TO OUR MEMBERS

99 §1. The purpose of our studies is to train Jesuits to proclaim and transmit the truth revealed in Christ and entrusted to the Church.[66] Our teaching, therefore, should faithfully adhere to what "was once given to the holy men of the faith," and should be such that, accommodating itself to changing ways of speaking and thinking, and adapting itself to the diverse cultures of the whole world, it can continually revivify that faith in human hearts.[67]

---

[61] See GC 34, d. 21, no. 10; ibid., d. 7, no. 19; GC 32, d. 6, no. 45; GC 31, d. 9, no. 18.

[62] See GC 32, d. 6, no. 40.

[63] GC 31, d. 8, no. 28, citing Vat. Council II, *Perfectæ caritatis*, no. 18.

[64] GC 31, d. 7, no. 7.

[65] See GC 34, d. 7, no. 17.

[66] GC 32, d. 6, no. 21.

[67] GC 31, d. 9, no. 41; GC 32, d. 6, nos. 26–27.

disputation within the college, with someone presiding in the manner already stated. 2The purpose is that the intellectual powers may be exercised more and that difficult matters occurring in these subjects may be clarified, for the glory of God our Lord.

[380]   12. 1Those who are studying humanities should also have their fixed times to discuss and debate about the matters of their subject in the presence of someone who directs them. 2After dinner on one Sunday (or other designated day) they will defend theses, 3and on another exercise themselves in writing compositions in prose or in verse, whether extemporaneously as a test of their facility or by bringing a composition previously written and reading it publicly there, 4with the topic being assigned beforehand in the one case and at the moment in the other.

[381]   13. 1All, particularly the students of humanities, should ordinarily speak Latin [K] and memorize what is assigned by their teachers. They should devote much exercise to style in their compositions [L] and have someone to correct them. 2Moreover, some with the approval of the rector may privately read other authors besides those on whom they have lectures. 3One day each week after dinner, one of the more advanced students should deliver a Latin or Greek oration on a subject likely to edify those within and without the college and to encourage them to things of greater perfection in our Lord.

[382]   K. 1In regard to the exercises of repetitions, disputations, and speaking Latin, if something ought to be changed because of circumstances of place, time, or persons, the decision will be left to the discretion of the rector, with authorization, at least in general, from his superior.

[383]   L. 1So that the students may be helped more, it would be wise to place together some of equal ability who with holy rivalry may spur one another on. 2From time to time it will also be helpful to send to the place where the provincial superior or the superior general is a specimen of their work, now from one student, now from another; for example some compositions from the students of the humanities, or theses from those studying arts or theology. 3It will also aid them to be reminded that upon their arrival at the houses after their studies they will have to be examined in all the subjects which they have learned.

[384]   14. 1Moreover, especially those studying the arts and theology, but also the rest, ought to have their own private and undisturbed study so that they may better and more profoundly understand the matters treated [M].

§2. Our formation must be such that a Jesuit can be one with the people to whom he is sent, capable of communicating with them. He must be able to share their convictions and values, their history, their experience and aspirations; at the same time he must be open to the convictions and values of other peoples, traditions, and cultures.[68]

100 Jesuits ought to put their trust in the strength of divine truth and in that inner unction of the Holy Spirit which leads the Church of Christ to all truth. Therefore they should strive to join to their studies a close familiarity with God; following this secure way, they will be safe from timidity as well as from thoughtless innovation. Let them in all matters see that their knowledge is well grounded, according to the norms which the Holy See has given to the Church and to the Society.[69]

101 Professors should bear in mind that they do not teach in their own name, but in the Church, in accordance with the mission received from the Church, and that they teach joined together in charity in the Society of Jesus. Hence, they should let themselves be guided by the mind and will of the Church, show proper respect for the teaching authority of the Church, and have regard for the building up of the faith in their students and in all the faithful. At the same time they should keep in mind those who are separated from us.[70]

102 Both professors and scholastics should faithfully adhere to and diligently study the written word of God along with sacred tradition. Let them also have high regard for the teaching of the holy fathers and other doctors, specifically St. Thomas, and for those authors of the Society who are highly regarded in the Church.[71]

103 §1. Professors should clearly distinguish between matters of faith to be held by all and teachings approved by the consent of theologians. Probable, new, and personal explanations are to be proposed modestly.[72]

§2. For more secure and profitable progress in doctrine, it will be very helpful if the professors freely and sincerely com-

---

[68] GC 32, d. 6, no. 27; see GC 34, d. 4, no. 17.

[69] GC 31, d. 9, no. 42; see GC 29, d. 27; GC 30, d. 44.

[70] GC 31, d. 9, no. 43.

[71] See GC 31, d. 9, no. 44.

[72] GC 31, d. 9, no. 45.

[385]   M. ¹In this private study (if the rector thinks it good), they could read a commentary. While they are attending lectures, this should ordinarily be a single commentary, carefully chosen. ²They could also write down what they think will be more helpful to them.

[386]   15. ¹Just as it is necessary to hold in those who run too rapidly, so is it proper to spur on, push, and encourage those who need it. ²For this purpose the rector ought to keep informed, through himself and through a person whom he will appoint as syndic or visitor of the students.

³When someone is seen to be wasting his time in the college because he is either unwilling or unable to make progress, it is better to remove him and let someone else enter in his place who will make better progress for the end sought, the service of God [N].

[387]   N. ¹If anyone should be unfit to study but fit for other ministries, he could be employed within the colleges or houses of the Society in something judged proper. ²But if he entered to become a scholastic and should be unfit for both study and the other ministries, he may be dismissed. ³However, it will be good for the rector, after considering the case, to inform the provincial or general and to follow his order.

[388]   16. ¹When the subject matter of one faculty has been completed, it will be good to review it, by reading, with the rector's approval, one or more authors than the one used the first time, ²and by making, also with his approval, an extract of what pertains to that subject, briefer and better organized than the notes he had made earlier when he lacked the understanding acquired with completion of his courses [O].¹⁹

[389]   O. ¹It is good that these extracts be made only by persons who have greater knowledge, clarity of mind, and judgment, of whose work the others could take advantage. ²It would also be good to have the extracts approved by the professor. ³The rest of the students will be able to draw help from the professor's explanations and from the noteworthy matters that they themselves have collected. ⁴It will render these extracts more useful if they have the topics indicated in the margin as well as a table of contents, to make it easier to find what is sought. ⁵Although these books of extracts and personal ideas or other writings of any sort be made, it is understood that no one may publish any book without examination and specific approval by the superior general, as has been said [273].

---

¹⁹ Clarified by CN 83.

municate to their colleagues their new ideas, even before they are published. Thus, if necessary, they can be corrected by them and can perhaps also be of benefit to them.[73]

104   If any of our professors in his teaching departs from doctrine in accord with the magisterium of the Church, superiors ought to speak with him in order to understand well both him and his thinking; and, if occasion warrants, they should admonish him. If he does not change, superiors should not hesitate even to remove him from his teaching position, if it eventually proves necessary, observing as far as possible the statutes of the institution or faculty.[74]

105   During their course of studies, scholastics should be taught, under the direction of their professors, to read critically and use prudently the works of those authors who have greater influence on present-day cultures. Thus they should learn how to retain what is good and to correct what is unacceptable.[75]

The text of the Norms resumes on page 167.

---

[73] GC 31, d. 9, no. 46.

[74] See *CollDecr* d. 102 (GC 30, d. 66; see GC 5, d. 56, no. 4; GC 12, d. 28; GC 26, d. 19, no. 3); d. 105 (GC 30, d. 66; see GC 25, d. 16, nos. 2, 4).

[75] See GC 31, d. 9, no. 47.

[390]   17. ¹At the times designated for them they should prepare themselves for the public acts of examinations and replies. **Those who after careful examination are found to deserve their degrees may receive them.**²⁰ ²But to avoid every appearance of ambition or inordinate desires, they should not take special places. Rather, they should place themselves in a group independently of rank, even though indications of rank are customarily given in the university where they are studying. ³Moreover, they should not make expenditures inappropriate for poor men when they take their degrees, which should be received, without detriment to humility, for the sole purpose of being better able to help one's neighbors for the glory of God.

[391]   18. ¹The superior should consider whether it is advisable for those who have finished their studies to lecture in private or in public for their own progress and for that of others. He should make provision according to what seems more expedient in our Lord.

CHAPTER 7

¹THE SCHOOLS MAINTAINED IN THE COLLEGES OF THE SOCIETY²¹

[392]   1. ²To take care that in our colleges not only our own scholastics may be helped in learning, but also those from outside in both learning and good habits of conduct, ³where schools [open to the public] can be conveniently had, they should be established at least in humane letters [A], and in more advanced subjects in accordance with the conditions found in the regions where the colleges are situated [B], looking always to the greater service of God our Lord.

[393]   A. ²*It will belong to the general to decide where it will be opportune to have such schools.*

[394]   B. ¹*The situation of the Society should also be taken into account.* ²*However, our intention would be that humane letters, languages, and Christian doctrine should ordinarily be taught in the colleges;* ³*if necessary, lectures on cases of conscience should be given.* ⁴*If persons are available for preaching and hearing confessions, this should be done, without entering upon higher branches of knowledge. For learning these,*

---

²⁰ **Clarified by** *CN* 92.

²¹ **Clarified (in a general way) by** *CN* 277–92.

students who have studied humane letters should be sent from the colleges to the Society's universities.

[395] 2. ¹In these schools measures should be taken that the extern students are well instructed in matters of Christian doctrine, go to confession every month if possible, attend the sermons, and, in sum, acquire along with their letters the habits of conduct worthy of a Christian. ²Since there must be great variety in individual cases, according to circumstances of places and persons, the treatment here will descend no further into particulars, except to state that there should be rules covering everything that is necessary in each college *[C].* ³The only recommendation made here is that {suitable correction should not be lacking *[D]* in the case of externs for whom it is necessary, and that this should not be given by the hand of any member of the Society}.²²

[396] *C.* ¹{*From the rules of the Roman College, the part which is suitable to the other colleges can be adapted to them*}.²³

[397] *D.* ¹*For this purpose there should be a corrector where this is possible. Where it is not, there ought to be some method of administering punishment, either through one of the students or in some other suitable way.*

[398] 3. ¹Since it is so proper to our profession not to accept any temporal remuneration for the spiritual ministries in which we employ ourselves according to our Institute to aid our fellowmen, ²it is not fitting for us to accept for a college any endowment with **an attached obligation of supplying** a preacher or a confessor or **a lecturer on theology** *[E].*²⁴ ³For, although the reason of equity and gratitude moves us to give more careful service in those ministrations proper to our Institute in those colleges which have been founded with greater liberality and devotion, ⁴there ought nevertheless to be no entering into obligations or agreements which impair the sincerity of our manner of proceeding, which is to give freely what we have freely received [Matt. 10:8]. ⁵However, for the sustenance of those who serve the common good of the colleges or who study for the sake of it, the endowment which the charity of the founders is wont to assign for the divine glory is accepted.

[399] *E.* ¹*When the superior general or the Society accepts the charge of a university, the fact that an obligation arises to give the ordinary*

---

²² **Abolished by GC 34.** (The non-corporal correction of students, when necessary, can be done in different ways in different places.)

²³ **Abolished.** (This norm is obsolete and cannot be applied.)

²⁴ (But it would not be illicit; see *CN* 186.)

lectures of the university will not be against the intention of this constitution, even if lectures on theology are included in them.

CHAPTER 8

¹THE INSTRUCTION OF THE SCHOLASTICS IN THE MEANS OF HELPING THEIR NEIGHBOR²⁵

[400]   1. ²In view of the objective which the Society seeks in its studies, towards their end it is good for the scholastics to begin getting accustomed to the spiritual arms they must employ in aiding their fellowmen; ³and this work can be begun in the colleges, even though it is more properly and extensively done in the houses.

[401]   2. ¹First of all, those who in the judgment of the superior should be ordained are to be taught how to say Mass not only with interior understanding and devotion but also with a good exterior manner, for the edification of those who hear the Mass. ²**All members of the Society should as far as possible use the same ceremonies,**²⁶ ³conforming, so far as the diversity of regions permits, to the Roman usage as being more universal and embraced in a special way by the Apostolic See.

[402]   3. ¹**Similarly, they will exercise themselves in preaching and delivering [sacred] lectures in a manner suited to the edification of the people, which is different from the scholastic manner [A]; ²they should strive to learn the vernacular language well, to have prepared and have ready at hand the topics most useful for this ministry [B], and to avail themselves of all appropriate means to perform it better and with greater fruit for souls [C].**²⁷

[403]   A. *²In their lectures, besides giving the interpretation, they should take care to treat matters helpful for morality and Christian living. ³They should do the same when teaching in their classes in the schools, but much more so when lecturing to the people.*

---

²⁵ (See *CN* 106–12.)

²⁶ (See CIC 846, §1. "Liturgical books approved by competent authority are to be faithfully observed in the celebration of the sacraments; therefore, no one on personal authority may add, remove, or change anything in them. §2. The ministers are to celebrate the sacraments according to their own rite"; CCEO 674, §§1–2.)

²⁷ (See *CN* 96.)

CHAPTER 6

APOSTOLIC FORMATION

106 §1. The whole process of formation through its various stages from novitiate to tertianship should favor integration into the apostolic body of the Society, so that it prepares our young men to fulfill the missions and perform the ministries which the Society may wish to assign to them.[76]

§2. Therefore, our style of life and its attendant circumstances, both personal and communitarian, ought to favor apostolic formation, so that young Jesuits can know and understand what the people among whom they live are seeking, what they suffer, and what they lack;[77] in a particular way they should foster solidarity with the poor, so that they learn from them how they can aid them.[78]

§3. A certain experience of living with the poor will sometimes be necessary for our young men, to help them both to overcome limitations that may perchance spring from their own social background and to strengthen their love for the poor. However, this should take place under such conditions that it will be genuine, free of illusions, and productive of a true conversion. For this purpose, contact with the poor should be extended rather than occasional, and must be accompanied by careful reflection and integrated into training in sociocultural analysis.[79]

107 A formation that is bound up with the activities of the province or region is also especially helpful for this. Therefore, the major superior himself or others designated by him should see that our young men are directed in this in progressive stages and by means of a variety of experiences, according to the talents

---

[76] GC 32, d. 6, no. 13.

[77] GC 32, d. 6, no. 9, c.

[78] See GC 32, d. 4, nos. 48–50; GC 34, d. 4, no. 28.4.

[79] See GC 32, d. 6, no. 10; GC 34, d. 3, no. 18.

[404] B. ¹It will be helpful if they have studied particularly and with a view to preaching the gospel passages that occur throughout the year, and have studied a portion of Scripture for purposes of lecturing; ²likewise, if they have considered in advance matters pertaining to the vices, motives for their abhorrence, and their remedies; and, on the contrary, in what pertains to the commandments and virtues and good works, motives for esteeming them and means for acquiring them. ³It will be better, if possible, to have this material in extracts, so as to have less need of books.

[405] C. ¹Some means are these: to have studied the precepts about the manner of preaching given by those who have performed this ministry well and to listen to good preachers; ²to practice preaching either in the house or in monasteries; and during this practice, to have a good corrector who points out defects either in the matter preached or in the voice, inflection, gestures, and movements. ³Finally, the scholastic himself, by reflecting on what he has done, can help himself more in every respect.

[406] 4. ¹They should also exercise themselves in administering the sacraments of confession [D] and Communion, ²keeping before their minds and striving to put in practice what regards not only the sacraments but the penitents and communicants also, ³so that they may receive and frequent these sacraments well and fruitfully, for the divine glory.

[407] D. ¹In regard to the confessions, in addition to the scholastic treatment and the cases of conscience, especially in the matter of restitution, it is good to have a summary containing the {reserved}²⁸ cases and censures ²so that one may know how far his jurisdiction extends, as well as the extraordinary forms of absolution which are needed. ³Moreover, it is good to have a brief list of questions about the sins and their remedies, and an instruction helping toward the good and prudent exercise of this ministry in the Lord without harm to oneself and with profit to one's neighbors. ⁴Especially at the beginning of the confessor's ministry, after hearing a confession he should make a practice of reflecting to see whether he has been deficient in any regard and to do better in the future.

[408] 5. ¹After they themselves have experienced the Spiritual Exercises, they should get practice in giving them to others. ²Each one should know how to give an explanation of them and how to make use of this spiritual weapon, since it is obvious that God our Lord has made it so effective for his service [E].²⁹

---

²⁸ **Abolished.** (In regard to sins [cases]: reserved sins as such no longer exist.)

²⁹ (See *CN* 108, §4; 271, §3.)

of each and with a view to the apostolic works of the province or region as well as of the whole Society.[80]

108 §1. Apostolic formation of all our members ought to be carried on in a progressive fashion under the direction of a competent coordinator, who should direct our men in formation in their apostolic activities, bring them to examine the activities critically, and help them to carry them out. This apostolic formation should be an integrated part of the curriculum of studies.[81]

§2. Apostolic activities, which are to be undertaken as a mission from superiors, should be so arranged that they lead to a deeper level of spiritual and intellectual reflection.[82]

§3. Scholastics should be trained for different priestly ministries.[83] Brothers, on the other hand, should be prepared to perform the works proper to their vocation, so that they fully participate in the apostolic mission of the Society in their distinctive way.

§4. All should grow accustomed to directing others in the Spiritual Exercises under the supervision of an experienced director.[84]

109 §1. Regency, whose purpose is to contribute to a fuller religious and apostolic maturity,[85] will be made after philosophy according to the ordinary practice in the Society; but, according to the judgment of the provincial, it may be deferred up to the time immediately preceding priestly ordination, or some other appropriate experiment may be substituted for it.[86]

§2. Without a serious reason, a provincial should not send scholastics to regency before the completion of philosophy or of two years of philosophical-theological studies; nor should he keep any one in regency for more than two or three years.[87]

§3. During the time of teaching or experiments, care is to be taken that the scholastics' spiritual life not only does not

---

80 See GC 32, d. 6, no. 16.

81 GC 32, d. 6, no. 47; see ibid., no. 28.

82 GC 32, d. 6, no. 47; see GC 31, d. 8, no. 41; d. 9, no. 4.

83 See P. IV, c. 8 [400–414].

84 See GC 32, d. 6, no. 47; see P. IV, c. 8, no. 5, E [408–9].

85 GC 31, d. 8, no. 39.

86 See GC 31, d. 9, no. 30.

87 *CollDecr* d. 84 (GC 30, d. 66).

[409]   E. ¹*They could begin by giving the Exercises to persons with whom less is risked, and consulting about their method of procedure with someone more experienced, noting well what he finds more appropriate and what less so.* ²*Their explanation of the Exercises should be such that it not only satisfies people but also moves them to a desire to take advantage of the Exercises.* ³*Generally, only the exercises of the First Week ought to be given. When the Exercises are given in their entirety, it should be to exceptional persons or those who desire to decide upon their state of life.*

[410]   6. ¹They should likewise bestow appropriate study upon the method of teaching Christian doctrine and of adapting themselves to the capacities of children or simple persons [F].

[411]   F. ¹*It will be helpful to have a written compendious explanation of the matters necessary for the faith and Christian life.*

[412]   7. ¹Just as the above is for helping one's neighbors live well, efforts should also be made to learn what helps to die well, ²along with the procedure to be employed at a moment so important for gaining or losing the ultimate end of eternal happiness [G].

[413]   G. ¹*It is good to have a compendium on the method of helping a person to die well, to refresh the memory when this holy ministry must be exercised.*

[414]   8. ¹In general, they ought to be instructed about the manner of acting proper to a member of the Society, who has to associate with so great a diversity of persons throughout such varied places. ²Hence they should foresee the difficulties which may arise and the opportunities which can be grasped for the greater service of God by employing this means or that. ³Although all this can be taught only by the unction of the Holy Spirit [1 John 2:20, 27] and by the prudence which God our Lord communicates to those who trust in his Divine Majesty, ⁴nevertheless the way can at least be opened by some suggestions which help and prepare for the effect that is to be produced by divine grace.

CHAPTER 9

¹REMOVAL FROM STUDIES

[415]   1. ²Some [A] are removed from the colleges for the reasons stated in Part II and in the manner explained there [209–30], so that others in their place may make better progress in the service of God our Lord, ³since the same reason holds true for removing from the colleges as from the houses.

thereby suffer damage but, on the contrary, that it derives therefrom a proper growth.[88] Accordingly, consideration should be given to the community where they live during regency, and their superior should have special concern for their formation.[89]

§4. But if they experience greater difficulties in prayer and work at this time, they should learn to overcome them with magnanimity and patience in the Lord.[90]

110   In the whole course of formation, especially during philosophical and theological studies, a deep and authentic involvement with the local culture should be fostered, according to regional differences, by sharing the life and experiences of those peoples among whom we work and by trying to understand their cultures from within.[91] Yet care should also be taken to promote unity of minds and hearts in the Society, based on genuine Ignatian spirituality;[92] and a truly universal spirit, proper to our vocation, is to be reinforced by various experiences, such as by participating in international meetings of those in formation, or by receiving part of one's training in a culture other than one's own.[93]

111   Besides enjoying the kind of communication among young men of different provinces and regions that leads to a true sense of the universality of the Society,[94] our members in formation should have suitable contacts, arranged with prudence, with young people of their own age—clerics, religious, laity—both of their own and other nations, so that, ridding themselves of nationalism and every other form of particularism, they will acquire the universality of mind and the openness toward different forms of

---

[88] GC 31, d. 8, no. 39.

[89] See Fr. Peter-Hans Kolvenbach, "Regency as a Stage of Formation," *ActRSJ* 20:362ff.

[90] GC 31, d. 8, no. 40.

[91] See GC 34, d. 4, no. 28.4; d. 3, no. 18.

[92] GC 32, d. 6, no. 29.

[93] See GC 34, d. 21, no. 8.

[94] GC 32, d. 6, no. 29.

[416]　A. ²{*Others are removed after seven years, namely, those who were admitted to the colleges for that length of time without a fixed resolution to enter the Society, as has been said [338]. ³But a dispensation could be given in regard to this period of seven years, by prolonging it when such students give much good example in such a way that much service of God is expected from them, or when they are useful to the college}.*³⁰

[417]　2. ¹Sometimes, too, they will be removed because a different place is useful for their better progress in spirit or in learning; or because it is useful for the universal good of the Society, ²**as is the case when someone is removed from one college where he has studied arts to lecture on them in another before he studies theology,**³¹ and similarly for other purposes of greater service of God our Lord.

[418]　3. ¹The usual manner of removal from a college where all the subjects are studied will be after a person has finished his studies, namely, after he has completed the course in arts and studied theology for four years. ²Near the end of this period the rector ought to furnish the general or provincial with a report on the man's competence, and then to follow the order given him for the glory of God our Lord.

CHAPTER 10
¹THE GOVERNMENT OF THE COLLEGES

[419]　1. ²In accordance with the bulls of the Apostolic See, the Professed Society will hold the superintendency over the colleges. ³For since it may not seek any gain from the fixed revenues nor employ them for itself, ⁴it may be expected in the long run to proceed with greater disinterestedness and a more spiritual attitude in regard to what ought to be provided in the colleges for the greater service of God our Lord and for the good government of the colleges.

[420]　2. ¹Except for what pertains to the Constitutions, and to suppression or alienation of such colleges, all the authority, the

---

³⁰ **Abolished by GC 34.** (This refers to students from outside, of whom there now are none in our colleges, or if there are any, they do not depend on the Society.)

³¹ **Clarified by** *CN* **109.** (Where there is question of the experiment of "regency.")

cultures, diverse civilizations, and differing mentalities that our apostolic vocation demands.[95]

112 Those who teach our men ought to manifest by their labor and living example this integration of the intellectual, spiritual, and apostolic life[96] and to help them identify problems and assume responsibilities flowing from our mission today.[97]   ∎

---

[95] GC 31, d. 9, no. 11.

[96] GC 32, d. 6, no. 30.

[97] See GC 32, d. 4, no. 43.

administration, and in general the execution of this superintendency will be vested in the superior general. ²He, keeping his mind fixed on the end of the colleges and of the entire Society, will see best what is expedient in them.

[421]   3. ¹Therefore the general, by himself or through another to whom he delegates his authority in this matter, {will appoint one of the coadjutors}³² in the Society as the rector who is to have the principal charge [A]. ²This rector will give account of his charge to the provincial or to whomever the general designates. The general will likewise have power to remove the rector, or to change him from this charge, as seems better to him in our Lord.

[422]   A. ²This does not prevent a professed member who has been sent to visit or reform the affairs of a college from dwelling there, or presiding over all those who live there, for a time or in some other manner, as may seem more expedient for the welfare of the college or for the universal good.

[423]   4. ¹Care should be taken that the rector be a man of great example, edification, and mortification of all his evil inclinations, and especially a man of proven obedience and humility. ²He ought likewise to be discreet, fit for governing, experienced both in matters of business and of the spiritual life. He should know how to blend severity with kindness at the proper times. ³He should be solicitous, stalwart under work, a man of learning, and finally, one in whom the higher superiors can confide and to whom they can with security delegate their authority. ⁴For the greater this delegated authority will be, the better will the colleges be governed to the greater divine glory.

[424]   5. ¹The function of the rector will be first of all to sustain the whole college by his prayer and holy desires, and then to see that the Constitutions are observed [B]. ²He should watch over all his subjects with great care, and guard them against difficulties from within or without the house by forestalling the difficulties or remedying them if they have occurred, in a way conducive to the good of the individuals and to that of all. ³He should strive to promote their progress in virtues and learning, and care for their health and for the temporal goods both stable and movable [C]. ⁴He should appoint officials discreetly, observe how they proceed, and retain them in office or change them as he judges appropriate in

---

³² **Abolished by GC 34.** (As a preceptive norm: since it has hardly ever been applied in a uniform way in the Society nor is it so applied now; in fact there was a somewhat contrary directive in *CollDecr* d. 244.)

the Lord. ⁵In general he ought to see to it that what has been stated about the colleges in the preceding chapters is observed.

⁶He should fully maintain the subordination he ought to keep not only toward the superior general but also to the provincial superior, ⁷informing and having recourse to him in the matters of greater moment and following his directions since he is his superior, as it is right that those in his own college should act toward him. ⁸These ought to hold him in great respect and reverence as one who holds the place of Christ our Lord, leaving to him with true obedience the free disposal of themselves and their affairs, ⁹not keeping anything closed to him [D], not even their own conscience. Rather, as has been stated in the Examen [93–97], they should manifest their conscience to him at fixed times, and more frequently when there is reason, without showing any repugnance or any manifestations of contrary opinion, ¹⁰so that by union of opinion and will and by proper submission they may be better preserved and make greater progress in the divine service.

[425] B. ¹Thus, just as it will pertain to the rector to see that the Constitutions are observed in their entirety, so it will be his to grant exemptions from them with authority from his own superiors (when he judges that such would be the intention of the one who enacted them, in a particular case ²according to occurrences and necessities and while keeping his attention fixed on the greater common good).

[426] C. ¹This statement includes appropriate care to retain friendships and to render adversaries benevolent.

[427] D. ¹Anything closed means a door, cabinet, and the like.

[428] 6. ¹For the good government of the house, the rector ought to appoint not merely as many officials as are necessary, but also such as are as well fitted as possible for their office [E]. ²He should give each one the rules of what he ought to do [F] and take care that no one interferes in the business of another. ³Furthermore, just as he ought to have help given to them when they need it, so when time is left over he ought to see to it that they employ it fruitfully in the service of God our Lord.

[429] E. ¹Fitted, I mean, in respect both to the competence of persons and to their occupations. ²For it would not be proper to give offices which demand much work to subjects much occupied with other things. Furthermore, since some offices require experience to be done well, their personnel ought not easily to be changed.

[430] *F.* ¹*Each one ought to read* **once a week**³³ *those of the rules that pertain to him.*

[431] 7. ¹The officials needed by the rector seem to be, first of all, a good minister, to be vice-rector or master of the house, who should provide for everything necessary for the common good; **a syndic for exterior matters**³⁴ and another person to superintend spiritual matters; ²and two or more persons in whose discretion and goodness the rector has much confidence, so that he can confer with them about the matters in which he finds difficulty and which he deems it right to discuss with them for the greater divine glory *[G]*. ³These are in addition to those needed for more particular offices *[H]*.

[432] *G.* ¹*If there are not that many persons, one could hold several offices.* ²*For example, the aforementioned minister or superintendent could have the charge of looking out for the rector or the novices, and so on.*

[433] *H.* ¹*Thus, there could be someone for clerical work, a porter, a sacristan, a cook, and a launderer.* ²*Other less burdensome offices could be distributed among the students when there is no one else to do them.*

[434] 8. ¹The rector should see that all in the college observe complete obedience towards each official in his own office, and the officials towards the minister and to the rector himself, in accordance with his directions to them. ²In general, those who have charge of others who must obey them ought to give the latter an example by the obedience they themselves observe towards their own superiors, as persons holding for them the place of Christ our Lord.

[435] 9. ¹A regular order of time for study, prayer, Mass, lectures, eating and sleeping, and so on, will be helpful for everything. ²Thus a signal will be given at designated times *[I]*. When it is heard, all should go immediately, leaving even a letter they have begun. ³When these hours ought to be changed because of the seasons or other unusual reasons, the rector or the one in charge should consider the matter and what he orders should be observed.

[436] *I.* ¹*The signal will be given by a bell*³⁵ *which will be sounded for retiring for sleep, for taking meals, and so forth.*

---

³³ **Modified by** *CN* **415.**

³⁴ (See note 11 to [271].)

³⁵ (This may be done according to local customs.)

[437] 10. ¹{The rector ought himself to explain or teach Christian doctrine for forty days} *[K]*.³⁶ ²He should also consider which of his subjects should deal with their neighbors inside the house or outside of it, and for what length of time they should do this, in spiritual conversations, conducting exercises, hearing confessions, and also in preaching or lecturing or in teaching Christian doctrine. ³They should do this work partly to gain practice themselves (especially when they are near the end of their studies), and partly for the benefit of the others inside and outside the house. ⁴After pondering all the factors, the rector should in everything provide what he thinks to be more pleasing to the Divine and Supreme Goodness and for his greater service and glory *[L]*.

[438] *K. ¹If for reasons of edification or for some other sufficient reason it does not seem proper for the rector to do this teaching himself, he may inform the provincial. ²If the provincial has the same opinion, the rector may have someone else do it for him.*

[439] *L. ¹The Constitutions which pertain to the colleges could be kept apart and* **read publicly two or three times a year.**³⁷

CHAPTER 11

²THE ACCEPTANCE OF UNIVERSITIES³⁸

[440] 1. ³The same considerations of charity by which colleges are accepted, in which public classes are held for the improvement in learning and in living both of our own members and even more of those outside the Society, ⁴can extend also to accepting charge of universities ⁵in which these benefits may be spread more universally, both through the subjects which are taught and the numbers of persons who attend and the degrees which are conferred ⁶so that the recipients may teach with authority elsewhere what they have learned well in these universities for the glory of God our Lord.

---

³⁶ **Abolished by GC 34, as a strict norm;** it may be retained rather as a counsel for the exercise of a humble pastoral ministry.

³⁷ **Modified by** *CN* **415.** (With regard to the public reading.)

³⁸ **Abolished in general by GC 34 are the concrete normative directives, contained in chapter 11–17, except for [440–42],** insofar as they have not already been abrogated by laws of the Church for ecclesiastical and Catholic universities. Found here, however, are appropriate and useful counsels and criteria to be considered in our apostolate of higher education. See also *CN* 289, 293–95.

[441]   2. ¹However, to decide under what conditions and obligations *[A]* and in what places universities should be accepted will be left to the judgment of the one who has the universal care of the Society. ²After he has heard the opinion of his assistants and of the others of whose counsel he may wish to avail himself, he will have the power to decide by himself upon the acceptance. ³{**But once such universities have been accepted, he cannot suppress them without the general congregation**}.³⁹

[442]   A. ²*When the founder desires that the Society should have to provide a certain number of lecturers, or to undertake some other obligations, it should be noted that if these obligations are accepted because this is deemed to be a lasting aid to the Society in achieving its ends for the service of God our Lord, there ought to be no failure to fulfill them.* ³*Conversely, more than what is obligatory in this regard (especially if this could be interpreted as inducing a new obligation) should not readily be done without the general's consent.* ⁴*Neither ought the general to be lenient in such a matter; rather, consulting his assistants he should take care that he does not burden the Society.* ⁵*If he makes a concession on some point, it should be made clear that no obligation is assumed but that what is added is something voluntary.*

[443]   3. ¹However, since the Society's religious tranquillity and spiritual occupations preclude the distraction and other detriments entailed in holding the office of judge in civil or criminal affairs, ²there should be no acceptance of such jurisdiction, which the Society would be required to exercise either by itself or through others who depend upon it. ³However, for what properly pertains to the well-being of the university, it is desirable that in regard to the students the ordinary civil or ecclesiastical ministry of justice should carry out the will of the rector of the university when he has expressed it in regard to punishing the students *[B]*; ⁴and that this ministry should in general give its support in matters pertaining to the studies, especially when such matters have been recommended to it by the rector *[C]*.

[444]   B. ¹*If a student has been so unruly or scandalous that it would be proper to expel him not only from the classes but also from the city, or to put him into prison, it would be a matter properly pertaining to the well-being of the university for the ordinary ministers of justice to be informed and take immediate action.* ²*For this and similar matters it would be wise to have the authorization in writing from the ruler or supreme power.* ³*Similarly, the recommendation from the rector in favor of a student*

---

³⁹ Abolished by *CN* 402, §3.

ought to carry weight with the ministers of justice toward preventing the students from being oppressed.

[445] C. ¹*Since exemption from ordinary magistrates cannot serve as a means to attract a large number of students,* ²*efforts should be made to compensate for this through other concessions and privileges.*

CHAPTER 12
¹THE SUBJECTS WHICH SHOULD BE TAUGHT IN THE UNIVERSITIES OF THE SOCIETY

[446] 1. ²Since the end of the Society and of its studies is to aid our fellowmen to the knowledge and love of God and to the salvation of their souls, ³and since the subject of theology is the means most suited to this end, in the universities of the Society the principal emphasis ought to be placed upon it. ⁴Accordingly, there should be diligent treatment by excellent professors of what pertains to scholastic doctrine and Sacred Scripture, as also to that part of positive theology which is conducive to the aforementioned end, ⁵without entering into the part of canon law directed toward court trials.

[447] 2. ¹Moreover, since both the learning of theology and the use of it require (especially in these times) knowledge of humane letters [A] and of the Latin, Greek, and Hebrew languages, there should be capable professors of these languages, and that in sufficient number. ²Furthermore, there may also be teachers of other languages such as Chaldaic, Arabic, and Indian where these are necessary or useful for the end stated, taking into account the diversities of place and the reasons for teaching them [B].

[448] A. ¹*Under the heading of humane letters is understood, in addition to grammar, what pertains to rhetoric, poetry, and history.*

[449] B. ¹*When a plan is being worked out in a college or university to prepare persons to go among the Moors or Turks, Arabic or Chaldaic would be expedient; and Indian would be proper for those about to go among the Indians;* ²*and the same holds true for similar reasons in regard to other languages which could have greater utility in other regions.*

[450] 3. ¹Likewise, since the arts or natural sciences dispose the intellectual powers for theology, and are useful for the perfect understanding and use of it, and also by their own nature help toward the same ends, ²they should be treated with fitting diligence and by learned professors. In all this the honor and glory of God our Lord should be sincerely sought [C].

[451] C. ¹*Logic, physics, metaphysics, and moral philosophy should be treated, and also mathematics, with the moderation appropriate to secure the end which is being sought.*

  ²*To teach how to read and write would also be a work of charity if the Society had enough members to be able to attend to everything. ³But because of the lack of members these elementary subjects are not ordinarily taught.*

[452] 4. ¹The study of medicine and laws, being more remote from our Institute, will not be treated in the universities of the Society, or at least the Society will not undertake this teaching through its own members.

CHAPTER 13

¹THE METHOD AND ORDER OF TREATING THE AFOREMENTIONED SUBJECT MATTERS

[453] 1. ²To provide such proper treatment of both the lower subjects and of theology, there should be a suitable arrangement and order both for the morning and the afternoon.

[454] 2. ¹And although the order and hours which are spent in these studies may vary according to the regions and seasons, ²there should be such conformity that in every region that is done which is there judged to be most conducive to greater progress in learning [A].

[455] A. ¹*Concerning the hours of the lectures, their order, and their method, and concerning the exercises both in compositions (which ought to be corrected by the teachers) and in disputations within all the faculties, and in delivering orations and reading verses in public—²all this will be treated in detail in a separate treatise [approved by the general]. This present constitution refers the reader to it, ³with the remark that it ought to be adapted to places, times, and persons, even though it would be desirable to reach that order as far as this is possible.*

[456] 3. ¹Furthermore, there should be not only public lectures but also different masters according to the capacity and number of the students [B]. ²These masters should take an interest in the progress of each one of their students, require them to give an account of their lessons [C], and make them hold repetitions [D]. ³They should also have the students of humane letters get practice in regularly speaking Latin, writing compositions [in a good style], and delivering well what they have composed. ⁴They should make them, and much more those studying the higher subjects, engage in disputa-

tions often. ⁵Days and hours should be designated for this; and in these disputations the students should debate not only with the members of their own class, but those who are somewhat lower down should dispute about matters they understand with students who are more advanced, ⁶and conversely those who are more advanced should debate with those lower down by coming down to subjects which these latter are studying. The professors too ought to hold disputations with one another. ⁷All should preserve the proper modesty, and there should be someone to preside, cut off the debate, and give the doctrinal solution.

[457]   B. ¹*Ordinarily, there will be three teachers in three different classes of grammar, another who is to lecture on humanities, and another on rhetoric. ²In the class of these last two groups there will be lectures on the Greek and Hebrew languages, and on any other if it is to be learned. Thus there will always be five classes. ³If there should be so much to do in one of them that a single teacher does not suffice, an assistant should be given to him. ⁴If the number of students makes it impossible for one teacher to attend to them even with assistants, the class can be divided into two sections so that there are two fifth classes or two fourth classes; ⁵and all the teachers, if possible, should be members of the Society, although in case of necessity there may be others. ⁶If the small number or the quality of the students is such that so many classes or teachers are not required, discretion will be used in everything to adjust the number by assigning those who suffice and no more.*

[458]   C. ¹*Whether in addition to the ordinary masters who have special care of the students there ought to be some one or several who in the capacity of public lecturers are to give lectures on philosophy or mathematics or some other subject with greater solemnity than the ordinary lecturers, ²prudence will decide, in accordance with the places and persons involved, looking always to the greater edification and the greater service of God our Lord.*

[459]   D. ¹*There will be repetitions not merely of the last lesson, but also of those of the week and of a longer time when it is judged that this ought to be the case.*

[460]   4. ¹Likewise, it will always be the function of the rector to see to it himself or through the chancellor that the newcomers are examined and placed in those classes and with those teachers that are suitable for them. ²Furthermore, it is left to his discretion (after he has heard the counsel of those deputed for this purpose) to decide whether they ought to be retained longer in the same class or to advance into another. ³So too in regard to the study of the languages other than Latin, he is to determine whether it should

precede the arts and theology or follow them, and how long each should study these languages. ⁴The same holds true for the other higher subjects. According to the difference of abilities, ages, and other circumstances that must be considered, it will be the rector's function to investigate to what extent each student should begin these subjects or continue in them, ⁵although it is better for those who have the age and ability to advance and distinguish themselves in all these areas for the glory of God our Lord *[E]*.

[461]   E.   ¹*It can happen that because of someone's age or capacity Latin, together with as much of the other subjects as is required to hear confessions and deal with his neighbor, suffices for him.* ²*Such might be certain persons who have a curacy of souls and are not capable of great learning.* ³*Likewise, others may advance farther in the sciences, although it will be up to the superior to decide to what extent some subjects should be dropped and others taken up.* ⁴*After he has explained this to the students from outside the Society and if they still desire to proceed differently, they should not be coerced.*

[462]   5.   ¹Just as steady application is necessary in the work of studying, so also is some relaxation. ²The proper amount and the times of this relaxation will be left to the prudent consideration of the rector to determine, according to the circumstances of persons and places *[F]*.

[463]   F.   ¹*At least one day during the week should be given to rest from dinner on.* ²*On the other points the rector should consult with the provincial about the order to be observed in regard to the vacations or ordinary interruptions of the studies.*

CHAPTER 14

¹THE BOOKS TO BE LECTURED ON

[464]   1.   ²In general, as was stated in the treatise on the colleges [358], those books will be lectured on which in each subject have been deemed to contain more solid and safe doctrine; books which are suspect, or whose authors are suspect, will not be treated *[A]*. But in each university these should be individually designated.

³In theology there should be lectures on the Old and New Testaments and on the scholastic doctrine of St. Thomas *[B]*; and in positive theology those authors should be selected who are more suitable for our end *[C]*.

[465]   A.   ¹*Even though the book be without suspicion of bad doctrine, when its author is suspect it is not expedient that it be lectured on.* ²*For*

through the book affection is acquired for the author; and part of the credence given to him in what he says well could be given to him later in what he says badly. ³*Furthermore, it is rare that some poison is not mixed into what comes forth from a heart full of it.*

[466]   B. ¹*The Master of the Sentences will also be lectured on.* ²*But if in time it seems that the students will draw more help from another author, as would be the case through the writing of a compendium or book of scholastic theology that seems better adapted to these times of ours, it will be permitted to make this book the subject of the lectures,* ³*after much consultation and study of the matter by the persons deemed most suitable in the whole Society and with the superior general's approval.* ⁴*In regard to the other subjects and humane letters too, if some books written in the Society are adopted as being more useful than those commonly used,* ⁵*this will be done after much consideration, with our objective of greater universal good always kept in view.*

[467]   C. ¹*For example, in connection with some section of canon law, the councils, and so on.*

[468]   2. ¹In regard to the books of humane letters in Latin or Greek, in the universities as well as in the colleges, lecturing to the adolescents on any book which contains matters harmful to good habits of conduct should be avoided, as far as possible, unless the books are previously expurgated of the indecent matters and words *[D]*.

[469]   D. ¹*If some books, such as Terence, cannot be expurgated at all, it is better that they should not be lectured on,* ²*in order that the nature of the contents may not injure the purity of the minds.*

[470]   3. ¹In logic, natural and moral philosophy, and metaphysics, the doctrine of Aristotle should be followed, as also in the other liberal arts. ²In regard to the commentaries, both on these authors and on those treating humanities, a selection should be made. Those which the students ought to see should be designated, and also those which the masters ought to follow by preference in the doctrine they teach. ³In everything which the rector ordains, he should proceed in conformity with what is judged throughout the whole Society to be more suitable to the glory of God our Lord.

CHAPTER 15

¹THE TERMS AND DEGREES

[471]   1. ²In the study of humane letters and the languages no definite period of time for their completion can be established, because of the difference in abilities and knowledge of those who

attend the lectures, ³and because of many other reasons which permit no other prescription of time save that which the prudent consideration of the rector or chancellor will dictate for each student [A].

[472]   A. ¹In the case of beginners of good ability, one should see whether a single semester in each of the four lower classes would be enough, and two semesters in the highest class spent in studying rhetoric and the languages. ²However, no definite rule can be given.

[473]   2. ¹In the arts, it will be necessary to arrange the terms during which the natural sciences are to be lectured upon. It seems that less than three years would be insufficient for them [B]. ²Another half year will remain for the student to review, perform his academic acts, and take the master's degree in the case of those who are to receive degrees. ³In this way the whole curriculum enabling a student to become a master of arts will last three years and a half. Each year with the help of God one such cycle of treatises will begin and another will come to its end [C].

[474]   B. ¹If someone has attended the lectures on some part of the arts elsewhere, this can be taken into account. ²But ordinarily, in order to be graduated one must have studied for the three years mentioned. ³This holds true also for the four years of theology, in regard to being admitted to the acts and receiving a degree in it.

[475]   C. ¹If because of insufficient personnel or for other reasons facilities for that arrangement are lacking, ²the best that will be possible should be done, with the approval of the general or at least of the provincial.

[476]   3. ¹The curriculum in theology will be one of six years. In the first four years all the matter which must be lectured on will be expounded. In the remaining two, in addition to the reviewing, the acts customary for a doctorate will be performed by those who are to receive it.

²Ordinarily, the cycle of the curriculum will be begun every fourth year, and the books to be lectured on distributed so that a student can enter the curriculum at the start of any one of the four years [D] ³and, by attending the lectures on the rest of the four-year curriculum and the next one up to that point, will have heard the lectures of the entire curriculum within four years.

[477]   D. ¹If in a college or university of the Society the situation is such that it appears better to begin the cycle of subjects every two years, or somewhat later than every four, with the consent of the general or of the provincial that which is found to be more suitable may be done.

[478] 4. ¹In the matter of the degrees, both of master of arts and of doctor of theology, three things should be observed. ²First, no one, whether a member of the Society or an extern, should be promoted to a degree unless he has been carefully and publicly examined [E] by persons deputed for this office, which they should perform well, and unless he has been found fit to lecture in that faculty. ³Second, the door to ambition should be closed by giving no fixed places to those who receive degrees; rather, they should "anticipate one another with honor" [Rom. 12:10], observing no distinction of places. ⁴Third, just as the Society teaches altogether gratis, so should it confer the degrees completely free, and only a very small expenditure, even if it is voluntary, should be allowed to the extern students, so that the custom may not come to have the force of law and no excess in this matter may creep in with time [F]. ⁵The rector should also take care not to permit any of the teachers or other members of the Society to accept money or gifts, either for themselves or for the college, from any person for anything he has done to help him. ⁶For according to our Institute, our reward should be only Christ our Lord who is "our reward exceedingly great" [Gen. 15:1].

[479] E. ¹If it appears, for sufficiently weighty reasons, that someone ought not to be examined publicly, with the permission of the general or provincial that may be done which the rector judges will be for the greater glory of God our Lord.

[480] F. ¹Thus, banquets should not be permitted, nor other celebrations which are costly and not useful for our end. ²Neither should there be any conferring of caps or gloves or any other object.

Chapter 16

¹What Pertains to Good Moral Habits

[481] 1. ²Very special care should be taken that those who come to the universities of the Society to obtain knowledge should acquire along with it good and Christian moral habits. ³It will help much toward this if all go to confession at least once every month, hear Mass every day and a sermon every feast day when one is given. ⁴The teachers will take care of this, each one with his own students [A].

[482] A. ¹When this can be done easily, students should be obliged to what has been said about confession, Mass, the sermon, Christian doctrine, and declamation. ²The others should be persuaded gently and not be

forced to it nor expelled from the classes for not complying, provided that dissoluteness or scandal to others is not observed in them.

[483] 2. ¹Furthermore, on some day of the week Christian doctrine should be taught in the college. Care should be taken to make the young boys learn and recite it; also, that all, even the older ones, should know it, if possible.

[484] 3. ¹Likewise each week, as was said about the colleges, one of the students will deliver a declamation about matters which edify the hearers and lead them to desire to grow in all purity and virtue. ²The purpose is not only practice in literary style but also the encouraging of moral habits *[B]*. ³All those who understand Latin ought to be present.

[485] B. ¹*Usually the one who must deliver this declamation should be a member of the highest class, whether a scholastic of the Society or one of the externs. ²At times, however, when it seems good to the rector, someone else could give it or deliver what another has composed. But no matter who delivers the declamation, since the performance is public, it ought to be such that it will not be judged unworthy of being given in that place.*

[486] 4. ¹In the classes no cursing, nor injurious words or deeds, nor anything immoral, nor anything indecent or dissolute should be allowed on the part of the externs who come to classes from elsewhere. ²The masters should make it their special aim, both in their lectures when occasion is offered and outside of them too, to inspire the students to the love and service of God our Lord, and to a love of the virtues by which they will please him. They should urge the students to direct all their studies to this end. ³To recall this to their minds, before the lesson begins, one of them should recite a short prayer which is ordered for this purpose, while the master and students stand attentive and have their heads uncovered *[C]*.

[487] C. ¹*The prayer should be recited in a manner which furthers edification and devotion, or else it should not be said, but the teacher should uncover his head, make the sign of the cross, and begin.*

[488] 5. ¹For those who are derelict either in proper diligence in their studies or in what pertains to good moral habits, and for whom kind words and admonitions alone are not sufficient, ²there should be a corrector from outside the Society. He should keep in fear and should punish those who need chastisement and are fit for it. ³When neither words nor the corrector avail and some student is seen to be incorrigible and a scandal to others, ⁴it is better to dismiss him from the classes rather than to keep him where he

himself is not progressing and others are receiving harm *[D]*. ⁵This decision will be left to the rector of the university, so that everything may proceed in a manner conducive to the glory and service of God our Lord.

[489]   *D. ¹If a case should arise in which dismissal from the classes is not enough to remedy the scandal, the rector will take care to provide what is more suitable. ²However, as far as possible he ought to proceed in a spirit of leniency and to maintain peace and charity with all.*

CHAPTER 17
¹THE OFFICIALS OR ADMINISTRATORS OF THE UNIVERSITY

[490]   1. ²The complete charge, that is, the supervision and government of the university, will belong to the rector *[A]*. ³He may be the same person who governs the principal college of the Society and should have the qualities that have been mentioned in his regard [423], so that he may be able to perform satisfactorily the office entrusted to him of directing the whole university in learning and habits of conduct. ⁴The task of selecting him will be vested in the general or in someone else to whom he entrusts it, such as the provincial or a visitor; but the confirmation of the appointment will always belong to the general. ⁵The rector will have four consultors or assistants who in general can aid him in matters pertaining to his office and with whom he discusses the matters of importance *[B]*.

[491]   *A. ¹However, the rector will not change the principal lecturers, nor officials such as the chancellor, without informing the provincial, or the general if he is nearer (unless the higher superior has entrusted the matter to the rector). The rector ought to keep the higher superior informed about all things.*

[492]   *B. ¹One of these consultors can be a collateral associate if this seems necessary to the superior general. ²If the personnel is not sufficient to have so many officials, the best that will be possible should be done.*

[493]   2. ¹There will also be a chancellor *[C]*, a person distinguished for learning and great zeal who is able to judge wisely in the matters which will be entrusted to him. ²It is his duty to act as general representative of the rector in carefully organizing the studies, in directing the disputations in the public acts, ³and in judging the competence of those to be admitted to the acts and degrees. He himself will confer the degrees.

[494]   *C. ¹If the rector can perform the office of chancellor in addition to his own, these two functions can be vested in one person.*

[495] 3. ¹There should be a secretary who is a member of the Society. He should keep a register in which are written the names of all the students who regularly attend the classes *[D]* ²and should receive their promise to obey the rector and to observe the constitutions, which he ought to propose to them *[E]*. He should keep the seal of the rector and of the university. ³But all this should be done without cost to the students.

[496] *D. ¹If they attend regularly for a week or longer, it is good to invite them to enter their names in the register. ²The constitutions should be read to them, not in their entirety, but those which each student ought to observe. A promise, but not an oath, should be exacted from them to obey and observe the statues proposed. ³If some should be unwilling either to bind themselves with a promise or to enter their names in the register, the door of the classes should not for that reason be closed to them so long as they behave peacefully and give no scandal in the classes. ⁴They should be told this, but also informed that more particular care is taken of the students entered in the register.*

[497] *E. ¹Later on, however, the constitutions which all ought to observe should be posted where they can be read publicly, and those pertaining to each class should be posted there.*

[498] 4. ¹There will also be a notary to give public certification to the degrees and other matters which will occur *[F]*; and two or three beadles, one in the faculty of languages, another in that of arts, and another in that of theology *[G]*.

[499] *F. ¹This notary can receive a fee from the extern students who desire to have their degrees certified. ²But this fee should be moderate and never redound to the gain of the Society. The letters patent of the rector will suffice for the members of the Society.*

[500] *G. ¹These beadles will not be members of the Society. However, since they will have much to do they should receive a good salary; and one of them can be the corrector.*

[501] 5. ¹The university will be divided into these three faculties. ²In each one of them there will be a dean and two others assigned as deputies, chosen from among those who better understand the affairs of that faculty; these, when called into consultation by the rector, can tell him what they think would be advantageous for the welfare of their faculty. ³When they perceive something of this kind while conferring among themselves, they should inform the rector even without being consulted.

[502] 6. ¹In regard to the matters pertaining to one faculty alone the rector will consult, in addition to the chancellor and his assis-

tants, the dean and the deputies of the faculty involved. ²In what pertains to all the faculties, the deans and deputies of all of them should be consulted *[H]*. ³If it seems wise to the rector, he may also consult others from within and without the Society, in order that by learning the opinions of all he may the better decide upon what is expedient.

[503]   *H. ¹Although the decision will not depend upon their votes, it is proper that they be consulted and heard. The rector should take fitting account of the opinion of those who are more cognizant. ²However, if all have an opinion contrary to his, he should not go against them all without consulting the provincial about the matter.*

[504]   7. ¹There will also be a general syndic who is to give information to the rector, the provincial, and the general about both the persons and the things which he will deem noteworthy *[I]*. He should be a person of great fidelity and judgment.

²In addition to this general syndic the rector will have his own particular syndic to refer to him what happens in each class and requires his intervention *[K]*. ³The rector will write about the teachers and other persons of the Society, and the collateral associate, the syndic, and the board of consultors will write about the rector and about the others once a year to the superior general and twice to the provincial *[L]*, who will inform the general about whatever seems appropriate, ⁴in order to proceed in everything with greater circumspection and care to do what each one should.

[505]   *I. ¹This office of syndic could be combined with that of collateral associate or consultor if this should seem fitting because no one better suited than one of them is to be found in the university.*

[506]   *K. ¹Even if the syndics have no business of moment, they should report this fact to the superior, at least every Saturday.*

[507]   *L. ¹These letters should be sent sealed in such a manner that one does not know what the other writes. ²When the superior general or the provincial desires more complete information, not only should the collateral associate, syndic, and board of consultors write about the rector and all the others, ³but each of the teachers and approved scholastics as well as of the formed coadjutors should write his opinion about all of them, the rector included. ⁴So that this may not seem to be something new, this report should be written as something ordinary at least every three years.*

[508]   8. ¹Whether the rector, chancellor, and beadles and also the doctors and masters ought to have some insignia in order to be recognized in the university or at least during the public acts and, ²if so, of what sort they ought to be, will be left to the consider-

ation of him who is general at the time when a given university is accepted [M]. ³After considering the circumstances he will order, either by himself or through someone else, what he judges to be for the greater glory and service of God our Lord and for the universal good, which is the only end sought in this matter and in all others.

[509] M. ¹However, what seems best for each place in regard to these insignia will be clearly stated in the rules of each university.

PART V
¹ADMISSION OR INCORPORATION INTO THE SOCIETY¹

CHAPTER 1
²ADMISSION: WHO SHOULD ADMIT, AND WHEN

[510] 1. ³Those who have been tested in the Society sufficiently and for a time long enough that both parties may know each other and if their remaining in it is conducive to the greater service and glory of God our Lord, ⁴ought to be admitted—not to probation as was the case in the beginning, but more intrinsically as members of one same body of the Society *[A]*. ⁵This is the case chiefly with those who are admitted to profession or into the ranks of the formed coadjutors. ⁶But since the **approved**² scholastics too are admitted in a different and more intrinsic manner than those received into the probation, in this Fifth Part we shall also state what we think in our Lord ought to be observed about the admission of these scholastics.

[511] *A. ²The Society, in the broadest sense of the term, includes all those who live under obedience to its superior general. ³Thus it comprises even the novices* **and the persons who, desiring to live and die in the Society, are in probation**³ *to be admitted into it under one of the other categories of membership about to be described.*

⁴In the second and less universal sense, the Society **includes** *not only the professed and the formed coadjutors but* **also the approved scholastics.**⁴ *For the body of the Society is composed of these three kinds of parts or members.*

---

¹ (In this entire Part V the words "admit to vows" are also used in the sense of "receive the vows." Each act is distinguished in *CN* 113, 114.)

² (The same holds for approved brothers; see *CN* 6.)

³ (Today there are no others besides novices who are in probation; see *CN* 6.)

⁴ (See note 2 to [510].)

PART V
ADMISSION INTO THE BODY
OF THE SOCIETY

CHAPTER 1
THE POWER OF ADMITTING TO AND RECEIVING VOWS

113 §1. The provincial has the power of admitting to first vows that the general habitually communicates to him; but the power of admitting to final vows the general reserves to himself.

§2. The general will not easily delegate to anyone, not even to a provincial, the power of admitting to solemn profession.[1]

114 §1. The general habitually substitutes for himself

1° For receiving first vows: the provincial of the place where the vows are taken, the local superior or another one of our men designated by either of them;

2° For receiving final vows: the provincial of the place where the vows are taken or another one of our men whom he will have designated; and if he has not designated anyone, the local superior.

§2. The person designated to receive the vows may validly substitute another one of our members for himself; but he should not use this faculty unless he is himself impeded.

§3. To receive any sort of vows validly, even one of our members who is not a priest can be designated, but this cannot be done licitly except in the case of necessity.[2]

115 The general, and he alone, can validly communicate the power to receive any of the Society's vows to someone who is not of the Society, such as a bishop or a person of ecclesiastical

---

[1] *CollDecr* d. 149 (GC 30, d. 67); see P. V, c. 2, A [517]; P. IX, c. 3, A [737].

[2] GC 27, *CollDecr* d. 150; see P. V, c. 3, A [526].

⁵*In the third and more proper sense, the Society comprises the professed and the formed coadjutors.* ⁶*This is the sense which is understood in regard to that entrance into the Society which the scholastics promise; that is, they promise to become either professed or formed coadjutors in the Society.*

⁷*The fourth and most proper meaning of this name, the Society, comprehends only the professed. The reason is, not that the body of the Society contains no other members, but that the professed are the principal members, some of whom, as will be explained later, have active and passive voice in the election of the superior general and in other such matters.*

⁸*No matter in which one of these four categories one finds himself in the Society, he is capable of sharing in the spiritual favors which, according to the grant of the Apostolic See, the superior general may dispense in the Society for the greater glory of God.* ⁹*Now admission to the Society in the first sense is the same as reception into probation, and has thus already been discussed above in Part I.* ¹⁰*This Fifth Part, therefore, deals with the subsequent three kinds of admission.*

[512]   2. ¹First of all, the authority to admit into the body of the Society those who ought to be admitted will be vested in whoever may be its head, as reason requires. ²But since the superior general cannot be everywhere, **he may communicate to other members of the Society as much of his authority as seems good to him for the welfare of the entire body of the Society** *[B]*.⁵

[513]   B. ¹*The others to whom he will more ordinarily and completely communicate this authority will be the provincial superiors.* ²*But the general may communicate it to some local superiors or rectors and to other visitors or important persons;* ³*and even, occasionally, to one who is not a member of the Society, such as a bishop or other person established in an ecclesiastical dignity, when no professed member of the Society itself is in the place where someone ought to be so admitted.*

[514]   3. ¹The period of time required for admission in the manner mentioned **should always be more than two years** *[C]*.⁶ ²But if one who was tested for a long time before being sent to his studies

---

⁵ **Clarified by** *CN* 113 (in regard to the faculty of admitting to vows) **and** *CN* 114, 115 (in regard to the faculty of receiving the vows.)

⁶ **Modified by** *CN* 119. (The time to be spent in the Society before final vows is determined.)

rank; however, this is licitly done only when there is no solemnly professed in the place where the vows are pronounced.[3]

CHAPTER 2

THOSE TO BE ADMITTED TO FIRST VOWS

116 Although the first vows are perpetual, they can be pronounced after the completion of one's nineteenth year of age; indeed, by obtaining a dispensation that only the general can grant, they can be pronounced after completion of one's eighteenth year, in such wise, however, that the time required by universal law to be spent in the novitiate has been fulfilled after the completion of the seventeenth year.[4]

117 §1. For a man to be admitted to first vows, he must be considered suited to living the life of the Society and to carrying out its ministry and offices; therefore, no one is to be admitted unless, after legitimately completing two years of novitiate and undergoing the examination prescribed in the Constitutions, both he himself and the Society are satisfied.

§2. However, if he is satisfied but the Society has doubts about his aptitude, the novitiate can be extended until both parties are clearly satisfied in the Lord.

1° Provincials can extend the novitiate for six months;

2° If a further extension seems to be required for truly serious reasons, the matter is to be proposed to the general, who can permit it.[5]

---

[3] *CollDecr* d. 151 (GC 8, d. 34); see P. V, c. 1, B [513].

[4] See *CollDecr* d. 152, §1 (GC 8, d. 35; GC 12, d. 13); see CIC 658, 1°; 648; CCEO 450, 4°.

[5] See *Examen,* c. 1, no. 12 [16]; c. 4, no. 43 [100]; c. 7, no. 1 [121]; P. V, c. 1, no. 3, C [514, 515]; CIC 653, §2. By a privilege granted by the Council of Trent, the Society is not bound by the prescription of universal law (CIC 648, §3; CCEO 461, §2) forbidding the time of probation to be extended beyond two years or beyond a year respectively (see above no. 56).

or during them, and **if he ought to be admitted to profession,**[7] **he will have another year**[8] after the completion of these studies to become still better known before pronouncing it. [3]As was stated in the Examen [100], **this period can be prolonged** when the Society, or he who in our Lord has this charge from it, **desires more complete satisfaction.**[9]

[515]   C.   [1]*However, just as this period may be prolonged, so too, according to the judgment of the superior general (who will have the power of dispensing), it may be shortened in some cases and for important reasons. But this power should be used rarely.*

Chapter 2

[1]The Qualities of Those Who Should Be Admitted

[516]   1.   [2]Inasmuch as no one should be admitted into any of the aforementioned categories **who has not been judged suitable in our Lord,**[10] [3]**those persons will be judged suited for admission to profession whose life is well-known** through long and thorough probations **and is approved**[11] by the superior general, to whom a report will be sent by the subordinate superiors or others from whom the general desires information *[A]*.

[4]For this purpose, it will be helpful **for those who had been sent to studies,**[12] **upon finishing the work and effort of intellectual formation, to apply themselves during the period of final probation to the school of the heart,**[13] [5]exercising themselves in spiritual and corporal pursuits which can engender in them greater humility, abnegation of all sensual love and will and judgment of their own, and also greater knowledge and love of God our Lord; [6]so that

---

[7] **Modified by** *CN* 125. (Also those to be admitted as spiritual coadjutors and as brothers make tertianship.)

[8] **Modified by** *CN* 125, §1. (Tertianship must be made by all, including the brothers, who pronounce final vows.)

[9] **Clarified by** *CN* 56; 117, §2.

[10] **Clarified by** *CN* 118–20. (Both general and particular requirements for different types of admission to final vows are declared.)

[11] **Clarified by** *CN* 121.

[12] **Modified** (see preceding note 8).

[13] **Clarified by** *CN* 125–26. (Concerning the purposes and way of making tertianship.)

CHAPTER 3

THOSE TO BE ADMITTED TO FINAL VOWS
(AND ABOUT TERTIANSHIP)

118   Because of the close connection between priestly ordination and definitive incorporation into the Society, none of our
scholastics is to be promoted to the priesthood unless it is clear
that he can eventually be definitively incorporated into the Society.

119   It is required that the one who is to pronounce final vows
will have spent at least ten full years in the Society.[6] However,
this prescribed time of religious life in the Society is not required
for validity and can be shortened or lengthened by the general
until the one to be admitted has fully proved himself.[7]

120   In the case of all who are to be admitted to last vows, they
must be outstanding in the following of Christ proposed to us in
the Gospels, since this is the ultimate norm of religious life; such
men are those who

1° Regularly and for the most part, in ordinary matters,
act according to the demands of virtue that is rooted in love of
Christ, and there is firm hope that they will do the same in more
difficult matters if such are encountered;

2° Humbly accept corrections concerning faults they
have committed in religious life and generously strive to correct
them;

3° Driven on by love, live more and more for Christ
and his Body which is the Church, and in the daily practice of
virtue bear witness both to our members and to others of the new
life gained through the redemption of Christ.[8]

121   For someone to be admitted to the solemn profession of
four vows the following are required:

1° An outstanding level of virtue in conformity with no.
120, one that is positively demonstrated and is so obvious that
the individual stands out by reason of his good example

---

[6] *CollDecr* d. 160, 7° (GC 31, d. 11, no. 2, modified by GC 32, d.
10, no. 1, b).

[7] *CollDecr* d. 157 (GC 4, d. 9; GC 5, d. 37); see Gregory XIV,
"Ecclesiæ catholicæ."

[8] *CollDecr* d. 158 (GC 31, d. 11, no. 1; see GC 9, d. 6).

when they themselves have made progress they can better help others to progress for the glory of God our Lord.

[517] *A.* ¹*In some very remote regions, such as the Indies, the general may leave it to the judgment of the provincial*¹⁴ *to decide whether or not certain subjects should be admitted to profession without awaiting approval from here [in Rome] (since it would not arrive for several years).* ²*However, in the regions where better communications exist he should not readily entrust admission to profession to any provincial, but should himself first be informed and give his consent individually for those who he thinks in our Lord should be admitted to profession.*

[518] 2. ¹Similarly, such persons ought to possess sufficient learning in humane letters and the liberal arts and, beyond that, in scholastic theology and Sacred Scripture. ²And while some might be able to progress as much in a shorter time as others in a longer one, nevertheless for the sake of a common standard a terminus will need to be set, and this will be four complete years of theology following the arts course *[B].* ³Thus, to be admitted to profession one should have spent four years in the study of theology and made good progress to the glory of God our Lord. ⁴**As evidence of his progress each one should before his profession defend theses in logic, philosophy, and scholastic theology. Four persons will be designated to object and to judge his sufficiency according to what they think in all truth and sincerity.**¹⁵ ⁵When the subjects are found not to have enough learning, it is better that they wait until they have it. Similarly, those also ought to wait who have not obtained fully adequate testimony to their self-abnegation and religious virtues.

[519] *B.* ¹*This standard period of four years of theology (beyond the study of humanities and the arts) should ordinarily be observed, as also the aforementioned examination of the progress made therein.* ²*Nevertheless one who has sufficient learning in canon law, or **other outstanding qualities***¹⁶ *which can make up for what he lacks in the study of theology, could be admitted to the profession of three vows without the latter. Furthermore, some outstanding persons could be admitted also to the profession of four vows, although this practice ought not to be extended.*

---

¹¹ **Clarified by** *CN* 113.

¹⁵ **Modified by** *CN* 93. (There will be a comprehensive examination in theology before three examiners approved by the major superior.)

¹⁶ **Clarified by** *CN* 121.

to others. A deficiency in this regard cannot be supplied by any other endowments.

2° Sound judgment and prudence in action, as well as basic virtue tested and necessary;

3° A more-than-average talent for our ministries, demonstrated for at least three years;

4° Complete availability and mobility for missions and ministries of the Society;

5° Sufficient physical and psychological health;

6° An outstanding level of learning in sacred studies or other outstanding endowments from God in conformity with §§2 and 3 below;

7° Priestly ordination.[9]

§2. The high level of learning in sacred sciences must be shown by a higher academic degree, at least the licentiate, or by having taught them or written about them with distinction, or by the examination for grade according to no. 93, §§ 1 and 2.[10]

§3. For other outstanding endowments from God (mentioned in §1, 6°, above) those men can be promoted who exhibit outstanding apostolic or ministerial capability for any post or ministry proper to the Society, demonstrated respectively by having earned higher academic degrees or by having exercised the ministry for at least three years (see §1, 3°, above), and always presupposing that adequate theological learning commonly required by the Church in a well-educated priest.

§4. Major superiors and their consultors must have proof that candidates proposed for profession of four vows have all the qualifications required for it.[11]

122 The provincial and his consultors, when they are treating of those to be advanced to final vows, should inquire whether some priests who have already taken final simple vows deserve to

[9] *CollDecr* d. 160, 161 (GC 31, d. 11, no. 2, 1°–5°, no. 3; GC 32, d. 10, nos. 1–2). Points 4° and 5° were added by GC 34.

[10] See *CollDecr* d. 161; GC 32, d. 6, no. 51 (modified by GC 34, *CN* 93, §1).

[11] See *CollDecr* d. 161, 163 (GC 31, d. 11, nos. 3, 4; see GC 7, d. 96; GC 20, d. 68; GC 6, d. 15; GC 7, d. 33, nos. 3, 6; GC 12, d. 19; GC 29, d. 33).

³The judgment about these qualities will be left exclusively to the superior general, or to another to whom he entrusts it by a special commission, so as to do what is for the greater glory of God our Lord.

[520] 3. ¹In addition to these, some can be admitted to the profession of only three solemn vows. But this will be done rarely and for special and important reasons. ²These members **should have been known in the Society for seven years**¹⁷ and have given therein great satisfaction by their talent and virtues, for the glory of God our Lord *[C]*.

[521] C. *¹Those admitted to the profession of three solemn vows should ordinarily possess sufficient learning, at least enough for them to be good confessors, or else some compensating exceptional qualities ²such that the superior general, or whomever he entrusts with the matter by special commission, judges their admission to profession expedient for the greater service of God and the good of the Society. ³These will ordinarily be persons of whom, because of their good services and great devotion and despite their lack of the learning and skill in preaching required by our Institute, it is judged in our Lord that they ought to be admitted.*

[522] 4. ¹**To be admitted among the formed coadjutors, a subject should likewise have given satisfaction in regard to his life and good example and his ability to aid the Society, ²either in spiritual matters by his learning or in exterior matters without the learning, each one according to what God has communicated to him.**¹⁸ ³By his discretion the superior general will have to appraise this matter too, unless it seems good to him to entrust it to the particular persons in whom he has much confidence in our Lord.

[523] 5. ¹For subjects to be admitted among the approved scholastics, proportionately the same set of requirements remains. Especially, in regard to their ability there should be hope that they will succeed in their studies, ²in the judgment of the general or of the one whom he designates, while confiding in the discretion and goodness which God our Lord has given to him.

Chapter 3

¹The Procedure in Admission to Profession

[524] 1. ²When certain members are to be admitted to the profession after they have completed the experiences and other

---

¹⁷ **Modified by** *CN* 119. (Ten years spent in the Society is required.)

¹⁸ **Clarified by** *CN* 123.

be proposed to the general for the grade of the professed of four vows in conformity with no. 121.[12]

123   No men should be admitted to final simple vows unless

1° They are outstanding in virtue in conformity with no. 120;

2° They have shown sufficient knowledge and talent for the works and ministries that are proper to the Society;

3° In the case of spiritual coadjutors, they have received ordination to the priesthood or, in the exceptional case mentioned in no. 124, ordination to the permanent diaconate.[13]

124   Those members who for good reasons approved by Father General are ordained permanent deacons will retain the grade they already have in the Society. If they are approved brothers, they are to be advanced to the grade of brother, after having fulfilled all requisites. If they are scholastics, they can also be admitted by Father General to the grade of spiritual coadjutors, by way of exception, once all requisites have been fulfilled; but they cannot be made superiors in the strict sense.[14]

125   §1. All members before pronouncing final vows must complete the third year of probation, exercising themselves in the school of the heart.[15] For priests this is not to be deferred beyond three years after priestly ordination except for a just reason in the judgment of the provincial.[16]

§2. The purpose of this probation is for each one, in concrete and personal contact with the things of the Society, to bring to completion a synthesis of spiritual, apostolic, and intellectual or technical formation, which makes for the fuller integration in the Lord of the whole personality, in keeping with the Society's objective as St. Ignatius described it: "that, since they

---

[12] *CollDecr* d. 163, a (GC 31, d. 11, no. 5; see GC 32, d. 8, no. 2, b).

[13] *CollDecr* d. 165, §§1–2 (GC 31, d. 11, no. 6, 1°–2°; GC 32, d. 10, no. 1; d. 9, no. 2).

[14] GC 32, d. 9, no. 2.

[15] See *CollDecr* d. 160, 6°; 165, §2, 1° (GC 32, d. 7, no. 2; d. 10, no. 2; GC 30, d. 42); Gregory XIII, *Ascendente Domino*; *Examen*, c. 1, no. 12 [16]; c. 4, no. 16 [71]; c. 6, no. 8 [119]; P. V, c. 1, no. 3 [514]; c. 2, no. 1 [516].

[16] See GC 32, d. 7, no. 3.

prescriptions contained in the Examen and after the Society or its superior is entirely satisfied in our Lord, the profession will be made in the following manner.

[525] 2. ¹First of all the superior general, or the one who with his authority **admits** the subject **to profession,**¹⁹ **will celebrate Mass in the church publicly**²⁰ before the members of the house and the others who happen to be present. Then with the most holy Sacrament he will turn toward the one who is making the profession *[A]*, ²and he, **after reciting the Confiteor and the words which precede Holy Communion,**²¹ **will in a loud voice read**²² his written vow (which he will have pondered for some days in advance) in this formula [527].

[526] A. ¹*These details and those which follow below are appropriate and should be observed when possible, but they are not necessary.* ²*For it could happen that the one who through the superior general's order is admitting to profession is not a priest or is unable to celebrate Mass.* ³*What is essential is that the vow be read publicly in the presence of the Society's members and the externs who are present,*²³ *and that it be made and received as a solemn vow.*

[527] 3. ¹"I, N., make profession, and I promise to Almighty God, in the presence of his Virgin Mother, the whole heavenly court, and all those here present, ²and to you, Reverend Father N., superior general of the Society of Jesus and the one holding the place of God, and to your successors (or, to you, Reverend Father N., representing the superior general of the Society of Jesus and his successors and holding the place of God), ³perpetual poverty, chastity, and obedience; and, in conformity with it, special care for the instruction of children *[B]*, according to the manner of living contained in the apostolic letters of the Society of Jesus and in its Constitutions.

---

¹⁹ (This refers to receiving the vows.)

²⁰ **Modified by a very ancient practice.** (See note 30 to *CN* 132. This is noted by Fr. Nadal in a scholion to this number; indeed, this was already the usage from the profession of the first fathers: see MHSI, MI, *Fontes narr.* I:21.)

²¹ **Modified because of a change in liturgical norms.** (See *CN* 132.)

²² (But see *CN* 130.)

²³ **Modified by** *CN* **130.** (For validity, some unambiguous expression of the vow that is taken is sufficient.)

themselves have made progress, they may better help others to make spiritual progress to the glory of God and of our Lord."[17]

126   Third probation should be made according to a program suitable for attaining these ends and approved by the general; in it experiments prescribed by the Constitutions should be diligently carried out and a study of the Institute and our way of proceeding should be fostered with great care.[18]

127   A provincial can dispense no one from making a complete tertianship. It is for the general, however, to judge whether for most serious reasons someone should be exempted from some part of it; but he will scarcely ever dispense someone from all of it.[19]

128   Those who are to be advanced to final vows

1° Are to make the renunciation of their property if that has not already been done;[20]

2° Are to make an account of conscience about thirty days before their final vows;[21]

3° Are to make the Spiritual Exercises for eight days; if, however, they have already done so within the past three months, it is sufficient that they recollect themselves for three days;[22]

4° Are to make a general confession;[23]

5° Are to spend some time in ministries among the poor and marginalized;

6° Are to reflect seriously on the Constitutions, the apostolic letters and the vows they are about to take.[24]

129   Ours who before final vows are elevated to the cardinalate or to the episcopacy, whether residential or titular, cannot be promoted to grade; neither, during the duration of their appoint-

---

[17] GC 31, d. 8, no. 43, 45; see P. V, c. 2, no. 1 [516].

[18] See GC 31, d. 8, no. 43; *CollDecr* d. 156 (GC 20, d. 15).

[19] *CollDecr* d. 155 (GC 16, d. 34; GC 18, d. 22, no. 5; GC 20, d. 12, no. 5; GC 22, d. 44, no. 1).

[20] See *CollDecr* d. 176 (see GC 7, d. 17, nos. 4–7; GC 15, d. 8).

[21] See *Examen,* c. 4, no. 38 [95].

[22] GC 27, *CollDecr* d. 166, 2°; see *Examen,* c. 4, no. 41 [98].

[23] See *Examen,* c. 4, no. 41 [98].

[24] See *Examen,* c. 4, no. 41 [98].

⁴"I further promise a special obedience to the sovereign pontiff in regard to the missions *[C]*, according to the same apostolic letters and the Constitutions.

⁵"Rome, or elsewhere, on such a day, month, and year, and in such a church."

[528] *B.* ¹*The promise to instruct children and uneducated persons in conformity with the apostolic letters and the Constitutions does not induce a greater obligation than the other spiritual exercises by which the neighbor is aided,* ²*such as confessions, preaching, and the like. Each one ought to employ himself in these as directed by the commands of his superiors.* ³*But the promise about the children is placed in the vow so that this holy practice may be held as something more especially enjoined and may be exercised with greater devotion, in view of the special service thereby given to God our Lord in aid of his souls* ⁴*and the greater danger of its being allowed to fall into oblivion and dropped than is the case with other more conspicuous services such as preaching and the like.*

[529] *C.* ¹*The entire purport of this fourth vow of obedience to the pope was and is with regard to missions;* ²*and this is how the bulls should be understood where they speak of this obedience in all that the sovereign pontiff may command and wherever he may send one, and so on.*

[530] 4. ¹Thereupon the one professed will receive the most Holy Sacrament of the Eucharist. ²When this has been done, his name should be written in the book of the Society which will exist for this purpose, along with the name of the person into whose hands he made the profession, with the day, month, and year in which it was made. ³His written vow should be preserved so that it may always be evidence of all this, to the glory of God our Lord.

[531] 5. ¹Those who are admitted to the profession of only three solemn vows **will read**²⁴ their written vow in the church before receiving the most holy Sacrament, in the presence of the members of the house and the others from outside who are present. The formula is as follows:

[532] 6. ¹"I, N., make profession, and I promise to Almighty God, in the presence of his Virgin Mother, the whole heavenly court, and all those here present, ²and to you, Reverend Father N., superior general of the Society of Jesus and the one holding the place of God, and to your successors (or, to you, Reverend Father N., representing the superior general of the Society of Jesus and his succes-

---

²⁴ (See *CN* 130.)

ment, can those who are delegates, vicars, and prefects apostolic, even though they are not elevated to episcopal status.[25]

CHAPTER 4

THE PRONOUNCING OF THE VOWS

130   For pronouncing the religious vows of the Society, it is required and sufficient for their validity that the one taking them expresses them in the presence of the one who receives them legitimately, using words or signs whose meaning cannot be doubted.[26]

131   §1. First vows are taken during a Eucharistic celebration, in the presence of some residents of the house, not excluding relatives, but avoiding too much solemnity, according to the formula prescribed in the Constitutions, P. V, c. 4, no. 4 [540], and in an approved vernacular translation; after the vows, those pronouncing them should receive the Body and Blood of the Lord.[27]

§2. The one taking vows should declare in writing that he has correctly understood the force of the fourth vow,[28] which is also simple, whereby he is obliged to pronounce the vows of formed coadjutors or even, if he is a scholastic, of the solemnly professed, when and as it seems good to the superior general for the greater service of God.[29]

132   Immediately after Communion in a public Mass, which may also be concelebrated by priests pronouncing their vows,[30] in the presence of those in the house and any others from outside who may be there, the one who is to receive the final vows should turn with the Holy Eucharist to the one who is to pronounce his vows. The one pronouncing his vows should read, in

---

[25] *CollDecr* d. 159 (GC 22, d. 40).

[26] See GC 27, *CollDecr* d. 168; P. V, c. 3, A [526].

[27] See P. V, c. 4, no. 4 [540]; GC 31, d. 12.

[28] *CollDecr* d. 153 (GC 5, d. 50, no. 1).

[29] See *CollDecr* d. 146 (GC 5, dd. 4, 5, 7, 50, no. 1; GC 7, dd. 32 and 39; GC 11, d. 39, 1°–4°; see *Examen*, c. 1, no. 10 [14]; c. 7, no. 1 [121]; P. V., c. 1, A [511]; c. 4, E [541].

[30] See GC 31, d. 12, a.

sors and holding the place of God), [3]perpetual poverty, chastity, and obedience; and, in conformity with it, special care for the instruction of children, according to the manner of living contained in the apostolic letters of the Society of Jesus and in its Constitutions.

"Rome, or elsewhere, on such a day, month, and year, and in such a church."

[4]Thereupon Holy Communion will follow and all the rest, as was stated above.

CHAPTER 4
[1]THE ADMISSION OF FORMED COADJUTORS AND SCHOLASTICS

[533]   1. [2]Those admitted as formed spiritual coadjutors with simple but not solemn vows will, in the church or the chapel of the house or in another fitting place, and in the presence of the members of the house and those from outside who are present, [3]make their vow into the hands [A] of the one who admits them, reading it to him in the following form [in 535 below]:

[534]   A. [1]*The vows are said to be made into the hands when they are made before one who receives them with authorization to do so.* [2]*And even though many persons happen to be present when these vows are taken, they do not for this reason cease to be simple vows.* [3]*For, in accordance with the authority of the Apostolic See granted to the Society, the intention of the one who makes them and of the one who receives them is this: that they are neither made nor received as solemn.* [4]*However, it will be left to the discretion of the one who receives them to take thought for the edification which might ensue, and he will accordingly direct that more or fewer persons be present.* [5]*In other respects the temporal coadjutors and spiritual coadjutors will have the same procedure, which in both cases will be outwardly quite similar to that of the professed.*

[535]   2. [1]"I, N., promise to Almighty God, in the presence of his Virgin Mother and the whole heavenly court, [2]and to you, Reverend Father N., superior general of the Society of Jesus and the one holding the place of God, and to your successors (or, to you, Reverend Father N., representing the superior general of the Society of Jesus and his successors and holding the place of God), [3]perpetual poverty, chastity, and obedience; [4]and, in conformity with it, special care for the instruction of children, [5]according to the manner indicated in the apostolic letters and Constitutions of the aforementioned Society [B].

a loud voice, his written vows, keeping intact the prescription in no. 130; after this he should receive the Holy Eucharist.[31]

133   In pronouncing final vows the formulas prescribed in the Constitutions (P. V, c. 3, nos. 3 [527] and 6 [532]; and c. 4, nos. 2 [535] and 3 [537]) are to be used, even in an approved vernacular translation.

134   One pronouncing the five simple vows of the solemnly professed should use the following formulas:

"I, N., a professed member of the Society of Jesus, promise to almighty God in the presence of his Virgin Mother and the entire heavenly court, and in the presence of Reverend Father N., superior general (or, in the presence of N., who is taking the place of the superior general), that I will never act in any way or consent that what has been ordained in the Constitutions of the Society concerning poverty should be changed unless, for justifiable cause flowing from the demands of life, it would seem that poverty ought to be made stricter.

"Further, I promise that I will never strive or seek, not even indirectly, to be chosen for or promoted to any prelacy or dignity within the Society.

"I promise further that I will never strive for or seek any prelacy or dignity outside the Society, or consent to my election thereto insofar as is in my power, unless compelled by obedience to him who has power to command me under pain of sin.

"I promise as well that if I become aware that anyone else is seeking or striving for either of the foregoing two preferments, I will manifest him and the entire matter to the Society or to its superior.

"I also promise that, if it should ever happen that, in spite of the third vow, I should be ordained bishop, I will never refuse to listen to the counsel which the superior general of the Society himself, or someone else of the Society whom he substitutes for himself, will deign to give me."[32]

---

[31] See P. V, c. 3, nos. 2, 4, 5 [525, 530, 531]; c. 4, nos. 1, 2 [533, 535].

[32] See *CollDecr* d. 169 (GC 1, d. 102; GC 3, d. 46), modified by GC 34.

"Rome, or elsewhere, in such a place, day, month, year, and so forth."

[1]Thereupon he will receive Holy Communion and all that was stated in regard to the professed [530] will be done.

[536] B. [1]*The reference to the bulls and the Constitutions makes clear that the coadjutors take these vows with a tacit condition in regard to the perpetuity. This condition is: if the Society will desire to retain them. [2]For although they on their own side bind themselves perpetually for their devotion and stability,* **the Society remains free to dismiss them,**[25] *as is explained in Part II [204, 205]; and in that case they are entirely freed from their vows.*

[537] [2]The procedure for the temporal coadjutors will be the same [C], with the reference to the instruction of children omitted.

[3]Those who, after finishing their first probation and two years' experiences, **are received as approved scholastics**[26] will make their vows in the presence of some members of the house, although not into the hands of anyone [D], according to the following formula [in 540 below]:

[538] C. [1]*If they are persons who do not know Latin, as some temporal coadjutors might not, the vow should be put into the vernacular, and they should read it, or someone else should read it for them while they follow it.*

[539] D. [1]*Just as this vow is made to God alone and not to a man,* {*so no man receives it*}.[27] *This is the reason why it is not said to be made into the hands of anyone.* [2]*And the tacit condition about the perpetuity which the vow of the coadjutors contains, as was stated [in 536], is present in this one too; it is, that is to say, if the Society will desire to retain them.*

[540] 4. [1]"Almighty and eternal God, I, N., though altogether most unworthy in your divine sight, yet relying on your infinite goodness and mercy and moved with a desire of serving you, [2]in the presence of the most holy Virgin Mary and your whole heavenly court, vow to your Divine Majesty perpetual poverty, chastity, and obedience in the Society of Jesus; [3]and I promise that I shall enter that same

---

[25] (See note 5 to [208].)

[26] (This is to be understood also for the pronouncing of the vows of approved brothers.)

[27] **Abolished.** (They are true public vows—see Gregory XIII, *Ascendente Domino*—and therefore received in the name of the Church by a legitimate superior [see CIC 1192, §1; CCEO 889, §4].)

135   The solemnly professed of three vows should pronounce the same five simple vows as do the solemnly professed of four vows.[33]

136   In the formula of final vows, the name of the one receiving the vows should always be mentioned; in regard to the superior general, however (or, after his death, the vicar general), only his office should be expressed and not his name, unless he himself receives the vows.[34]

CHAPTER 5

THE SIMPLE VOWS OF THE SOLEMNLY PROFESSED

137   §1. The matter of the vow not to relax poverty, reserved to the Holy See,[35] is completely defined in this statement of the Constitutions: "To alter what touches upon poverty would be to mitigate it by allowing some fixed revenue or possession for personal use, or for the sacristy, or for the building, or for some other purpose, apart from what pertains to the colleges and houses of probation."[36] Therefore, in virtue of the vow the solemnly professed are obliged only to this: not to grant a stable income or any possession for its own use to houses and churches, notwithstanding other more general expressions that are found in the same declaration of the Constitutions.[37]

   §2. This practice of poverty is now applied to all apostolic communities as distinct from institutions, according to the norm of no. 191, §1.

138   In regard to the second vow of not ambitioning prelacies or, what comes to the same thing, dignities in the Society, prelacies are understood to mean the office of General, Vicar General, Provincial, Superior of a Region (or Mission), even a dependent one, and Local Superior.[38]

---

[33] *CollDecr* d. 147 (GC 4, d. 54; see ibid., d. 19).

[34] *CollDecr* d. 170 (GC 12, d. 56, no. 7; see GC Pol. 4, d. 6).

[35] See Gregory XIII, *Ascendente Domino;* Paul V, *Ex incumbenti;* Urban VIII, *Vota quæ Deo;* P. VI, c. 2, no. 1 [553].

[36] P. VI, c. 2, A [554].

[37] See GC 31, d. 18, no. 14.

[38] See *CollDecr* d. 205, §2 (GC 7, d. 44).

Society *[E]* in order to lead my entire life in it, understanding all things according to its Constitutions. ⁴Therefore I suppliantly beg your immense Goodness and Clemency, through the blood of Jesus Christ, to deign to receive this holocaust in an odor of sweetness; ⁵and that just as you gave me the grace to desire and offer this, so you will also bestow abundant grace to fulfill it.

⁶"Rome, or elsewhere, in such a place, day, month, year, and so forth."

⁷After this he will likewise receive Holy Communion and all the rest will be done as is stated above [530].

[541] E. ¹*The promise to enter the Society, as was stated in the beginning [511], means:* **to become one of its professed or its formed coadjutors, according to what its general judges to be for greater service to God.**²⁸

[542] 5. ¹After anyone has been incorporated into the Society in one grade he should not seek to pass to another *[F]*, ²but should strive to perfect himself in the first one and to serve and glorify God our Lord in it, leaving the care of everything else to the superior whom he holds in place of Christ our Lord.

[543] F. ¹*To represent his thoughts and what occurs to him is permissible. Nevertheless, as is stated in the Examen [130–32], he should be ready in everything to hold as better that which his superior judges to be so.*

[544] 6. ¹Just as the scholastics ought to take their vows at the end of two years and bind themselves to Christ our Lord, ²so also those who are in the houses without any intention of their studying and of whom it is nevertheless judged that they should not so soon be admitted as formed coadjutors or professed ought to take **their vows in the same manner**²⁹ as the scholastics.

³If someone because of his personal devotion takes the vows before the end of the two years, he may use the same formula. ⁴Handing in one copy *[G]*, he may retain the other copy of his vow that he may know what he has offered to God our Lord. ⁵For the same purpose too and for an increase of devotion, it is good that at certain times which will appear fitting these persons should renew their vows *[H]*. To do this is not to take on a new obligation but to remind themselves of the one they already have in our Lord and to confirm it.

---

²⁸ **Clarified by** *CN* 131, §2.

²⁹ (Today all novices at the end of the novitiate take public vows and become approved scholastics or brothers; see *CN* 6, §1, 2°.)

139   §1. The third vow, also reserved to the Holy See, not to ambition or accept prelacies or dignities outside the Society[39] extends to the episcopate and to the office of Vicar General and Episcopal Vicar;[40] but not to the office of Judicial Vicar or *Officialis* and to Diocesan Judge[41] nor to lay prelacies.[42]

§2. In regard to accepting the office of Vicar General and Episcopal Vicar, the superior general, by a faculty received from the Holy See, can grant a dispensation in particular cases.[43]

§3. In regard to accepting the episcopal office, the first response on the part of the one whose appointment is being proposed should always be to make a representation of our vow. This can more easily be done, since the Holy See does not impose an episcopal appointment without the consent of the candidate. But if in a particular case the Holy See insists or some member remains anxious because he has not positively responded immediately to the will of the Holy Father expressly manifested to him,[44] he should refer the matter either directly or through his provincial to the superior general, so that together they may examine the more appropriate way of responding to what is proposed, according to the spirit of our Institute and for the greater glory of God.[45]

140   The actions that are prohibited by the second and third simple vow of the solemnly professed are to be understood as external acts.[46]

141   The fourth vow of denouncing anyone who is ambitioning honors obliges one to make a denunciation even though the one who is ambitioning is not solemnly professed.[47]

---

[39] See Gregory XIII, *Ascendente Domino;* Paul V, *Ex incumbenti;* Urban VIII, *Vota quæ Deo;* P. X, no. 6 [817].

[40] See CIC 475, 476; CCEO 245, 246.

[41] See CIC 1420; CCEO 1086.

[42] Approved by Pope John Paul II, Letter of June 10, 1995, from the Secretariat of State.

[43] See *ActRSJ* 19:1099.

[44] See P. VI, c. 1, no. 1 [547].

[45] See *ActRSJ* 19:1099–100.

[46] GC 27, *CollDecr* d. 205, §1.

[47] *CollDecr* d. 206 (GC 9, d. 13); see Gregory XIII, *Ascendente Domino;* P. X, no. 6 [817].

[545] G. ¹The record of these vows ought to be kept in a book, just as that of the others, for good reasons.

[546] H. ¹In regard to the scholastics, the times at which they ought to renew their vows have already been stated in Part IV [346–47]. ²The same holds true of those in the houses who will have them. That is, **they should renew them** to the superior **on two principal feasts of the year.**³⁰ ³They will not make them into the hands of anyone, but each one will read his own before the most blessed Sacrament, with the other members of the Society, or some of them, present, ⁴in order to be stirred to greater devotion in observing what they have promised to God our Lord and holding more clearly before their eyes their obligations toward him.

---

³⁰ **Clarified by** CN **75.**

142 The fifth vow concerns listening to the superior general, by which the one making the vow promises that if he should be promoted to the episcopate, he would not refuse to listen to the counsel which the general himself or someone else of the Society whom he substitutes for himself would see fit to give him.[48]

---

[48] See P. X, no. 6 [817].

PART VI
[1]THE PERSONAL LIFE OF THOSE ALREADY ADMITTED AND INCORPORATED INTO THE BODY OF THE SOCIETY

The text of the Constitutions begins on page 220.

PART VI

THE PERSONAL LIFE OF THOSE ALREADY ADMITTED AND INCORPORATED INTO THE BODY OF THE SOCIETY

SECTION 1: THE APOSTOLIC CHARACTER OF OUR VOWS IN GENERAL

143 §1. Our consecration by profession of the evangelical counsels, by which we respond to a divine vocation, is at one and the same time the following of Christ poor, virginal, and obedient and a rejection of those idols that the world is always prepared to adore, especially wealth, pleasure, prestige, and power. Hence, our poverty, chastity, and obedience ought visibly and efficaciously to bear witness to this attitude, whereby we proclaim the evangelical possibility of a certain communion among men and women that is a foretaste of the future kingdom of God.[1]

§2. Our religious vows, while binding us, also set us free:

▶ free, by our vow of poverty, to share the life of the poor and to use whatever resources we may have, not for our own security and comfort, but for service

▶ free, by our vow of chastity, to be "men for others," in friendship and communion with all, but especially with those who share our mission of service

▶ free, by our vow of obedience, to respond to the call of Christ as made known to us by him whom the Spirit has placed over the Church, and to follow the lead of all our superiors[2]

---

[1] See GC 32, d. 4, no. 16; see GC 31, d. 16, no. 4; d. 17, no. 2; d. 18, no. 3.

[2] GC 32, d. 2, no. 20.

SECTION 2: CHASTITY

144   §1. By the vow of chastity, we devote ourselves to the Lord and to his service in such a unique love that it excludes marriage and any other exclusive human relationship, as well as the genital expression and gratification of sexuality. Thus the vow entails the obligation of complete continence in celibacy for the sake of the kingdom of heaven. Following the evangelical counsel of chastity, we aspire to deepen our familiarity with God, our configuration to Christ, our companionship with our brother Jesuits, our service to our neighbors whoever they may be; and at the same time we aspire to grow in our personal maturity and capacity to love.[3]

§2. Hence in the Society chastity, which is before all else God's gracious gift,[4] is essentially apostolic and the source of radical availability and mobility for mission,[5] and not at all to be understood as directed exclusively to our own personal sanctification. Its precious apostolic fruitfulness, besides providing freedom for greater mobility in God's service, in imitation of the angels,[6] is a mature, simple, anxiety-free dealing with the men and women with whom and for whom we exercise our ministry for building up the body of Christ.[7]

§3. Especially in our times, when people tend to put whole classes of their fellow human beings beyond the margins of their concern, while at the same time identifying love with eroticism, the self-denying love that is warmly human, yet freely given in service to all, especially to the poor and the marginalized, can be a powerful sign leading people to Christ, who came to show us what love really is, namely, that God is love.[8]

145   This consecration of ourselves to Christ involves a certain affective renunciation and solitude of heart; namely, a renunciation of conjugal intimacy and the possibility of having children of one's own; and of an affective bonding that is a normal condition for achieving human growth and establishing a family of one's

---

[3] GC 34, d. 8, no. 13; see GC 31, d. 16, nos. 3–4; GC 32, d. 11, no. 26.

[4] See GC 34, d. 8, no. 7.

[5] See GC 34, d. 8, no. 11.

[6] See P. VI, c. 1, no. 1 [547].

[7] See GC 31, d. 16, no. 4; 8, b; GC 34, d. 8, nos. 6, 8–9.

[8] GC 32, d. 11, no. 26; GC 34, d. 8, no. 10.

own. But this is part of the cross offered to us by Jesus Christ as we follow his footsteps, and closely associates us with his paschal mystery and makes us sharers of the spiritual fruitfulness that flows from it. But not only does it not diminish our personality or hamper human contacts and dialogue, it expands affectivity instead, assists people fraternally, and brings them to a fuller charity.[9]

146   §1. That the love once consecrated by chastity may grow unceasingly, all should before all else cultivate intimate familiarity with God and friendship with Christ through contemplation of his mysteries and through life-giving assimilation to him in the sacraments both of penance and of the Eucharist.[10]

§2. It is also very important, as the Society has learned from the experience of Ignatius himself,[11] to renew incessantly the strong desire of persevering, by means of humble and simple devotion to the Blessed Virgin Mary, who by her chaste assent obtained divine fecundity and became the mother of fair love.[12]

§3. Chastity is more safely preserved "when in common life true fraternal love thrives among its members," by fostering charity and the ready union of souls, which disposes us to bear one another's burdens; and when we feel a generous love for one and all and at the same time engage in a helpful and fruitful dialogue with all and are true brothers and friends in Christ,[13] leading the community life proper to the Society, as described in Part VIII, nos. 311–30.[14]

147   §1. With humble awareness that love consecrated by chastity must constantly grow in order to come to maturity, we should use all the supernatural and natural helps available for this. Among these, however, we prefer those that are positive, such as probity of life, generous dedication to one's assigned task, great desire for the glory of God, zeal for solid virtues and spiritual concerns, openness and simplicity in dealing with and

---

[9] See GC 31, d. 16, no. 5; GC 32, d. 2, no. 20; GC 34, d. 8, nos. 14–16.

[10] See GC 31, d. 16, nos. 7, a; 8, a; GC 34, d. 8, nos. 18–19.

[11] See *Autobiography,* no. 10.

[12] See GC 31, d. 16, no. 7, e; GC 34, d. 8, no. 20.

[13] See GC 31, d. 16, no. 7, b; no. 10; d. 19, no. 4; GC 32, d. 11, no. 14; Vat. Council II, *Perfectæ caritatis,* no. 12.

[14] GC 34, d. 8, nos. 21–23.

consulting with superiors, rich cultural attainments, spiritual joy, and above all true charity.[15]

§2. We should know how to participate with moderation in the human contacts that our ministry involves, our visits and recreations, our reading and study of problems, our attendance at shows, and our use of what is pleasurable, so that our consecration to God through chastity may be strengthened and its testimony may shine forth inviolate.[16]

§3. Also in order to foster this, our men should take into account and, according to the custom of different places where they deal with individual persons, they should take appropriate steps with a view to the edification of all.[17] It is especially important that those in ministries like spiritual direction or counseling keep appropriate "professional boundaries."[18]

§4. Nevertheless, mindful of our frailty, which throughout our whole life accompanies the development of chaste love, we cannot omit observance of the ascetical norms confirmed by the Church and the Society in their wide experience and required by today's dangers to chastity. These include, above all, examination of conscience, spiritual direction, internal self-discipline, and custody of the senses, by which with the help of God's grace we diligently moderate desires and impulses that might lessen a just and wholesome dominion over our senses and affections.[19]

148   §1. All our members should share in a common responsibility seriously to safeguard chastity and to further it through their mutual support and friendship as well as through the aid they offer superiors in their care for their companions and for the Society.[20]

§2 Superiors and spiritual directors should

1° Manifest the utmost solicitude for the spiritual life of each individual, accompanying him dependably and helping him to overcome fatigue, difficulties, and temptations that he may experience on the path of a life dedicated to chastity.

---

[15] GC 31, d. 16, nos. 7, b; 8, c; GC 34, d. 8, nos. 24, 32, 38.

[16] See GC 31, d. 16, no. 8, e; GC 34, d. 8, nos. 25–26, 30.

[17] See *CollDecr* d. 172 (see GC 6, d. 39, no. 1); GC 34, d. 8, no. 23.

[18] See GC 34, d. 8, nos. 25–26.

[19] See GC 31, d. 16, no. 8, b, c, d; GC 34, d. 8, nos. 28–29.

[20] GC 34, d. 8, no. 38; see *CN* no. 235; *Examen*, c. 4, no. 8 [63].

2° See to it that our members in the course of their formation are educated and strengthened in the matter of sex in a suitable, positive, and prudent manner, so as to be able vigorously to surmount the various crises attending maturation. If serious psychological problems emerge, a member should be advised to visit a counselor, psychologist, or psychiatrist.[21]

3° Firmly exercising true charity toward our members, take care that those who are unfit or doubtfully suitable for observing chastity are not admitted to the Society and, even more, that they are not admitted to vows or promoted to orders.

4° Solicitously, attentively, and with much trust be at the service of newly ordained priests and younger brothers who are beginning to work in the vineyard of the Lord, and also of those who for a long time engage in arduous special studies. They should lovingly endeavor to lead back those whom they see or sense to be drawing away from the community.[22]

---

[21] GC 34, d. 8, no. 33.

[22] See GC 31, d. 16, no. 9, b, c, d, e; GC 34, d. 8, nos. 36–44.

Chapter 1

2What Pertains to Obedience

[547] 1. ³In order that those already admitted to profession or as formed coadjutors may be able to employ themselves more fruitfully according to our Institute in the service of God and the aid of their neighbors, they need to observe certain things in regard to themselves. ⁴And although the most important of these are reduced to the vows which they offer to God our Creator and Lord in conformity with the apostolic letters, nevertheless, in order that these points may be further explained and commended, they will be treated in this present Part VI.

⁵**What pertains to the vow of chastity requires no interpretation,**¹ since it is evident how perfectly it should be preserved, by endeavoring to imitate therein the purity of the angels in cleanness of body and mind. ⁶Therefore, with this presupposed, we shall now treat of holy obedience.

All should strongly dispose themselves to observe obedience and to distinguish themselves in it, not only in the matters of obligation but also in the others, even though nothing else be perceived except an indication of the superior's will without an expressed command. ⁷They should keep in view God our Creator and Lord, for whom such obedience is practiced, and endeavor to proceed in a spirit of love and not as men troubled by fear. Hence all of us should be eager to miss no point of perfection which we can with God's grace attain in the observance of all the Constitutions [A] and of our manner of proceeding in our Lord, ⁸by applying all our energies with very special care to the virtue of obedience shown first to the sovereign pontiff and then to the superiors of the Society.

⁹Consequently, in all the things into which obedience can with charity be extended [B], we should be ready to receive its command just as if it were coming from Christ our Savior, since we are practicing the obedience [to one] in his place and because of love and reverence for him. ¹⁰Therefore we should be ready to leave unfinished any letter or anything else of ours which we have begun, and in the Lord to bend our whole mind and energy so that holy obedience, in regard to the execution, the willing, and the understanding, may always be perfect in every detail [C], ¹¹as we perform with great alacrity, spiritual joy, and perseverance whatever has

---

¹ Clarified by *CN* 144–48.

SECTION 3: OBEDIENCE

149   Impelled by love of Christ, we embrace obedience as a distinctive charism conferred by God on the Society through its founder, whereby we may be united the more surely and constantly with God's salvific will, and at the same time be made one in Christ among ourselves. Thus, through the vow of obedience our Society becomes a more fit instrument of Christ in his Church, to assist souls for God's greater glory.[23]

150   §1. Obedience is always an act of faith and freedom whereby the religious recognizes and embraces the will of God manifested to him by one who has authority to send him in the name of Christ. But both the superior who sends and the companion who is sent gain assurance that the mission is really God's will if it is preceded by special dialogue.[24]

§2. Therefore if we are to receive and to fulfill our mission through obedience, we must be faithful to that practice of spiritual apostolic discernment, both personal and in community, so central to our way of proceeding, as rooted in the Spiritual Exercises and the Constitutions. This discernment grows and gains strength by the examination of conscience, personal prayer and brotherly dialogue within our community, and the openness to superiors through the account of conscience that inclines us toward obedience.[25]

151   §1. All receive their mission from the superior, but the superior himself expects the community to discern in union with him and in conformity with his final decision, the concrete ways whereby that mission is to be accomplished and the procedure by which it is to be evaluated and revised in the light of actual performance.[26]

§2. If, therefore, the question at issue is of some importance and the necessary preconditions have been verified, the use of communal and apostolic discernment is encouraged as a privileged way to find God's will.[27]

---

[23] GC 31, d. 17, no. 2.

[24] GC 32, d. 11, no. 31; GC 31, d. 17, no. 11.

[25] GC 33, d. 1, nos. 11, 39; see GC 32, d. 11, nos. 31, 38; GC 31, d. 17, no. 8; *Examen*, c. 4, no. 35 [92].

[26] GC 32, d. 11, no. 18.

[27] GC 32, d. 11, no. 50.

been commanded us, [12]persuading ourselves that everything is just [13]and renouncing with blind obedience any contrary opinion and judgment of our own in all things which the superior commands and **in which** (as is stated [549]) **no species of sin can be judged to be present.**[2] [14]We ought to act on the principle that everyone who lives under obedience should let himself be carried and directed by Divine Providence through the agency of the superior [15]as if he were a lifeless body, which allows itself to be carried to any place and treated in any way; or an old man's staff, which serves at any place and for any purpose in which the one holding it in his hand wishes to employ it. [16]For in this way the obedient man ought joyfully to employ himself in any task in which the superior desires to employ him in aid of the whole body of the religious order; [17]and he ought to hold it certain that by so doing **he conforms himself with the divine will more than by anything else he could do while following his own will and different judgment.**[3]

[548]   *A.* [2]*These first Declarations, which are published along with the Constitutions, bind with the same authority as the Constitutions. Therefore in the observance equal care should be given to both.*

[549]   *B.* [1]*Such things are all those in which some sin is not manifest.*

[550]   *C.* [1]*The command of obedience is fulfilled in regard to the execution when the thing commanded is done; in regard to the willing when the one who obeys wills the same thing as the one who commands; in regard to the understanding when he forms the same judgment as the one commanding and regards what he is commanded as good.* [2]*And that obedience is imperfect in which there does not exist, in addition to the execution, also that agreement in willing and judging between him who commands and him who obeys.*

[551]   2. [1]Likewise, it should be strongly recommended to all that they should have and show great reverence, especially interior reverence, for their superiors, by considering and reverencing Jesus Christ in them; and from their hearts they should warmly love their superiors as fathers in him. [2]Thus in everything they should proceed in a spirit of charity, keeping nothing exterior or interior hidden from the superiors and desiring them to be informed about everything, so that the superiors may be the better able to direct them in everything along the path of salvation and perfection. [3]For that reason, once a year and as many times more as their superior

---

[2] Clarified by *CN* 154. (For cases of a conflict of conscience.)

[3] Clarified by *CN* 152, 153.

§3. In the Society the discerning community is not a deliberative or capitular body but a consultative one, whose object, clearly understood and fully accepted, is to assist the superior to determine what course of action is for God's greater glory and the service of humankind. It is up to him to make the final decision in the light of the discernment, but freely, as the one to whom both the grace and the burden of authority are given.[28]

152   In offering personal obedience, all should leave to superiors the full and completely free disposal of themselves, desiring to be guided, not by their own judgment and will, but by that indication of the divine will that is offered to us through obedience; and they should make their own the superior's command in a personal, responsible way and with all diligence "bring to the execution of commands and the discharge of assignments entrusted to them the resources of their minds and wills, and their gifts of nature and grace."[29]

153   Obedience by its very nature and perfection supposes in the subject the obligation of personal responsibility and the spirit of ever seeking what is better. Consequently, he can, and sometimes should, set forth his own reasons and proposals to the superior.[30] But a subject may not refuse to obey in those things where there is not manifestly any sin, because he thinks something better should be done or because he believes he is led along other lines by the inspiration of the Spirit.[31]

154   If it should happen that a member sincerely considers himself bound by a dictate of conscience not to follow the superior's will and thinks that in a given case he is morally obliged to act contrary to it, the following norms are to be observed:

1° After prayer and appropriate consultation, the individual should enter into a sincere dialogue with his superior, to whom he explains his reasons according to the Ignatian principle of representation.

2° He is always free to have recourse to a higher superior.

---

[28] GC 32, d. 11, no. 24.

[29] GC 31, d. 17, no. 9; Vat. Council II, *Perfectæ caritatis,* no. 14.

[30] GC 31, d. 17, no. 11; see *Examen,* c. 4, no. 35 [92], c. 8, no. 1, A [131]; P. V, c. 4, no. 5, F [543]; P. VII, c. 2, no. 1, K [627].

[31] See GC 31, d. 17, no. 10.

thinks good, all the professed and formed coadjutors should be ready to manifest their consciences to him {in confession},⁴ or in secret,⁵ or in another manner, for the sake of the great profit this practice contains, as was stated in the Examen [91, 92, 97]. ⁴Thus too they should be ready {to make a general confession, from the last one they made, to the one whom the superior thinks it wise to designate in his place}.⁶

[552] 3. ¹All should have recourse to the superior for the things which they happen to desire; ²and without his permission and approval no individual should directly or indirectly request, or cause to be requested, any favor from the sovereign pontiff or from another person outside the Society, either for himself or for someone else. ³He should be convinced that if he does not get what he desires through the hands of the superior or with his approval, it is not useful to him for the divine service; ⁴and that if it is useful to him for that service, he will get it with the consent of the superior, as from the one who holds the place of Christ our Lord for him.

---

⁴ **Abolished by GC 34.** (As a consequence of CIC 984, §2, and CCEO 734, §2, insofar as a manifestation of conscience thus made is directly opposed to this purpose as defined in the Examen [92].)

⁵ (See *CN* 155, §2.)

⁶ **Abolished.** (See note 23 to [200].)

3° But if the superior continues to urge the command and the conflict cannot be resolved either through dialogue with the superior or through recourse to a higher superior, other persons—some of whom may be from outside the Society—may be invited by mutual consent to assist in forming the individual's conscience more clearly. This should be done privately and without publicity.

4° This procedure cannot be imposed on either the superior or the member. It is entirely voluntary and unofficial, and is nothing more than a new effort to find the divine will. The opinion of those consulted has no juridical effect on the authority of the superior. It is merely advisory.

5° If, after following this procedure, the member still feels he cannot obey in good conscience, the superior, having consulted higher superiors as the case may merit, should determine what is to be done in view of the good both of the whole Society and of the individual's conscience. But a man who, time after time, is unable to obey with a good conscience, should give consideration to some other path of life wherein he can serve God with greater tranquility.[32]

155   §1. The account of conscience, by which the superior becomes able to take part in each one's discernment and to help him therein,[33] is to retain intact its value and vitality as an element of great moment in the spiritual governance of the Society.[34] Therefore, all should give an account of conscience to their superiors, according to the norms and spirit of the Society, inspired by charity, with any obligation under pain of sin always precluded.[35] In addition, the relationships between superiors and their brethren in the Society should be such as to encourage the manifestation of conscience and conversation about spiritual matters.[36]

§2. No one, without exception, may directly or indirectly make known what has been revealed in an account of conscience

---

[32] GC 32, d. 11, no. 55; GC 31, d. 17, no. 10; see *Examen,* c. 3, no. 12, D [48–49].

[33] GC 32, d. 4, no. 67.

[34] GC 32, d. 11, nos. 31–32; see GC 31, d. 17, no. 8; *CollDecr* d. 58 (see GC 26, d. 14), *Examen,* c. 4, no. 35 [92].

[35] GC 31, d. 17, no. 8; see CIC 630, §5; *ActRSJ* 5:88–89.

[36] GC 32, d. 11, nos. 31, 46; see GC 31, d. 17, no. 8.

Chapter 2

¹What Pertains to Poverty and Its Consequences

[553] 1. ²Poverty, as the strong wall of the religious institute, should be loved and preserved in its integrity as far as this is possible with God's grace. ³The enemy of the human race generally tries to weaken this defense and rampart which God our Lord inspired religious institutes to raise against him and the other adversaries of their perfection. ⁴Into what was well ordered by their first founders he induces alterations by means of interpretations and innovations not in conformity with those founders' first spirit. ⁵Therefore, so that provision may be made in this matter as far as lies in our power, all those who make profession in this Society should promise not to take part in altering what pertains to poverty in the Constitutions *[A]*, **unless it be in some manner to make it more strict,**⁷ according to the circumstances in the Lord.

[554] *A.* ¹*To alter what touches upon poverty would be so to mitigate it as to have any fixed revenue or possession for personal use, or for the sacristy, or for the building, or for some other purpose, apart from what pertains to the colleges and the houses of probation.*⁸ ²*To prevent the Constitutions from being changed in so important a matter, each one after making his profession will make this promise in the presence of the superior general and those who happen to be present with him:* ³*In the sight of our Creator and Lord he will promise to take no part in altering what pertains to poverty in the Constitutions, either in a congregation assembled from the entire Society or by attempting this himself in any manner.*

---

⁷ (See *CN* 137.)

⁸ **Clarified by** *CN* **137; 191, §1.** (In regard to the matter of the vow not to relax poverty.)

unless it is with the express consent of the one rendering the account.[37]

156   Ours should neither seek to have externs intercede for them with superiors nor allow this to happen in any instance.[38]

SECTION 4: POVERTY
CERTAIN GENERAL PRINCIPLES

157   Voluntary religious poverty is the attempt of fallen human beings, in the radical following of the humble and poor Christ, to achieve that freedom from every inordinate attachment which is the condition for a great and ready love of God and neighbor.[39]

158   The principle and foundation of our poverty is found in a love of the Word of God made flesh and crucified.[40] Therefore in the Society that way of life is to be maintained which is as far as possible removed from all infection of avarice and as like as possible to evangelical poverty, which our first fathers experienced as more gratifying, more undefiled, and more suitable for the edification of the neighbor.[41]

159   §1. Our poverty in the Society is apostolic: our Lord has sent us "to preach in poverty."[42] Therefore our poverty is measured by our apostolic purpose, so that our entire apostolate is informed with the spirit of poverty.[43]

§2. Efficiency in the apostolate and the witness of apostolic poverty are two values that are closely united and must be held in an ongoing tension; this is a rule for apostolic institutes as well as for individuals.[44]

---

[37] *CollDecr* d. 59 (GC 12, d. 15; see GC 23, d. 16, no. 1); see GC 31, d. 17, no. 8.

[38] *CollDecr* d. 173 (GC 5, dd. 14, 19; GC 7, d. 20); see P. VI, c. 1, no. 3 [552].

[39] See GC 32, d. 12, no. 9.

[40] GC 32, d. 12, no. 2. See *SpEx* nos. 98, 147, 167; "Deliberation on Poverty," MHSI, *Const.* I, pp. 78ff.; "Diary of St. Ignatius," ibid., pp. 86ff.; *FI* of Paul III and Julius III, no. 7; P. VI, c. 2, no. 1ff. [553ff.].

[41] See *FI* of Paul III and Julius III, no. 7.

[42] MI, *Letters* I, p. 96.

[43] GC 31, d. 18, no. 4; see GC 32, d. 12, no. 9; GC 34, d. 9, no. 4.

[44] See GC 32, d. 12, no. 9; GC 34, d. 9, no. 17.

[555]   2. ¹In the houses or churches which the Society accepts to aid souls, it should not be licit to have⁹ any fixed revenue,¹⁰ even for the sacristy or building or anything else, in such a manner that any administration of this revenue is in the control of the Society *[B]*. ²But the Society, relying on God our Lord whom it serves with the aid of his divine grace, should trust that without its having fixed revenue he will cause everything to be provided which can be expedient for his greater praise and glory.

[556]   *B. ¹If a founder of houses or churches should wish to leave some amount by way of fixed income for the maintenance of the building, this would not be at variance with the Society's poverty, so long as this revenue is not at the disposition of the Society and the Society is not in charge of it—even if the Society does take care that the person who has that charge does his duty. The same would apply to other similar cases.*

[557]   3. ¹The professed should live on alms¹¹ in the houses (when they are not sent away on missions), ²{and they should not hold the ordinary office of rectors of the colleges or universities of the Society} *[C]*,¹² (unless this is necessary or notably useful for these institutions); and in the houses they should not avail themselves of the fixed revenues of these colleges *[D]*.¹³

[558]   *C. ¹The statement that the professed should not live in the colleges is understood to mean a prolonged stay. But they may remain*

---

⁹ **Clarified by** *CN* 191, §1. (GC 32, d. 12, no. 41, authentically declared which revenues were forbidden to apostolic communities.)

¹⁰ **Modified by** *CN* 191. (A distinction is made between communities dedicated to the apostolate and churches on the one hand, and apostolic institutes on the other. These communities and churches follow the principles of the Constitutions set down for houses, while apostolic institutes follow those of colleges. Seminaries for our own members retain their own principles of poverty, as do houses or infirmaries for the care of the elderly and the sick.)

¹¹ **Clarified by** *CN* 181-87. (GC 31, d. 18, nos. 15–16, authentically declared that, besides alms and revenues, the fruit or remuneration of labor is a legitimate source of the material goods that are necessary for our life and apostolate.)

¹² **Abolished.** (See note 32 to [421].)

¹³ (But there remains the concession granted by Julius III—*Sacræ religionis*—in favor of those professed and formed coadjutors who are elderly or ill: see *CN* 196, §2. Moreoover, those who work for the formation of our men can live from the revenues of the colleges and houses of formation; see *CN* 197; 205, 1°.)

160   Our poverty is the condition of our apostolic credibility,[45] as the total expression of our trust in God and our freely given service to others,[46] when we are made witnesses of the freely bestowed love of God, who gave his Son for us in the total emptying of the incarnation and the cross.[47]

161   The forms of our poverty must truly suit the mentality, life, and apostolate of our times and give a visible witness to the Gospel. Therefore, our contemporary poverty must be especially characterized by these qualities: sincerity, by which our lives are really poor; devotion to work, by which we resemble workers in the world; and charity, by which we freely devote ourselves and all we have for the service of the neighbor.[48]

162   Let our poverty, sincerely and profoundly renewed, be

▶ simple in community expression and joyous in the following of Christ

▶ happy in sharing all goods among ourselves and with others

▶ apostolic in its active indifference and readiness for any service

▶ inspiring our selection of ministries and turning us to those most in need

▶ spiritually effective, proclaiming Jesus Christ in our way of life and in all we do[49]

163   The preferential option for the poor, as proposed by the Church, which the Society wishes to make its own, should find some concrete expression directly or indirectly in the life of every companion of Jesus, as well as in the orientations of our existing apostolic works and in our choice of new ministries.[50]

---

[45] See GC 34, d. 9, no. 6; GC 33, d. 1, no. 48.

[46] See P. VI, c. 2, no. 2 [555]; no. 7 [565].

[47] GC 34, d. 9, no. 6.

[48] GC 31, d. 18, no. 6.

[49] GC 32, d. 12, no. 14.

[50] See GC 33, d. 1, no. 48.

there in passing for a day or some fitting time. ²They could also live there for a longer time when this is necessary or expedient for the good of the same college or university, ³for example, if they are necessary for the administration of the studies, or if they lecture or devote themselves to the spiritual activities of confessions and preaching in order to relieve the scholastics who would have to do this, or in order to supply what the scholastics cannot do, ⁴or if they are sent to make a visitation of these colleges or universities and to set things right in them; ⁵and also when it is necessary or fitting for the universal good, for example, if someone with an explicit commission from the superior general retires there for a time for the purpose of writing.

[559] D. ¹Very small things are counted for nothing; ²and thus, to avoid scruples, this explanation is made: When the rector by means of some provisions for a journey helps someone who is passing through a college and who lacks those provisions, thus giving him an alms, it may be accepted. ³Also the fact that the colleges supply certain expenditures which the houses would otherwise make if they could, for example, expenditures for clothing and the giving of provisions for traveling to those who are sent from the houses to the colleges, ⁴even though it is or seems to be an aid to the house, is not against the intention of this constitution which states that these members should not avail themselves of the fixed revenues of the college for their food or clothing or other expenses which are proper to the house. ⁵Likewise, the fact that the sick or the well from the houses take some recreation in a garden of the college is not understood to be against the constitution, provided that these persons are not supported at the expense of the college during the time when they are members of the houses. ⁶The same judgment can be made in regard to similar matters.

[560] 4. ¹The coadjutors dwelling in the houses will live on alms according to the manner of living in these houses. ²In the colleges, if they are rectors or lecturers or helping in things necessary or highly useful to these same colleges, they will live on the fixed revenues of the colleges just as the other persons, as long as the need for them lasts. ³When it ceases, they should not reside in the colleges but in the houses of the Society, as has been said about the professed.

[561] 5. ¹Not only fixed revenue **but also stable goods of any kind are forbidden to be possessed by the houses or churches of the**

CHAPTER 1

THE POVERTY OF INDIVIDUALS

Article 1: The Vow of Poverty

164   §1. After their first vows Ours retain ownership of their goods and the capacity to acquire other goods for themselves, but only those that constitute their patrimony or capital or pertain to it either by their very nature or by the will of the donors or for some other special reason. Other goods they acquire for the Society.[51]

§2. They act against the vow of poverty who without permission exercise an act of proprietorship over their goods.[52]

165   §1. Without explicit permission of the superior, Ours are sternly prohibited from

1° Accepting a loan of money from someone outside the Society, either for themselves or for another, even if it is to be spent for pious purposes

2° Investing money for profit, on any pretext whatever, in their own name or in another's, with due regard for no. 57, §2, 2°[53]

§2. The prohibition against anyone's having money either in his possession or in the possession of another[54] includes the sort of money or other goods that some one of Ours uses as he pleases, but whose ownership, indeed, remains with someone else; no superior can permit such a practice.[55]

§3. If on occasion just reasons seem to suggest that someone should be allowed to have money received from a person outside the Society, he should keep these funds in the possession of the superior or the treasurer. Such a deposit is always subject to the authority of superiors, with due regard for the intentions of

---

[51] *CollDecr* d. 175, §1 (see GC 6, d. 39, no. 1); see CIC 668, §§3; CCEO 529, §3; Gregory XIII, *Quanto fructuosius*; id., *Ascendente Domino*; P. IV, c. 4, E [348]. The special personal obligations flowing from **final vows** are expressed in the Constitutions themselves: P. VI, c. 2, esp. nos. 3, 4, 7, 11, 12 [557, 560, 565, 570, 572].

[52] See *CollDecr* d. 175, §2 (GC 5, d. 50, no. 4, d. 59).

[53] *CollDecr* d. 186, 1°, 2° (GC 16, d. 28, d. 16).

[54] See *Examen*, c. 4, no. 4 [57]; P. VI, c. 2, no. 11, H [570, 571].

[55] *CollDecr* d. 184 (GC 12, d. 41; GC 16, d. 35).

Society, either in particular or in common,[14] except for what is necessary or highly expedient for the members' habitation and use [E]. ²Such would be the case if a place apart from the common habitation should be accepted for those who are convalescing and those who withdraw there to devote themselves to spiritual matters, because of the better air or other advantages which it may have. ³In such a case it should not be a property which is let out to others or brings profits equivalent to fixed revenue [F].

[562] E. ¹For, as the bull states, **the Society will not have the civil right to retain any stable possession beyond what is opportune for its habitation and use.**[15] ²*The Society should be obliged to dispossess itself as soon as possible of any stable possession which is given to it, selling it to relieve the penury of the needy inside or outside the Society.*

But this does not exclude waiting for an opportune time to sell; ³and it should be understood as referring to when the stable possession is not necessary for the use of the house, such as some things among those mentioned above. ⁴In regard to other goods which are movable, such as money or books or what is connected with food and clothing, **the Society may in common have property for its use.**[16]

[563] F. ¹*There would be such profits if the aforementioned possessions yielded wine or oil or wheat, or if the fruits or vegetables of the garden were being sold. But none of this will be licit, although the residents should be able to enjoy the fruit or a part of it for the use of the house. ²If the Society should have a gardener or lay person who has charge of the garden or lands which the above houses possess, he ought not to be prohibited from doing what seems proper for his own profit, ³provided that in such cases no profit accrues to the houses or individual members of the Society.*

---

[14] **Clarified** *CN* **190.** (In regard to goods and rights destined for apostolic institutes, whose communities can be juridical subjects, but in such a way that neither the capital nor the interest of the institutes can be of financial benefit to our members or communities, with the exception of the approved amount for work done in them and for services rendered: see *CN* 190, §2.)

[15] **Modified by** *CN* **203–5.** (The Society, provinces, and regions, dependent and independent, as distinguished from communities and apostolic institutes, can possess even revenue-bearing capital and enjoy stable and assured revenues within the limits defined there.)

[16] (It must be noted, however, that the property of each community is proper to it and distinct from the property of the Society and the province and also of other communites; see P. IV, c. 2, no. 5 [326]; P. VI, c. 2, no. 5 [561].)

the donors. Superiors should be careful, however, that such funds on deposit do not become in some sense permanent and that a sort of *peculium* is not gradually introduced.[56]

166   §1. Our members are forbidden to accept any responsibility for administering the goods of nonmembers of the Society, even of relatives.

§2. No one except the general can grant a dispensation from this prohibition.[57]

167   All should faithfully exercise dependence upon superiors in the use of temporal goods, both in seeking permission and in giving an account of expenditures and, where applicable, of administration.[58]

Article 2: Renunciation of Property

168   A renunciation of goods made after first vows[59] without permission of the superior involves a violation of the vow of poverty of the Society.[60]

169   The renunciation before final vows should be

1° Universal, such that it embraces all goods and rights which one actually has, and any right to or control over property that could come to him

2° Absolute, such that the one making the renunciation deprives himself of all hope of recovering the goods at any time[61]

170   The formula of renunciation should be drawn up in such language that all avenues of escape are cut off; and every required formality should be attended to, so that the renunciation will to the extent possible have its effects even in civil law.[62]

171   Specifically, according to our Institute,

---

[56] See *CollDecr* d. 185, §§1–3 (GC 22, d. 26, nos. 1–3, see GC 30, d. 69).

[57] *CollDecr* d. 236, §2, 3°; §3 (GC 7, d. 13); see P. VI, c. 3, no. 7, D [591, 592].

[58] See *CollDecr* d. [106] (GC 28, d. 25, 2°); GC 32, d. 12, 8.

[59] See *CN* no. 32.

[60] *CollDecr* d. 177 (GC 5, d. 59).

[61] *CollDecr* d. 178, §1 (GC 7, d. 17, no. 4; GC 20, d. 7, no. 4); see *Examen*, c. 4, no. 1 [53]; P. III, c. 1, F [255].

[62] *CollDecr* d. 178, §2 (GC 10, d. 2; GC 20, d. 7, no. 4).

[564] 6. ¹Although it is praiseworthy to induce others to do good and holy works, especially those which endure perpetually, nevertheless, with a view to greater edification, no one of the Society ought to or may induce any person to establish perpetual alms for the houses or churches of the Society itself. ²Moreover, if some persons do of their own accord establish such alms, no civil right should be acquired which makes it possible to claim these alms through a court of justice; but rather, let the persons give these alms when charity moves them for the sake of service to God our Lord.

[565] 7. ¹All who are under the obedience of the Society **should remember that they ought to give gratuitously what they have gratuitously received** [Matt. 10:9], ²**without demanding or accepting any stipend or alms as compensation for Masses or confessions or preaching or lecturing or visiting or any other ministry among those which the Society may exercise according to our Institute *[G]*,**¹⁷ ³so that thus it may proceed in the divine service with greater liberty and greater edification of the neighbor.

[566] G. ¹*Although all those who wish may give an alms to the house or the church (whether they receive spiritual help from it or not),* ²*nothing ought to be accepted as a stipend or alms for what is given to them solely out of service to Christ our Lord, in such a manner that the one is given or received in exchange for the other.*

[567] 8. ¹To avoid all appearance of avarice, especially in the spiritual ministries which the Society exercises in order to aid souls, in the church there should not be a box in which those who come to the sermons, Masses, confessions, and so on customarily place their alms.

[568] 9. ¹For the same reason, the members should not give small presents to important persons as is customarily done to elicit greater gifts from them. ²Neither shall they make a practice of visiting important persons of this kind, unless it is for spiritual purposes of doing good works or when the persons are so intimately benevolent in our Lord that such a service seems due to them at times.

[569] 10. ¹The members should be ready to beg from door to door when obedience or necessity requires it. ²Some person or persons should be designated to request alms by which the members of the Society may be supported. These persons should ask for them with simplicity, for the love of God our Lord.

---

¹⁷ **Clarified by** *CN* 181–87.

1° Goods and rights that are actually possessed, even if perhaps unknown, are to be applied to a particular purpose or person, whether individual or moral; the same should be done with goods that happen to come to one during the brief interval of time that, according to no. 32, §3, elapses between the renunciation and final vows.[63]

2° Ours are not to dispose of hereditary posessions that might come to them after final vows; rather, they should simply abdicate them. (By this practical rule, however, the Society does not intend to set forth any theoretical conclusions on the legitimacy of such a disposition in civil law.) And whatever goods come to Ours under title of gift or bequest after final vows are acquired for the Society.[64]

3° Hereditary succession, which according to the norm of the Constitutions,[65] neither Ours after their last vows nor the Society itself is capable of accepting, is understood to mean only that succession by which, according to local civil law, a person is an heir, not the recipient of a bequest or legacy unless it is known that the intention of the deceased was to benefit the Society either directly or by way of the religious. In case of doubt this intention can be presumed.[66]

4° The one making a renunciation can express to parents and relatives his wish that a certain part of the goods which would have come to him as an inheritance had he not taken final vows should be given to the Society or to some other pious work in the form of a gift or a bequest. But he should first inform them that the Society has no right to such goods and that they have complete freedom in the matter.[67]

5° But if someone, with the permission of the general, does make an early renunciation taking effect immediately, he should even then explicitly renounce in favor of some third party (even, if he so chooses, the Society) those goods that under

---

[63] *CollDecr* d. 179, 1°.

[64] *CollDecr* d. 179, 2°; GC 32, d. 12, no. 8.

[65] *FI* of Paul III and Julius III, no. 7; Gregory XIII, *Quanto fructuosius;* Id., *Ascendente Domino; Examen,* c. 1, nos. 3–4 [4–5]; P. VI, c. 2, nos. 4, 11, H, 12 [560, 570, 571, 572].

[66] *Statutes on Poverty* (Sept. 8, 1976), no. 84 (*ActRSJ* 16:939–40).

[67] *CollDecr* d. 179, 3° (see GC 3, d. 39).

[570]   11. ¹Just as no one may have within the house anything as his own property, so no one may have anything outside of that house in the hands of another *[H]*. Each one should be content with what is given to him from the common supply as necessary or proper for his use without any superfluity.

[571]   *H.* ¹*This is understood absolutely about the professed and the formed coadjutors.* ²*But in the case of the scholastics and others who are in the time of their probation, it should be understood to refer to things which are at present within their disposition,* ³*so that they do not have anything unless the superior knows it and agrees to it.* ⁴*It does not refer to the goods which they may happen to have far away in houses or other properties. But even with respect to these houses or properties,* **they ought to be ready to dispossess themselves of them whenever the superior thinks this wise,***¹⁸ as was said in the Examen* [54, 59].

[572]   12. ¹So that poverty may be the better preserved in all its integrity, and also the tranquility which it brings with it, ²not only will the individual professed or formed coadjutors be incapable of receiving an inheritance, but not even the houses or churches or colleges will be able to do so on their account. ³In this way all lawsuits and contentions will be more effectively eliminated and charity with all will be preserved to the glory of God our Lord.

[573]   13. ¹When the sovereign pontiff or the superior sends such professed and coadjutors to labor in the vineyard of the Lord, they may not demand any provision for the journey; ²but they should generously offer their persons so that these superiors may send them in the manner which they think will be for the greater glory of God *[I]*.

[574]   *I.* ¹*That is to say, on foot or on horseback, with money or without it; and they should be completely ready to do what the sender judges to be more fitting and for greater universal edification.*

[575]   14. ¹To proceed here too in a manner conformed to what poverty requires, {in the houses of the Society ordinarily no mount will be kept for any member of the Society itself, either superior or subject} *[K]*.¹⁹

[576]   *K.* ¹*Unless it should be because of constant infirmities or of urgent necessities in regard to public business, especially in large towns.*

---

¹⁸ **Clarified by** *CN* **32.** (See note 5 to [254].)

¹⁹ **Abolished by GC 34.** (This cannot be applied in modern circumstances, but the reason given here can be applied to modern means of transportation; see *CN* 178.)

whatever title, in accord with the norm in no. 164, §1, could come to him before final vows.[68]

6° Revenues from property and pensions accruing to our members by reason of patrimony or family that by law cannot be renounced are similarly to be applied to some definite purpose, in such a way that although they are retained in the name of the beneficiary, he nevertheless maintains no right to them.[69] It is not permissible to arrange that such revenues and pensions should follow from one place to another the one who renounced them, or that some part of the goods should be reserved for some pious use that the one making the renunciation designates as he pleases.[70]

172   §1. A written document of renunciation should be drawn up, declaring

1° In whose favor disposition is made of goods and rights actually possessed, even if these are unknown, in accord with the norm in no. 171, 1°; if there are no goods or rights, that fact should be noted;

2° That hereditary goods are simply being abdicated, in accord with the norm in no. 171, 2°.

§2. Agreements that have perchance been made with parents or other persons or promises that they have made in conformity with no. 171, 4°, should be put in writing.[71]

173   §1. The acceptance of renunciations made in favor of the Society, which is always necessary for validity, and their application pertain to the general. Both of these acts, however, are permitted to the provincial if the value does not exceed the sum that, with the general's permission, he may spend for extraordinary expenses. The general, and the provincial as well, have power to accept and ratify, even after the last vows or the death of the donor, a gift made previously; if the gift is not accepted, the goods are to be considered simply abdicated.[72]

§2. If goods are left to the disposition of the provincial, they are to be applied to uses within the province of the one

---

[68] *CollDecr* d. 179, 4°.

[69] See *CollDecr* d. 179, 5° (GC 7, d. 17, no. 4).

[70] See *CollDecr* d. 179, 6° (GC 23, d. 31).

[71] *CollDecr* d. 180 (see GC 3, d. 39; GC 4, d. 65).

[72] *CollDecr* d. 181, §1 (GC 28, d. 42; see GC 11, d. 17).

²*For then more account should be taken of the universal good and the health of the individuals than of whether the use of the mount is for a limited or an indefinite period, or of the fact of going on foot or by other means.* ³*The consideration should always be need and decorum, and in no way ostentation.*

[577]   15. ¹The clothing too should have three characteristics: first, it should be proper; ²second, conformed to the usage of the country of residence *[L];* and third, not contradictory to the poverty we profess, as would happen through the wearing of silk or expensive cloths *[M].* These ought not to be used, ³in order that in everything fitting humility and lowliness may be preserved for greater divine glory.

[578]   L. ¹*Or at least, it should not be altogether different.*

[579]   M. ¹*This refers to those to whom the house supplies new clothing. But in the case of those who are entering the Society, if they bring some expensive fabrics or the like, there is no difficulty in allowing their use.* ²*Nor is there any difficulty in someone's wearing better but proper garments in some circumstance or necessity; but these ought not to be used for ordinary wear.* ³*Nevertheless it should be observed that all do not have the same bodily strength, nor does health of body belong to all, nor an age which favors it. Therefore care should be taken both for the greater particular good of such persons and for the universal good of many others; and what provision is possible should be made for the greater glory of God.*

[580]   16. ¹What **pertains to food, sleep, and the use of the other things necessary or proper for our life will be ordinary and not different from that which appears good to the physician of the place of residence** *[N],* ²**in such a manner that what each one subtracts from this will be withdrawn through his own devotion and not through obligation.** ³**Nevertheless there should be concern for the humility, poverty, and spiritual edification which we ought to keep always in view in our Lord.**[20]

[581]   N. ¹*In individual cases it will be left to the discretion of those in charge to provide as is fitting for the greater or smaller needs of the individual persons according to their circumstances.*

The text of the Constitutions resumes on page 254.

---

[20] (See *CN* 176–79.)

making the renunciation, unless in particular cases another course is advisable.[73] If the one making the renunciation is transcribed to a different province when he pronounces his last vows, the beneficiary is understood to be the province to which the individual is transcribed.

§3. In general, the same holds true if goods are left to the disposition of the general; but the latter can, for serious reasons and in accord with the intent of the Constitutions, also apply them to other needs of the Society.[74]

Article 3: Common Life

174   In the Society "common life" should be understood as follows:

1° As to food, clothing, and other necessities of life, superfluities are always to be avoided and the same standard of living of different communities and of the members in them are to be maintained, insofar as differences of ministries and of places allow. But if something special is judged necessary for someone because of ill health or some other just reason, this is in no sense contrary to common life.[75]

2° All these items superiors should provide for Ours; it is not allowed for anyone to procure these items for himself in some other way; nor may any superior give permission to do so.[76]

3° If externs should of their own initiative offer anything of this sort, it should be accepted for common use; however, in particular cases the superior in his prudence should judge what ought to be done.[77]

4° Since in modern life there are many procedures that can make the use of money almost invisible, all should be fully honest with superiors in the use of such means.[78]

---

[73] *CollDecr* 181, §2 (GC 2, dd. 23, 38, 41, 43; GC 3, d. 16).

[74] *CollDecr* d. 181, §3 (see GC 2, dd. 23, 38, 41; GC 3, dd. 16, 48); see P. III, c. 1, no. 9 [258].

[75] See *CollDecr* d. 183, 1° (GC 12, d. 43; GC 20, d. 7, no. 3); see GC 31, d. 19, no. 7, d.

[76] *CollDecr* d. 183, 2° (GC 12, d. 43; GC 16, d. 27; GC 22, d. 7, no. 3; GC 20, dd. 25, 26, no. 2; see GC 18, d. 22, 2°).

[77] *CollDecr* d. 183, 3° (GC 6, d. 21); see also *CollDecr* d. [107] (GC 28, d. 25, 3°).

[78] GC 34, d. 9, no. 9.

175   Our members who are attached to some community for reasons of study, health, or other special purposes, and those as well from another province who are not applied to this one but are attached to one of its communities, should be considered not guests but true members of the community who share fully its common life, with consequent rights and obligations according to the norm of no. 174. The provincials concerned should clearly determine whatever has to do with expenses and income, without prejudice to the requirements of common life.[79]

Article 4: Our Common Way of Living in External Matters

176   §1. Our community poverty includes two aspects: that "common life" which St. Ignatius derived from a centuries-old tradition and current Church law still sanctions as an essential element for all religious families; and that mode of living which, in the following of Christ as he preached with the apostles, bears the mark of the special calling that ought to characterize the Society's efforts as it works among people for the redemption of the world.

§2. Moreover, it is of the utmost importance that an apostle, always following the poor Christ, in some manner accommodate himself to the manner of life of those whom he helps, becoming all things to all people. Therefore our every use of material things should be such that, by sharing these goods in common, we not only express and strengthen the unity of heart and mind of all members of the Society but also, by the tenor of our life, signify to the world our will, both common and personal, to give a witness of evangelical poverty, humbly and fraternally serving all, especially the poor, so that we may gain all for Christ, living in a manner that is poor and common in its externals.[80]

177   The dictum in our Institute that the manner of life in the Society should be "common" and not unlike the life of "good priests in the same locality" is to be understood as follows: The Society does not assume as obligatory any austerities in the external way of life, as other institutes customarily do. The life of good priests should be understood according to the norms on evangelical and religious poverty given in nos. 160–63, 176–80.[81]

---

[79] See *CollDecr* d. [411] (GC 30, d. 47, no. 1).

[80] GC 31, d. 18, no. 13; GC 34, d. 4, no. 28.2; d. 9, nos. 14–15.

[81] See CollDecr. d. [407] (GC 30, d. 46, 2°); *FI* of Julius III, no. 8;

178 §1. Our manner of living, therefore, with respect to food, clothing, habitation, recreation, vacations, travel, working facilities, and so forth should be appropriate to "disciples of the poor Christ" and not beyond what people of modest means can afford, those who must work hard to support themselves and their families. In this regard, those who have influential and well-salaried positions must be especially alert. If we must undertake travels or use equipment exceeding such limits, these must really be, and as far as possible should clearly be seen to be, means necessary for our apostolate alone, means that we employ within the limits imposed by our poverty and never as belonging to ourselves alone.[82]

§2. Ours should not be allowed things that are unusual, unnecessary, excessively elegant, or in any way incompatible with religious poverty and simplicity. In making a journey, Ours should refrain from side trips and from expenditures that are less in keeping with our poverty, and when possible they should stay in our houses.[83]

179 §1. The buildings of the Society should be suitable for our ministries and useful for living purposes; they should be sound and strongly built. But they ought to be such that it will be clear that we are mindful of poverty. Consequently, they should not be luxurious or too elaborate.[84] In them, especially in the part reserved to Ours, and in any of our works, we are to avoid too exquisite a refinement and ornamentation and every type of extravagance, always keeping in mind both the purpose of our institutions[85] and our religious poverty.

§2. It can be a great help to the simplicity and intimacy of community life as well as to poverty if the house or place where we live and the house or place where we work or even where

---

Examen, c. 1, no. 6 [8]; c. 4, no. 26 [81]; P. VI, c. 2, no. 16 [580]; Letter of Fr J. B. Janssens, Sept. 15, 1951, no. 8 (*ActRSJ* 12:114ff.).

[82] See *CollDecr* d. [409] (GC 30, d. 46, 4°); GC 31, d. 19, no. 7, d); GC 32, d. 12, no. 7; GC 34, d. 9, no. 9; *Examen,* c. 4, nos. 44, 46 [101, 103]; Letter of Fr. J. B. Janssens, Sept. 15, 1951 (*ActRSJ* 12:117).

[83] See *CollDecr* d. 187 (GC 22, dd. 24, 25; see GC 7, d. 82, no. 7; GC 25, d. 11, no. 1; see GC 3, d. 37).

[84] *CollDecr* d. 212 (GC 1, d. 113).

[85] See GC 32, d. 12, nos. 5, 9, 33.

we study can be properly separated, provided that this can be done without harm to poverty or apostolic work.[86]

180   Unless there are evident considerations suggesting the contrary, provincials should encourage those communities which, in union and charity with the rest of the province, choose to practice a stricter poverty or to live among the poor, serving them and sharing something of their experience,[87] in such a way that these communities may be a visible sign of the application of our option for the poor and thus may contribute by means of fraternal exchange to increasing the social sensitivity of the province. Moreover, it is recommended to all our members that in accord with the constant tradition of the Society, they have at least some ministry with the poor.[88]

CHAPTER 2

POVERTY IN COMMON

Article 1: Sources of Revenues Needed for Support and Apostolate

181   The gratuity of ministries proper to our Institute[89] is to be explained especially from its purpose, which is both inner freedom (refraining from seeking one's own temporal advantage), outer freedom (independence from the bonds of undue obligation), and the edification of the neighbor that arises from this freedom and from the love of Christ and humankind.[90]

182   §1. Preaching the word of God and spiritual and sacramental ministry, by which the Society carries out its purpose, of their very nature completely transcend all consideration of material remuneration and urge us toward a perfect gratuity.[91]

§2. With the exception of the special norms for parishes and of a legitimate recompense for travel and other expenses, including sustenance, Jesuits may demand no stipend for their

---

[86] See GC 31, d. 19, no. 7f.

[87] GC 32, d. 12, no. 10.

[88] See GC 32, d. 12, no. 5; GC 34, d. 9, no. 16.

[89] See *Fl* of Paul III (1540) and Julius III (1550), no. 1; *Examen,* c. 1, no. 3 [4]; P. VI, c. 2, no. 7 [565].

[90] GC 31, d. 18, no. 16, a.

[91] See *Statutes on Poverty* (Sept. 8, 1976), no. 34 (*ActRSJ* 16:927).

work in spiritual ministries, especially for those mentioned in the beginning of the Formula of the Institute of Julius III (1550); they may accept only those stipends that are offered to them.[92]

183 As to the prescriptions of the Constitutions concerning the gratuity of our ministries, no superior, not even the general, can validly give a dispensation.[93]

184 §1. We may accept stipends or offerings given for the celebration of Mass, according to the current law of the Church. But where it can be done, gratuity should be practiced both in and outside the Society, taking account of edification of the people of God and of charity especially toward the poor.[94]

§2. The Masses to be offered for the intention of the general cannot be applied by him in such a way that someone outside the Society is freed from an obligation that he has incurred in accepting a stipend or an alms.[95]

185 In addition to the alms and income that different types of communities and apostolic institutes can accept (see nos. 191, §§2–3; 196; 199), gain from or remuneration for work done according to the Institute is also a legitimate source of material goods that are necessary for the life and apostolate of Jesuits. But we are to select these works according to the obligations of obedience and the nature of our ministries, avoiding every desire of monetary gain or temporal advantage.[96]

186 The royalties due authors, emoluments, honoraria, personal pensions, grants, and other gifts that are considered to be the fruit of the talents and industry of Jesuits may be accepted, as also the remuneration attached to certain stable ministries, such as those of hospital chaplains, catechists, and the like.[97]

187 With due regard for nos. 57, §2; 164, §1; 171, 1° and 6°, all yearly pension payments, even small ones, that are assigned to Ours must not be used as they choose, but rather are to be

---

[92] GC 31, d. 18, no. 16, c.

[93] See *CollDecr* d. 198 (GC 12, d. 39).

[94] See GC 31, d. 18, no. 16, b.

[95] *CollDecr* d. 199 (see GC 12, d. 8).

[96] GC 31, d. 18, no. 15.

[97] GC 31, d. 18, no. 16, c, d; emended by GC 32, d. 12, no. 42; approved by letter of Card. Secr. of State, June 6, 1966 (*ActRSJ* 14:1006).

applied by the provincial in accord with norms approved by the general.[98]

Article 2: Distinction between Communities and Apostolic Institutes

188   §1. Community is here taken to mean any group of Jesuits legitimately constituted under the authority of the same local superior.

§2. Apostolic institutes are those institutions or works belonging to the Society that have a certain permanent unity and organization for apostolic purposes, such as universities, colleges, retreat houses, reviews, and other activities of this kind in which our members carry on their apostolic work.

§3. All communities can have attached to them one or more apostolic institutes in which the whole community or some of its members exercise the apostolate.[99]

189   §1. A clear distinction is to be established between communities and apostolic institutes, at least with regard to specifying the use of their goods and the profit therefrom [ususfructus] and between the financial accounts of each.

§2. A distinction of moral persons, canonical or civil, is also recommended where this can be effected without great inconvenience, preserving always the apostolic finality of the institutes and the authority of the Society to direct them to such ends.[100]

Article 3: The Poverty of Communities

190   §1. Communities may be the juridical subject of all rights, including ownership, pertaining to the apostolic institutes attached to such communities.[101]

§2. The goods of apostolic institutes of the Society may not be diverted to the use or profit of our members or communities, except for a suitable remuneration to be approved by the provin-

---

[98] *CollDecr* d. 182 (see GC 3, d. 39; GC 4, d. 65).

[99] GC 32, d. 12, nos. 16–18. GC 33, d. 2, no. 2, definitively confirmed decree 12 of GC 32, which later received pontifical confirmation by the letter of the Card. Secr. of State, Nov. 3, 1983 (*ActRSJ* 18:1100).

[100] GC 32, d. 12, nos. 19–20.

[101] GC 32, d. 12, no. 22.

cial, for work in such institutes or for services rendered to them.[102]

191 §1. All communities dedicated to pastoral work or to any other apostolic functions are held to the practice of poverty that is indicated in the Constitutions for "houses";[103] and therefore, these communities are forbidden these and these only assured and permanent sources of income; namely, those that are derived from moveable and immoveable property that either belongs to the Society or is invested in foundations in such a way that the Society has a legal claim to it.[104]

§2. Therefore, all other forms of fixed and stable revenues are licit, such as revenues from insurance, pensions, or temporary investments permitted according to the norm of no. 195.

§3. Those of our communities that may accept fixed revenues are not allowed to receive them on the condition that a certain part of them will be paid in perpetuity to some other community that may not accept revenues; this, however, is permitted if these funds are applied to the construction of a house or church, although this is not to be prolonged beyond the time needed for construction.[105]

§4. In virtue of a faculty granted by the Holy See, the general, with the deliberative vote of his council, can in individual cases where it seems necessary, dispense both communities and churches from the prohibition of having stable revenues, when revenues not deriving from investment with the intention of gain are involved and when these are judged necessary or very useful.[106]

192 §1. Communities are allowed to rent out for a short time an adjoining house that it has purchased and that will eventually be needed for housing its members or for building a church, and it can enjoy the revenue it realizes. And if the purchase of this building has entailed some indebtedness, it can apply the income from the rental to retire this debt until such time as it has been repaid in full.

---

[102] GC 32, d. 12, no. 21.

[103] GC 32, d. 12, no. 22; see P. VI, c. 2, nos. 2, 5 [555, 561].

[104] GC 32, d. 12, no. 41.

[105] *CollDecr* d. 189 (GC 7, d. 50; GC 11, d. 20).

[106] See GC 32, d. 12, no. 43; Letter of Card. Secr. of State, May 2, 1975 (*ActRSJ* 16:456).

§2. As long as communities devoted to the apostolate do not already possess what they may legitimately own,[107] they may save money to buy what they lack and may administer and invest this money until it is spent when occasion arises. From the revenue they may rent a house as long as they are without one of their own.[108]

193   The community farm, if there is one, should be of such a type and size that it cannot become a source of revenue.[109]

194   In each community, after community discernment about its lifestyle, which ought to bear credible witness to the counter-cultural values of the Gospel,[110] the responsible administrators each year at the appointed times, according to norms established by the provincial and the criteria given in no. 178, should draft a projected budget as well as a statement of revenues and expenses. These will be communicated to the community as soon as convenient and are to be approved by the provincial.[111]

195   That the life of our communities may be "removed as far as possible from all infection of avarice and conformed as closely as possible to evangelical poverty,"[112] the surplus of each community is to be distributed yearly, according to the provision of nos. 210–11, except for a moderate sum to be approved by the provincial for unforeseen expenses. This sum is never to exceed the ordinary expenses of one year.[113]

Article 4: The Poverty of Seminaries for Our Members and Infirmaries

196   §1. Seminaries for our members, that is, houses of probation and formation, can possess stable goods and fixed revenues.[114]

---

[107] See *FI* of Julius III, no. 7; P. VI, c. 2, no. 5, E [561, 562].

[108] See *CollDecr* d. 190 (GC 7, d. 51).

[109] *CollDecr* d. 188, §3; see P. VI, c. 2, F [563].

[110] See GC 34, d. 9, no. 12; GC 34, d. 4, no. 28.2.

[111] GC 32, d. 12, no. 24.

[112] *FI* of Paul III and Julius III, no. 7.

[113] GC 32, d. 12, no. 25; see P. VI, c. 2, E [562]; see *FI* of Julius III, no. 7.

[114] GC 32, d. 12, no. 23; see *FI* of Paul III and Julius III, no. 8; Gregory XIII, *Ascendente Domino; Examen*, c. 1, no. 4 [5]; P. IV, c. 2, nos. 5, 6 [326, 331]; c. 7, no. 3 [398].

§2. Houses or infirmaries for the care of our aged or sick members are subject to the same norms as the above.[115]

197 None of our formed members may live from the goods and revenues of the seminaries or infirmaries unless they are engaged in serving them. But the aged and the sick may live from the goods and revenues of these houses.[116]

198 §1. Dependent communities forming part of seminaries for our members can be sustained by the revenues either of the principal house or of goods that they have been given, provided that the ownership of these goods rests with the principal house.[117]

§2. It is within the general's power to unite communities with seminaries of Ours, complying with the requirements of both the common law and our own.[118]

§3. Such a union takes place legitimately only when the community, for reasons intrinsic to itself, can truly be said to be part of the seminary.

§4. The goods of a community united in this fashion pertain entirely to the seminary,[119] although the intentions of the donors are to be honored.

Article 5: The Poverty of Apostolic Institutes

199 Apostolic institutes, churches excepted, can have revenue-bearing capital and stable revenues, adequate to their purposes, if this seems necessary to the provincial.[120]

200 §1. Superiors and directors, mindful that we are sent to preach in poverty, will take great care that our apostolic institutes avoid every manner of extravagance and limit themselves strictly to the functional, attentive to the standards of similar institutes or works of the region and to their apostolic finality.

---

[115] GC 32, d. 12, no. 23.

[116] See *CollDecr* d. 192; *Examen*, c. 1, no. 4 [5]; P. IV, c. 2, no. 5, F. [326, 330]; c. 10, A [422]; P. VI, c. 2, nos. 3–4, D [557, 559, 560]; P. IX, c. 3, no. 18 [763]; c. 4, no. 7 [774]; P. X, no. 4 [815]; Julius III, *Sacræ religionis*.

[117] *CollDecr* d. 195, §2 (GC 24, d. 15, 1°).

[118] CollDecr d. 195, §3 (GC 24, d. 15, 3°).

[119] *CollDecr* d. 195, §§4–5 (GC 24, d. 15, 1°).

[120] GC 32, d. 12, no. 32.

§2. It is the responsibility of the provincial to determine what is required so that the apostolic institutes belonging to the Society manifest this character and mark of apostolic evangelical poverty.[121] Whether it is fitting to retain rich and powerful institutions requiring great capital resources is to be weighed prudently and spiritually.[122]

201 Those responsible for the administration of apostolic institutes will present to the provincial at the appointed times the annual budget of the institute, a statement of the year's revenues and expenses, and, if required, a balance sheet.[123]

202 If an apostolic institute is suppressed, superiors, according to their respective competence, will take care to devote its assets to another apostolic work or place them in the fund for apostolic works of the province, of the region, or of the Society, respecting always, if this applies, the statutes of the institute and the will of benefactors. Such assets may never be diverted to the use or benefit of a community, of a province, of a region, or of the Society.[124]

Article 6: The Poverty of the Society as a Whole and of Provinces and Regions

203 The Society, provinces, and regions (missions), even dependent ones, as distinguished from communities and apostolic institutes, are capable of possessing even revenue-bearing capital and of enjoying fixed and stable revenues, within the limits defined in nos. 204–5, provided always that such goods and revenues are not applied to the support of our formed members, except as permitted in no. 205, 1° and 2°.[125]

204 §1. The Society may possess such revenue-bearing capital and fixed and stable revenues only to promote certain apostolic works of a more universal kind or to relieve the needs of regions (missions) and provinces.

§2. The Society is owner of the Charitable and Apostolic Fund mentioned in no. 213.[126]

---

[121] GC 32, d. 12, no. 33.

[122] GC 32, d. 12, no. 9.

[123] GC 32, d. 12, no. 35.

[124] GC 32, d. 12, no. 36.

[125] GC 32, d. 12, no. 40, 1.

[126] GC 32, d. 12, no. 40, 2.

205   Provinces and regions (missions) dependent and independent, can possess revenue-bearing capital and can enjoy fixed and stable revenues only for the following purposes:

1° For the support and education of those in probation or engaged in studies, as well as for the support of those engaged in serving them (Seminary Fund, *Arca seminarii*)[127]

2° For the care of the aged and the sick (Retirement Fund, *Arca prævisionis*)

3° To set up or develop houses and foundations, whether these have already been established or are yet to be established, according as necessity or opportunity may indicate (Foundations Fund, *Arca fundationum*)

4° To promote certain works, such as retreat houses especially for non-Jesuits, centers for the social apostolate or for the diffusion of Catholic teaching by means of the media of social communication, for charitable enterprises both in and outside the Society, and for other apostolates that otherwise would lack sufficient resources (Apostolic Works Fund, *Arca operum apostolicorum*)[128]

206   Provinces are permitted to provide insurance for old age and for sickness, either through their own *arca* or with other provinces, or by participation in governmental or private plans.[129]

207   When in the judgment of the general severe need makes it necessary, Ours can be supported by alms that have already been applied to the *Arca fundationum* or by common funds set aside for community expenses, if the consent of the donors can reasonably be presumed.[130]

208   Common expenses of the Society as a whole or of the province should be met, not from fixed revenues, but either from alms given to the Society or province or from contributions that the general imposes on provinces and regions and that, with his

---

127 *CollDecr* d. 192 (GC 23, d. 33); see *FI* of Paul III and Julius III, no. 8; Gregory XIII, *Ascendente Domino; Examen,* c. 1, no. 4 [5]; P. IV, c. 2, nos. 5, 6 [326, 331]; c. 7, no. 3 [398].

128 GC 32, d. 12, no. 40, 3).

129 GC 32, d. 12, no. 30.

130 *CollDecr* d. 197, §5 (GC 24, d. 17).

permission, major superiors impose on communities in proportion to their resources.[131]

209 The general, visitors, provincials, regional superiors, and their socii and assistants should be supported by the houses in which they are residing for the benefit of those houses; when not in such houses, they should be supported from the common funds.[132]

Article 7: The Sharing of Goods

210   §1. According to norms to be established by the provincial and approved by Father General, there is to be provision for the distribution of the communities' surplus mentioned in no. 195, for the benefit of those communities or works of the province that are in greater need.

§2. The first beneficiary of such surplus in each community will be the apostolic institute or institutes attached to it if these stand in need, unless the provincial, with his consultors, should decide otherwise.

§3. In this sharing of resources, the needs of other provinces, of the whole Society, and of non-Jesuits are to be considered.[133]

211   Major superiors can require that individual communities, according to their capacities, contribute a certain sum of money to the relief of the needs of other communities or apostolic institutes of the province or of the region even if this should require some reduction in their standard of living, which in any case must always be frugal.[134]

212   With due respect for the needs of apostolic institutes and, if this applies, for the statutes of the institute and the will of benefactors, provincials, with the approval of the general, will provide for a more equitable and apostolically effective sharing of resources among the apostolic institutes of the province, looking always to God's greater service.[135]

213   §1. A Charitable and Apostolic Fund of the Society is to be established for the benefit of communities and works of the

---

[131] *CollDecr* d. 197, §2 (GC 24, d. 17).

[132] *CollDecr* d. 213, §2 (GC 2, d. 82; see GC 2, d. 83; GC 4, d. 18).

[133] GC 32, d. 12, nos. 26–28; see GC 31, d. 48, no. 4.

[134] GC 32, d. 12, no. 29; see GC 31, d. 18, no. 9.

[135] GC 32, d. 12, no. 34.

Society and, should need arise, for externs as well. Money received is not to be permanently invested.

§2. Father General is to determine the sources of this fund, its administration, and the manner of distributing its benefits, with the assistance of advisers from different parts of the Society.[136]

214   It is not allowed to collect alms in another province or region without the permission of the respective major superior.[137]

CHAPTER 3

AVOIDING EVERY APPEARANCE OF AVARICE AND COMMERCE

215   §1. We must carefully avoid even the appearance of engaging in commerce or of seeking profit.[138]

§2. In the Society the general is the competent authority to permit any commercial activity that is necessary or useful for the apostolate, for example, a printing press.[139]

CHAPTER 4

TEMPORAL ADMINISTRATION

216   §1. The Society's temporal goods are regarded as the property of our Lord Jesus Christ and as the patrimony of Christ's poor; on these goods the spiritual activities and the well-being of the Society greatly depend, and without them our spiritual ministries themselves could scarcely take place.[140]

§2. Superiors and other officials should with great diligence and fidelity exercise the management of temporal goods, not as owners who can use their own goods as they please, but as men with the mandate to administer the goods entrusted to their care in accord with the laws of the Church and of the Society.

§3. Superiors should take care that in administrative tasks committed to them, officials make no changes without permission or depart from received norms of procedure; and superiors them-

---

[136] GC 32, d. 12, no. 31.

[137] See *CollDecr* d. 203 (GC 23, d. 35).

[138] *CollDecr* d. 204, §1 (GC 2, d. 61; GC 7, d. 84).

[139] See CIC 286, 672: CCEO 385, §2.

[140] *CollDecr* d. 207, §1; see P. III, c. 2, no. 7 [305].

selves should make or permit no changes of any significance without consulting the provincial.

§4. Superiors who are negligent or wasteful in the management of their houses should be corrected.[141]

217   All superiors and officials should be particularly vigilant that in their temporal administration, especially when investing the money of the Society, of provinces, of communities, and of apostolic institutes, social justice is not violated or insufficient attention paid to fostering that same justice.[142]

218   Provincials should not use their faculty to enter into contracts for the benefit of houses of the province if the local superior is unwilling or unaware, unless an urgent need advises the contrary course; in that case he should advise the general of the reasons for his action.[143]

219   Local superiors should not accept from externs any deposit of money, whether in the form of cash or in negotiable paper, unless for a very serious reason, with all due precautions taken and with the prior permission of the provincial; superiors can, indeed, presume this permission in an urgent case, but with the obligation of notifying the provincial afterwards.[144]

220   §1. None of Ours should initiate litigation without the permission of the provincial or of whomever the provincial has explicitly substituted for himself in a particular case unless the matter is so urgent that he cannot wait for a reply; in this case he is to inform the provincial later. However, the latter should first try to resolve the matter by negotiation.

§2. If Ours are threatened with a lawsuit, the provincial can permit them to defend themselves in court; but unless it is clearly a case of a right manifestly belonging to us and it is not opportune that we renounce it, they should always show themselves willing to resolve the matter by negotiation. Moreover, they should inform the general about the entire matter as soon as possible.[145]

---

[141] See *CollDecr* d. 207, §§2–4 (GC 7, d. 82, no. 6; GC 7, d. 15; GC 14, d. 12); see *CollDecr* d. [110] (GC 28, d. 26, 2°).

[142] GC 32, d. 12, no. 39, a.

[143] *CollDecr* d. 208 (GC 8, d. 54).

[144] *CollDecr* d. 209 (GC 16, d. 32).

[145] *CollDecr* d. 211 (GC 2, d. 55).

221   It belongs to the competence of the general to prescribe the form and style of our buildings; but he can communicate to the provincials the faculty of approving the plans for constructing new buildings.[146]

222   When leaving office, local superiors and treasurers should, in the presence of the minister, hand over to their successors a written and signed account of the house's economic status.[147]

---

[146] *CollDecr* d. 212 (GC 2, d. 84; GC 31, d. 55, no. 3).

[147] See *CollDecr* d. 214 (GC 8, d. 60, no. 4; see GC 30, d. 69).

CHAPTER 3

¹THE OCCUPATIONS WHICH THOSE IN THE SOCIETY SHOULD UNDERTAKE AND THOSE WHICH THEY SHOULD AVOID

[582] 1. ²Given the length of time and approbation of their life which are required before admission into the Society among the professed and also the formed coadjutors, ³it is presupposed that those so admitted will be men who are spiritual and sufficiently advanced that they will run in the path of Christ our Lord ⁴to the extent that their bodily strength and the exterior occupations undertaken through charity and obedience allow. ⁵Therefore, in what pertains to prayer, meditation, and study, and also in regard to the bodily practices of fasts, vigils, and other austerities or penances, it does not seem proper to give them any other rule than that which discreet charity dictates to them [A], ⁶provided that the confessor always be informed and also, when a doubt about advisability arises, the superior.²¹ Only this will be said in general: On the one hand, they should take care that the excessive use of these practices not weaken their bodily strength and or take up so much time that they are rendered incapable of helping the neighbor spiritually according to our Institute; ⁷on the other hand, they should be vigilant that these practices not be relaxed to such an extent that the spirit grows cold and the human and lower passions grow warm.

[583] A. ¹If the superior thinks it expedient to give some subjects a prescribed time to keep them from exceeding or falling short in their spiritual exercises, he may do so. ²So too in regard to the use of the other means: if he judges that one ought to be employed without leaving it to the discretion of the individual, he will proceed in accordance with what God our Lord leads him to think proper. ³And the part of the subject will be to accept with complete devotion the order which is given to him.

[584] 2. ¹The frequentation of the sacraments should be highly recommended; ²and Holy Communion or the celebration of Mass should not be postponed beyond eight days without reasons legitimate in the opinion of the superior.²² ³{All should confess to

---

²¹ Clarified by *CN* 225.

²² Modified by *CN* 227, according to the changed sacramental practice of the Church. (See CIC 663, §2; 664; CCEO 473, 474.)

SECTION 5: OTHER MATTERS CONCERNING OUR WAY OF LIVING

CHAPTER 1

THE SPIRITUAL LIFE OF OUR FORMED MEMBERS

223   §1. Since the goal to which the Society rightly aspires is "to aid its own members and their fellow men and women to attain the ultimate end for which they were created,"[148] "what might be called, in contemporary terms, the total and integral liberation of man, leading to participation in the life of God himself,"[149] our life must be undividedly apostolic and religious. This intimate connection between religious and apostolic aspects ought to animate our whole way of living, praying, and working in the Society and to impress on it an apostolic character.[150]

§2. The service of faith and the promotion of justice must be the integrating factor of our inner life as individuals, as communities, and as a worldwide brotherhood.[151]

§3. Hence, all Ours are urged to strive each day, personally and communally, toward an even greater integration of our spiritual life and apostolate, by which they will find God in all things,[152] the God who is present in this world,[153] in its struggle between good and evil, between faith and unbelief, between the yearning for justice and peace and the growing reality of injustice and strife.[154] We should also seek to be enriched in our own spirituality by the spiritual experiences and ethical values, theological perspectives, and symbolic expressions of other religions.[155]

§4. If we are thus to hear and respond to the call of God in this kind of world, we must have a discerning attitude both individually and in community. We cannot attain this discerning

---

[148] P. IV, *Pream.,* no. 1 [307].

[149] GC 32, d. 2, no. 11.

[150] GC 31, d. 13, no. 3.

[151] GC 32, d. 2, no. 9; GC 34, d. 2, no. 14.

[152] See P. III, c. 1, no. 26 [288].

[153] See GC 34, d. 4, nos. 14–18; d. 8, no. 7.

[154] GC 33, d. 1, no. 11.

[155] GC 34, d. 5, no. 9.1.

the confessor who is assigned to them,}[23] or according to the order which each one has from the superior.

[585]   3. [1]Of the particular rules in use in the houses where they happen to be, it is good that they strive to observe the part which is appropriate and is appointed them according to the judgment of the superior either for their own progress and edification or for that of the rest among whom they happen to be.

[586]   4. [1]Because the occupations which are undertaken for the aid of souls are of great importance, proper to our Institute, and very frequent; and because, on the other hand, our residence in one place or another is so uncertain, [2]they will not regularly hold choir for the canonical hours or sing Masses and offices [B]. For those whose devotion urges them to hear such will have no lack of places to satisfy themselves, [3]and our members ought to apply their efforts to the pursuits that are most proper to our vocation, for the glory of God our Lord.

[587]   B. [1]If it should be judged advisable in some houses or colleges, at the time when an afternoon sermon or lecture is to be given, Vespers alone could be recited to occupy the people before these sermons or lectures. [2]This could also be done regularly on Sundays and feast days, without measured music or plain chant but on a devout, smooth, and simple tone. [3]This is done for the purpose of attracting the people to more frequent attendance at the confessions, sermons, and lectures and to the extent that it is judged useful for this, and in no other manner. [4]In Holy Week, the Tenebrae service with its ceremonies could be recited in the same tone.

   [5]In the principal Masses which are celebrated (even though they are low Masses), there could be, for the sake of devotion and propriety, two assistants vested in surplices, or one, with everything done according to what may be possible in the Lord.

[588]   5. [1]Likewise, because the members of this Society ought to be ready at any hour to go to any part of the world where they may be sent by the sovereign pontiff or their own superiors, **they ought not to take on the care of souls,**[24] [2]**and still less ought they to take charge of religious women or any other women whatever to be their regular confessors or to direct them.**[25] However, noth-

---

[23] Abolished by the universal law of the Church: CIC 630, §1; CCEO 473, §2, 2°; 474, §2.

[24] Clarified by *CN* 274. (In regard to accepting parishes.)

[25] Modified by *CN* 237.

attitude without self-abnegation, which is the fruit of our joy at the approach of the Kingdom and results from a progressive identification with Christ.[156]

224   §1. To achieve such integration, it is crucial for us to use all means to foster that familiarity with God in both prayer and action which St. Ignatius considered absolutely essential[157] to the very existence of our companionship.[158] But we cannot achieve this familiarity with God unless we regularly engage in personal prayer.[159]

§2. The Jesuit apostle goes forth from the Exercises, at once a school of prayer and of the apostolate, a man called by his vocation to be a contemplative in action.[160] We must contemplate our world as Ignatius did his, that we may hear anew the call of Christ dying and rising in the anguish and aspirations of men and women.[161]

225   §1. Therefore, the traditional hour of prayer is to be adapted so that each Jesuit, guided by his superior, takes into account his particular circumstances and needs, in the light of that discerning love which St. Ignatius clearly presupposed in the Constitutions.[162]

§2. All should recall that the prayer in which God communicates himself more abundantly is the better prayer, whether it is mental or even vocal, whether it consists in meditative reading or in an intense feeling of love and self-giving.[163] Prayer thus becomes a truly vital activity whose progressive growth makes increasingly evident in us the action and presence of God, whereby we are enabled to seek, love, and serve him in all things.[164]

§3. Ours are also to give sufficient time to preparation for prayer and to spiritual reading.[165]

---

[156] GC 33, d. 1, nos. 12, 13; GC 32, d. 11, nos. 11, 38.

[157] See P. X, no. 2 [813].

[158] GC 32, d. 11, no. 7; see GC 31, d. 14, nos. 4, 8.

[159] GC 33, d. 1, no. 11; GC 32, d. 11, no. 8; GC 31, d. 14, no. 11.

[160] GC 31, d. 14, no. 4; GC 32, d. 11, no. 8.

[161] GC 32, d. 4, no. 19; GC 34, d. 2, no. 6.

[162] See GC 31, d. 14, no. 11; see P. VI, c. 3, no. 1, A [582, 583].

[163] GC 31, d. 14, no. 11; see GC 32, d. 11, nos. 9–10, 36.

[164] GC 31, d. 14, no. 7.

[165] *CollDecr* d. 52, §5 (GC 31, d. 14, no. 14).

ing prohibits them on a single occasion from hearing the confessions of a whole monastery for special reasons.

[589] 6. ¹Neither should the members take on obligations of Masses which are to be celebrated perpetually in their churches, or similar burdens which are incompatible with the freedom required for our manner of proceeding in the Lord [C].

[590] C. ¹In regard to the colleges, what is admissible in this matter is treated in Part IV [324, 325]. ²In regard to the houses, not to undertake such burdens is altogether proper.

[591] 7. ¹So that the Society may be able to devote itself more entirely to the spiritual pursuits pertaining to its profession, it should abstain as far as possible from all secular employments, (such as those of being executors of wills or of mandates or of being procurators of civil affairs or of any such business), ²through not accepting such burdens and not employing itself in them because of any requests [D]. ³If such business affairs occur in connection with the colleges, they should have a procurator to take care of them and defend their rights. ⁴If such affairs arise in connection with the houses of the Society or its whole body, to enable the Society itself to preserve its peace, the same procurator, or another {coadjutor},²⁶ or some person from outside the Society, or a family which undertakes the protection of the house could defend the Society's rights for the greater glory of God.

[592] D. ¹This should be observed as far as possible. But the authority to dispense for a time, in a case of necessity and importance for the end of the divine service which is sought, should be left to the superior. ²This superior will be the general or the one to whom he delegates his authority in this matter.

[593] 8. ¹For the same reason, and to avoid occasions of unrest foreign to our profession, and also the better to preserve the peace and benevolent relations with all unto the greater glory of God, ²no professed or coadjutor or scholastic of the Society will consent to be interrogated in criminal trials or even in civil trials [E] (unless he is compelled to do so by someone who can oblige him under sin), without permission of the superior. ³The superior will not give the permission except in the trials which touch upon the Catholic religion, or in other pious cases which are favorable to one party in such a way that they do not do damage to another.²⁷ ⁴For it is

---

²⁶ Abolished by GC 34.

²⁷ Clarified by CN 239.

226   §1. The local superior is also responsible for the spiritual vitality of the community. He should therefore consider it part of his duty to provide the conditions that foster personal and community prayer, the sacramental life, and communication on a spiritual level. He should also take care that every Jesuit finds in the organization of community life whatever is necessary for recollection and for a suitable balance between work and rest.[166]

§2. He should also provide at times, in a way that is appropriate for each apostolic community, a longer period for prayerful interchange as an opportunity for reflecting before God on the mission of the community and, at the same time, for expressing the apostolic character of our prayer.[167]

227   §1. Every community of the Society is a faith community that comes together in the Eucharist with others who believe in Christ to celebrate their common faith. More than anything else, our participation at the same table in the Body and Blood of Christ makes us one companionship totally dedicated to Christ's mission in today's world.[168]

§2. According to the prescriptions of their own rite,[169] all should take part in the daily celebration of the Eucharist and consider it as the center of their religious and apostolic lives. Communitarian celebrations of the Eucharist are encouraged, especially on days when the community can more easily gather.[170] Moreover, for the faithful fulfillment of their apostolic vocation, both communities and individuals should cherish daily converse with Christ the Lord in visiting the Blessed Sacrament.[171]

§3. Likewise, so that they might increase in purity of soul and in freedom in God's service, all should also frequently receive the sacrament of reconciliation; they should also willingly participate in community penitential services and strive to promote the spirit of reconciliation in our communities.[172] Each one

---

[166] GC 32, d. 11, no. 41; see GC 31, d. 14, no. 9; GC 33, d. 1, no. 13.

[167] GC 32, d. 11, no. 37.

[168] See GC 32, d. 11, no. 12; GC 33, d. 1, no. 11.

[169] See CIC 663, §2; CCEO 473, §1.

[170] See GC 32, d. 11, no. 35; GC 31, d. 14, no. 10.

[171] GC 31, d. 14, no. 15.

[172] See GC 32, d. 11, no. 39.

proper to our Institute to serve all in our Lord without offense to anyone, as far as this is possible.

[594] E. ¹*If the superior gives permission to anyone in regard to a civil trial out of respect for a person he thinks cannot be refused, a restriction will be needed prohibiting him, should any criminal or defamatory question occur, from being questioned about it.* ²*For no superior ought to give permission for this.*

The text of the Constitutions resumes on page 266.

should have his own fixed confessor to whom he ordinarily confesses.[173]

228   In the recitation of the Liturgy of the Hours, to which they are obligated by the reception of ordination,[174] our priests and deacons should try to pray attentively and at the appropriate time that wonderful song of praise which is truly the prayer of Christ to the Father, in union with his Body.[175]

229   Twice daily the examination of conscience should be made, which, in accord with Ignatius's intent, contributes so much to discernment regarding our entire apostolic life, to purity of heart, and to familiarity with God in the midst of an active life. In accord with the approved tradition of the Society, it is recommended that it last a quarter of an hour.[176]

230   Insofar as their apostolic character permits, Jesuit communities should come together daily for some brief common prayer.[177]

231   §1. Because it is especially in the Spiritual Exercises that we experience Christ and respond to him calling us to the Society, they are the source and center of our vocation[178] and an altogether special means both for fostering renewal and union in the Society and for carrying on our apostolic mission in a more profound way. Hence, they should be made for eight successive days each year; certain adaptations may be allowed, of which the provincial is to be the judge.[179]

§2. In addition, it is recommended that

1° Especially at the time of the annual visitation, the provincials inquire about the way our members are making the Spiritual Exercises

2° Those who are already formed be encouraged to make the full Exercises even extended over a month

---

[173] *CollDecr* 57, §1 (GC 23, d. 30, no. 1); see P. III, c. 1, n. 11, Q [261, 278]; P. VI, c. 3, no. 2 [584].

[174] See CIC 276, §1, 3°; 1174, §1; CCEO 377.

[175] See GC 31, d. 14, no. 10; see *General Instruction on the Liturgy of the Hours,* no. 29.

[176] See GC 32, d. 11, no. 38; GC 31, d. 14, no. 13; see GC 33, d. 1, no. 40.

[177] GC 31, d. 14, no. 15; see GC 32, d. 11, no. 37.

[178] GC 31, d. 4, no. 2.

[179] See GC 32, d. 11, nos. 37, 42; GC 31, d. 14, no. 16.

3° In the provinces the greatest care be given to the formation of those who have the talent to direct the Exercises

4° Those already formed should at times make the annual retreat under the personal direction of a skilled director[180]

232   Since dialogue with a spiritual director on a regular basis is a great help for growing in spiritual insight and learning discernment, all of Ours, even when engaged in an active apostolate, should highly esteem spiritual direction and should openly and frequently speak with a spiritual director.[181]

233   We should make the love of Christ, symbolized in the devotion to the Sacred Heart of Jesus, the center of our own spiritual lives, so as more effectively to proclaim before all people the unfathomable riches of Christ and to foster the primacy of love in Christian life.[182]

234   All of Ours should consider, as something most earnestly recommended to them, devotion to the Blessed Virgin Mary, whom our Society has always honored as a mother.[183]

CHAPTER 2

FRATERNAL CONCERN

235   The prescriptions of the General Examen[184] on the manifestation of faults are to be understood in this way:

1° Since the purpose of a manifestation of the defects of others to the superior is both the common good and the spiritual progress of individuals, it should proceed only from the motivation of charity and be done in such a way as to manifest love and charity.

2° All are allowed to manifest to the superior as to a father any defect, small or great, of another; but this does not refer to those things that the person reveals about himself to another in an account of conscience or in secret or for the sake

---

[180] GC 32, d. 11, no. 42.

[181] GC 32, d. 11, no. 40.

[182] See GC 31, d. 15, no. 3; GC 32, d. 11, no. 43.

[183] GC 27, *CollDecr* d. 224; see GC 32, d. 11, no. 43; GC 31, d. 16, no. 7, e.

[184] *Examen,* c. 4, no. 8 [63].

of seeking advice, so that he might be directed or helped; nor need Ours wait until they are asked by the superior.

3° Each one not only can but should manifest to the superior as to a father matters about to cause serious harm to the common good or imminent danger to some third party, so that he may secretly and prudently provide for both the good of the subject involved and for religious life in general.

4° The manifestation should be made to the immediate superior unless serious reasons suggest that it should be made to the mediate one, in which case these reasons are to be made known to the latter.[185]

5° Superiors should not lightly give credence to those who report the fault of another; rather, they should inquire into each such matter. In particular, they should listen to the one who was reported, so that he can defend himself; and if he is found innocent, the one who reported him should be reprehended or punished, in accord with the gravity of the matter.[186]

236 This fraternal concern for permanent conversion and the human and spiritual progress of our members can also be shown by fraternal correction, both in a personal conversation and at a community gathering when the appropriate spiritual circumstances are present.

CHAPTER 3

CERTAIN ACTIVITIES TO BE AVOIDED

237 Our members may not undertake the care of institutes of consecrated life, societies of apostolic life, or similar associations; consequently, they are forbidden to govern them or to involve themselves in their concerns.[187]

238 §1. In accord with the Constitutions, Ours should refrain as far as possible from all secular business, such as the task of making wills or being executors thereof, being agents in civil matters, or other occupations of this sort; and they should not be led by any entreaties to undertake these things or to engage in them.

---

[185] See *CollDecr.* d. 62 (GC 6, d. 32, nos. 2–7; can. 10, nos. 2–4; GC 7, d. 12); *CollDecr* d. [119] (GC 28, d. 27, 5°).

[186] See *CollDecr* d. 63, §1 (GC 7, d. 12).

[187] See *CollDecr.* d. 234, §1 (GC 7, d. 56; GC 8, d. 11; GC 23, d. 40; see GC 20, d. 12, no. 9); P. VI, c. 3, no. 5 [588]; modified by GC 34.

§2. In the matter of this prohibition, no one but the general can grant a dispensation, and he should show himself most reluctant to do this.[188]

239   The prohibition of the Constitutions against Ours' giving testimony in civil litigation, and much more so in criminal proceedings, without permission of the superior,[189] is to be understood of a case where neither an order of a legitimate superior nor the good of religion or public edification or justice obliges us. Even when we are not free in the matter, the advice of the superior is always required.[190]

CHAPTER 4

SPIRITUAL PROGRESS AND ONGOING FORMATION

240   Especially in our times a truly contemporary apostolate demands of us a process of permanent and continuing formation. Thus formation is never ended, and our "first" formation must be seen as the beginning of this continuing process.[191]

241   All, even those who have already completed their formation, should strive constantly to nourish and renew their own spiritual lives from those sources that the Church and the Society give us (biblical study, theological reflection, liturgy, Spiritual Exercises, recollections, spiritual reading, and the like). Thus, with the advance of years, each one should experience constant rejuvenation in his spiritual life, and his apostolic activity should increasingly become able to respond more effectively to the needs of the Church and of men and women.[192]

242   §1. Ours achieve continuing formation especially through a constant evaluation of and reflection on their apostolate, in the light of faith and with the help of their apostolic community. Our professors and experts should also assist in this, shedding the light of their theories on our praxis, even while they themselves are led to more profound reflection by the apostolic experience of their companions.

---

[188] See *CollDecr* d. 236 (GC 5, dd. 48, 80; GC 8, d. 56); see P. VI, c. 3, no. 7, D [591, 592].

[189] P. VI, c. 3, no. 8 [593].

[190] See *CollDecr* d. 237.

[191] GC 32, d. 6, no. 18; see GC 34, d. 3, no. 18; ibid., d. 6, nos. 23–29.

[192] See GC 31, d. 8, no. 46; see GC 34, d. 8, no. 32.

§2. This continuing formation demands that definite periods of time be given to formal courses or simply to private study, whether in theology or other disciplines, as required for one's apostolate.[193] As far as foreign languages are concerned, insofar as possible our formed members are encouraged to follow what is prescribed in no. 97 for those in formation.[194]

§3. Continuing formation should also foster an attitude of universalism by providing an opportunity for members to experience the international character of the Society.[195]

243   §1. In accord with the resources and the apostolic needs of the different provinces and regions, major superiors should provide for the spiritual, intellectual, and apostolic renewal of all our members. At determined times let Ours be given sufficient opportunity to apply themselves seriously to this sort of renewal according to a program to be approved by the major superiors.[196]

§2. An appropriate course or program on spiritual and doctrinal formation should also be set up each year for the brothers, especially for those who have not yet completed their final probation. On such occasions, lectures are to be offered on Sacred Scripture, liturgy, theology, and social doctrine.[197]

§3. It is suggested that our members, priests and brothers alike, after completing about ten years in apostolic ministries and offices be given the opportunity for more intensive spiritual, psychological, and apostolic renewal during a period of at least three months.[198]

---

[193] GC 32, d. 6, nos. 18–20; see GC 31, d. 8, nos. 46–48; GC 33, d. 1, nos. 21, 41; see GC 34, d. 3, no. 18.

[194] See GC 34, d. 21, no. 10.

[195] See GC 34, d. 21, no. 9.

[196] See GC 32, d. 6, no. 35.

[197] See GC 31, d. 8, no. 30.

[198] See GC 32, d. 6, no. 36.

CHAPTER 4

¹THE HELP GIVEN TO THE DYING MEMBERS OF THE SOCIETY AND THE SUFFRAGES AFTER DEATH

[595]   1. ²As during his whole life, so also and even more at the time of his death, each member of the Society ought to strive earnestly that through him God our Lord may be glorified and served and his neighbors may be edified, ³at least by the example of his patience and fortitude **along with his living faith, hope, and love of the eternal goods which Christ our Lord merited and acquired for us by those altogether incomparable sufferings of his temporal life and death.**²⁸ ⁴But sickness is often such that it greatly impairs the use of the mental faculties; and through the vehement attacks of the devil and the great importance of not succumbing to him, the passing away is itself such that the sick man needs help from fraternal charity. ⁵Therefore with great vigilance the superior should see to it that the one who in the physician's opinion is in danger should, before being deprived of his judgment, receive all the holy sacraments ⁶and fortify himself for the passage from this temporal life to that which is eternal, by means of the arms which the divine liberality of Christ our Lord offers.

[596]   2. ¹He ought likewise to be aided by the very special prayers of all the members of the community, until he has given up his soul to his Creator. ²Besides others who may come in to witness the sick man's death, in greater or lesser number as the superior judges [A], ³some ought to be especially assigned to keep him company. They should encourage him and afford him the reminders and helps which are appropriate at that moment. ⁴When in time he can no longer be helped, they should commend him to God our Lord, until his soul now freed from the body is received by him who redeemed it by that price so high, his blood and life.

[597]   A. *¹With sick persons who fall into delirium and lose the use of their reason, so that there is neither blame nor merit to what they say, or with someone who fails to give as much edification in his infirmity as he ought to, those assisting could be few and chosen from among those in whom more confidence is placed.*

[598]   3. ¹From the hour when one has expired until his interment, his body should be kept decently for the proper time [B] and

---

²⁸ (See *CN* 244, §4.)

CHAPTER 5

SICKNESS, OLD AGE, AND DEATH

244 §1. Our elderly and infirm members continue to be apostolically fruitful and make others sharers in their own wisdom, acquired by the experience of serving our mission. They ought to take care that others are encouraged by the example of their filial and confident dedication to God in sickness and failing strength.[199]

§2. We should all have a special spiritual and human care for them, with profound gratitude and fraternal charity. Superiors have a special responsibility to do this.[200]

§3. Major superiors should give to our elderly and infirm members a special mission to pray for the Church and the Society and to unite their personal suffering and limitations to the worldwide salvific ministry of the Church and the Society.

§4. In the light of present-day progress in medical science and, in particular, the possibility on the one hand of prolonging human life beyond its normal natural limits and on the other hand of helping others in certain circumstances by donating one's own bodily organs, each one should determine—according to the laws of each region—what in conscience he considers to be the better expression, the one enlightened by faith in Jesus Christ, of his own personal dignity and a sense of solidarity with others, at the moment of his transition from earthly to eternal life in the Lord.[201]

---

[199] See P. III, c. 1, no. 16 [272]; see GC 34, d. 6, no. 29.

[200] See P. III, c. 2, no. 6, G [303, 304].

[201] See P. VI, d. 4, no. 1 [595].

then, after the office has been recited in the usual manner in the presence of the members of the community *[C]*, it should be buried. ²On the first morning after his death all the priests of the community should celebrate a Mass for his soul and the rest should offer a special prayer asking God's mercy for him. ³They should continue this subsequently, according to the judgment of the superior, the devotion of each one, and the obligations which exist in our Lord.

[599]   B. *¹On occasion it could be a few hours less than a full day when, because of the bad odor, especially when the weather is very hot, the superior judges it expedient to wait a shorter time. But ordinarily what was stated will be done.*

[600]   C. *¹The practice should be that of reciting the office in a moderately loud voice and with the members of the community present in the church with their candles lit, and so on.*

[601]   4. ¹Likewise, notice that the same should be done ought to be sent to the other places of the Society which the superior thinks proper, so that charity toward the departed no less than toward the living may be shown in our Lord.

CHAPTER 5

¹THE CONSTITUTIONS DO NOT OBLIGE UNDER PAIN OF SIN

[602]   ²The Society desires that all the Constitutions and Declarations and its regime of living should be observed in every regard according to our Institute, without deviation in anything; ³and on the other hand it also desires that its individual members may be safe, or aided against falling into any occasion of sin which could arise on account of the said Constitutions or ordinances. ⁴For that reason it is our considered opinion in our Lord that, apart from the express vow which the Society has with respect to the currently reigning sovereign pontiff, and apart from the other three essential vows of poverty, chastity, and obedience, ⁵no constitutions, declarations, or regime of living can oblige under mortal or venial sin, unless the superior orders the subjects in the name of Christ our Lord or in virtue of obedience, ⁶which may be done in regard to things and persons where it is judged to be highly expedient for the particular good of each one or for the universal good. ⁷Thus the fear of sin should give place to the love and desire of all perfection and of contributing to the greater glory and praise of Christ our Creator and Lord.

PART VII

[1]THE RELATIONS TO THEIR NEIGHBOR OF THOSE ALREADY INCORPORATED INTO THE SOCIETY WHEN THEY ARE DISPERSED INTO THE VINEYARD OF CHRIST OUR LORD

The text of the Constitutions begins on page 276.

PART VII

THE MISSION AND MINISTRIES OF THE SOCIETY

CHAPTER 1

THE MISSION OF THE SOCIETY TODAY

245   §1. The mission of the Society today is participation in the total evangelizing mission of the Church,[1] which aims at the realization of the Kingdom of God in the whole of human society, not only in the life to come but also in this life.[2] This mission is "a single but complex reality, which is expressed in a variety of ways";[3] namely, through the interrelated dimensions of the witness of one's life; of proclamation, conversion, inculturation, and of the establishment of local churches; and also through dialogue and the promotion of the justice desired by God.[4]

§2. Within this framework and in accordance with our original charism approved by the Church, the contemporary mission of the Society is the service of faith and the promotion in society of that justice of the Gospel that is the embodiment of God's love and saving mercy.[5]

§3. In this mission, its aim (the service of faith) and its integrating principle (faith directed toward the justice of the Kingdom) are dynamically related to the inculturated proclamation of the Gospel and to dialogue with other religious traditions as integral dimensions of evangelization.[6]

246   Conditions for carrying out this mission are the following:

---

[1] See GC 34, d. 11, no. 19.

[2] GC 34, d. 2, no. 3.

[3] John Paul II, Encyclical *Redemptoris missio*, no. 41 (*AAS* [1991], p. 289).

[4] See John Paul II, ibid., nos. 41–59.

[5] See GC 34, d. 2, no. 3.

[6] GC 34, d. 2, no. 15; see ibid., dd. 3, 4, 5; GC 32, d. 4, no. 36.

1° A continuing personal conversion, finding Jesus Christ in the brokenness of our world, living in solidarity with the poor and outcast, so that we can take up their cause under the standard of the cross. Our sensitivity to such a mission will be most affected by frequent direct contact with these "friends of the Lord," from whom we can often learn much about faith. Some insertion into the world of the poor should therefore be part of the life of each member, and our communities should be located among ordinary people wherever possible.[7]

2° A dialogue, born of respect for people, especially the poor, in which we share their cultural and spiritual values and offer our own cultural and spiritual resources, in order to build up a communion of peoples instructed by God's Word and enlivened by the Spirit as at Pentecost.[8] In such a dialogue, we come into contact with the activity of God in the lives of other men and women, and we try to enable people to become aware of God's presence in their culture.[9] This dialogue is also necessary in the so-called "post-Christian" cultures, based upon a sharing of life, a shared commitment to action for human development and liberation, a sharing of values and a sharing of human experience.[10]

3° A deep respect for everything that has been brought about in human beings by the Spirit who blows where he wills;[11] attention to the global desire for a contemplative experience of the divine; a desire to be enriched by the spiritual experiences and ethical values, theological perspectives, and symbolic expressions of other religions.[12]

4° A desire to embody Christ's ministry of healing and reconciliation in a world increasingly divided by economic and social status, race and ethnicity, violence and war, cultural and religious pluralism.[13]

---

[7] GC 34, d. 3, no. 17; see d. 6, no. 20; d. 9, no. 16; GC 32, d. 4, nos. 35–36, 48; GC 33, d. 1, no. 41; NC nos. 180, 273.

[8] GC 34, d. 4, no. 8.

[9] See GC 34, d. 4, no. 17; d. 6, no. 20; GC 33, d. 1, no. 41; John Paul II, Encyclical Redemptoris missio, nos. 52–57 (pp. 299ff.).

[10] See GC 34, d. 4, no. 23.

[11] See John 3:8.

[12] See GC 34, d. 5, no. 9.1.

[13] GC 34, d. 6, no. 14; see FI no. 1.

5° A closer collaboration with others, especially with the laity, with other members of local churches, with Christians of other denominations, with adherents to other religions, and all "who hunger and thirst after justice"; in short, with all who strive to make a world fit for men and women to live in, a world where the brotherhood of all opens the way for the recognition and acceptance of Christ Jesus and God our Father.[14]

6° A more profound spiritual experience through the Spiritual Exercises, by which we continually renew our faith and apostolic hope by experiencing again the love of God in Christ Jesus. We strengthen our commitment to be "companions of Jesus" in his mission, to labor with him in solidarity with the poor for the establishment of the Kingdom.[15]

7° All the major problems of our time have an international dimension. On our part, great solidarity and availability and real openness to change will be necessary, even as we remain firmly rooted in our own culture, in order to foster the growth of cooperation and coordination throughout the whole Society, in the service of the worldwide mission of the Church.[16]

8° We must therefore have an operative freedom: open, adaptable, even eager for any mission that may be given us. Our desire is an unconditional consecration to mission, free of all worldly interest and free to serve all men and women. Our mission extends to the creation of this same spirit of mission in others.[17]

247 §1. As far as the promotion of justice is concerned, we must become more aware, as the Church itself has done, of its more recent and new exigencies for our mission;[18] such are, among others, protection of the human rights of persons and peoples (individual, socioeconomic, civil and political, the right to peace, to progress, to cultural integrity); the disturbing consequences of the interdependence of peoples, causing grave dam-

---

[14] See GC 32, d. 4, no. 37; d. 2, no. 29; GC 33, d. 1, no. 47; GC 34, d. 4, no. 8; d. 13.

[15] GC 32, d. 4, no. 38; see GC 33, d. 1, nos. 39–40, 42.

[16] See GC 32, d. 4, nos. 69, 81; GC 34, d. 21.

[17] GC 34, d. 26, no. 24.

[18] See John Paul II, Encyclical *Sollicitudo rei socialis,* no. 26 (*AAS* [1988], 544ff.); id., *Centesimus annus,* nos. 28, 36–39 (*AAS* [1991], 638ff.).

age to the quality of life and culture of poor peoples, especially of "indigenous" peoples;[19] safeguarding human life itself, from its beginning to its natural end, life that is severely threatened by the so-called "culture of death"; the influence of the media in the service of justice, which requires coordinated action of Christians and other persons in different areas;[20] protection of the environment; the tragic marginalization of not a few nations, especially on the African continent at this time; the need of the peoples of Eastern Europe to find a sure way to a future in freedom, peace, and security; the problem of the socially marginalized in every society; the very grave worldwide situation of refugees.[21]

§2. The situation of women in the world today merits special attention.[22] Our contribution to overcoming unjust structures and experiencing our solidarity with women include the following: teaching the essential equality of women and men; supporting women in opposing situations of exploitation and violence; fostering an appropriate presence of women in our ministries and institutions and involving women in decision making in our ministries; promoting the education of women and elimination of all forms of discrimination in it; using appropriately inclusive language in speaking and writing.[23]

§3. All these efforts must be concentrated on transforming the cultural values that sustain an unjust and oppressive social order.[24]

248   Father General, with the help of his council, has the task of stimulating the entire Society to serve the cause of the Gospel and its justice. But all our members, especially major superiors, should strenuously collaborate with him, even if this might shake up their settled habits or even disturb their peace of mind, when they are accustomed instead to work of a less universal scope.[25]

---

[19] See GC 34, d. 4, no. 11.

[20] See GC 34, d. 15, no. 5.

[21] See GC 34, d. 3, nos. 5–16.

[22] See John Paul II, Apos. letter *Mulieris dignitatem,* no. 10 (*AAS* [1988], 1674ff.); Apos. exhortation "Christifideles laici," n. 49 (*AAS* [1989], 486ff.).

[23] See GC 34, d. 14, nos. 12–13.

[24] GC 34, d. 4, no. 28.3.

[25] GC 32, d. 4, no. 69.

249   §1. Any realistic desire to engage in the promotion of justice in our mission will mean some kind of involvement in civic activity;[26] but this will make our preaching of the Gospel more meaningful and its acceptance easier.[27]

§2. Communities and superiors should help each one of us to overcome the difficulties, fear, and apathy that block us from truly comprehending the cultural, social, economic, and political problems existing in our city, country, or region, as well as in the world at large. In this way let each identify and assume the responsibilities to society that are his, and let each in his own proper way participate in the efforts needed to promote genuine justice.[28]

§3. In each of our different apostolates, we must create communities of solidarity in seeking justice. Working together with our colleagues, we can and should engage in every ministry of the Society to promote justice in one or more of the following ways: directly serving and accompanying the poor, developing awareness of the demands of justice joined to the social responsibility to achieve it, and participating in social mobilization for the creation of a more just social order.[29]

250   All our members, but especially those who belong to the affluent world, should endeavor to work as much as is appropriate with those who form public opinion, as well as with international organizations, to promote justice more effectively among all peoples.[30]

251   Finally, in carrying out this mission of ours with exactitude, we should ever keep in mind that "the means which unite the human instrument to God and so dispose it that it may be wielded dexterously by his divine hand are more effective than those which equip it in relation to men."[31]

---

[26] GC 32, d. 4, no. 80.

[27] GC 32, d. 4, no. 46.

[28] GC 32, d. 4, no. 43, see ibid., nos. 42, 45–46.

[29] GC 34, d. 3, no. 19.

[30] GC 32, d. 4, no. 81.

[31] See GC 32, d. 4, no. 12; P. X, no. 2 [813].

CHAPTER 1

[2]MISSIONS FROM THE SUPREME PONTIFF[1]

[603]   1. [3]Just as Part VI treats of what each member of the Society needs to observe in regard to himself, so this Part VII deals with what the members need to observe in regard to their neighbor (which is an end eminently characteristic of our Institute) [4]when they are dispersed throughout Christ's vineyard to labor in that part of it and in that work which have been entrusted to them, [5]whether they have been sent to some places or others by either the supreme vicar of Christ our Lord or the superiors of the Society, who for them are similarly in the place of his Divine Majesty; [6]or whether they themselves choose where and in what work they will labor, having been commissioned to travel to any place where they judge that greater service of God and the good of souls will follow; [7]or whether they carry on their labor not by traveling but by residing steadily and continually in certain places where much fruit of glory and service to God is expected [A].

[8]And to treat the missions from His Holiness first as being most important, [9]it should be observed that **the vow which the Society made**[2] to obey him as the supreme vicar of Christ without any excuse meant that the members were to go to any place where he judges it expedient to send them for the greater glory of God and the good of souls, whether among the faithful or unbelievers [B]. [10]The Society did not mean the vow for a particular place, but rather for being dispersed to various regions and places throughout the world, wishing to make the best choice in this matter by having the sovereign pontiff make the distribution of its members.

[604]   A.   [1]These are the four more general ways of distribution into the vineyard of Christ our Lord. Each of them is treated in its own chapter in this Part VII.

[605]   B.   [1]The intention of the fourth vow pertaining to the pope was not for a particular place but for having the members dispersed throughout the various parts of the world. [2]For those who first united to form the Society were from different provinces and realms and did not know into which regions they were to go, whether among the faithful or the unbelievers; [3]and therefore, to avoid erring in the path of the Lord, they made the promise or vow in order that His Holiness might distribute them for

---

[1] (See *CN* 252-54.)

[2] (By this vow are bound directly and personally each of those who in the Society make profession of the four vows: see *FI* no. 3.)

CHAPTER 2

MISSIONS FROM THE SUPREME PONTIFF

252   §1. To be truly Christian, our service to the Church must be anchored in fidelity to Christ, who makes all things new; to be proper to the Society, it must be done in union with the successor of Peter.[32]

§2. Out of love for Christ and in virtue of the fourth vow of special obedience to his vicar concerning missions,[33] the Society offers itself completely to the Church, so that the Supreme Pontiff may send all its members into the vineyard of the Lord to carry out his mission.[34]

§3. Missions that the Supreme Pontiff may wish to entrust to our Society at any time and in any part of the world[35] in fulfillment of our mission, we must place in the category of the highest priority of our apostolic activity.[36]

253   The calls that have come to the Society from recent popes are the following:

1° To contribute effectively to the implementation of the Second Vatican Council

2° To confront with all our forces the problem of atheism and cooperate in that profound renewal of the Church needed in a secularized age

3° To better adapt our traditional apostolates to the different spiritual necessities of today: the renewal of Christian life, the education of youth, the formation of the clergy, the study of philosophy and theology, research into humanistic and scientific cultures, and missionary evangelization

4° To pay particular attention to ecumenism, interreligious dialogue, and the task of authentic inculturation

5° In a manner consonant with our priestly and religious Institute and within the Church's evangelizing action, to promote the justice "connected with peace, which is the aspiration of all peoples"

---

[32] GC 34, d. 11, no. 28.

[33] See *FI* no. 3; P. VI, c. 1, no. 1, B [603, 605].

[34] See GC 31, d. 1, no. 6; GC 34, d. 11, no. 28; d. 26, no. 12.

[35] See P. V, c. 3, no. 3, C [529]; P. VII, d. 1, no. 1, B [605].

[36] GC 31, d. 21, no. 12.

the greater glory of God, in conformity with their intention to travel throughout the world 4and, when they could not find the desired spiritual fruit in one place, to pass on to another and another, ever seeking the greater glory of God our Lord and the greater aid of souls.

[606]   2. 1In this matter, the Society having placed its own judgment and will wholly under that of Christ our Lord and his vicar, 2neither the superior for himself nor any individual member of the Society will be permitted to arrange for himself or for another, or to try to arrange, directly or indirectly, with the pope or his ministers to reside in or to be sent rather to one place than another. 3The individual members will leave this entire concern to the supreme vicar of Christ and to their own superior [C]; and in regard to his own person the superior will in our Lord leave this concern to His Holiness and to the Society [D].

[607]   C. 1When one of the subjects has been designated for some place or undertaking, and it is judged that the supreme vicar of Christ, if well informed, would not send him to it, 2the superior general may give him better information, while finally leaving the entire matter to the decision of His Holiness.

[608]   D. 1"The Society" should be understood to mean those members of it who happen to be in the place where the general is.3 2These could give good information to the sovereign pontiff if, because of different reports from other persons, he seemed about to send the general to some place which is not conducive to the common good of the Society and greater service of God.

[609]   3. 1Moreover, he who has been designated by His Holiness to go to some region should offer his person generously, without requesting provisions for the journey or causing a request for anything temporal to be made, 2but rather leaving it to His Holiness to have him sent in the manner that he judges to be the greater service of God and of the Apostolic See, without taking thought about anything else in his case [E].

[610]   E. 1Representation may well be made, and even should be, through the prelate or person through whom His Holiness issues the command to go somewhere, by asking how he wishes him to make the journey and stay in the place, 2namely, by living on alms and begging for the love of God our Lord, or in some other manner. 3This is so that what His Holiness deems best may be done with greater devotion and security in our Lord.

---

3 (The assistants for provident care are understood.)

6° To foster the vigorous impulse toward missionary work and church union and to serve our prophetic mission to promote the new evangelization[37]

254   The pontifical mandate entrusted to the Society of resisting atheism should permeate all the accepted forms of our apostolate, in such wise that we may both cultivate among believers true faith and an authentic awareness of God and also zealously direct our efforts to nonbelievers of every type.[38]

The text of the Norms resumes on page 283.

---

[37] GC 33, d. 1, no. 37; see GC 31, d. 3, no. 1; John Paul II, Homily to Fathers of GC 33, nos. 4, 6, 7 (*ActRSJ* 18:1093–99); allocution to delegates of GC 34, Jan. 5, 1995.

[38] See GC 31, d. 3, no. 11: GC 32, d. 4, nos. 24–26.

[611]   4. ¹If His Holiness does not designate the person but orders that one or more should go to one region or another, and if he thus leaves it to the superior to judge who would be the most fit for such a mission, ²the superior, in conformity with His Holiness's order, will designate those who are more appropriate or more suitable for it, ³with a view to the greater universal good and the least damage possible to the other enterprises which are undertaken in the service of God our Lord.

[612]   5. ¹It is highly expedient that the mission be fully explained to the one who is thus sent, as well as the intention of His Holiness and the result in hope of which he is sent. ²This should be given to him in writing, if possible [F], so that he may be better able to accomplish what is entrusted to him [G]. ³The superior too will try to help him by what further instructions he can [G], so that in everything God our Lord and the Apostolic See may be better served.

[613]   F. ¹If this is not feasible, at least an effort should be made to procure an oral explanation of His Holiness's intention, whether given by himself directly to the one who is to go, or through the agency of the superior, some prelate, or another person.

[614]   G. ¹The superior will also be able to help with some instruction, not only in his own missions but also in those of His Holiness, in order to attain better the end which is sought in the service of Christ our Lord.

[615]   6. ¹When they are sent to particular places without the time being fixed by His Holiness, it should be understood that the stay ought to last three months, ²and longer or shorter depending on the greater or lesser spiritual fruit which is seen to be reaped there or is expected elsewhere, or as seems most expedient for some universal good. ³All this will be done according to the judgment of the superior, who will consider the holy intention of the pontiff for the service of Christ our Lord.

[616]   7. ¹When it is necessary to prolong residence in a determined place, and where this can be done without prejudice to the principal mission and intention of the sovereign pontiff, it will not be improper to make some excursions—²if the person can do so and deems that they would be fruitful in service to God our Lord— in order to aid the souls of neighboring regions, and afterwards to return to his residence.

³Similarly, in the territory where he resides, in addition to what has been specifically enjoined upon him, which he must attend to with special care and not neglect for other opportunities

in the divine service, even good ones, ⁴he can and should consider—without prejudice to his mission, as has been said—what other activities he can undertake for the glory of God and the good of souls, ⁵not losing the opportunity for this which God may send him, to the extent that he will judge expedient in the Lord.

[617]   8. ¹In order to achieve better the end of our profession and promise, he who happens to be the superior general when a new vicar of Christ takes office ²should be obliged, either himself or through another and within the year after the pontiff's election and coronation, to manifest to His Holiness the profession and express promise which the Society has to be obedient to him, ³especially in regard to the missions, to the glory of God our Lord.

CHAPTER 2

¹THE MISSIONS RECEIVED FROM THE SUPERIOR OF THE SOCIETY

[618]　1. ²The more readily to be able to meet the spiritual needs of souls in many regions, as also with greater security for those who go for this purpose *[A]*, ³the superiors of the Society, in accord with the faculty granted by the sovereign pontiff, will have authority to send any of the Society's members *[B]* to whatsoever place these superiors think it more expedient to send them *[C]*, although these members, wherever they are, will always be at the disposition of His Holiness.

⁴Now there are many who make requests more with a view to their own spiritual obligations to their flocks, or to other less immediate advantages, rather than to those that are common or universal. Hence, the superior general, or whoever holds this authority from him, ought to bestow much careful thought on missions of this kind, ⁵so that, in sending subjects to one region rather than to another *[D]*, or for one purpose rather than for another *[E]*, or one particular person rather than another or several of them *[F]*, in this manner or in that *[G]*, or for a longer or shorter time *[H]*, that may always be done which is conducive to the greater service of God and the universal good.

⁶With this thoroughly right and pure intention in the presence of God our Lord, and—should he think it advisable because of the difficulty or importance of the decision—⁷commending the matter to his Divine Majesty and causing it to be commended in the prayers and Masses of the house, ⁸as well as discussing it with one or more members of the Society who happen to be present and whom he thinks suitable, the superior will on his own authority decide about sending or not sending, and about the other circumstances, as he will judge to be expedient for the greater glory of God.

⁹The part of the one who is sent will be, without interposing himself in favor of going or remaining in one place rather than another, to leave the disposition of himself completely and very freely to the superior who in the place of Christ our Lord directs him in the path of his greater service and praise *[I]*. ¹⁰In similar manner, too, no one ought to try by any means to bring it about that others will remain in one place or go to another, unless he does so with the approval of his superior, by whom he should be governed in our Lord *[K]*.

CHAPTER 3

MISSIONS FROM THE SUPERIORS OF THE SOCIETY AND OUR CHOICE OF MINISTRIES

255 §1. All members of the Society of Jesus, even though dispersed in various local communities and ascribed to individual provinces and regions, are inserted directly and primarily into the single apostolic body and community of the whole Society. It is at this level that the overall apostolic decisions and guidelines are worked out and established, for which each one should feel responsible. This demands of all of us a high degree of availability and a real apostolic mobility in the service of the universal Church.[39]

§2. This solidarity with the body of the Society ought to take precedence over any other loyalties (those binding a man to any type of institution, within or outside the Society). It ought to mark any other commitment, transforming it thereby into a "mission." For a "mission" as such is bestowed by the Society through the superior and is always subject to its review. The Society can confirm or modify it as the greater service of God may require.[40]

256 §1. As we continue to respond to our mission today as it is described by recent general congregations, traditional apostolates, appropriately updated, take on fresh importance, while new needs and situations make new demands on us, so that all our works may contribute to strengthening the faith that does justice.[41]

§2. Hence all our ministries, both traditional and new, must be reviewed by means of apostolic spiritual discernment, both personal and communitarian,[42] with great attention to the role they can play in the service of faith and the promotion of

---

[39] See GC 32, d. 4, nos. 68–69, 81; see *Examen*, c. 4, no. 35 [92]; P. III, c. 2, no. 6, G [304]; P. IV, *Pream.* A [308]; P. VII, c. 1, no. 1, B [603, 605].

[40] GC 32, d. 4, no. 66.

[41] GC 33, d. 1, no. 43; see GC 32, d. 4, nos. 11, 18, 51–52, 57–58; GC 31, d. 27.

[42] GC 33, d. 1, no. 39.

[619]   A. ¹The superior of the Society can more easily and more expeditiously make provision for many places (especially those remote from the Apostolic See) than would be the case if those who need members of the Society must always approach the sovereign pontiff. ²For the individual members, too, there is greater security in going under obedience to their superiors rather than on their own initiative, even supposing they could act in this way and not as sent by the one charged with directing them in the place of Christ our Lord, as the interpreter of his divine will.

[620]   B. ¹Just as the general can perform the other functions by himself and through persons under him, so too can he perform this one of sending his subjects on missions, by reserving to himself the missions which he thinks should be thus reserved.

[621]   C. ¹The sending of subjects "to whatsoever place these superiors think it expedient" means either among the faithful, even though it be in the Indies, or among the unbelievers, especially where there is a community of believers, as in Greece and elsewhere. ²Where the inhabitants are more exclusively unbelievers, the superior should ponder seriously in the sight of God our Lord whether he ought to send subjects or not, and where, and whom. ³The part of the subject will always be to accept his mission joyfully as coming from God our Lord.

[622]   D. ¹To make the best choice in sending persons to one place or another while having the greater service of God and the more universal good before one's eyes as the guiding norm, ²it would appear that in the ample vineyard of the Lord one ought to select, other things being equal (and this should be understood in everything that follows), that part of the vineyard which has greater need, ³both because of lack of other workers, and because of the wretchedness and infirmity of the people there and their danger of eternal condemnation.

⁴Consideration should also be given to where greater fruit is likely to be reaped through the means usual in the Society; as would be the case where one sees the door more widely open and a better disposition and readiness among the people to be profited. ⁵This would consist in their greater devotion and desire (which can be judged in part by the insistence they show), or in the condition and quality of the persons who are more capable of making progress and of preserving the fruit produced, to the glory of God our Lord.

⁶In places where our indebtedness is greater, for example, where there is a house or college of the Society, or members of it engaged in study, who are recipients of charitable deeds from the people there, ⁷and assuming that the other considerations pertaining to spiritual progress are equal, it would be more suitable to have some laborers there, preferring

justice, in solidarity with the poor,[43] so that, if need be, they may be replaced by others which are more effective.[44]

257   Our institutions can use the following means to help them implement our mission more effectively: institutional evaluation of the role they play in society; discernment whether the institution's own internal structures and policies reflect our mission; collaboration and exchange with similar institutions in diverse social and cultural contexts; continuing formation of personnel regarding mission.[45]

258   §1. All our members, especially superiors, to whom the choice of ministries belongs "as the most important task of all,"[46] must make great efforts to bring about this review of our ministries. The criteria for review, found in the Constitutions themselves and illuminated by the decrees of the general congregations and the instructions of the superiors general, retain their perennial validity, but none the less must always be rightly applied to historical circumstances.[47]

§2. We should always keep in mind social conditions and pastoral programs, the apostolic forces available or hoped for, the more pressing pastoral and apostolic needs, and the help that ought to be given to Father General for more universal works.[48]

§3. Social and cultural analysis of the true state of affairs should also be employed from a religious, social, and political point of view, based on serious and specialized studies and on an accurate knowledge of those matters.[49]

§4. According to this way of proceeding, which is to be used by local, provincial, and regional communities, superiors can employ the customary consultations and then draw up apostolic options to be submitted to Father General.[50]

---

[43] GC 32, d. 4, no. 76.

[44] GC 32, d. 4, no. 77.

[45] GC 34, d. 3, no. 21; ibid., d. 4, no. 28.7.

[46] Fr. J. B. Janssens, "Letter on Our Ministries" (*ActRSJ* 11:299–336).

[47] See GC 31, d. 21, no. 4; GC 33, d. 1, no. 40.

[48] GC 31, d. 22, no. 2; see GC 32, d. 4, nos. 44, 67; GC 34, d. 21, no. 28.

[49] See GC 33, d. 1, no. 41; GC 32, d. 4, no. 44.

[50] GC 33, d. 1, no. 41; see GC 32, d. 4, no. 69.

these places to others for these considerations in conformity with perfect charity.

⁸The more universal the good is, the more is it divine. Hence preference ought to be given to persons and places which, once benefited themselves, are a cause of extending the good to many others who are under their influence or take guidance from them.

⁹For that reason, the spiritual aid which is given to important and public persons ought to be regarded as more important, since it is a more universal good. This is true (whether these persons are laymen such as princes, lords, magistrates, or administrators of justice, or whether they are clerics such as prelates). ¹⁰This holds true also of spiritual aid given to persons who are distinguished for learning and authority, for the same reason of the good being more universal. ¹¹For that same reason, too, preference ought to be shown to the aid which is given to large nations such as the Indies, or to important cities, or to universities, which are generally attended by numerous persons who, if aided themselves, can become laborers for the help of others.

¹²Similarly, in places where the enemy of Christ our Lord is seen to have sown cockle [Matt. 13:24–30], particularly where he has spread bad opinion about the Society or stirred up ill will against it so as to impede the fruit which it might produce, the Society ought to exert itself more, ¹³especially if it is an important place of which account should be taken; persons should be sent there, if possible, who by their life and learning may undo the evil opinion founded on false reports.

[623]   E. ¹For making a better choice of the undertakings on which the superior sends his men, the same rule should be kept in view, namely, that of considering the greater divine honor and the greater universal good. This consideration can quite legitimately suggest sending persons to one place rather than to another.

²To touch upon some motives which can exist in favor of one place rather than another, we mention these:

³First of all, where members of the Society have the possibility of engaging in works aimed at spiritual benefits and also in works aimed at corporal benefits where mercy and charity are exercised; ⁴or of helping persons in matters of greater perfection and also of lesser perfection, and, in fine, in things which are in themselves more good and also less good; ⁵then, if both things cannot be done simultaneously (everything else being equal), the first ought always to be preferred to the second.

⁶Likewise, when there are matters in the service of God our Lord which are more urgent, and others which are less pressing and can better

259   Keeping ourselves available to the Holy See above all, let all our members and especially superiors propose to themselves to follow the plans, judgments, and works of the local hierarchy; to implement them; and to be animated by the spirit and impulse toward fellowship, by which our works are harmonized with the pastoral programs of particular churches,[51] according to the constant tradition in the Society of serving the Church by explaining, propagating, and defending the faith.[52]

260   §1. To promote the better choice of ministries and to foresee to some extent future developments, a commission should be set up as an aid to the provincial and under his authority; the task of this commission will be, after careful study and in view of the priorities established by the general or the Conference of Major Superiors,[53] to give advice on an overall review of ministries. This will involve suggesting which ones ought to be kept or dropped and which others ought to be undertaken for the first time. Each year the provincial should report to Father General what has been done in this regard.

   §2. In order to achieve a more effective coordination of the apostolate in a given region, the Conferences of Major Superiors can be greatly helped by a commission of the entire conference, linked with the provincial and regional commissions. In regions that are sufficiently homogeneous, a single general commission can be instituted in place of commissions for the individual provinces or regions.[54]

261   §1. Not only should our structured activities undergo review but so should our individual apostolates, and by means of the same criteria.[55]

   §2. So that our energies may not be dispersed but instead be well organized into a single whole, superiors should bear in mind that they are placed in charge not only of their subjects themselves but also of their works. Hence, they should not be afraid to require subjects to obey them in the choice of ministries. Subjects, however, if some ministry is offered to them, should on

---

[51] See GC 31, d. 21, no. 7; GC 33, d. 1, no. 47; GC 34, d. 6, no. 18.

[52] See GC 32, d. 3, no. 3.

[53] GC 34, d. 21, no. 28.

[54] See GC 31, d. 22, nos. 1–6; see *CollDecr* d. [415, 416] (GC 30, d. 50, nos. 1–2); GC 32, d. 4, no. 77; GC 33, d. 1, no. 40.

[55] GC 32, d. 4, no. 76.

suffer postponement of the remedy, even if they are of equal importance, the first should be preferred to the second.

⁷Similarly too, when there are matters that are especially incumbent upon the Society, or clearly without anyone else to attend to them, and others for which other persons do have a care and means of providing, the first kind should rightly be preferred to the second in selecting missions.

⁸Likewise, among pious works of equal importance, urgency, and need, when some are safer for those engaged in them and others more dangerous, ⁹and when some are dispatched more easily and quickly, whereas others are more difficult and take longer time, the first should be similarly preferred to the second.

¹⁰All things mentioned above being equal, when there are occupations which are of more universal good and extend to the aid of greater numbers of our neighbors, such as preaching or lecturing, ¹¹and others aimed more at individuals, such as hearing confessions or giving the Exercises, ¹²and it is impossible to accomplish both at once, then preference should be given to the first, unless there should be circumstances through which it would be judged that it would be more expedient to take up the second.

¹³Similarly too, when there are pious works that continue longer and are permanently profitable, such as are certain pious foundations for the aid of our neighbors, and others that are less durable and give help only on a few occasions and for a short time, then it is certain that the first ought to be preferred to the second. ¹⁴Hence the superior of the Society ought to employ his subjects more in the first than in the second, always as being for the greater divine service and greater good for our neighbors.

[624]   F. ¹Although it is the supreme providence and direction of the Holy Spirit that must efficaciously bring us to make the right decision in all matters, and to send to each place those who are best fitted and suited to the people and tasks for which they are sent, ²still this much may be said in general. ³First, that for matters of greater moment and where it is more important to avoid mistakes, so far as this depends on the one who with God's grace is to provide, persons ought to be sent who are more select and in whom greater confidence is had.

⁴In matters that involve greater bodily labors, persons more strong and healthy.

⁵In matters which contain greater spiritual dangers, persons more proven in virtue and more reliable.

their own initiative refer the matter to the superior, so that all is arranged in accord with his counsel. They should be willing to join their work to that of others and to subordinate themselves to others, in order to attain the more universal good.[56]

262   The Society recognizes how apostolically important it can be for the fulfillment of our mission today that some of our members are present and work with others in certain sectors of secular activity; therefore, engaging in a secular job or profession, especially in an area that is de-Christianized or underprivileged, can at times, because of its apostolic meaning, be part of the Society's mission, provided that the mission is both given by superiors and can be carried out according to our way of proceeding.[57]

The text of the Norms resumes on page 293.

---

[56] See *CollDecr* d. [415] (GC 30, d. 50, §1).

[57] See GC 32, d. 4, nos. 78–79.

⁶*To go to astute persons who hold posts of spiritual or temporal government, those members seem most suitable who excel in discretion and grace of conversation, and who (while not lacking interior qualities) have an outward appearance which may enhance their authority;* ⁷*for their counsel can be of great moment.*

⁸*To deal with persons of subtle intelligence and learning, those are more suitable who are especially gifted with intelligence and learning; for these persons can be of more assistance in lectures and conversations.*

⁹*For the ordinary people, those will generally be most apt who have talent for preaching, hearing confessions, and so on.*

¹⁰*The number and combination of laborers to be sent should also receive consideration.* ¹¹*First of all, it would be wise when possible not to send one person by himself, but instead at least two persons,* ¹²*so that they may be of greater aid to one another in spiritual and bodily matters, and also, by dividing up among themselves the labors in the service of their neighbor, be of more benefit to those to whom they are sent.*

¹³*Moreover, if two are to go, it seems that a preacher or lecturer could well be accompanied by someone who through confessions and spiritual exercises could gather in the harvest which the other prepares for him, and could assist him by conversations and the other means used in dealing with our neighbors.*

¹⁴*Likewise, when a person is sent who is less experienced in the Society's manner of proceeding and of dealing with the neighbor, it seems that he ought to be accompanied by another who has more experience therein, whom he can imitate, consult, and get advice from in matters where he is uncertain.*

¹⁵*With a person who is very ardent and daring it seems that there could well go another who is more circumspect and cautious. The like holds for other combinations of this kind,* ¹⁶*in such a way that their difference, united by the bond of charity, may be helpful to both and not be able to engender contradiction or discord between the two of them or with their neighbors.*

¹⁷*To send more than two when the importance of the work intended in the service of God our Lord is greater and requires a larger number, and when the Society can provide more laborers without prejudice to other things conducive to the greater divine glory and universal good,* ¹⁸*is something which the superior will have authority to do, accordingly as the unction of the Holy Spirit inspires him or as he judges in the sight of his Divine Majesty to be better and more expedient.*

[625]   G. ¹*In regard to the manner in which he is to send them (after the proper instruction), the superior should deliberate whether he will send*

them in the manner of the poor, so that they would go on foot and without money, or with better facilities; whether with or without letters to aid toward winning acceptance and benevolence at their destination; and whether these letters should be addressed to individuals, or the city, or its head. ²In regard to all the details, the superior will consider the greater edification of the neighbor and the service of God our Lord and then decide what should be done.

[626]   H. ¹With regard to the length of time for which various persons are sent to different places, it would seem that, when no limitation has been set by the sovereign pontiff, the time ought to be gauged on the one hand by consideration of the nature and greater or lesser importance of the spiritual affairs in question, taking into account the need and the fruit reaped or anticipated; ²and on the other by consideration of what occasions emerge elsewhere, what obligation there is to respond to them, and what resources the Society possesses to provide for this or that undertaking. ³One should also weigh the contingencies which can intervene to shorten or lengthen the time. ⁴Finally, in view of the original design of our Institute, which is to travel through various regions, staying for longer or shorter times in accordance with the fruit that is seen, it will be necessary to judge whether it is expedient to give more time or less to certain missions or to others. ⁵So that this may be perceived, it is important that those who are sent keep the superior informed by frequent reports about the fruit which is gained.

⁶When someone has to be moved, the superior should take care in recalling him to do everything possible to see that the persons from among whom he is taken are left quite well disposed rather than in any way disedified, and persuaded that in everything the honor and glory of God and the universal good are being sought.

[627]   I. ¹This prescription is not violated if someone represents the motions or thoughts that occur to him contrary to an order received, meanwhile submitting his entire judgment and will to the judgment and will of his superior, who is in the place of Christ our Lord.

[628]   K. ¹By this it is clearly forbidden that any member should influence a prince, community, or person of authority to write to a superior requesting some member of the Society or to ask this of him by word of mouth, unless the member has first communicated the matter to the superior and understood this procedure to be his will.

[629]   2. ¹Wherever the superior sends someone, he will give him complete instructions, ordinarily in writing [L], about the manner of proceeding, and the means which he wishes to be used for the end he has in view. ²Moreover, by maintaining frequent communication

through letters and receiving the fullest possible information about what is going on, the superior will, as persons and affairs require, furnish advice and whatever other assistance he can from his place of residence *[M]*, ³so that God our Lord may be better served and the common good promoted by the members of the Society. ⁴This should be done with all the more care the more it is demanded by the character of the enterprise, as being important or difficult, or that of the persons sent, as standing in need of advice and instruction *[N]*.

[630]   *L.* ¹*The word "ordinarily" is used because sometimes the person sent is so instructed and capable that this writing is unnecessary. But in a word, these instructions should be given whenever necessary.*

[631]   *M.* ¹*Such assistance would be prayers and Masses, applied especially at the start of undertakings or when greater need of such aid is experienced because of the importance of the affair or major difficulties which may occur.* ²*Thus in this matter, as in other helps such as letters patent or bulls and the like which may be necessary, the superior will provide as reason and charity require.*

[632]   *N.* ¹*This counsel and instruction can be useful not only regarding the business but also regarding the persons, as each one may need to be encouraged or restrained. This should also be applied to everything else.*

CHAPTER 3

¹A MEMBER'S FREE MOVEMENT FROM ONE PLACE TO ANOTHER

[633]   1. ²Although it is the part of those who live under the Society's obedience not to involve themselves, directly or indirectly, with how they are sent on mission, either by His Holiness or by their own superior in the name of Christ our Lord, ³nevertheless, someone who is sent to a large territory such as the Indies or other provinces, and for whom no particular region is assigned, may remain for longer or shorter periods in one place or another, ⁴going off to whatever places he deems—after having weighed the various factors, found himself indifferent as to his will, and made his prayer—to be more expedient for the glory of God our Lord.

⁵From this it is clear that, without swerving from the chief and primary obedience due to His Holiness, in missions of this type the superior will be all the more able to direct a member to one place rather than another as he judges in the Lord to be expedient.

[634]   2. ¹Wherever anyone is, if he is not limited to the use of some means such as lecturing or preaching, he may use the means

CHAPTER 4

THE MINISTRIES BY WHICH THE SOCIETY FULFILLS ITS MISSION

1. Missionary service

263   §1. By reason of their vocation to the Society, all our members, and not only those who so petition, may be sent to evangelize peoples. But those who were born in former mission lands ought to be aware of their serious responsibility to promote the faith and the life of the Church with deep roots in their own cultures.[58] But even they should be prepared to undertake mission service among other peoples.[59]

§2. Superiors ought to select for the missions those who are men of solid virtue, who are quite flexible, and who are capable of fitting into a new culture,[60] so that their proclamation

---

[58] See GC 32, d. 4, no. 55.

[59] GC 31, d. 24, no. 4.

[60] GC 31, d. 24, no. 4.

which he judges more suitable among those which the Society employs. They have been mentioned in Part IV, chapter 8 [402–14] and will be mentioned again in the following chapter [A]. ²Similarly, he will avoid what those passages disapprove, for the greater service of God.

[635]   A. ¹However, it will always be safer for him to confer with his nearest superior about the means which he ought to use.

CHAPTER 4
¹WAYS IN WHICH THE HOUSES AND COLLEGES CAN HELP THEIR NEIGHBORS

[636]   1. ²Since the Society endeavors to aid its neighbors not only by traveling through various parts of the world but also by residing continually in certain places, as is the case with the houses and colleges, ³it is important to have an clear idea of the ways in which souls can be helped in those places, so as to put into practice those of them which are possible for the glory of God our Lord.

[637]   2. ¹The first is by giving the good example of a thoroughly upright life and of Christian virtue, striving to edify those with whom one deals no less, but rather even more, by good deeds than by words.

[638]   3. ¹Likewise, the neighbor is aided by desires in the presence of God our Lord and by prayers for all the Church, ²especially for those persons in it who are of greater importance for the common good [A]. They should also pray for friends and benefactors, living and dead, whether they request these prayers or not; ³and likewise for those for whose particular benefit they and the other members of the Society are working in diverse places among believers or unbelievers, ⁴that God may dispose them all to receive his grace through the weak instruments of this least Society.

[639]   A. ¹Examples of such persons are ecclesiastical and secular princes, and other persons who have great power to promote or impede the good of souls and the divine service.

[640]   4. ¹Furthermore, aid can be given by saying Masses and other divine services, but **without accepting any alms for them** [B],¹ whether they are said at the request of particular persons or the devotion of the persons saying them. ²In regard to the Masses,

---

¹ Clarified by CN 182, 184.

of the Gospel may be sensitive to the religious situation of those to whom they address it.[61]

264   §1. Provinces entrusted with the evangelization of peoples should consider this ministry an integral part of the province, on the same level as their other works. They should help this work with men and money, according to their means, and with a greater enthusiasm where the needs are more pressing. This applies as well to those areas that have already been erected as independent entities.

§2. Our men should diligently promote the work of evangelization of peoples among all the faithful and foster vocations for it.[62]

2. Interreligious dialogue

265   §1. In the context of the divisive, exploitative, and conflictual roles that religions, including Christianity, have played in history, dialogue seeks to develop the unifying and liberating potential of all religions, thus showing the relevance of religion for human well-being, justice, and world peace.[63]

§2. Dialogue is "an activity with its own guiding principles, requirements, and dignity";[64] and it should never be made a strategy to elicit conversions, since a positive relationship with believers of other faiths is a requirement in a world of religious pluralism.[65]

266   §1. The culture of dialogue should become a distinctive characteristic of our Society, sent into the whole world to labor for the greater glory of God and the help of human persons.[66]

§2. The Society should foster the fourfold interreligious dialogue recommended by the Church; namely,

"a. The dialogue of life, where people strive to live in an open and neighborly spirit, sharing their joys and sorrows, their human problems and preoccupations

---

[61] See GC 34, d. 5, no. 9.4.

[62] GC 31, d. 24, no. 8.

[63] GC 34, d. 5, no. 3; see no. 8.

[64] John Paul II, Encyclical *Redemptoris missio*, no. 56 (p. 304).

[65] GC 34, d. 5, no. 3.

[66] GC 34, d. 5, no. 17.

beyond those said for the founders, one or two or more Masses (according to the number of priests and their convenience) **should be ordered each week for the benefactors living and dead,**[5] [3]in which God our Lord should be begged to accept this Holy Sacrifice on their behalf and, in his own infinite and sovereign generosity, to requite with eternal recompense the generosity that they have shown the Society out of love and reverence for him.

[641]   *B. ¹As was explained in Part VI [565, 566].*

[642]   5. ¹Further still, the neighbor can be aided through the administration of the sacraments, especially the hearing of confessions (with some priests being assigned by the superior for this function *[C]*) and the administration of Holy Communion **{except in Easter time}**[6] in their church *[D]*.

[643]   *C. ¹Apart from those assigned as ordinary confessors, it will be up to the superior, as spiritual needs may arise, to decide where others should attend to the administration of these sacraments, and to make the appropriate arrangements.*

[644]   *D. ¹{Easter time is understood to mean the eight days before and after the feast. However, one may admit to Communion during this time persons who have received permission, pilgrims, and others exempted by the law, ²as well as those who have fulfilled their duty in their own parish and wish to communicate one or more times in our churches during these fifteen days}.*[7]

[645]   6. ¹In the church the word of God should be constantly proposed to the people by means of sermons, lectures, and the teaching of Christian doctrine, by those whom the superior approves and designates for this work ²and at the times and in the manner which he judges to be most conducive to the greater divine glory and edification of souls *[E]*.

[646]   *E. ¹Since on occasion it could happen in some places that it is inexpedient to employ these means, or a part of them, this constitution obliges only when the superior judges that they ought to be used. ²It indicates, however, the Society's intent in the places where it takes up residence, namely, to employ these three means of proposing God's word, or two of them, or whichever one seems more suitable.*

---

⁵ **Modified by** *CN* 413.

⁶ **Abolished.** (This exception no longer obtains, once the universal law of the Church was changed in this matter.)

⁷ (See note 6 to [642].)

"*b.* The dialogue of action, in which Christians and others collaborate for the integral development and liberation of people

"*c.* The dialogue of theological exchange, where specialists seek to deepen their understanding of their respective spiritual heritages and to appreciate each other's religious values

"*d.* The dialogue of religious experience, where persons who are rooted in their own religious traditions share their spiritual riches; for instance, with regard to prayer and contemplation, faith, and ways of searching for God and the Absolute"[67]

267   The Society must prepare members able to become experts in the third aspect of interreligious dialogue. Since this dialogue is becoming a global concern, such preparation should include an interprovincial and international exchange of persons and be done in collaboration with other groups.[68]

3. Ecumenical activity

268   Faith which does justice is necessarily committed to ecumenical dialogue and cooperation. Ecumenism is not only a specific work for which some Jesuits must be trained and missioned, it is a new way of living as a Christian. It seeks, namely, what unites rather than what divides; it seeks understanding rather than confrontation, it seeks to know, understand, and love others as they wish to be known and understood, with full respect for their distinctiveness, through the dialogue of truth, justice, and love.[69]

269   §1. In choosing the path of ecumenism, the Society is responding not only to its discernment of the signs of the times

---

[67] GC 34, d. 5, no. 4; see Pontifical Council for Interreligious Dialogue and Congregation for the Evangelization of Peoples, "Dialogue and Proclamation," May 19, 1991, no. 42.

[68] GC 34, d. 5, no. 11.

[69] See GC 34, d. 12, nos. 1–3; GC 32, d. 4, no. 37.

[647]   7. ¹The same may also be done outside the Society's church, in other churches, squares, or places of the region, when the one in charge judges it expedient for God's greater glory.

[648]   8. ¹They will likewise endeavor to benefit individual persons in spiritual conversations, giving counsel and exhorting to good works, and in giving the Spiritual Exercises *[F]*.

[649]   F. ¹*The Spiritual Exercises should not be given in their entirety except to a few persons, namely, those of such a character that from their progress notable fruit is expected for the glory of God. ²But the exercises of the First Week can be made available to large numbers; and some examinations of conscience and methods of prayer (especially the first of those which are touched on in the Exercises) can also be given far more widely; for anyone who has goodwill seems to be capable of these exercises.*

[650]   9. ¹They will also occupy themselves in corporal works of mercy, to the extent that the more important spiritual activities permit and their own energies allow; ²for example, by assistance to the sick, especially in hospitals, through visits and sending persons to serve them; by the reconciliation of quarreling parties; and likewise by doing what they can for the poor and for prisoners in the jails, both personally and by getting others to do so *[G]*. ³How much of all this it is expedient to do will be regulated by the discretion of the superior, who will keep always in view the greater service of God and the universal good.

[651]   G. ¹*However, it is not expedient that the Society, or its houses or colleges, should become mingled with any other association, or that such groups should meet on its premises for a purpose different from that proper to these houses or colleges in the service of God our Lord.*

[652]   10. ¹As much as possible of what has been said regarding the houses will be done in the colleges and in the churches belonging to them, according to the opportunity which the superior judges to be present, as has been mentioned.

[653]   11. ¹One who has talent to write books useful for the common good and who has written them ought not to publish any writing **unless the superior general sees it first** ²**and has it read and examined,**⁸ so that if it is judged apt to edify, it may be published, and otherwise not.

[654]   12. ¹What pertains to domestic offices and other more detailed matters will be seen in the rules of the house; hence nothing further will be added here regarding missions or the distribution of the Society's members in the vineyard of Christ our Lord.   ∎

---

⁸ **Modified by** *CN* 296. (In regard to the intervention of the general himself.)

but also to the repeated calls of the Church[70] and preceding general congregations.[71]

§2. To foster such work, superiors should see to it that some of our members are prepared as experts in ecumenical matters according to the requirements of different regions. They are to learn to grasp fully the doctrine and the spiritual life of both Catholics and other Christians.[72]

§3. In ecumenical activity Jesuits are faithfully to observe all the prescriptions and directives of the Holy See and of those whose duty it is to direct the ecumenical movement.[73]

4. Pastoral services and works

270   §1. Those pastoral works or services that have been initiated in the past are to be renewed and energetically promoted, provided they still fulfill the end for which they were intended and are approved by the hierarchy.

§2. According to the tradition and spirit of the Society, our members should also diligently look for new forms of pastoral services and works that answer contemporary needs, even those of other religions.[74]

§3. Our pastoral service ought to prepare Christian communities for carrying on dialogue with believers of other religions and help them experience God's compassionate love in their lives.[75]

271   §1. The Spiritual Exercises, carefully adapted in different ways, should be presented to every type of person insofar as individuals are capable of them, not excluding simple folk, in order to form Christians who are enriched by a personal experience of God as Savior and are led to an intimate knowledge of

---

[70] See especially Vat. Council II, *Unitatis redintegratio, Lumen gentium, Orientalium Ecclesiarum, Dignitatis humanæ;* John Paul II, Allocutions to GC 33 (Sept. 2, 1983), no. 6, and to GC 34 (Jan. 5, 1995), no. 5; Pontifical Council for Christian Unity, "Ecumenical Directory," *AAS* (1993), pp. 1039–119.

[71] GC 34, d. 12, no. 4; see GC 31, d. 26; GC 33, d. 1, no. 37; GC 34, d. 6, no. 20.

[72] See GC 31, d. 26, nos. 1, 8.

[73] GC 31, d. 26, no. 13.

[74] See GC 31, d. 27, no. 1.

[75] GC 34, d. 5, no. 9.9.

the Lord, so as to love and follow him more.[76] Thus wherever necessary they can play a constructive part in the reform of social and cultural structures.[77]

§2. The same thing should be done, as far as possible and with appropriate adaptations, for believers of other religions.

§3. Our members are to be trained to give the Spiritual Exercises in a true and correct way; others too among the diocesan and religious clergy, as well as lay women and men, are to be helped to do the same.[78]

272 Superiors should insist that

1° The directors of works sincerely adapt themselves to contemporary pastoral practice;

2° Our members have a high esteem for teaching Christian doctrine to children and the uneducated, in accordance with the tradition of the Society and the vows they have taken; for the promotion of new forms of modern catechetics and introduction to the faith by suitable means; for the giving of spiritual assistance in hospitals and prisons;

3° Our members cooperate with the program of renewal of both the Christian Life Communities and the Apostleship of Prayer.[79]

273 In accordance with the spirit of the Society, and especially in accordance with the repeated wish of the Church, residences should be encouraged among the more neglected groups of people. There our members should carry on their apostolate in different ways, with the special motivation that they are living their lives with the poor Christ.[80]

274 §1. Now that the discipline of the Church in regard to parishes entrusted to religious institutes has been changed,[81] the care of souls in a parish is no longer considered contrary to the

---

[76] See GC 31, d. 27, no. 2, 1°; *SpEx* [104]; P. IV, c. 8, no. 5, E [408–9].

[77] See *CollDecr* d. 221–22 (GC 24, d. 20, 4°; see GC 5, d. 46; GC 22, d. 23); GC 32, d. 4, no. 58; see P. VII, c. 4, no. 8, F [649].

[78] See GC 31, d. 27, no. 2, 1°.

[79] See GC 31, d. 27, no. 11, 2° and 3°.

[80] See GC 31, d. 27, no. 8; *CollDecr* d. [129], [263] (GC 28, d. 29, no. 8; GC 29, d. 29, no. 5); GC 32, d. 4, nos. 34–35, 47–50; GC 33, d. 1, no. 41.

[81] See CIC 538, §2, 681–82; CCEO 284, §3, 1°; 297; 543.

principles of our Constitutions.[82] In fact, under certain circumstances it can assist our mission of serving the faith and promoting justice as well as foster interreligious and cultural dialogue.[83] It belongs to the general to judge whether any particular parishes are to be accepted or given back.[84]

§2. Parishes accepted by the Society must be in accordance with its proper charism and mission; therefore, committed to the pastoral goals and policies of the local church, they also participate in the apostolic priorities of the Society and in the mission plan of the province, according to our way of proceeding.[85]

§3. Those who are appointed pastors must have special training, especially in such skills as homiletics, catechesis, sociocultural analysis, social communication, and conflict management. In addition, opportunities for contact with model parishes and appropriate pastoral-training centers must be available to them for ongoing formation.[86]

275 Worthy of particular esteem are apostolic labors among Eastern churches, whether Catholic or not Catholic, undertaken by our members by the will of the Holy See. Our members destined for this work should either retain or assume an Eastern rite, and houses and stations of an Eastern rite should be established in the Society.[87]

276 §1. All should have a high regard for, and be keenly mindful of, the mystery of the Heart of Christ in the life of the Church. It should be so much a part of their own lives that they can promote it among others in their every apostolic activity, as a most pleasant responsibility entrusted to the Society by Christ our Lord. In this way the results of our varied ministries may daily increase.

§2. They should also trust in the patronage of the Blessed Virgin Mary in their assigned tasks and activities, and everywhere

---

[82] See P. VI, c. 3, no. 5 [588].

[83] GC 34, d. 19, no. 1.

[84] See *CollDecr* d. 230, a (GC 31, d. 27, no. 10).

[85] See GC 34, d. 19, no. 3.

[86] GC 34, d. 19, no. 9; see CIC 521, §§2–3; CCEO 285, §1.

[87] See *CollDecr* d. [145] (GC 28, d. 32, 1°).

show more and more clearly the role of the mother of our Savior in the economy of salvation.[88]

5. Educational apostolate

a. General remarks about the educational apostolate

277 §1. The educational apostolate in all its ramifications, recommended in a special way by the Church in our day, is to be valued as of great importance among the ministries of the Society for promoting today's mission in the service of faith from which justice arises. For this work, when carried out in the light of our mission, contributes greatly to "the total and integral liberation of the human person, leading to participation in the life of God himself."[89]

§2. Our members can exercise this apostolate in various ways either in our own institutions or by collaborating with other institutions. The Society should have its own educational institutions where resources and circumstances permit this and where there is well-grounded hope for the greater service of God and the Church.[90]

§3. Those who work in schools of whatever kind or level or who are engaged in nonformal or popular education can exercise a deep and lasting influence on individuals and on society.[91]

§4. All educational initiatives of the Society must look to the plurality of cultures, religions, and ideologies as well as to local socioeconomic needs.

278 Keeping intact our preferential option for the poor, we must not neglect students expected to make greater progress and to exercise greater influence on society in the service of the neighbor, no matter to what social class they belong.[92]

---

[88] See GC 31, d. 27, no. 2, 2°; CollDecr d. 223 (see GC 26, d. 21).

[89] GC 33, d. 1, no. 44: see GC 32, d. 2, no. 11; d. 4, no. 60; GC 31, d. 28, no. 6.

[90] GC 31, d. 28, no. 5.

[91] GC 33, d. 1, no. 44.

[92] See GC 31, d. 28, no. 10, a.

279   §1. We must in a special way help prepare all our students effectively to devote themselves to building a more just world and to understand how to labor with and for others.[93]

§2. When dealing with Christian students, we should take particular care that along with letters and sciences they acquire that knowledge and character which are worthy of Christians, and that animated by a mature faith and personally devoted to Jesus Christ, learn to can find and serve him in others.[94] For this, it will help to establish groups of Christian Life Communities in our schools.

§3. Regarding all other students of other religions, we must take care throughout the whole course of studies and especially in the teaching of ethics courses to form men and women who are endowed with a sound moral judgment and solid virtues.[95]

§4. In our educational work we must sensitize our students to the value of interreligious collaboration and instill in them a basic understanding of and respect for the faith vision of those belonging to diverse local religious communities.[96]

280   In this new communications-media culture, it is of great importance to educate our students to a critical understanding of the news transmitted by the media, so that they can learn to be selective in personally assimilating such news. Therefore, our educators should be among the best-trained people in media.[97]

281   Young people who travel abroad for their education, as is common nowadays, should be attentively helped.[98]

282   For its part, the Society should help those many children of the Church who are being educated in non-Catholic schools, collaborating insofar as we are able, in directing Catholic centers for students, serving as chaplains, and also teaching in these schools.[99]

---

[93] GC 32, d. 4, no. 60.

[94] GC 31, d. 28, no. 12, a; GC 32, d. 4, no. 60; see P. IV, c. 7, nos. 1, 2 [392, 395].

[95] See GC 31, d. 28, no. 12f.

[96] GC 34, d. 5, no. 9.8.

[97] See GC 34, d. 15, no. 6.

[98] *CollDecr* d. [418] (GC 30, d. 51, §2); GC 31, d. 28, no. 15, a.

[99] GC 31, d. 28, no. 14.

283   We should continue to relate to and advise our former students, so that imbued with gospel values they may take their place in society and help one another in their respective tasks to work for its good.[100]

284   To foster a close collaboration with the laity in the work of education, we should hand over to them, as far as is possible, the roles they are prepared to assume, whether these are in teaching, in academic and financial administration, or even on the board of directors.[101]

b. Educational institutions of the Society

285   §1. Documents on our educational apostolate, elaborated by the Central Secretariat for Education and approved by Father General,[102] allowing for different local and cultural differences and adapted to the nature of different institutions, should inspire school mission statements, policies, teaching programs, and the entire academic milieu of the educational institutions of the Society.

§2. In order to ensure the proper character of our schools and a fruitful Jesuit-lay cooperation, it is altogether necessary to carefully select administrators and teachers, both Jesuits and others, and to form them adequately in Ignatian spirituality and pedagogy, especially those who will assume positions of major responsibility.[103]

286   In many places, primary schools can be one of the most effective services we offer to people, especially the poor, because they can provide a solid academic and religious foundation during the formative early years.[104]

287   §1. So-called nonformal education, by which both youths and adults are educated outside the traditional school system in both rural and urban areas of developing countries, is a very apt means to promote justice; hence, it is fully in accord with the mission of the Society and has greatly enriched it.[105]

---

[100] See GC 31, d. 28, no. 15, b.

[101] See GC 31, d. 28, no. 27.

[102] See "The Characteristics of Jesuit Education," Dec. 8, 1986 (*ActRSJ* 19:767ff.); "Ignatian Pedagogy Project," July 31, 1993 (*ActRSJ* 20:911ff.).

[103] GC 34, d. 18, no. 2.

[104] GC 34, d. 18, no. 3; see *CollDecr* d. 132 (GC 31, d. 28, no. 16).

[105] See GC 34, d. 18, no. 4.

§2. Cooperation is to be fostered between centers for nonformal education conducted by Ours and schools, universities, and social centers of the Society, since such cooperation is beneficial to all.[106]

288   §1. Secondary schools should improve continually both as educational institutions and as centers of culture and faith for lay collaborators, for families of students and former students, and through them for the whole community of a region. Our members should also foster close cooperation with parents of students, who bear the primary responsibility for education.[107]

§2. Where need or great utility suggests it, other schools, such as technical and agricultural schools, may well be opened.[108]

§3. In establishing coeducation in our secondary schools for the greater good of souls, ecclesiastical and civil norms existing in various places are to be observed.[109]

289   §1. Universities and institutions of higher learning play an increasingly important role in the formation of the whole human community, for in them our culture is shaped by debates about ethics, future directions for economics and politics, and the very meaning of human existence.[110] Accordingly, we must see to it that the Society is present in such institutions, whether directed by itself or by others, insofar as we are able to do so.[111] It is crucial for the Church, therefore, that dedicated Jesuits continue to engage in university work.[112]

§2. We must continue to work strenuously, with imagination and faith and often under very difficult circumstances, to maintain and even to strengthen the specific character of each of our institutions of higher education both as Jesuit and as university, and bring it about that both of these aspects always remain fully operative.[113]

---

[106] See GC 34, d. 18, no. 4.

[107] GC 31, d. 28, no. 18.

[108] GC 31, d. 28, no. 19, c.

[109] See GC 31, d. 28, no. 23.

[110] See GC 34, d. 17, no. 2.

[111] See GC 31, d. 28, no. 24, a.

[112] See GC 34, d. 17, no. 12.

[113] See GC 34, d. 17, nos. 5–6.

§3. Universities of the Society, participating in its mission, must discover in their own proper institutional forms and authentic purposes a specific and appropriate arena, consonant with their nature, for fostering the faith that does justice.[114]

§4. The complexity of a Jesuit university today can require new structures of government and control in order to preserve its identity and at the same time allow it to relate effectively to the academic world and the society of which it is a part, including the Society of Jesus and the Church. Periodic evaluation and accountability are necessary to judge whether or not its dynamics are being developed in line with the mission of the Society. Jesuits who work in these universities should actively involve themselves in directing them toward the objectives desired for them by the Society.[115]

§5. A Jesuit university must be outstanding in its human, social, spiritual, and moral formation, as well as in its pastoral attention to its students and to the different groups of people who work in it or are related to it.[116]

§6. Among the faculties of our institutions of higher learning, theology and philosophy should especially exercise their proper role, to the extent that they contribute to the greater service of God according to local circumstances.[117] Interdisciplinary work should also be promoted, which implies a spirit of cooperation and dialogue among specialists within the university itself and with those of other universities.[118]

290 The education of priests, as a work of the highest value, is to be considered one of the chief ministries of the Society. Therefore, seminarians who attend our universities are to be cared for with special attention, and directors and teachers chosen from among our best men are to be assigned to those clerical seminaries whose direction the Society has accepted. But if there is question of accepting diocesan seminaries, a definite agreement

---

[114] See GC 34, d. 17, no. 7; see d. 3, no. 21.

[115] See GC 34, d. 17, no. 9.

[116] GC 34, d. 17, no. 11.

[117] See GC 31, d. 28, no. 24, a, b; *CollDecr* d. [417] (GC 30, d. 51, §1); P. IV, c. 12, no. 1 [446].

[118] GC 34, d. 17, no. 10.

should be made with the bishop with the approval of Father General.[119]

291   Not only youth but adults also are to be educated both in advancements made in their professions and in steps that can be taken to make their conjugal, family, and social life more human and, where appropriate, more Christian and therefore just; they are to be educated also in what will serve to develop a better understanding of their own religious life.[120]

292   Our colleges and universities may have protectors, that is, friends who undertake to protect the work; however, names connoting jurisdiction should be avoided when and where these have no place.[121]

6. Intellectual apostolate

293   §1. Research in philosophy and theology, in the other sciences and in every branch of human culture is extremely necessary to fulfill our mission today and to help the Church to understand the contemporary world and speak to it the Word of salvation.[122]

§2. Ours whom superiors assign to this scholarly work are to give themselves to it entirely and with a strong and self-denying spirit, for in one way or another such work makes demands upon the whole person. They should know that they are making an invaluable contribution to the contemporary mission of the Society. At the same time they should do this in such a way that they do not lose touch with other apostolic activities of the Society and should cooperate with our members who are engaged in more direct social and pastoral ministries.[123]

294   Among all the ways of being engaged in the intellectual apostolate in the service of the Kingdom of God, theological research and reflection, when undertaken with the seriousness of research and the creativity of imagination that they merit, within the broad spectrum of Catholic theology and in the midst of the varied circumstances in which Jesuits live and work, have a

---

[119] GC 31, d. 28, no. 25; see CIC 681, §2.

[120] See GC 31, d. 28, no. 26.

[121] See *CollDecr* d. 216 (GC 1, d. 112).

[122] GC 33, d. 1, no. 44; see GC 31, d. 29; GC 32, d. 4, nos. 59–60; GC 34, d. 16, nos. 1–3.

[123] See GC 31, d. 29, no. 2; GC 33, d. 1, no. 44; GC 34, d. 16, no. 5.

special place because of their unique value to discern, illuminate, and interpret the opportunities and problems of contemporary life and thus to respond to the broadest questions of the human mind and the deepest yearnings of the human heart.[124]

295   In the elaboration and expression of our theological views and in our choice of pastoral options, we must always actively seek to understand the mind of the hierarchical Church, having as our goal the Society's objective to help souls. At the same time, we must try to articulate the *sensus fidelium* and help the magisterium discern in it the movements of the Spirit in accord with the teaching of Vatican II.[125]

296   The office of writer should be regarded as a ministry that is most profitable to souls and altogether appropriate to the Society; therefore, it is to be diligently encouraged by superiors.[126] Regulations enacted both by the common law of the Church and our own Institute with regard to the publishing of books should be exactly and fairly put into practice.[127]

297   We must never forget the distinctive importance of the intellectual quality of all our ministries.[128] Therefore we must all insist on the ongoing development of our capacity to analyze and evaluate our mission, which is indispensable if we wish to integrate the promotion of justice with the proclamation of faith, and if we hope to be effective in our work for peace, in our concern to protect life and the environment, in our defense of the rights of individual men and women and of entire peoples.[129]

7. Social apostolate

298   In the planning of our apostolic activities, in fulfilling today's mission of the Society in the service of faith, the social apostolate should take its place among those of prime importance. Its goal is to build, by means of every endeavor, a fuller

---

[124] See GC 34, d. 16, nos. 7–9; d. 4, nos. 19–24; d. 6, no. 12; d. 11, no. 27.

[125] GC 34, d. 11, no. 20; see Vat. Council II, Dogmatic constitution *Lumen gentium,* no. 12.

[126] See *CollDecr* d. 230 (GC 5, d. 9); GC 22, d. 20).

[127] See "An Ordination on Writings and Other Works Intended for Publication," *ActRSJ* 19:1016ff.

[128] See GC 34, d. 6, no. 21; ibid., d. 16, no. 1.

[129] See GC 34, d. 16, no. 3.

expression of justice and charity into the structures of human life in common.[130]

299 §1. The social apostolate, like every form of our apostolate, flows from the mission "for the defense and propagation of the faith and the progress of souls in Christian life and learning."[131]

§2. Moreover, all should understand that they can and ought to exercise the social apostolate in their spiritual ministries by explaining the social teaching of the Church, by stimulating and directing the souls of the faithful toward social justice and social charity, and, finally, by establishing social projects by means of the members of our organizations.[132]

300 §1. Provinces or regions should sponsor social centers for research, publications, and social action according to a plan that will seem better suited to the concrete circumstances of each region and time. They should be in close contact with one another both to garner information and to supply every kind of practical collaboration;[133] and in particular to identify and promote the liberating dynamics of the local religions and cultures, and to initiate common projects for the building of a just social order.[134]

§2. Social centers and direct social action for and with the poor will be more effective in promoting justice to the extent that they integrate faith into all dimensions of their work.[135]

301 §1. Our members should promote those things that, in the light of the social teaching of the Church, tend to infuse Christian principles into public life; they should not, however, become involved in partisan politics.[136]

§2. Whether any of our members, in truly exceptional circumstances, may be permitted to take some active part in offices entailing a participation in the exercise of civil power or in

---

[130] GC 31, d. 32, nos. 1; 4, a; GC 32, d. 4, nos. 40, 59–60; see also *CollDecr* d. [122–37; 258–63; 419–22] (GC 28, d. 29; GC 29, d. 29; GC 30, dd. 52–53).

[131] See GC 31, d. 32, no. 3.

[132] GC 29, d. 29, no. 3 (*CollDecr* d. [261]).

[133] GC 31, d. 32, no. 4, d, e.

[134] GC 34, d. 5, no. 9.7.

[135] GC 34, d. 3, no. 20.

[136] See GC 31, d. 32, no. 3; *CollDecr* d. [137] (GC 28, d. 29, no. 16).

political parties or in the direction of labor unions is for the general to decide; he will take into account the universal law of the Church and the opinion of competent ecclesiastical authority.[137]

302   In the entire course of our training, both theoretical (by serious study of the social sciences) and practical, the social dimension of our whole modern apostolate must be taken into account and members who are to be specifically destined for this apostolate should be chosen in good time and appropriately trained.[138]

8. Social communications

303   §1. The Society should acknowledge that communication is not primarily a sector restricted to a few Jesuit "professionals," but rather a major apostolic dimension of all our apostolates. Therefore, every Jesuit, in order to be apostolically effective, must be aware of and well versed in the language and symbols, as well as the strengths and weaknesses, of modern communication culture.[139]

§2. We must cooperate with the media, so that the Church's true face can appear and the Gospel can be inculturated in this new mass culture as well. Though we remain always loyal to the truth, our Ignatian sense of *sentire cum ecclesia* will lead us to present what is praiseworthy in the Church.[140]

§3. In no way detracting from the general formation to be given to all, according to no. 96, §2, in order that we may more efficaciously use the social-communications media in a way that is adapted to the needs and opportunities of our apostolate in fulfilling our mission, major superiors should in good time choose and assign some men endowed with a religious spirit and other gifts, so that after they have become expert at various levels of specialization and have acquired academic degrees, they may become competent in practicing these skills and in directing others.[141]

---

[137] See GC 32, d. 4, no. 80; CIC 672 compared with 285, §3, and 287, §2; CCEO 383, 1°; 384, §2.

[138] See GC 31, d. 32, no. 4, b, c; GC 32, d. 4, nos. 35, 44.

[139] See GC 34, d. 15, nos. 1, 3.

[140] GC 34, d. 11, no. 26.

[141] See GC 31, d. 35, no. 3; GC 34, d. 15, no. 9.

9. Interprovincial works and houses in Rome

304 §1. In the spirit of our fourth vow, the Society confirms its commitment to the interprovincial Roman works entrusted to it by the Holy See: the Pontifical Gregorian University and its associated institutes, the Pontifical Biblical Institute and the Pontifical Oriental Institute, as well as the Pontifical Russicum College, the Vatican Radio, and the Vatican Observatory, all of which are common works of the whole Society, placed directly under the superior general. Recognizing the very valuable service that these institutions have offered and continue to offer today, it calls upon major superiors who share Father General's responsibility for them to continue their help through subsidies and especially by training and offering professors and other personnel to them.

§2. Also recommended to the care of all the provinces are those other works or houses in Rome that render a service to the entire Society, such as the Historical Institute of the Society of Jesus and the international colleges of the Society in Rome.[142]

CHAPTER 5

OUR COOPERATION WITH THE LAITY IN MISSION

1. Cooperation with the laity in general

305 §1. The Society recognizes as a grace of our day and a hope for the future[143] the laity's taking "an active, conscientious, and responsible part in the mission of the Church in this great moment of history."[144] Therefore, we seek to respond to this grace by cooperating with them to realize their mission fully,[145] accommodating ourselves in our way of conceiving and exercising "our" apostolate.[146]

§2. In order to achieve this, all our members should become more keenly aware of the meaning of the state and vocation of the laity and their apostolate in the Church and the world,

---

[142] See GC 34, d. 22, no. 1; GC 31, d. 31, nos. 1–3.

[143] See GC 34, d. 13, nos. 18–20.

[144] See John Paul II, Apostolic exhortation *Christifideles laici,* no. 3 (p. 398).

[145] See GC 34, d. 13, nos. 1, 26.

[146] See GC 34, d. 13, no. 20; d. 6, no. 19; d. 14, nos. 12–13; d. 26, nos. 18–19.

according to the new teaching of the ecclesiastical magisterium.[147] By means of fraternal dialogue with them, we should make efforts to understand better their life, their ways of thinking and feeling, their aspirations and their religious mentality; and along with them we should strive to share our spiritual heritage, conscious that we can receive from the laity much to strengthen our own vocation and mission.[148]

2. Cooperation with the laity in their works

306 §1. The Society places itself at the service of the mission of the laity by offering them what we are and have received; namely, formation in our apostolic spirituality, especially—to the extent this is desired—the experience of the Spiritual Exercises and spiritual direction and discernment,[149] educational resources for developing their pastoral and apostolic capacities, and our friendship.[150]

§2. We intend to cooperate with them as true companions, serving together, learning from and responding to each other's concerns and initiatives, dialoguing with one another on apostolic objectives,[151] always ready to serve as counselors, assistants, or helpers in works that the laity promote.[152]

§3. For our part, this cooperation in these works should be in accord with the Society's criteria for the choice of ministries, especially service of the faith and promotion of justice and the other integral dimensions of our mission; our members should be missioned to this cooperative work with clear apostolic objectives and should remain in continuous discernment with their superior and apostolic community.[153]

§4. This cooperation requires from all of us formation and renewal, to take place early in our training and throughout our

---

[147] See GC 31, d. 33, no. 2; Conc. Vat. II, Dogmatic constitution *Lumen gentium*, nos. 30–38; Decree *Apostolicam actuositatem;* John Paul II, Apostolic letter *Mulieris dignitatem* and apostolic exhortation *Christifideles laici.*

[148] See GC 31, d. 33, no. 3; GC 33, d. 1, no. 47; GC 34, d. 13, no. 4.

[149] See GC 34, d. 13, no. 8.

[150] See GC 34, d. 13, no. 8.

[151] See GC 34, d. 13, no. 7.

[152] See GC 31, d. 33, no. 6.

[153] See GC 34, d. 13, no. 15.

lives. By means of this we will be aided both in understanding and respecting the distinctive lay vocation as well as in appreciating our own.[154]

3. Cooperation with the laity in works of the Society

307 §1. Cooperation with the laity in works of the Society, namely, those works whereby the Society realizes its mission, manifests Ignatian values, and in various ways assumes and retains "ultimate responsibility,"[155] must be guided by a clear mission statement that outlines the purposes of the work and forms the basis for collaboration in it. This mission statement should be proposed and clearly explained to all those with whom we cooperate.[156]

§2. Programs are to be provided to enable these lay people to acquire a greater knowledge of the Ignatian tradition and spirituality and to grow in their personal vocations.[157]

§3. We must not only fully observe the demands of justice toward those who work with us but also maintain a cordial cooperation based on love. We must open up to them in various ways a wide participation in, as well as responsibility for, the organization, implementation, and administration of our works, presupposing that our coworkers have assimilated the principles of Ignatian spirituality which inspire our mission; of course, we must also keep the power of ultimate decision in the hands of the Society where it has the ultimate responsibility.[158]

§4. Where these conditions are verified, a lay person can be the director of a work of the Society. When this is the case, members of the Society receive from the provincial their mission to work in the institution, and they carry out this mission under the direction of the lay director. In institutions where Jesuits are a small minority, special attention should be given both to the leadership role of lay colleagues and to appropriate means for the Society to assure the Jesuit identity of the work.[159]

---

[154] See GC 34, d. 13, no. 9.

[155] See GC 31, d. 33, no. 6; GC 34, d. 13, no. 11.

[156] See GC 34, d. 13, nos. 11–12.

[157] GC 34, d. 13, no. 12.

[158] See GC 31, d. 33, no. 6; GC 34, d. 13, no. 13.

[159] GC 34, d. 13, no. 13; see no. 20.

308   In order to foster the responsibility of the laity in the Church, the Society should examine at the proper moment whether some works begun by us might be turned over to competent lay men and women for the greater good of the Church.[160]

4. Lay associations of Ignatian inspiration

309   §1. Many lay persons desire to be united with us through participation in apostolic associations of Ignatian inspiration. The Society views positively this growth of lay associations. They give witness to the Ignatian charism in the world, enable us to undertake with them works of greater dimensions, and help their members to live the faith more fully. The Society encourages its members to study these various associations, to know them through personal contact, and to develop a genuine interest in them.[161]

§2. Among such associations the Society actively promotes and fosters with special care the following, and it encourages provinces to do the same: Christian Life Communities, Jesuit Volunteers and similar programs, Jesuit Former Student Associations, the Apostleship of Prayer, and the Eucharistic Youth Movement, recommended by the Holy See. This list does not in any way intend to exclude other communities or movements with which the Society has very privileged and fruitful links in a number of countries.[162]

§3. That so many persons share with us the inspiration of Ignatian spirituality as they realize their own lay vocation in the Church impels us to work with them more decisively, so that after careful discernment we may strengthen the organic bonds among all these persons and groups. Thus we will foster better communication and provide stronger personal and spiritual support among them and provide an example of the sort of specific contribution the Society can make to "the new evangelization."[163]

---

[160] GC 31, d. 33, no. 6.

[161] GC 34, d. 13, no. 16; see John Paul II, Apostolic exhortation *Christifideles laici,* nos. 29–31 (p. 443ff.).

[162] See GC 34, d. 13, no. 17.

[163] See GC 34, d. 13, nos. 21–22.

5. Closer bonds of certain laity with the Society

310   One possibility among others for the Society to cooperate with the laity in mission is to set up a special personal "juridical bonding" of certain persons, whether or not they form an association among themselves, for the attainment of apostolic purposes. Such experimentation is recommended, according to directions given by the general congregation, and should be evaluated in the future.[164]

---

[164] See GC 34, d. 13, nos. 23–25.

PART VIII

¹HELPS TOWARD UNITING THE DISPERSED MEMBERS WITH THEIR HEAD AND AMONG THEMSELVES

CHAPTER 1

²AIDS TOWARD THE UNION OF HEARTS

[655] 1. ³The more difficult it is for the members of this congregation to be united with their head and among themselves, since they are so spread out in diverse parts of the world among believers and unbelievers [A], the more should means be sought for that union. ⁴For the Society cannot be preserved or governed or, consequently, attain the aim it seeks for the greater glory of God unless its members are united among themselves and with their head. Therefore the present treatise will deal first with means towards the union of hearts, and then towards the union of persons in congregations or chapters. ⁵With respect to the union of hearts, some things will be helpful on the side of the subjects, others on the side of the superiors, and others on both sides.

[656] A. ¹*There are also other reasons, for example, the fact that they will ordinarily be learned men who enjoy the favor of princes or important persons, or of peoples, and so forth.*

[657] 2. ¹On the side of the subjects, it will be helpful not to admit a mob of persons to profession, and to retain only selected persons **even to be formed coadjutors or scholastics** [B].¹ ²For a crowd of persons whose vices are not well mortified is incapable of order and likewise of unity, so necessary in Christ our Lord for preserving the Society's well-being and proper functioning.

[658] B. ¹*This is not to exclude even a large number of persons suitable for profession or admission as formed coadjutors or approved scholastics. Rather, the injunction is against too easily passing as suitable those persons who are not, especially for admission among the professed. ²If what was stated in Parts I and V is properly observed, it will suffice;*

---

¹ Approved brothers are included with the scholastics; see CN 6, §1, 2°.)

PART VIII
FOSTERING UNION IN THE SOCIETY

CHAPTER 1
UNION OF MINDS AND HEARTS

311 §1. Our members fulfill their mission in companionship with others, for they belong to a community of friends in the Lord who have desired to be received under the standard of Christ the King.[1]

§2. It is our community-life ideal that we should be not only fellow workers in the apostolate but truly brothers and friends in Christ.[2]

312 Given the wide dispersion of our apostolic enterprises, the need for us to acquire highly specialized skills for highly specialized works, and in many places the need to make a distinction between our apostolic institutions and our religious communities, the preservation of unity of purpose and direction becomes a prime necessity.[3]

313 §1. Within limits imposed by our profession of poverty, communication and union among members of the Society should be strengthened in the following ways, besides those other useful ways already begun:

a. Gatherings of communities in the same city or region or in the whole province should be encouraged;

b. Task forces and workshops for reflection should be established in the provinces for each area of the apostolate or, where it can easily and usefully be done, also among provinces;

c. The superiors of each province and the provincials of each assistancy or major region should hold regular meetings.[4]

---

[1] GC 32, d. 2, no. 15; see GC 34, d. 7, no. 4.

[2] GC 32, d. 11, no. 14.

[3] GC 32, d. 11, no. 27; see ibid. , no. 4.

[4] GC 32, d. 11, no. 53.

such persons, even if numerous, would be considered a select group, not a mob.

[659] 3. ¹Since this union is produced in great part by the bond of obedience, this virtue should always be maintained in its vigor; and those who are sent out from the houses to labor in the Lord's field should as far as possible be persons practiced in this virtue *[C]*. ²Those who are more important in the Society should give a good example of obedience to the others, by being closely united to their own superior and by obeying him promptly, humbly, and devoutly. ³Thus too one who has not given much evidence of this virtue ought at least to go in the company of someone who has, for in general a companion more advanced in obedience will help one who is less so, with the divine favor. **⁴And even apart from such a purpose, a person sent with some charge can be given a collateral associate *[D]* if the superior thinks that he will thus better fulfill the task entrusted to him. ⁵The collateral and the one in charge will act towards each other in such a way that the obedience and reverence of the others is not weakened, and that the one in authority has in his collateral a true and faithful help and relief, for his own person and for the others who are under his charge.²**

[660] *C. ¹When experience reveals that some of those sent are not proceeding correctly in regard to obedience, either they ought to be recalled or a companion who is advanced in it ought to be sent to them, even though one was not sent in the beginning.*

[661] *D. ¹Even though the collateral associate is not under obedience to the superior or person to whom he is given, he ought to have interior and exterior reverence for him and to give an example in this to the others who are under his obedience. ²Similarly he should with all possible diligence assist the one in charge in all matters of his office on which his help is requested.*

³And even if not asked anything, when he sees that he ought to say something to the superior regarding his person or matters pertaining to his office, he ought to tell him faithfully and express his opinion with Christian freedom and modesty. ⁴But once he has presented his thoughts and reasons, if the superior judges otherwise, the collateral ought to submit his personal judgment and conform himself to the superior, unless he sees with great clarity that he is wrong, ⁵in which case he ought to inform their superior.

---

² (This office, used at times in the early Society, was never in use later, nor was it ever abrogated.)

§2. What especially helps toward fostering communion among all members of the Society is an attitude of mind and heart that esteems and welcomes each member as a brother and friend in the Lord, because "[w]hat helps most . . . toward this end must be, more than any exterior constitution, the interior law of love and charity which the Holy Spirit writes and engraves in our hearts."[5]

CHAPTER 2
COMMUNITY LIFE OF THE SOCIETY

314 §1. Community in the Society of Jesus takes its origin from the will of the Father joining us into one; it is constituted by the active, personal, united striving of all members to fulfill the divine will and is ordered to a life that is apostolic in many ways.[6]

§2. Our community is the entire body of the Society itself, no matter how widely dispersed over the face of the earth. The particular local community to which one belongs at any given moment is, for him, simply a concrete—if, here and now, a privileged—expression of this worldwide brotherhood.[7]

315 A local Jesuit community is an apostolic community, whose focus of concern is the service that Ours are bound, in virtue of their vocation, to give to people. It is a community *ad dispersionem,* since its members are ready to go wherever they are sent; but it is also a *koinonia,* a close sharing of life and goods, with the Eucharist at its center, and a community of discernment with superiors, to whom belong the final steps in making decisions about undertaking and accomplishing missions.[8]

316 §1. When community life flourishes, the whole religious life is sound; and unity and availability, universality, full personal dedication, and gospel freedom are also strengthened for the assistance of souls in every way.[9]

---

[5] GC 34, d. 7, no. 22; *Pream.,* no. 1 [134].

[6] GC 31, d. 19, no. 2.

[7] GC 32, d. 2, no. 16.

[8] See GC 32, d. 2, nos. 17–19.

[9] See GC 34, d. 8, nos. 21–22.

⁶The collateral should also endeavor to bring the subjects to agree among themselves and with their immediate superior as far as this is possible, acting as an angel of peace among them and getting them to hold the proper esteem and love toward their superior, whom they have in the place of Christ our Lord.

⁷The collateral should also report to his own superior, whether superior general or provincial superior, about whatever the latter enjoins on him, as well as about whatever may be enjoined on him by the one to whom he is assigned as collateral. ⁸Furthermore, he ought also on his own initiative to supply for the one in charge, reporting when the latter fails to do so because of illness, occupations, or other reason.

⁹On the other hand, the one in charge ought to observe certain things in regard to his collateral. ¹⁰First, seeing that the collateral is assigned to him not as a subject but as one to assist him and lighten his burden, he ought to have and show special love and respect for him, conversing familiarly with him so that he in turn may have more courage and ease in expressing his opinion and may see more clearly the matters where he can render help. ¹¹He should also strive to enhance the collateral's credit and get him to be loved by those under his authority, ¹²for he will thereby have in him a more valuable instrument in his dealings with them.

¹³He would do well to discuss with the collateral matters in which he finds difficulty, asking his opinion and urging him to say what he thinks even unasked, and to call his attention to anything that may come up regarding his person or office. ¹⁴Having heard what his collateral says, he will then be better able to make his own decision.

¹⁵In what pertains to his carrying out his duty of governing those in his charge, he should employ the collateral as a faithful instrument in matters of greater importance, whether general ones concerning the houses or particular ones concerning the individual brethren.

¹⁶He should likewise employ the collateral's help in what pertains to the superior general and is owed to him; and in everything except his authority he should look and rely upon the collateral as another self, in unity of spirit in our Lord.

¹⁷It should be noted that there are two principal cases where a collateral ought to be assigned. ¹⁸The first is when considerably more help is desired for the person being sent with the principal charge because of his lack of practice or experience in such government or other reasons, even though he is a man of highly approved desires and life for the greater divine glory. ¹⁹The second case occurs when one of those who will be accompanying the person in charge is looked upon as someone who

§2. Community life itself is a manifold testimony for our contemporaries, especially since it fosters brotherly love and unity by which all will know that we are disciples of Christ.[10]

317   §1. The more one is exposed to situations and structures alien to the faith, the more one must strengthen his own religious identity and his union with the whole body of the Society as represented by the local community to which he belongs.[11] Therefore, all our members, even those who must live apart because of the demands of their apostolate or for other justifiable reasons, should take an active part as far as possible in the life of some community.[12]

318   Every community of the Society should have its own superior,[13] who should maintain it in love and obedience.[14]

319   The following are necessary for fostering community life in the Society of Jesus: exchange of information between superiors and subjects;[15] consultation by which experts share their insights and all members of the community actively engage in the process of coordinating and promoting the apostolate and other things that pertain to the good of the community;[16] delegation by superiors in favor of their subjects;[17] collaboration of various kinds transcending every sort of individualism; a certain daily order;[18] a feeling for the whole Society on the part of its members that transcends local and personal limits.[19]

320   All should associate with one another easily, in sincerity, evangelical simplicity, and courtesy, as is appropriate for a family gathered together in the name of the Lord.[20]

---

[10] GC 31, d. 19, no. 4.

[11] GC 33, d. 1, no. 33.

[12] See GC 32, d. 11, no. 44.

[13] GC 32, d. 11, no. 45.

[14] See GC 32, d. 11, no. 29.

[15] See P. VIII, c. 1, no. 9 [673].

[16] See P. VII, c. 2, no. 1 [618].

[17] See P. VIII, c. 1, no. 6, G [667].

[18] See GC 32, d. 11, no. 47; GC 31, d. 19, no. 7, g.

[19] See GC 31, d. 19, no. 5.

[20] GC 31, d. 19, no. 7, c; see Vat. Council II, *Perfectæ caritatis*, no. 15.

*would be more helpful to him as a companion than under his obedience,
and who possesses the qualities needed for helping him.*

[662] 4. ¹To the virtue of obedience also pertains the properly
observed subordination of some superiors to others and of subjects
to superiors, in such wise that the individuals who dwell in a house
or college have recourse to their local superior or rector and are
governed by him in all things. ²Those who are spread throughout
the province refer to the provincial or another local superior who is
closer, according to the orders they have received; ³and all the local
superiors or rectors should communicate often with the provincial
and thus too be directed by him in everything; and the provincials
in their turn will deal in the same way with the general. This
subordination, when thus observed [E], will uphold union, which to
a very great extent consists therein, with the grace of God our Lord.

[663] E. ¹*When in particular cases the provincial superior thinks it more
expedient for the divine service that someone dwelling in a house or
college should be under direct obedience to himself, he may exempt him
from obedience to the rector or local superior. ²Similarly the general may
make certain individuals and local superiors or rectors directly dependent
on himself. ³But ordinarily, the more fully the aforementioned subordination is observed, the better it is.*

[664] 5. ¹Anyone seen to be a cause of division among those who
live together, estranging them either among themselves or from
their head, ought with great diligence to be separated from that
community, as a pestilence which can infect it seriously if a remedy
is not quickly applied [F].

[665] F. ¹*To separate can mean either expelling the person from the
Society altogether or transferring him to another place if this seems
sufficient and more expedient for the divine service and the common good
in the judgment of the one responsible for it.*

[666] 6. ¹On the side of the superior general, what will aid toward
this union of hearts are the qualities of his person [C], to be treated
in Part IX [723–25], with which he will perform his office, ²which is
to be for all the members a head from which the influence required
for the end sought by the Society ought to descend to them all. ³It
is thus from the general as head that all authority of the provincials
should flow, from the provincials that of the local superiors, and
from the local superiors that of the individual members. ⁴And from
this same head, or at least by his commission and approval, should
likewise come the appointing of missions. And the same should
apply to communicating the graces of the Society. ⁵For the more

321   The standard of living with regard to food, clothing, and furniture should be common to all, so that, poor in fact and in spirit, differences may be avoided as far as possible. This does not prevent each one from having what is necessary for his work or for his health, with the permission of the superior.[21]

322   Customs that are more suitable for monastic life are not to be introduced into our community life, nor those that are proper to seculars; much less should those that manifest a worldly spirit. Let our relationship with all other men and women be such as can rightly be expected from men consecrated to God and seeking the good of souls above all things, and such as includes a proper regard for genuine fellowship with all our members.[22]

323   Since our communities are apostolic, they should be oriented to the service of others, particularly the poor, and to cooperation with those seeking God or working for greater justice in the world. For this reason, under the leadership of superiors, communities should periodically examine whether their way of living supports their apostolic mission sufficiently and encourages hospitality. They should also consider whether their style of life testifies to simplicity, justice, and poverty.[23]

324   §1. To the extent possible, superiors should strive to build an Ignatian apostolic community in which many forms of open and friendly communication on a spiritual level are possible.[24]

§2. Taking into account the mission it has been given, every community should after mature deliberation under the direction of the superior establish a daily order for community life, to be approved by the provincial and periodically reviewed.[25]

§3. The daily order of the community should include, besides a brief prayer every day as mentioned in no. 230, occasionally a longer period for prayerful discussion;[26] when the will of God is seriously sought concerning the life and work of

---

[21] See GC 31, d. 19, no. 7, d.

[22] GC 31, d. 19, no. 7, e.

[23] GC 32, d. 11, no. 48.

[24] GC 32, d. 11, no. 50.

[25] GC 32, d. 11, no. 47; GC 31, c. 19, no. 5; f, no. 7; g.

[26] See GC 32, d. 11, no. 37.

the subjects are dependent upon their superiors, the better will the love, obedience, and union among them be preserved.

[667]   G. ¹*Very especially helpful, among other qualities, will be his credit and prestige among his subjects, as well as his having and showing love and concern for them, in such a way that the subjects hold the opinion that their superior has the knowledge, desire, and ability to rule them well in our Lord.* ²*For this and many other matters he will find it useful to have with him persons able to give good counsel (as will be stated in Part IX [803, 804]), whose help he can employ in what he needs to ordain for the Society's good proceeding in various different regions for the divine glory.*

³*It will further help if his commanding is well thought out and ordered; he should endeavor to keep up obedience among the subjects in such wise that the superior on his part employs all possible love, modesty, and charity in our Lord* ⁴*so that the subjects may be disposed always to have greater love than fear for their superiors, though at times both are useful.* ⁵*He should also leave some matters up to them when it appears likely they will be helped by this;* ⁶*and at other times he should go along with them in part and sympathize with them when this might seem best.*

[668]   7. ¹That the location may be favorable for communication between the head and his members, it can be a great help for the general to reside for the most part in Rome *[H]*, where communications with all regions can more easily be maintained. ²Similarly, for the greater part of the time the provincials should be in places where they can communicate with their subjects and with the superior general *[I]*, as far as they find this possible in our Lord.

[669]   H. ¹*He may visit his subjects in other places, according to the circumstances and necessities which arise.* ²*Likewise, he may at times live near Rome, in accordance with what is judged to be for the greater glory of God.*

[670]   I. ¹*What has been said about the general will hold true of **the provincial superior's visits**,*³ *namely, that he may make such visits when he thinks that God our Lord will be better served thereby;* ²*and it is something quite proper to his office.* ³*But when he must reside in a place for a longer time, he should if possible choose a location where communication with his subjects and the general is possible.*

---

³ (See *CN* 391, §3.)

the community, elements of true spiritual discernment in common can be included.[27]

325 §1. Each member should contribute to community life and give sufficient time and effort to the task. Only in this way can a certain "atmosphere" be created that makes communication possible and in which no one is neglected or looked down upon.[28]

§2. As far as apostolic work or other occupations for the greater glory of God permit it, all of us, "esteeming the others in their hearts as better than themselves,"[29] should be ready to help out in the common household chores.[30]

326 §1. As the most effective means of strengthening the sense of being part of one mission and of increasing the high regard we have for one another,[31] fraternal union and communication are to be fostered more and more among all our members (priests, scholastics, and brothers) by all the means that a discerning love may dictate.[32]

§2. To achieve more effectively the integration and participation of brothers in the common vocation and mission of the Society, important changes have been introduced in our proper law.[33]

§3. Communities that include priests, brothers, and scholastics are to be encouraged. If everyone in them shares in all aspects of community life, including faith, domestic tasks, relaxation, prayer, apostolic discernment, the Eucharist, and the Spiritual Exercises, more and more we will truly become "friends in the Lord." This sharing of life will help to build up communities of shared responsibility in our common following of Jesus and complementarity in the one mission. To make this sharing a reality among us, we need human and spiritual maturity and a better formation in interpersonal communication.[34]

---

[27] GC 32, d. 11, no. 23; see above, no. 151.

[28] See GC 32, d. 11, no. 49.

[29] See P. III, c. 1, no. 4 [250].

[30] GC 31, d. 19, no. 7, c.

[31] See GC 33, d. 1, no. 18.

[32] See GC 31, d. 7, no. 5.

[33] See GC 34, d. 7, no. 21.

[34] GC 34, d. 7, no. 11.

[671] 8. ¹On both sides, the chief bond to cement the union of the members among themselves and with their head is the love of God our Lord. ²For when the superior and the subjects are closely united to his Divine and Supreme Goodness, they will very easily be united among themselves, through that same love which will descend from the Divine Goodness and spread to all other persons, and particularly to the body of the Society. ³Thus charity will come to further this union between superiors and subjects, and in general all goodness and virtues through which one proceeds in conformity with the spirit. ⁴Consequently there will be also total contempt of temporal things, in regard to which self-love, the chief enemy of this union and universal good, frequently induces disorder.

⁵Still another great help can be found in uniformity, both interior uniformity of doctrine, judgments, and wills, as far as this is possible [K], and exterior uniformity in respect to clothing, ceremonies of the Mass, and other such matters, to the extent that the different qualities of persons, places, and the like permit.

[672] K. ¹In the case of those who have not studied, it is good to strive that all normally follow a single doctrine, that selected in the Society as the best and most suitable for its members. ²A person who has already finished his studies should also take care to keep diversity from harming the union of charity, and to accommodate himself in what is possible to the doctrine that is more common in the Society.

[673] 9. ¹Another very special help will be **communication by letter**[1] between subjects and superiors [L], and their learning frequently about one another and hearing the news [M] and reports [N] which come from the various regions. ²The superiors, especially the general and the provincials, will take charge of this, making arrangements so that each region can learn from the others whatever promotes mutual consolation and edification in our Lord.

[674] L. ¹The local superiors or rectors in a province, and those who are sent to bear fruit in the Lord's field, should write to their provincial superior once a week if facilities for this exist. ²The provincial and the others should likewise write to the general every week if he is near. ³If they are in a different kingdom where such facilities are lacking, both the said persons who have been sent to bear fruit as well as the local superiors and rectors will, like the provincials, write once a month to the general. ⁴The general will have a letter written to them ordinarily once a month, at least to the provincials; and the provincials once a month to

---

[1] **Modified by** CN 359–60. (In regard to particular determinations contained in [674–75].)

§4. To this end it will also be conducive

    a. To give brothers a share in consultations

    b. To observe what is set down about participation of brothers in congregations and about assigning to them offices of direction[35]

    c. In the future to use the term "brother" or "Jesuit brother," but not the term "temporal coadjutor," in our official or ordinary texts[36]

327 §1. Keeping in mind apostolic poverty and our witness to those among whom we must live, our houses should be made suitable for apostolic work, study, prayer, relaxation of mind, and a friendly spirit, so that our members will feel at home in their own house and so more efficaciously carry on our apostolic mission.[37]

§2. In our houses a certain part should be reserved for our members,[38] in which enclosure adapted to our mission is to be observed.[39] This is to be fully observed in houses yet to be built; in houses that have already been constructed, it is to be carried out as far as possible.[40]

§3. Ours should be mindful that a quite generous hospitality toward our own men rightly figures among the primary and most effective causes of mutual union among ourselves; therefore, our houses should never cease to be open and welcoming to Ours.[41] Our houses should also be open in genuine hospitality to others, especially to religious and to those who work with us, according to the customs in different places.[42]

328 No one should spend a notable period of time outside the house without the permission of at least the local superior.[43]

---

[35] See GC 31, d. 7 nos. 5–6; see no. 3.

[36] GC 34, d. 7, no. 12.

[37] GC 31, d. 19, no. 7, f; see GC 32, d. 11, no. 52.

[38] See GC 34, d. 8, no. 23.

[39] See CIC 667, §1; CCEO 541.

[40] See *CollDecr* d. 171 (GC 24, d. 220, no. 3).

[41] *CollDecr* d. 213, §1 (GC 7, d. 18); see GC 31, d. 19, no. 6, a.

[42] GC 31, d. 19, no. 7, e; see GC 34, d. 8, no. 23.

[43] See *CollDecr* d. 73 (see GC 16, d. 25; GC 18, d. 7); CIC 665, §1; CCEO 478.

the local superiors, rectors, and individuals where this is required; and more frequently from one side and the other as need for this may arise in our Lord.

[675]   M.   ¹So that news about the Society can be communicated to everyone, the following procedure should be followed. ²At the beginning of every four-month period, those under a provincial who is over various houses or colleges should write a letter containing only matters of edification in the vernacular language of the province, as well as another of the same tenor in Latin. ³They should send the provincial two copies of each, so that he can send one copy of the Latin and the vernacular to the general, along with a letter of his own stating anything noteworthy or edifying that was not mentioned by the individuals, ⁴and can have the second recopied as often as is needed to inform the others of his own province. ⁵In cases where much time would be lost by sending these letters to the provincial, local superiors and rectors may send their Latin and vernacular letters directly to the general, with a copy to the provincial. ⁶Also, when the provincial thinks it advisable he may charge some of the local superiors with informing the others in his province by sending them copies of what they write to the provincial.

⁷However, so that what pertains to one province may be known in another, the general will order that sufficient copies of the letters sent to him from the provinces should be made to provide for all the other provincials; and these provincials will likewise have copies made for the members of their own province.

⁸When there is much interchange between one province and another, like that between Portugal and Castile or between Sicily and Naples, the provincial of the one province may send to the provincial of the other the copy of those letters which he sends to the general.

[676]   N.   ¹For fuller knowledge of everyone, every four months the provincial should be sent, from each house and college, a brief list in duplicate of all who are in that house, and of those who are now missing because of death or some other cause, from the time of the last list sent until the date of the present one, with a brief account of the qualities of these persons. ²In the same manner, every four months the provincial will send to the general the copies of the lists from each house and college. ³For in this way it will be possible to have more information about the persons and to govern the whole body of the Society better, for the glory of God our Lord.

329   Solidarity among all communities in a province or region, which should also extend beyond their limits,[44] as well as fraternal charity require that communities be open to men of different ages, talent, and work.[45]

330   Particular norms, adapted to local circumstances, that are to be observed in the houses of a province or region can be determined by individual provincials or by a regional group of provincials, with the approval of the general; if they are published, all the major superiors to whom they apply should maintain them with equal vigor.[46]

---

[44] See GC 31, d. 19, no. 6.

[45] GC 32, d. 11, no. 51.

[46] See GC 31, d. 19, no. 7, h; GC 32, d. 11, no. 54, b.

CHAPTER 2

¹THE OCCASIONS FOR HOLDING A GENERAL CONGREGATION⁵

[677] 1. ²As we come to the union of persons which occurs in congregations of the Society, consideration must be given to the occasions on which they ought to assemble, which persons should assemble, who ought to assemble them, ³the place, time, and manner of their assembling, and the specification of what should be treated in the congregation.

⁴To begin with the explanation of the first point, namely, **the occasions on which the general congregation** and chapter **should take place:**⁶ It is presupposed that for the present it does not seem good in our Lord that such a congregation should be held at definite intervals [A] or very frequently; ⁵for the superior general, through the communication which he has with the whole Society [B] and through the help he gets from those near him, will spare the Society as a whole from that work and distraction as far as possible. ⁶Yet on some occasions a general congregation will be necessary; for example, for the election of a general, whether because of the death of the preceding general or because of any of the reasons for which a general may relinquish that office and which will be treated further on [774, 782].

[678] A. ¹*An example would be: every three or six years, or more or less.*

[679] B. ¹*This communication is maintained through letters* **and through the persons who should come from the provinces, at least one every three years from each province**⁷ *and {every four years from the*

---

⁵ (Note in regard to the rest of this part: *(a)* What is determined in this and the following chapters of this part concerning congregations is to be applied according to the determinations set down in the various formulas for congregations; namely, in the *Formula of a General Congregation,* the *Formula for Electing a Temporary Vicar General,* the *Formula of a Congregation of Procurators,* the *Formula for a Province Congregation: CN* 331; for many points from the Constitutions have been declared, modified, or abolished. *(b)* All **penalties inflicted by the law itself** [latæ sententiæ] contained in this part have been **abolished** by the superior general after General Congregation 31 by mandate and authority of that congregation—GC 31, d. 53 [*AR* 14:993]—on the occasion of the revision of the *Formula of a General Congregation* in 1973 [*AR* 16:142–78]. *(c)* Changes of a more procedural nature are not annotated here.)

⁶ (See *Form. of Gen. Cong.,* no. 1.)

⁷ **Modified by GC 34, d. 24, C, 2.** (A congregation of procurators will be held every fourth year.)

CHAPTER 3

UNION OF PERSONS IN THE CONGREGATIONS

331 What is prescribed in the Constitutions concerning congregations is to be understood and put into practice according to what is laid down in the respective formulas by a general congregation or by its authority (Formula of a General Congregation, of a Congregation to Elect a Temporary Vicar General, of a Congregation of Procurators, of a Province Congregation).

332 §1. With due observance of the prescriptions concerning the proximate preparation for a general congregation as contained in its formula (nos. 10–14), the superior general together with his general counselors should take care of all long-term questions and problems that refer to a future general congregation.[47]

§2. It is the duty of the superior general and the general counselors to see to it that these questions and problems, whether noted by themselves or indicated by province congregations preceding congregations of procurators, are put in suitable order and with the assistance of experts carefully studied and prepared for a future general congregation. When the time has been fixed for a general congregation, these questions and problems, together with the studies made about them, should be sent to all the provincials for communication in a suitable way to the province congregation.

§3. There should be a sufficiently long interval between all the province congregations and the start of the general congregation.[48] ∎

---

[47] See GC 31, d. 38, no. 1.

[48] GC 31, d. 38, nos. 3, 5.

Indies},[8] *having been elected by the votes of the professed and rectors of the province, to inform the general about many things. ²Through this communication it will also be possible to learn, when needed, the opinions of those throughout the Society whom the general will consider to have the soundest judgment. ³And thus, with those he has close to himself for purposes of consultation, he will be able to decide many matters without assembling the whole Society. ⁴For to a great extent the congregation is an aid toward making good decisions, either through the greater information which it possesses or through some more distinguished persons who express their opinion. In many cases it will be possible to accomplish all this without a general congregation, as has been stated.*

[680]   2. ¹The second occasion arises when it is necessary to deal with long-lasting and important matters *[C],* {as would be the suppression or transference of houses or colleges};[9] ²or with other very difficult matters pertaining to the whole body of the Society or its manner of proceeding, for greater service to God our Lord.

[681]   *C. ¹Long-lasting matters of any sort do not suffice for holding a general congregation unless they are also important. ²However, some matters of importance, even if not long-lasting, could suffice. The decision about importance will be left to the superior general. ³But when matters arise which are urgent and of great importance,* **so that the assistants to the general, the provincials, and the local superiors judge by a majority of votes that a general congregation should be held,**[10] *as is treated in Part IX [773, 786], it ought to be convoked; ⁴and the general should acquiesce and order the congregation to be held with great diligence.*

Chapter 3

¹Those Who Should Assemble

[682]   1. ²Those who should assemble in a general congregation are not all the subjects under obedience to the Society, nor even the approved scholastics, ³but the professed *[A],* and some coadjutors if it seems opportune in our Lord to summon them;[11] and

---

⁸ **Abolished by GC 26, d. 16** (*AR* 2:37.) (There is now no difference among provinces on this point; see *Form. of Cong. of Proc.,* n. 3.)

⁹ **Abolished by CN 402, §3.** (This is now in the ordinary power of the general, after hearing his council.)

¹⁰ **Clarified by CN 366, §§2–3.** (See notes 12 to [773] and 19 to [786].)

¹¹ **Modified by Form. of Gen. Cong.,** nos. 6–7. (Moreover GC 34, d. 23, A, 2, 1°, determined that formed coadjutors could be chosen as electors and

even from among all these, those who can come conveniently. ⁴Thus it is clear that those who are physically ill are not included, nor those who are in places very distant, for example, in the Indies, nor those who have in hand undertakings of major importance which cannot be forsaken without serious harm. ⁵This matter will be left to the judgment of the superior general if he calls the congregation, or of those who assemble in a province to elect those who are to come.

⁶By way of norm, **three will come from each province**¹² when the congregation is for electing a general or dealing with what pertain to him; namely, the provincial *[B]* and two others chosen by the rest in a province congregation which will be held for this purpose prior to the general congregation. ⁷In this province congregation the following will assemble and have a right to vote: **all the professed**¹³ who are able to come, the superiors of houses, the rectors of colleges, and the procurators, or those they send in their place.

⁸**When the congregation is held for other matters, the provincial may, without convoking a provincial congregation, select two members of his province, with the approval of the general;** ⁹**it will be up to the latter to determine according to the circumstances whether the provincial congregation should be held for the election of the two or whether the provincial superior should select them without a congregation, as shall seem good to him in the Lord.**¹⁴

¹⁰Those remaining will leave things to these three and to the general congregation *[C]*. ¹¹And if, in addition to these three, some individuals are named by the superior general, or if the provincial thinks that they ought to come, their status will be the same as that of the others. ¹²However, if the provincial does name any in addition to the three, they should be no more than two, so that altogether they are five at the most.

---

and substitutes for a general congregation, although there is a limitation on the number of them who can take part in it.)

¹² Modified by GC 33, d. 3, 1. (See *Form. of Prov. Cong.,* no. 60, §1; *Form. of Gen. Cong.,* no. 6, §1.)

¹³ Modified by *Form. of Prov. Cong.,* nos. 15–17, and GC 34, d. 23, D, 4–5.

¹⁴ Modified by GC 4, dd. 37–39. (See *Form. of Prov. Cong.,* no. 3, §1; province congregations are always held to elect those who will go to a general congregation.)

[683]   A. ¹*When the one holding the principal charge of the Society summons the congregation, he will determine whether some of the professed of three vows or some coadjutors ought to come for discussion of matters to be treated in the congregation.*¹⁵ ²*For it seems that this could be useful at times, particularly in the case of rectors and procurators from the colleges and other officials, who will possess a great deal of information about what pertains to their offices.* ³*In addition, these officials could hold active and likewise passive voice, except for positions of authority over the professed of four vows.* ⁴*If the congregation is held for the election of a general, no one who is not professed of four vows will have active or passive voice in that election.*¹⁶

[684]   B. ¹*That the provincial should come means if he is able. If he is unable, he will send someone else in his place whom he judges the most fit among three elected in that province congregation.*

[685]   C. ¹*Although those who remain behind may not send their vote in writing, if the subject matter was communicated to them they may express their opinion in writing; and those who go will state that opinion in the general congregation.*

[686]   2. ¹Of the professed who take part in the congregation, each one will have a single vote, and the general two; ²but if the number of votes is equal, the provincial will be preferred over the others. If there is a tie among the provincials, the side which is favored by the general (or if he is no longer alive, by his vicar) will prevail. ³For, since they have greater need of the divine assistance because of the charge they hold, it is to be hoped that God our Lord will bestow it upon them more copiously for thinking and saying what will be for his service.

CHAPTER 4

¹WHO SHOULD CONVOKE A GENERAL CONGREGATION

[687]   1. ²When the Society must convene to elect a superior general after the death of the former general, the duty of informing the other members will fall upon one of the professed whom the general before his death will have designated as his vicar in that respect [A]. ³Ordinarily this professed will be one of those who assist the general and reside with or near him. It will be his office to summon the Society for a specified place and date.

---

¹⁵ (See note 11 to [682].)

¹⁶ Modified by GC 34, d. 23, no. 2, 1°–2°.

[688]   A. ¹If none of the professed is present with the general and he designates one of those nearby, the same arrangement holds for him. ²But if, overtaken by death or an equivalent illness, he does not name a vicar, **the professed who are near him**¹⁷ (even though not living in the same place as he but in a neighboring one) will elect a vicar by a majority of votes. ³Whether the general has named someone absent but nearby or whether he has named no one, in either case **he who holds the principal charge in the house where the general dies or,** in case he dies outside a house of the Society, he who holds it **in the nearest house,**¹⁸ will immediately send word informing the neighboring professed that they should come, ⁴either to appoint a vicar (as was stated) or to recognize him who clearly was named. This vicar should hold the place of the general until a new one is elected.

[689]   2. ¹When the assembly is not held for the election of a general, in the other situations it is the general himself who should convoke it, except in the cases to be described in Part IX [782]. ²As has been stated [677], he shall not summon the Society frequently, but when necessity compels. ³Nevertheless, when the congregation does convene for the election of a general, it may, after electing him, deal with other matters which require consideration beyond that of the general and those who are with him.

Chapter 5

¹The Place, Time, and Manner of Assembling

[690]   1. ²The place to which the Society will be summoned for the election of a general should ordinarily be, it seems, the curia of the sovereign pontiff, where the general will more commonly reside, ³unless the members agree to meet somewhere else that is more convenient for all of them. This might be a central location amid the various regions where the Society is, or another which they think more suitable. ⁴If it is the general who is convoking the congregation to transact other business, he will be the one to select and designate the place which he thinks in our Lord to be most suitable.

[691]   2. ¹When the business is the election of a general, the time which will be allowed for assembling will be five or six months from

---

¹⁷ Modified by *Form. for Electing a Temporary Vicar General,* no. 3, according to GC 34, d. 23, B, 2–3.

¹⁸ Modified by *CN* 366, §2.

the date of the letters of notification; and this time may be prolonged according to necessity. ²When the members must convene
for the other cases, the superior general will designate the time
which seems good to him.

[692]   3. ¹The manner of assembling will be this. The one with this
responsibility should immediately, through several channels, inform
the provincials and any other individual professed who are to be
called, ²indicating as fully as he deems sufficient the reason, the
place, and the time of the congregation; and prescribing that
Masses and prayers be offered everywhere for a good election.
³Then the provincials, unless they alone will have to do the choosing, will have the duty of informing the professed and the rectors
and local superiors in their province who will be able to come.
⁴When those conveniently able to do so have assembled in a provincial congregation, they will choose by a majority of votes, with the
provincial having two votes, those who are to go to the general
congregation. ⁵These will be the persons who are most fit to take
part in the congregation and whose absence will cause less harm.
⁶As soon as they can they will depart for the designated place, after
making the proper provisions in their own provinces and appointing
a vicar.

[693]   4. ¹The superiors should also order that all those under the
Society's obedience should offer prayers daily, and be mindful in
their Masses to commend earnestly to God our Lord those going to
the congregation and whatever matters will be treated in it, ²so
that everything may turn out as may be for his greater service,
praise, and glory.

CHAPTER 6

¹THE MANNER OF REACHING A DECISION IN THE ELECTION
OF A GENERAL

[694]   1. ²When the congregation has convened that was summoned to elect a new general after the death of his predecessor, he
who has been given the function of vicar should address all its
members, four days before the election of the new general, ³exhort-
ing them to make it in a way conducive to the greater service of
God and the good governance of the Society. ⁴In addition to this
day, they will have another period of three days to commend
themselves to God and reflect better upon who in the whole Society might be most suitable for that office. ⁵They will seek to be

informed by those capable of supplying good information, ⁶but make no decision until they have entered and been locked into the place of the election.

[695] 2. ¹During this period each one will be obliged {under pain of automatic excommunication *(latæ sententiæ)*}¹⁹ to manifest to the vicar **or to one of those professed the longest,**²⁰ who will inform the vicar, if he knows that someone has directly or indirectly sought this office or is seeking it, either by trying to get it or by giving indications in that direction. ²One who is convicted of this charge **should be deprived of active and passive voice and thus disqualified to elect and to be elected;**²¹ and he should not be admitted to a congregation either on this occasion or any other *[A]*.²²

[696] A. ¹*For one charged with such ambition to be deprived of voice as someone disqualified, it would be necessary that he have been clearly convicted through the testimony of witnesses, or that the truth of the alleged offense has become sufficiently evident in any other possible way.* ²*However,* {*when the indications afford strong suspicion but not certain proof, the person will be unsuitable for election*},²³ *and an occasion ought to be sought to remove him from it; however, he will not be deprived of voice as though disqualified, and the suspicion should not be made public,* ³*much less so if it is found to be unsupported; for in such a case it must cause no detriment to the person wrongly charged, nor will he cease to be in the congregation and have voice like the rest.*

⁴*The one who must judge this case will be the vicar, after he has sought aid from three others of those professed the longest.* **The condemnation requires a vote of at least three.**²⁴ {***Those who vote inconsistently with their opinion will by that very fact incur excommunication***}.²⁵

---

¹⁹ **Abolished.** (In regard to the penalty, by the superior general in virtue of authority granted by GC 31, d. 53, 2°; see *Form. of Gen. Cong.*, no. 52.)

²⁰ **Clarified by** *Form. of Gen. Cong.*, **no. 54.** ("Judges concerning ambition are the vicar and the elector professed the longest from each of the assistancies except the assistancy of the vicar.")

²¹ **Clarified by** *Form. of Gen. Congr.*, **no. 56, §1.**

²² **Modified by** *Form. of Gen. Cong.*, **no. 56, §4.** (He should be deprived of active and passive voice only in any election of a superior general.)

²³ **Abolished by** *Form. of Gen. Cong.*, **no. 56, §2.** ("To pronounce that [sentence] moral certitude is required in the mind of the judge, certitude based on proved acts, about the sentence to be passed.")

²⁴ **Modified by** *Form. of Gen. Cong.*, **no. 56, §2.** (A condemnation cannot be pronounced except by a majority of votes, and in case of a tie a deciding vote is not given to the vicar.)

²⁵ **Abolished.** (In regard to the penalty, by the superior general in virtue

⁵*If the charge is brought against the vicar himself or one of the oldest professed, there will be four judges, always drawn from those who made the profession earliest, excluding the one charged.* ⁶*Any of these to whose ears such an infamous imputation has come should call the others to investigate it.*

[697] 3. ¹On the day of the election, which will be that following the three mentioned, the Mass of the Holy Spirit should be said, and all should attend and receive Communion.

[698] 4. ¹Later at the sound of the bell those with the right to vote *[B]* should be summoned to the place of assembly. ²One of them should deliver a sermon in which he exhorts them in a general way, with no suggestion of alluding to any individual, to choose a superior such as is required for the greater divine service. ³After all together have recited the hymn *Veni Creator Spiritus,* ⁴they should be locked inside the place of the congregation by one of the superiors or rectors or another member of the Society charged with this in the house where the assembly is held. ⁵They are enclosed in such a manner that they may not leave nor be given any food except bread and water until they have elected a general.

[699] B. ¹*Only those professed of four vows, as has been said [511, 683], will have the right to vote in the election of the general,*²⁶ *even if others are summoned to give further information where needed and to treat of other matters once the general has been elected.* ²*In these matters rectors and local superiors who are professed of three vows or formed coadjutors will, if summoned, have the right to vote, as was stated above* [683].

[700] 5. ¹**If all by a common inspiration should choose someone without waiting for the voting procedure, let him be the superior general,**²⁷ ²for the Holy Spirit who has moved them to such an election supplies for all procedures and arrangements.

[701] 6. ¹When the election does not take place in that manner, the following procedure should be followed. ²First, each one should pray privately and, without speaking with anyone else *[C],* make his decision in the presence of his Creator and Lord on the basis of the information he has. ³He will write on a piece of paper the name of

---

of authority granted by GC 31, d. 53, 2°; see *Form. of Gen. Cong.,* no. 56, §3.)

²⁶ (See note 16 to [683].)

²⁷ **Clarified by** *Form. of Gen. Cong.,* **no. 77.** ("And that [election] should be accepted, made in a way so clear and obvious, with no one abstaining, that by no subterfuge could its divine inspiration be denied.")

the person whom he chooses for superior general, and sign it with his name. ⁴One hour at most should be given for this. ⁵Thereupon all should assemble in their seats. ⁶The vicar, together with a secretary to be chosen for this purpose from among the professed and by another to assist [D], should arise and attest his wish to admit no one he should not, nor to exclude anyone. ⁷He should give to all general absolution from all censures for purposes of the canonical election [E]. ⁸After the grace of the Holy Spirit has been invoked, he should go with his companions to a table placed in the center. ⁹The three should request their votes from one another; and before handing it over each should pronounce an oath that he is naming the man whom he judges in our Lord most fit for the office [F]. The votes should be kept together in the hands of the secretary. ¹⁰Then they should request each member of the congregation to hand in his vote by himself and in the sight of all, similarly in writing and preceded by the same oath.

¹¹Afterwards in the presence of all the secretary should read the votes aloud, naming only the person chosen. ¹²Then the numbers should be compared with each other, and the person found to have more than half of all the votes is to be the superior general. ¹³Accordingly, {he who first named him, or the vicar, should ask the others if they agree on the one who has been chosen by the greater part; and no matter how they reply},²⁸ he will formulate the decree of election, saying:

¹⁴"In the name of the Father and of the Son and of the Holy Spirit. I, N., in my own name and the name of all those who have the same opinion, elect N. as superior general of the Society of Jesus." ¹⁵This done, all should immediately step forward to do him reverence; kneeling on both knees they should kiss his hand [G]. ¹⁶The person elected will not be able to refuse either the election or the reverence, calling to mind in whose name he is obliged to accept it. ¹⁷Then all should recite together the *Te Deum laudamus*.

[702] C. ¹*In their locked enclosure, all will preserve silence until the general is elected, in such wise that no one speaks to another about anything pertaining to the election unless it is something which he thinks it necessary to say, and that in the presence of all.*

---

²⁸ **Abolished.** (Since it is omitted in the *Form. of Gen. Cong.*, no. 82, §1. This inquiry seems never to have been used; see GC 1, d. 16 before the election—*Inst. S.I.*, II, 157—where no mention is made of it.)

[703] D. ¹During the four days before entering the locked room, all **the professed present**²⁹ in the place of the congregation will meet and choose a secretary and an assistant. Each professed gives in writing the name of the one he chooses. ²The vicar, together with the two longest professed, will publicly examine who has received more votes. ³In a tie, the three will be able to vote, and he who receives the vote of two of them will be the secretary and the assistant.

[704] E. ¹He absolves from all censures except those incurred through defects regarding this election.

[705] F. ¹The formula of the oath may be this: ²"With all reverence, I call upon Jesus Christ, Eternal Wisdom, to witness that I, N., choose and name as superior general of the Society of Jesus the one I think most fit to bear this burden." ³He thus swears to two things: first, that he is giving his own name as the one making the choice; second, that he is giving as the name of the person chosen the one he thinks most fit. ⁴He will then hand in his declaration in writing. Each one should have this formula of oath written on the outside of the paper containing his vote; and as he hands it to the three designated persons he should recite the formula aloud. ⁵The place where each one will deposit his vote, individually and in the presence of the others, will be the table in the center at which the vicar and his assistants are.

[706] G. ¹The vicar and his assistants will begin, or, if one of them was elected, the other two; the rest will follow.

[707] 7. ¹If no one receives more than half of the votes, another way should be taken, that of delegation to arbiters. From among all those present **three or five should be chosen as electors by a plurality vote**³⁰ *[H]*; **and whoever receives the majority of votes from these three or five**³¹ should be the superior general. ²His election should be proclaimed, the reverence should be paid to him, and thanks should be given to God our Lord, as is stated above [701].

---

²⁹ (See note 16 to [683].)

³⁰ **Modified by** *Form. of Gen. Cong.*, **no. 83, §2.** ("Electors, each from a different assistancy, are to be chosen from the electors by a majority of secret votes.")

³¹ **Modified by** *Form. of Gen. Cong.*, **no. 83, §7.** (A majority of votes is required; and, in addition, "if after three votes by these electors, no one receives a majority of votes of the electors, the Congregation is to decide what should be done.")

[708] *H.* ¹*The method of choosing these electors will be this. Each one should write down the names of those whom he thinks ought to be elected, and those receiving the most votes will be the electors.* ²*And as each one writes down the electors' names, he will take his oath, using the following form:* ³*"I call upon Jesus Christ, Eternal Wisdom, to witness that I, N., choose and name as superior general of the Society of Jesus the one whom the electors who have been constituted for this purpose will have chosen and named."*

[709] 8. ¹After the proclamation no one may change his vote or, once the election has been completed, attempt to have a new one. ²What has been stated should be observed by everyone who does not wish to be held as a schismatic and wrecker of the Society, and to {incur the penalty of excommunication *latæ sententiæ* [imposed by the law itself]}³² and other grave censures at the discretion of the Society *[I]*, whose interests require complete unity and conformity to the glory of God our Lord, as was stated above [701].

[710] *I.* ¹*The vicar after getting the opinion of the majority, or the one who has been elected superior general, will have the power to decree the censures which will seem expedient in our Lord.*

CHAPTER 7

¹THE MANNER OF REACHING A DECISION ABOUT MATTERS OTHER THAN THE ELECTION OF A GENERAL

[711] 1. ²When the business of the congregation is not the election of a general but other important matters concerning the state of the Society, the enclosure will be unnecessary, although an effort should be made to conclude whatever needs to be treated as speedily as possible. ³But since the light to perceive what decisions should be taken must come down from the First and Supreme Wisdom, ⁴Masses will be said first of all and prayer offered in the place where the congregation is being held as well as throughout the Society, for as long as the congregation continues and the matters it needs to settle are being discussed, ⁵in order to obtain grace to decide these matters as may be for the greater glory to God our Lord.

[712] 2. ¹Later the congregation will meet in one or several sessions. The superior general first and after him the provincials,

---

³² **Abolished.** (In regard to the penalty, by the superior general in virtue of authority granted by GC 31, d. 53, 2°.)

rectors, **and other persons summoned to the congregation**[33] will, in the presence of all, propose the matters which they think should be discussed, briefly giving the reasons for their opinions; ²and after they have seriously pondered all this and commended it to God our Lord, each one ought to put it in writing *[A]*. ³After he has spoken his opinion he may place his written text in the center *[B]*, so that those who wish to see it may state what they think in the following session.

[713] *A.* ¹*Those who come in the place of an absent provincial will speak in the same order as he would. ²However, the order to be observed is that the first to speak will be the one longest professed, from whatever province, who is a provincial or comes in the place of a provincial. ³After him the rest from his province will speak in the order of seniority from profession or of vows as a spiritual coadjutor. ⁴Then the longest professed among the remaining provincials will speak, and with him those from his province. ⁵After these, if there are any who are not under a provincial or who were called extraordinarily, they too will speak in the order of seniority.*

[714] *B.* ¹*He will place his written text upon the table which will be placed in the center. ²The secretary will be responsible for having copies made if necessary, or each one will bring already prepared copies of his arguments so that they may be read by those who are to express their opinion about them.*

[715] 3. ¹When the questions have been discussed from one side and the other during one or more sessions, if a solution in favor of one opinion does not become manifest and win **agreement from all or nearly all,**[34] then four definitors ought to be chosen by majority vote from among those present and having the right to vote in the congregation. ²These, authorized by the rest as arbiters,[35] will meet with the superior general as often as needed and conclude whatever matters are to be treated. ³Should they not all agree, the side

---

[33] **Modified by** *Form. of Gen. Cong.,* no. 116. ("Not only province congregations but all members of the Society can send postulates to the general congregation.")

[34] **Clarified by** *Form. of Gen. Cong.,* no. 126, §1. (Definitors of the first class cannot be elected unless the congregation by a two-thirds vote determines to do so; nor definitors of the second class unless decreed by a majority vote.)

[35] **Modified by** *Form. of Gen. Cong.,* no. 126, §3. ("The number of definitors should be chosen which is determined by the congregation.")

to which the majority inclines will prevail and the whole congregation will accept it as from the hand of God our Lord.

[716] 4. ¹If the superior general should not find himself well enough to handle all these matters, he could appoint someone else in his place. ²In this way the matters will be settled point by point according to the opinion of the majority, and the decision will be written down and read in the full congregation. ³**If even then someone thinks he ought to express his opinion, he may do so;**³⁶ but in the end he should defer to what is decided by the general together with the definitors.

[717] 5. ¹After the matter about which a difficulty was raised has been reconsidered and resolved in the aforementioned manner, the secretary will write the final decision in the book provided for this purpose and afterwards it will be promulgated *[C]*.

[718] *C.* ¹*The promulgation will take place before the whole house,*³⁷ *and subsequently throughout the houses and colleges. This refers to ordinances or statutes which were decided on to be observed in all places;* ²*for what pertains to a single college, house, or person need not be promulgated elsewhere, even should the matters not be secret. But if they are, much more ought their divulgence to be forbidden, under penalty of grave censures at the discretion of the superior general.*

³*The decrees passed in the congregation remain in force unless they are revoked in another general congregation, even if the superior general under whom they were enacted has departed this life.*

---

³⁶ **Clarified by** *Form. of Gen. Cong.,* **no. 128.** (Concerning intercessions, even after a decree enacted by definitors.)

³⁷ **Modified by** *Form. of Gen. Cong.,* **no. 144, §2, 1°.** ("Unless the congregation itself establishes otherwise, for the promulgation of decrees it is required and suffices that the superior general in the name of the congregation communicates them to the provinces for the purpose of being circulated to the houses.")

PART IX

¹THE SOCIETY'S HEAD, AND THE GOVERNMENT WHICH DESCENDS FROM IT

The text of the Constitutions begins on page 356.

PART IX
GOVERNANCE OF THE SOCIETY

SECTION 1
GOVERNANCE IN GENERAL

CHAPTER 1
POWER OF THE SOCIETY AND SUBJECTS OF POWER

333 §1. A general congregation alone has full legislative power.[1]

§2. To a general congregation is reserved the aggregation of an institute of consecrated life to the Society.[2]

§3. A congregation of procurators has the power in case of necessity to suspend a decree of a previous general congregation until the next general congregation, according to the norm of its formula. However, no legislative power, properly speaking, is within its competence.[3]

§4. A province congregation has no power other than what is explicitly given to it in its formula.[4]

334 §1. Superiors general can establish general rules, particular rules for specific offices, and ordinances for both a particular territory only or for the entire Society.[5]

---

[1] *CollDecr* d. 3, §1 (GC 4, d. 19; GC 7, d. 76); see *FI* of Paul III and Julius III, no. 2; Paul III, *Iniunctum Nobis*.

[2] See CIC 580; CCEO 439–40.

[3] GC 32, d. 13, no. 5; *Form. of Cong. of Proc.*, no. 2, §4.

[4] *CollDecr* d. 241 (GC 5, d. 2); *Form. of Prov. Cong.*, no. 31, §1.

[5] *CollDecr* d. 4, §1 (GC 1, d. 143; GC 7, d. 76); see *FI* of Julius III, no. 2; P. IX, c. 3, no. 20 [765]; c. 6, C [796].

§2. Without the consent of the general, provincials do not have power to make rules or ordinances binding an entire province for an indeterminate period of time.[6]

335 Even when they are absent, all superiors retain the jurisdiction they possess when present.[7]

336 §1. With due regard for the prescriptions of no. 345, §4, and those concerning temporary vice-provincials and vice-superiors in the Formula of a General Congregation, no. 8, §§3–4, and the Formula of a Province Congregation, no. 17, §1, 1° and 3°,

1° Vice-superiors who substitute for a superior in a stable manner (which, however, should not continue for a long time without necessity) have the same rights and obligations as superiors of the same title.

2° If a superior is not deprived of his jurisdiction but rather is prevented from exercising it by reason of sickness, absence, or some other similar reason, temporary vice-superiors exercise their office solely according to the superior's mind and, to the extent possible, dependently upon him; and they should consult him in matters of any moment.

3° However, if a superior is deceased or is completely deprived of his jurisdiction, the temporary vice-superiors have the same rights and duties as fixed superiors; however, they should make no changes in governance.[8]

§2. For those who take the place of local superiors according to no. 346, §§1–2, the prescriptions of §1, 2° and 3°, apply, according to the situation.

337 §1. Commands in virtue of holy obedience should not be given except for a very serious reason and only, generally speaking, after the consultors have given their advice.

§2. Commands imposed on an entire community retain their force even after the superior who gave them has died or has finished his term of office, until such time as they are revoked by his successor or by higher superiors.[9]

338 §1. Permissions and dispensations granted by major superiors are valid even though given orally; for the most part, how-

---

[6] *CollDecr* d. 4, §4 (GC 1, d. 143).

[7] *CollDecr* d. 248 (GC 12, d. 53, no. 1).

[8] *CollDecr* d. 249 (GC 12, dd. 35, 53).

[9] *CollDecr* d. 250 (GC 4, d. 3; GC 7, d. 72; GC 17, d. 12).

ever, particularly in the matter of poverty, they should be given in writing and they should be shown in writing to immediate superiors; those that have been granted in writing by visitors should be shown to provincials.

§2. As local superiors and especially provincials begin their term of office, they should caution their subjects that permissions of whatever kind granted by previous superiors must be made known to them, so that they can confirm them or abrogate them; after this announcement, those not made known before the deadline to be set by superiors are to be considered as automatically abrogated.[10]

339 §1. The Society is not accustomed to use its judiciary power unless the requirement of law compels it or unless in some truly rare case serious reasons make it advisable.

§2. Keeping intact the precepts of the formulas of congregations in regard to ambitious behavior, if ever it seems advisable to begin a judicial process, recourse must be had to the general, who, in keeping with the norm of the law and taking due account of the Society's privileges, will determine whether and how the matter should proceed.[11]

CHAPTER 2

APPOINTMENT OF SUPERIORS AND THEIR TERM OF OFFICE

340 §1. Such men should be appointed superiors who, first of all among other gifts of God, enjoy a good reputation and authority among their subjects so that they can promote their voluntary obedience, and so care for them that "they are convinced that superiors know them and both wish to and can govern them well in the Lord" and willingly agree to be guided by them.[12]

§2. A suitable consultation is always to precede the appointment of superiors.[13]

---

[10] *CollDecr* d. 251 (GC 23, d. 39; GC 7, d. 36).

[11] *CollDecr* d. 252 (GC 6, d. 45; GC 7, d. 94).

[12] See GC 31, d. 17, no. 4; see P. VIII, c. 1, no. 6, G [666, 667]; P. X, no. 8 [820].

[13] See CIC 625, §3.

341   §1. In the Society, superiors ordinarily constituted are of three categories:

1° He who is at the head of the whole Society and is called "superior general" (or general).[14]

2° Those at the head of provinces and regions (missions), who are called "provincial superior" or "provincial" and "regional (mission) superior."[15]

3° Those who are at the head of houses, and are called "superiors" or "local superiors" (by whatever other title they are called in ordinary life).[16] Similar to these is a "vice-superior" of a house not canonically erected and dependent on another house, according to the norm of no. 405.

§2. Those in §1, 1°–2°, are "major superiors."[17]

342   The following are constituted in extraordinary circumstances and for a time:

1° "Vicars of the superior general";

2° "Visitors";

3° "Vice-provincials," "regional (mission) vice-superiors," "local vice-superiors"; for a time these take the place of provincials or other superiors who have died, are absent, or otherwise impeded.[18]

343   Superiors are ordinarily constituted in this way:

1° By a general congregation: the superior general;

2° By the general: all major superiors and other superiors whose appointment the general reserves to himself because of the importance of their office;

3° By the provincial in virtue of a faculty habitually communicated to him by the general, but with his prior approval: other superiors.[19]

---

[14] See P. IX, c. 1 [719].

[15] See P. IX, c. 3, no. 14 [757]; c. 6, no. 6 [797].

[16] See P. IX, c. 3, no. 14 [757]; P. IV, c. 10, no. 3 [421].

[17] See CIC 620; CCEO 441.

[18] *Institute,* passim.

[19] See Gregory XIV, *Ecclesiæ catholicæ;* S. C. for Propagation of the Faith, Feb. 23 and Apr. 4, 1880; P. IV, c. 10, no. 3 [421]; c. 17, no. 1 [490]; P. IX, c. 3, nos. 3, 14, 15 [740, 757, 759]; c. 5, no. 1 [778]; GC

344   §1. For anyone to be validly appointed a major superior in the Society, he must have been professed of four vows after having spent the period of time in the Society that our law requires, according to no. 119.[20]

§2. From those professed of four vows must also be chosen the vicar general, temporary vice-provincials, and vice-superiors of regions (missions).[21]

345   §1. A provincial superior of a province or superior of a region (mission) who is going to be away from the province or region (mission) or who is seriously ill or has some other similar reason can name a temporary vice-provincial or vice-superior if the general has not designated anyone.

§2. If a provincial superior of a province or a superior of a region (mission) dies without designating a vice-provincial or vice-superior, then until the general makes provision his place will be taken by

1° The socius, if he is professed of four vows

2° If the socius is not professed of four vows, the one who has been province consultor for the longest time and is also professed of four vows

3° If even in this way no provision can be made, then the superior appointed by the general who has been in office for the longest time and is professed of four vows

§3. In the instances in §2, 2° and 3°, if more than one made their profession on the same day, the one older in religion is to be chosen, then the one more advanced in age.

§4. What is said about certain superiors in §2, 3°, applies also to vice-superiors of the same name, provided they are appointed by the general on a stable basis.[22]

346   §1. The minister of the house, if he is a priest, takes the place of the local superior when the latter is absent, impeded by illness, or has died; if the minister is also absent or impeded, then the house consultor who is longest in office and who is a priest

---

32, d. 14, no. 7, a.

[20] See CIC 623; CCEO 513, §1.

[21] See *CollDecr* d. 244 (GC 4, d. 32).

[22] See *CollDecr* d. 242 (see GC 9, d. 35).

will take his place. However, local superiors are permitted to substitute some other priest than the minister for themselves if some particular reason urges it and if the provincial cannot be informed in time to provide for the case; but they have the obligation of referring the matter as soon as possible to the provincial.[23]

§2. When a member who is not a priest is appointed minister of the house, at the same time a priest is to be designated by the provincial to take the place of the superior when he is absent, impeded by illness, or has died, whose duty it will be to care for those matters requiring the power of orders or the power of ecclesiastical governance.[24] If such an acting superior was not designated and cannot in an urgent case be constituted by the superior himself, or if he is absent, then the priest consultor who has been longest in office takes his place until the provincial makes provision.

§3. If it seems that a superior of a house who is ordinarily appointed by the general ought to be changed and immediately deprived of jurisdiction and the matter cannot be referred to the general, the provincial can appoint a temporary vice-superior until the general has been informed and provides for the case.

347 §1. The authority of superiors of lesser rank than the general begins from the time officially designed for the beginning of their office, even if they happen to be absent. In extraordinary cases, however, the appropriate superiors are to provide for them.[25]

§2. Unless a legitimate superior decides something else, the authority of these superiors does not cease until that of the successor begins.[26]

348 §1. With due regard for the special norms that pertain to the superior general,[27] the assistants for provident care,[28] and the

---

[23] See *CollDecr* d. 243 (GC 8, d. 20; GC 17, d. 9; see GC 12, d. 17, no. 1).

[24] See CIC 274, §1; 129, §1; 588, §2; CCEO 979, §1.

[25] See *CollDecr* d. 246, §1 (GC 8, d. 43; GC 19, d. 9; GC 9, d. 10).

[26] *CollDecr* d. 246, §2 (GC 17, d. 7).

[27] See GC 31, d. 41, no. 1; P. IX, c. 1 [719–22]; Paul V, *Quantum religio*.

[28] GC 31, d. 23, E, III, 1; see *CN*, no. 376, §§1–5.

general's admonitor,[29] a strictly determined duration of office is not assigned to any superior or official of the Society.[30]

§2. Provincials according to the Constitutions and local superiors as a matter of practice usually hold office for three years, but in such a way that they do not need confirmation to continue their office beyond three years; they can, however, be removed from office at any time. It is to be hoped that local superiors will not continue to hold office for too long a period.[31]

CHAPTER 3

COMMON OBLIGATIONS OF SUPERIORS[32]

349 §1. After the example of Christ, whose place they hold, superiors should exercise their authority in a spirit of service, desiring not to be served but to serve. Government in the Society should always be spiritual, whereby superiors direct our members with discerning love rather than through external laws, conscious before God of personal responsibility and of the obligation to rule their subjects as sons of God and with regard for the human personality. Government should also be strong where it needs to be, open and sincere.[33]

§2. Superiors should devote themselves with a true sense of responsibility to the task of government entrusted to them, not seeking to avoid making plans or decisions by themselves, but with a courageous spirit embarking on great undertakings for the divine service and remaining constant in carrying them out.[34]

350 §1. It is the role of superiors to promote the mission of the Society[35] and observance of the Institute, and to apply it to indi-

---

[29] See *CollDecr* d. 272, §2 (GC 3, d. 42; GC 4, d. 24; GC 6, d. 27, no. 2; GC 17, d. 8).

[30] *CollDecr* d. 247, §1 (GC 2, d. 68; GC 5, d. 35).

[31] *CollDecr* d. 247, §§2, 3 (see GC 2, d. 68; GC 12, d. 30; GC 5, d. 16); see P. IX, c. 3, no. 4, I [757–58].

[32] See "Some General Norms for the Use of Provincials and Local Superiors to Foster Better Governance," Oct. 8, 1975 (*ActRSJ* 16:561–610).

[33] GC 31, d. 17, no. 4; see also 8.

[34] GC 31, d. 46, no. 2; see P. IX, c. 2, no. 5 [728].

[35] See GC 32, d. 11, no. 29.

viduals as circumstances require. In order to do this, they should especially set an example to their subjects as a living norm by which others are constantly drawn to fidelity and generosity in the service of the Lord.

§2. Religious discipline in the Society supposes and produces mature obedient Christian men, superiors as well as members. It is the task of superiors diligently to search for the will of God, also making use of the help of others in regard to the more appropriate means, to decide what is to be done,[36] and to express it definitively in words.[37]

§3. Their greatest duty is to guide all their subjects, especially the younger ones, to ever increasing responsibility and freedom, so that they observe the provisions of our institute not in the spirit of fear[38] but from an intimate personal conviction rooted in faith and charity.[39] Therefore, they should promote religious discipline both paternally and forcefully; they should warn and if necessary correct those who neglect or violate it— even those who are older and respected, and even superiors if they are deficient in their office.[40]

351 Superiors should reckon their governance of our members, both as a community and as individuals, more important than any other tasks.[41]

352 In the exercise of authority, the gift of discretion or of discerning love is most desirable.[42] To acquire this virtue, the superior should be free from ill-ordered affections[43] and be closely united and familiar with God,[44] so that he will be docile to the will of Christ, which he should seek out with his subjects and authoritatively make manifest to them. He ought to know thoroughly our way of proceeding according to our Institute, and he

---

[36] See Vat. Council II, *Perfectæ caritatis,* no. 14.

[37] See GC 31, d. 17, no. 6.

[38] See P. VI, c. 1, no. 1 [547]; c. 5 [602].

[39] See GC 31, d. 19, no. 12.

[40] See *CollDecr* d. 254 (GC 20, d. 16; GC 21, d. 27).

[41] GC 31, d. 17, no. 4.

[42] See P. I, c. 2, no. 13 [161]; P. II, c. 3, A [219]; P. III, c. 1, no. 15 [269]; P. IV, c. 10, no. 4 [423]; P. VII, c. 2, F [624]; P. IX, c. 2, no. 3 [726].

[43] See P. II, c. 3, no. 4 [222]; P. IX, c. 2, no. 3 [726].

[44] See P. IX, c. 2, no. 1 [723].

should command the things that he knows will contribute towards attaining the end proposed by God and the Society,[45] keeping in mind persons, places, times, and other circumstances.[46]

353 The superior should endeavor to make his mind clearly known to his confreres and understood by them; and he should take care that they, according to the nature and importance of the matter and in proportion to their own talents and duties, share more fully in his knowledge and concern both for the personal and community life of our members and for their apostolic labors.[47]

354 §1. Superiors should readily and often ask for and listen to the counsel of their brethren, of a few or of many, or even of all gathered together, according to the importance and nature of the matter, and even by means of spiritual discernment carried out in common (according to no. 151, §2). They should gratefully welcome suggestions that their brothers offer spontaneously, but the duty of superiors themselves to decide and enjoin what ought to be done remains intact.[48]

§2. "Directors of works," of whom nos. 406 and 407 speak, should do the same; they should be altogether alert to the advice and suggestions of their brethren, so as to be helped by them in carrying out their offices.[49]

§3. It is also advantageous to the Society that the superior leave much to the prudence of his confreres, and that he allow them suitable freedom in the Lord to the extent that they have made the spirit of the Society their own, especially if they are men long proven in humility and self-denial. And finally, the universal good itself will sometimes demand that, in the manner of urging what has been commanded, those in charge should also take human frailty into account.[50]

---

[45] See *FI* of Paul III and Julius III, no. 2.

[46] See GC 31, d. 17, no. 5; P. X, c. 2, no. 3 [726].

[47] See GC 31, d. 17, no. 8.

[48] See GC 31, d. 17, no. 6.

[49] GC 32, d. 11, no. 29.

[50] See GC 31, d. 17, no. 7.

§4. All superiors should work together with the general and all officials with local superiors, in order to encourage implementation of what has been decided, in such a way that all will understand that there is in the Society but a single, identical spirit.[51]

CHAPTER 4

ASSISTANCE GIVEN TO SUPERIORS BY CONSULTORS AND OTHER OFFICIALS

355   §1. In order that they may more easily discover the will of God, all superiors should have their own consultors and should often hear their opinions, ordinarily when all are gathered for a common consultation. They should also use the service of experts in reaching decisions on complex matters.[52]

§2. However, in the Society the consent or advice of consultors is never required in order to act validly, apart from those particular cases specified in the law;[53] but superiors should not act against the unanimous advice of their consultors without the approval of their major superior.[54]

356   §1. With due regard to what pertains to the general counselors and the general's admonitor, consultors and admonitors of other superiors are appointed by the immediate higher superior of the one whose consultors and admonitors they are.

§2. In order that members may take an effective part in the selection of consultors of the house and of the province,

1° Generally at the time of his visitation of the houses, the major superior should inquire into the opinion of members of the community concerning the current or prospective consultors.

2° In their official letters to the general and after hearing the views of their own consultors and other members of the community, local superiors are to submit their opinion of the province consultors. If the present consultors are not satisfactory,

---

[51] *CollDecr* d. 256 (GC 6, d. 37, no. 4); see P. VIII, c. 1, nos. 4, 6 [662, 666].

[52] See GC 31, d. 17, no. 6; P. IV, c. 10, no. 7 [431]; P. IX, c. 6, nos. 10, 14, F, I [803, 804, 810, 811].

[53] See Gregory XIV, *Ecclesiæ catholicæ;* Pius XI, *Paterna caritas;* P. IX, c. 6, no. 14 [810].

[54] See P. IV, c. 17, H [503].

they should indicate others who may seem to be suited for this position.[55]

357 Superiors should show justified severity towards those who inappropriately communicate to others what occurred in a consultation, even to the point of their being removed as consultors, if necessary.[56]

358 §1. With due regard to what is said about the socius of major superiors in no. 393, other officials of the provincial curia are appointed by the provincial himself; but the province treasurer and the revisor of the *arcas* of the province are to be approved by the general.

§2. All stable officials of the houses (minister, treasurer, spiritual director) are appointed by the provincial, with the exception of those whose appointment he has left to the local superior. The tertian instructor and novice director are to be approved by the general.[57]

CHAPTER 5

OFFICIAL LETTERS AND OTHER DOCUMENTS

359 It is up to the superior general according to changing circumstances to determine the norms for writing official letters, as well as letters or news for spiritual edification and catalogues that are to be prepared.[58]

360 It is also up to the general to make determinations regarding confidential information to be obtained before superiors take certain decisions concerning persons.[59]

361 Those who reveal confidential information are to be reproved according to the gravity of the deed.[60]

---

[55] GC 31, d. 47.

[56] *CollDecr* d. 257 (GC 7, d. 99; GC 8, d. 45).

[57] See P. IV, c. 10, no. 6 [428].

[58] See *CollDecr* d. 291 (GC 3, d. 33); P. VIII, d. 1, no. 9, L [673–74]; P. IX, c. 6 A, no. 3 [790, 792].

[59] See *CollDecr* d. 258, §1 (GC 7, d. 98; GC 8, d. 45; GC 9, d. 37), see P. V, c. 2, no. 1 [516]; P. IX, c. 3, A [737].

[60] See *CollDecr* d. 258, §3 (GC 7, d. 23).

CHAPTER 1
²THE NEED OF A SUPERIOR GENERAL AND HIS LIFELONG TERM OF OFFICE

[719] ³In all well-organized communities or congregations there must be, besides the persons who take care of their particular goals, one or several whose proper duty is to attend to the universal good. ⁴So too in this Society, in addition to those who have charge of individual houses or colleges and of the individual provinces where the Society has these houses or colleges, there must be someone with responsibility for the entire body of the Society, ⁵a person whose duty is the good government, preservation, and growth of the whole body of the Society. This person is the superior general. ⁶While he could be elected in either of two ways, namely, for a fixed period or for his whole life, ⁷nevertheless, since experience and practice in government, a knowledge of the individual members *[A]*, and the enjoyment of authority with them *[B]* constitute a great aid in performing this office well, **his election will be for life and not for a fixed period.**¹ ⁸In this way too, the Society, which is commonly occupied with important matters in the divine service, will be less wearied and distracted by general congregations *[C]*.

[720] A. ¹*Besides the reasons mentioned in this constitution, there are still others for having a general who is elected for life.* ²*One is that thoughts and occasions of ambition, which is the pestilence of such offices, will be banished farther than if the general were to be elected at specified intervals.*

³*Another reason is that it is easier to find one capable person for this charge than many.*

⁴*Still another reason is the example of the common practice among the more important governmental offices, which are held for life. So it is with the pope and bishops among churchmen and with princes and lords among laymen.* ⁵*With regard to certain disadvantages which could ensue from holding such a charge for life, the remedy will be treated below in Chapter 4 [773–77].*

[721] B. ¹*The superior's authority will be greater if he cannot be changed than if he is elected for one or a few years: greater with the externs because he will be better known by all, and greater with the*

---

¹ **Clarified by** *CN* **362, 366.** (Concerning possible resignation of a general and his possible substitution in case of grave and perpetual incapacity for governing the Society.)

SECTION 2

GOVERNANCE OF THE WHOLE SOCIETY

CHAPTER 1

THE OFFICE OF SUPERIOR GENERAL

362 §1. Although the superior general is elected for life and not for any determined time,[61] he may nonetheless in good conscience and by law resign from his office for a grave reason that would render him permanently unequal to the labors of his post.[62]

§2. When the superior general, either of his own accord but after consultation with the assistants for provident care, or after he has been so advised by them, will have judged that it is proper to resign his office, he should ask these assistants and the provincials of the whole Society to take a secret vote on the seriousness of the causes. These votes should all be counted in the presence of the assistants for provident care and the secretary of the Society. If a majority judges that a general congregation ought to be convoked for the purpose of making provision for the supreme government of the Society, the superior general ought then to summon it.[63]

§3. But if a majority does not so judge, it is left entirely to the superior general to do what in conscience seems best to him according to our Institute.

§4. When a general congregation is in session for other business, the general may propose his resignation to it, for a grave reason that would render him permanently unequal to the labors of his post and after consultation with the assistants for provident care.

§5. The superior general's resignation from office does not take effect until it has been accepted by the Society in a general congregation.[64]

Text of the Norms resumes on page 367.

---

[61] See P. IX, c. 1 [719].

[62] *CollDecr* d. 260, §1 (GC 31, d. 41, no. 2, §1).

[63] *CollDecr* d. 260, §4 (GC 31, d. 41, no. 2, §4).

[64] *CollDecr* d. 260, §5 (GC 31, d. 41, no. 2, §5).

members of the Society for the same reason. ²*On the contrary, the knowl-edge that he must relinquish his office and be equal or inferior to the others, as also his being new in the office, can lessen his authority.*

[722]   C.   ¹*It is certain that congregations of the whole Society will occur less frequently if the superior general holds office for life. For the majority of congregations will be convoked to elect him, and other occasions will be few.*

CHAPTER 2
¹THE KIND OF PERSON THE SUPERIOR GENERAL OUGHT TO BE

[723]   1.   ²In regard to the qualities which are desirable in the superior general [A], the first is that he should be closely united with God our Lord and have familiarity with him in prayer and in all his operations, ³so that from him, the fountain of all good, he may so much the better obtain for the whole body of the Society a large share of his gifts and graces, as well as great power and effective-ness for all the means to be employed for the help of souls.

[724]   A.   ¹*The six qualities treated in this chapter are the most impor-tant, the rest being reduced to them.* ²*For they comprise the general's perfection in relation to God, together with what perfects his heart, understanding, and execution; and also the corporal and external gifts helpful to him.* ³*Morever, the order of their listing indicates the impor-tance at which they are rated.*

[725]   2.   ¹The second quality is that he be a person whose example in all the virtues will be a help to the other members of the Soci-ety. ²Charity towards all his neighbors should particularly shine forth in him, and in a special way toward the members of the Society; likewise a genuine humility which will make him highly beloved of God our Lord and of human beings.

[726]   3.   ¹He ought also to be free from all inordinate affections, having them tamed and mortified so that interiorly they will not disturb the judgment of his intellect, ²and so that exteriorly he will be so composed and, in particular, so circumspect in speaking ³that none, either members of the Society (who should regard him as a mirror and model) or externs, will observe any thing or word in him that is not edifying.

[727]   4.   ¹However, he should know how to mingle the required rectitude and severity with kindness and gentleness in such a way that he neither lets himself be deflected from what he judges to be more pleasing to God our Lord nor fails to have proper sympathy

for his sons. ²Thus even those who are reprimanded or punished will recognize that he proceeds rightly in our Lord and with charity in what he does, even if it is against their liking according to the lower man.

[728]   5.   ¹Magnanimity and fortitude of soul are likewise highly necessary for him, so that he may bear the weaknesses of many, initiate great undertakings in the service of God our Lord, and persevere in them with the needed constancy, ²neither losing courage in the face of the contradictions, even from persons of high rank and power, nor allowing himself to be deflected by their entreaties or threats from what reason and the divine service require. ³He should be superior to all eventualities, not letting himself be exalted by success or cast down by adversity, ⁴and being quite ready to accept death, when necessary, for the good of the Society in the service of Jesus Christ our God and Lord.

[729]   6.   ¹The third quality is that he ought to be endowed with great intelligence and judgment, so that he is not lacking in this talent in either speculative or practical matters which may arise. ²And although learning is highly necessary for one who will have so many learned men in his charge, still more necessary is prudence along with experience in spiritual and interior matters, so that he may be able to discern the various spirits and to give counsel and remedies to so many who will have spiritual necessities. ³He also needs discretion in exterior matters and a manner of handling such diverse affairs as well as of conversing with such various persons from within and without the Society.

[730]   7.   ¹The fourth quality, one highly necessary for the execution of business, is that he should be vigilant and solicitous in undertaking enterprises and vigorous in carrying them through to their completion and perfection, rather than careless and remiss about leaving them begun but unfinished.

[731]   8.   ¹The fifth quality concerns the body. ²As regards health, appearance, and age, account should be taken on the one hand of dignity and authority, ³and on the other of the physical strength demanded by his charge *[B]*, so as to be able therewith to fulfill his office to the glory of God our Lord.

[732]   *B.*   ¹*Thus it seems that he ought to be neither of very advanced age, which is generally unsuited for the labors and cares of such a charge,* ²*nor of great youth, which generally is not accompanied by the proper authority and experience.*

[733]   9. ¹The sixth quality regards external things *[C]*. Among these preference should be given to those which help more toward edification and the service of God our Lord in such a charge. ²Such are normally esteem, a good reputation, and whatever else contributes toward authority among those within and without.

[734]   C. ¹*Nobility, wealth which was possessed in the world, honor, and the like are external endowments. Other things being equal, these are worthy of some consideration;* ²*but even if they are lacking, there are other things more important which could suffice for election.*

[735]   10. ¹Finally, he ought to be one of those who are most outstanding in every virtue, most deserving in the Society, and known as such for the longest time. ²If any of the aforementioned qualities should be wanting, he should at least not lack great probity and love for the Society, nor good judgment accompanied by sound learning. ³In other matters, the aids which he will have (and which will be treated below [789–808]) will be able through God's help and favor to supply for much.

CHAPTER 3

THE SUPERIOR GENERAL'S AUTHORITY OVER THE SOCIETY AND HIS FUNCTIONS

[736]   1. ²It is judged altogether proper for the good government of the Society that the superior general should have complete authority over it, in order to build it up. This authority (from which the general's functions also become manifest) is that described below.

   ³First of all, the superior general will have the power, personally and through others, to admit those whom he thinks suitable for the Institute of the Society in the houses and colleges or anywhere else, both to probation and to profession *[A]* and also as formed coadjutors and approved scholastics. ⁴He will likewise have power **to let them depart and to dismiss them** *[B]*.²

[737]   A. ¹*When he admits one or several to profession through a third party, he should first receive information about them individually and be satisfied about their qualifications;* ²*or he should give a special commission to someone in whom he has confidence as in himself to admit those judged fit, in accordance with what was said in Part V [513, 517].*

[738]   B. ¹*This is in conformity with what was stated about dismissing, in Part II [206].*

---

² (See notes 5–7 to [208].)

[739]   2. ¹He will also have authority to send those whom he decides upon to studies, at the place which he thinks proper; ²and likewise to recall them before or after they have finished their studies, and to change them from one place to another, as he judges to be more expedient in our Lord for their personal good and for the universal good of the Society.

[740]   3. ¹He will have the entire superintendence and government of the colleges in regard to the students, teachers, and officials. Among these the principal person is the rector, ²whom the general may appoint and remove, and give him the authority which he thinks is expedient in our Lord. ³Through these rectors he will exercise the administration with respect to the material and temporal affairs of the colleges for the benefit of the students, as is stated in the bull [*Exposcit debitum*, no. 5].

[741]   4. ¹He will require them to give an account of their office in the manner which seems best to him *[C]*. ²What holds true of the colleges is also valid for the universities which are in the Society's charge, namely, ³that the direction of the matters which concern life and doctrine will be vested in the superior general; and he will exercise it through the officials whom he appoints, in conformity with the Constitutions, and so on.

[742]   C. ¹*Whether they are to give this account to him, to the provincial superior, or to someone else who has an authoritative commission to receive it.*

[743]   5. ¹In the superior general is vested all the authority to make **contracts for the purchase or sale of any** movable temporal goods whatsoever of the colleges and houses of the Society, ²**and to charge or redeem any annuities**³ whatsoever on their immovable goods, for the utility and benefit of the same colleges, with the right to redeem the debt by restoring the money which was given. ³{**However, without a general congregation of the Society he may not alienate or completely suppress colleges or houses of the Society that are already established**}.⁴

[744]   6. ¹The general will also have the power to dispose of anything that is left in undetermined fashion to the Society's disposition, whether immovable goods such as a house or property that is not applied or incorporated into a determined house or college by

---

³ (Note in regard to CIC 638, §3, and CCEO 1036, §4: the permission of the Holy See may be required.)

⁴ **Abolished by** *CN* **402, §3.**

the one leaving it, ²or movable goods such as money, grain, or any other things. ³**He may sell, or retain, or apply**⁵ whatever he thinks wise to one place or another as he judges it to be for the greater glory of God our Lord.

[745] 7. ¹Moreover, the provincial and local superiors, rectors, and other commissaries of the general will have such part of this authority as the general communicates to them, ²and will not need to assemble the members of the colleges collegially for such actions.

[746] 8. ¹Just as it pertains to the general to see to it that the Constitutions of the Society are everywhere observed, so too he will have power to **grant dispensations**⁶ in particular cases which require such dispensation, account being taken of persons, places, times, and other circumstances *[D]*. ²He will do this with the discretion which the Eternal Light gives him, looking to the purpose of the Constitutions, which is the greater divine service and the good of those who live in this Institute. ³He may use this power in regard to the experiences of those in probation *[E]* as well as in other matters where such dispensation is deemed to be according to the intention of those who enacted the Constitutions, for the glory of God our Lord.

[747] *D.* ¹*The general ought to exercise this authority personally. He will also be able to exercise it through someone else in urgent cases in which delay is impossible without notable inconvenience, or in which he has given a special commission to someone in whom he has confidence as in himself, especially in far-distant places such as the Indies.* ²*It is also understood that he may dispense where, in view of the particular circumstances, he judges in our Lord that such is within the intention of the Constitutions, and not otherwise.*

[748] *E.* ¹*It will be within the general's power to have all the experiences undergone, and even more than the six mentioned in the Examen [64–71], or to have one or some of them omitted or replaced by others,* ²*when in a particular case what is generally fitting is now inexpedient; for example, the hospital, or pilgrimage, or lecturing, or some of the other experiences.*

[749] 9. ¹The same general will also have complete authority over missions, in no case contravening those from the Apostolic See, as is stated in Part VII [618]. ²From those under his obedience, professed or not professed, he may send all he thinks right to any part of the world *[F]*, for whatever time seems good to him, whether it

---

⁵ **Clarified by** *CN* 173.

⁶ **Clarified by** *CN* 19, §1.

is definite or indefinite, to exercise any of the means employed by the Society to aid its neighbors. ³Similarly, he may recall those sent *[G]*, entirely as he judges to be for the greater glory of God our Lord.

⁴Knowing the talent of those who are under his obedience, he should distribute the offices of preachers, lecturers, confessors *[H]*, and the like, ⁵assigning each subject to the office which he judges in our Lord to be more expedient for the divine service and the good of souls.

[750]   F. ¹*Thus he may send them, for example, among the faithful in the Indies and among the unbelievers where there are Christian inhabitants. In some cases or urgent necessities he may even send them where there are no Christians; but he should do this only after much previous deliberation.*

[751]   G. ¹*He may recall not only those sent by his predecessor or himself but also those whom the sovereign pontiff sent without determining the length of their stay. This is granted in the bull of favors which was issued by our Holy Father Paul III in 1549.*

[752]   H. ¹*The general may make this distribution through his officials, whether they are local superiors or not, as will be the case also with many matters mentioned or still to be mentioned.*

[753]   10. ¹The general will also have the task of using the privileges granted by the Apostolic See, and of communicating to each subject under his obedience the portion of those privileges which he judges will be well placed in him for the divine service, the end which is sought. ²It will also belong to him to revoke or restrict these privileges, keeping in view the same norm of the greater service of God.

[754]   11. ¹He will also have the task of giving correction and imposing the penances which he judges suitable for any faults whatsoever, with attention given to the persons and other circumstances. ²The consideration of these is entrusted to his prudent charity, which he will use for the glory of God our Lord.

[755]   12. ¹It is his task to summon the Society to a general congregation when one must be convoked for other matters than the election of the general; ²and to order **the convocation of a province congregation when he judges one expedient;**⁷ and to direct those

---

⁷ **Modified by** *Form of Prov Cong.,* no. 3, §1. (Cases when a province congregation is to be called are reduced to two: (1) when a general congregation has been convoked; (2) when a congregation of procurators has been convoked.)

who attend and **to dismiss them**[8] at the appropriate time when the agenda has been concluded.

[756] 13. [1]Without his permission and approval, no one may accept any dignity outside the Society; nor will he give permission or approval if the command of the Apostolic See does not compel him.

[757] 14. [1]Furthermore, he (as has been said [740, 741]) should personally appoint those whom he judges best fitted for the purpose as the rectors of colleges and universities, and similarly as the local superiors of the houses. [2]He will also appoint the provincials, normally for three years, although he may shorten or lengthen this period when he thinks that this will be conducive to the greater glory of God our Lord *[I]*. [3]He will give to them the power which he judges wise.

[758] *I. [1]With those who perform their office well and are able to satisfy him in it, nothing is lost by the limitation of three years, since the period can be shortened or lengthened. [2]With those who do not prove apt, something is gained by relieving them without embarrassment when their term is over, unless the general thinks that for the sake of the general good such a person ought to be relieved earlier.*

[759] 15. [1]Likewise, he may revoke, extend, or restrict their authority, and require from them an account of their administration. [2]Furthermore, if he communicates his own authority to the provincial for the appointment of local superiors and rectors, it will remain his part **to confirm**[9] or remove them.

[760] 16. [1]He should appoint the other officials necessary for the government of the Society, such as the procurator general and the secretary of the Society *[K]*. He should give them the power which he judges in our Lord to be expedient according to the nature of the business and the persons.

[761] *K. [1]Although in regard to these choices and other important or doubtful matters he may hear the advice of other persons he considers in the Lord will judge soundly, the power to decide will ultimately be his.*

[762] 17. [1]He may, without waiting for a general congregation, accept houses, colleges, and universities for the Society; [2]and admit to the rank of founders with the privileges mentioned in Part IV [309–319] those who, he judges in our Lord, should be so admitted;

---

[8] **Modified** by *Form. of Gen. Cong.*, no. **143**. (The conclusion of a congregation is not left to the judgment of the general alone, but only to the consent of the assembled members expressed by a majority vote.)

[9] **Clarified** by *CN* 343, 3°.

and provide for lecturers, priests, and whatever else is needed. ³He should endeavor to have all this done with conditions such that the Society experiences advantage for the end of the divine service which it pursues, and not detriment. ⁴{However, if experience reveals that the Society has been burdened rather than helped, and the general provides no remedy, the next congregation of the Society could deal with whether the house, college, or university thus burdened ought to be given up or retained}.¹⁰

[763] 18. ¹{To transfer or suppress houses or colleges already founded, or to convert the fixed revenue from those institutions to the use of the professed Society, will not be within the general's power, as was stated in Part IV [322, 419]}.¹¹

[764] 19. ¹He should know the consciences, as far as possible, of those whom he has in his charge, especially of the provincial superiors and others to whom he entrusts important responsibilities.

[765] 20. ¹To speak in general, he may command in virtue of obedience all the members in regard to everything conducive to the end which the Society seeks, the perfection and aid of its neighbors for the glory of God. ²And although he communicates his authority to other superiors or visitors or commissaries, he may approve or revoke the actions they take and in all matters ordain what seems good to him. ³At all times he should be obeyed and reverenced as one who holds the place of Christ our Lord.

---

¹⁰ Abolished by *CN* 402, §3.
¹¹ Abolished by *CN* 402, §3; see 190.

CHAPTER 4

¹THE AUTHORITY OR PROVIDENT CARE WHICH THE SOCIETY SHOULD EXERCISE IN REGARD TO THE SUPERIOR GENERAL

[766] 1. ²The authority or provident care which the Society will have in regard to the general, looking always to the universal good and greater edification, will comprise six points which can help toward the glory of God our Lord [A].

[767] A. ¹The Society will exercise this authority through the assistants, who will be discussed later [779].

[768] 2. ¹The first point regards external matters such as clothing, food, and any expenditures touching upon the general's person. ²The Society will be able to extend or restrict all of these as it may judge to be appropriate for the general, the Society, and the greater service to God; and the general ought to be content with what is provided.

[769] 3. ¹The second pertains to the care of his body, to prevent him from going beyond measure in labors or excessive severity. ²And the superior will allow himself to be restrained and will be satisfied with what the Society orders.

[770] 4. ¹The third pertains to his soul, in the case of some necessity which might arise, even among perfect men, regarding his person or his office. The Society should have a person with the general (and this can also be practiced with subordinate superiors) who will be obliged, after recurring to God in prayer and taking counsel with his Divine Goodness, if he judges it right, ²to admonish the general with due modesty and humility about what in him he thinks would be for the greater service and glory of God. ³**This could be the general's confessor, or someone else appointed by the Society**¹² who seems fit for this purpose.

[771] 5. ¹The fourth is this. If pressure should be exerted upon the general, although without obliging him under sin, to accept a dignity which will require him to relinquish his office [B], he may not accept the dignity without the consent of the Society. ²And the Society, looking to what is for the greater service and glory of God our Lord, will never give its consent unless compelled by a command of the Apostolic See.

---

¹² **Clarified by** *CN 379* (The general's admonitor will be such.)

CHAPTER 2

PROVIDENT CARE OF THE SOCIETY
FOR THE SUPERIOR GENERAL

363   The obligation that binds the provincials in the sight of God to consider and do what they ought to do for the universal good of the whole Society in those matters that concern the superior general they will generally fulfill through the assistants for provident care, unless the matter should be extremely urgent.[65]

364   §1. A general congregation according to its formula must elect,[66] from among the professed of four solemn vows, four assistants for provident care from different assistancies, keeping in mind the general counselors appointed by the general, but with the freedom of the congregation remaining intact to choose other persons.[67]

§2. They should be upright men, faithful, lovers of the Society and of the common good, endowed with the gift of discretion, adept at conserving peace and union among themselves and with the general.[68]

§3. Since, by decision of the general congregation, they are also general counselors,[69] they should be men experienced in matters of business, suited for dealing with people, and best equipped to proffer counsel on behalf of the entire Society.[70]

365   Every third month, the assistant who has been professed for the longest time should convoke the others, and they should consider among themselves whether it seems that the general should be warned about any matter, whether in regard to his own person or to his governance; they should caution him if at least half of them so judge.[71]

366   §1. If at least a majority of the assistants for provident care, out of their knowledge and love of the Society, will have

---

[65] See *CollDecr* d. 260, §3 (GC 31, d. 41, no. 2, §2); see P. IX, c. 5 nos. 1, 4 [778, 782].

[66] *CollDecr* d. 268, §1 (GC 1, d. 80).

[67] GC 34, d. 23, E, II, no. 1, 2°–3°.

[68] *CollDecr* d. 268, §1 (GC 1, d. 80); see P. IX, c. 5, no. [779].

[69] GC 34, d. 23, E, I, no. 2.

[70] See *CollDecr* d. 268, §1; GC 33, d. 4, no. 3; *Form. of Gen. Cong.*, no. 130; see P. IX, c. 5, no. 2, A [779, 780].

[71] *CollDecr* d. 266 (GC 12, d. 7).

[772] *B.* ¹*This case would occur if a secular ruler sought to have him accept some dignity, and the pope ordered it but not so absolutely as to indicate an intention of obliging him to accept the charge.* ²*For in such cases, where there is no obligation, the general should not and may not accept the dignity without the approval of the Society; and the Society should not and may not approve if the pope does not compel it by a precept obliging under sin.*

[773] 6. ¹The fifth is this. If the general through illness or advanced age should be quite careless or remiss in the important matters of his office, without hope of his improvement in this regard and with the result that the common good suffers notably, **a coadjutor or vicar should be chosen who is to perform the office of the general.** ²**This vicar may be chosen by the general himself (with the approval of the provincial superiors); or the provincials, each with the approval of two local superiors or rectors of his province, may by means of letters elect the vicar by a majority of votes, that he may govern the Society** ³**with the authority which the general thinks it proper to give him or which the Society thinks proper should it choose him.**¹³

[774] 7. ¹The sixth is this. In certain cases (which we trust in the Divine Goodness will by his grace never occur), as where mortal sins involving external actions are present—²namely, sexual intercourse, infliction of a wound *[C]*, appropriation of the fixed revenues of the colleges for his own expenses or giving them to someone outside the Society *[D]*, alienation of immovable goods of the houses or colleges, or holding false doctrine—³the Society can and should depose him from office when the evidence is altogether sufficient *[E]* and dismiss him from the Society if necessary, ⁴acting in all matters as may be judged to be for the greater divine glory and the universal good of the Society.

[775] *C.* ¹*As with a weapon or knife or object capable of inflicting a notable wound.*

[776] *D.* ¹*What is specifically intended is to prevent him from giving anything to relatives or persons connected with him according to the world;* ²*the door is not closed against the general's having alms or whatever is appropriate given to persons he judges should receive them, for the glory of God our Lord.*

[777] *E.* ¹*Since those who hold an office, especially one so universal, can be calumniated by many persons for various reasons, much care must*

---

¹³ **Modified by** *CN* **366, §§2–4.**

judged that the superior general ought for a grave reason to resign his office, they should advise him of this through the admonitor.[72]

§2. But if, because of grave illness or senility, the superior general shows himself to be very negligent or remiss or even useless in important matters referring to his office and where there is no hope of improvement in the case, and if a majority of the assistants for provident care, after having earnestly recommended the matter to God and sought necessary advice from experts, judge that grave harm might come to the Society from it,[73] they should ask him to resign his office.

§3. But if the general in this case cannot resign his office or is unwilling to do so,

1° Let the one whom the superior general had previously designated for this eventuality, according to the norm of no. 368, be installed as temporary vicar general; but if the general had not done this, such a vicar should be elected according to the Formula for Electing a Temporary Vicar General.[74]

2° The temporary vicar general so constituted should, after consulting with the assistants for provident care, convoke a general congregation as soon as possible to provide for the situation.[75]

§4. If the general congregation thus convoked, after being fully informed by the vicar general and the assistants for provident care, will have declared the superior general definitively incapable of governing the Society without serious damage, for the reasons given in §2, it should elect a new superior general who will completely take the place of the former in his office; otherwise it should provide for the situation with appropriate means, avoiding the election of a perpetual vicar general.[76]

The text of the Norms resumes on page 373.

---

[72] *CollDecr* d. 260, §3 (GC 31, d. 41, no. 2, §3).

[73] See P. IX, c. 4, no. 6 [773]; c. 5, no. 6 [786].

[74] See *CollDecr* d. 260, §6, 1° (GC 8, dd. 28–29; GC 12, d. 55).

[75] See *CollDecr* d. 260, §6, 2°.

[76] See P. IX, c. 5, no. 6 [786], abolished by GC 34.

be taken that the proofs for these faults are as strong as is morally possible.

CHAPTER 5

[1]THE SOCIETY'S MANNER OF PROCEEDING IN WHAT PERTAINS TO THE GENERAL

[778]   1. [2]First of all, the **provincial superiors** personally appointed by the general **are bound**[14] in the sight of God our Lord to consider and carry out what they owe to the universal good of the Society in regard to the above points having to do with the superior general, as they judge in our Lord.

[779]   2. [1]Secondly, in regard to what pertains to his expenses, the care of his person, and other easily handled matters, there will be no need of a congregation. [2]Instead, the Society should have four assistants, persons of discretion and zeal for the good of the Society, who are deputed to remain close to the general [A] [3]with the duty in the sight of their Creator and Lord of saying and doing whatever they think to be for the greater glory of God in regard to the first three matters mentioned in the preceding chapter [768–71].

[780]   A. [1]*They should be professed fathers* {*if this is conveniently possible*}.[15] [2]*If one or some of these assistants should on occasion be absent from the general, having being sent somewhere or other to return soon, it will be unnecessary to replace them; if they have to stay for a long time,* **others should be appointed.**[16] [3]*However, the superior general ought not to send them far from himself without serious reason or necessity.*

[781]   3. [1]The election of these four persons will be vested in the same persons who elect the superior general **when they are in the congregation held for that purpose.**[17] [2]If one of the assistants dies or for important reasons must be away from the general for a long time, and there is no opposition from the provincials of the Society, the general will choose another **who, with the approval of all or**

---

[14] **Clarified by** *CN* **363.** (The provincials ordinarily do this by means of the assistants for provident care.)

[15] **Abolished by** *CN* **364, §1.**

[16] **Clarified by** *CN* **376, §3, 5°; §4.**

[17] **Modified by** *CN* **376, §1.** (They are to be elected in every general congregation.)

the greater part of the provincials, will take the place of the one who is missing.[18]

[782]   4. [1]Thirdly, if one of the sins sufficient for deposing the general from office should occur (and may God never permit this) and the case becomes evident through sufficient testimony or the general's own admission, then the four assistants should be obliged under oath to bring the matter to the attention of the Society, [2]and under their four signatures, or those of three of them, to summon the Society to a congregation. That is to say, they must summon the provincials and two persons with each of them, and these will be obliged to convene *[B]*. [3]When the offense is public and commonly known, **the provincials**[19] ought to come without waiting for the summons of the four assistants but instead summoning one another. [4]On the first day when they are locked within the place of the congregation, with the four who convoked them present together with those who came at their summons, the person best informed should arise and explain the accusation. [5]After the general has been heard he should leave the room. Then the senior provincial, with the secretary and another assistant, should conduct the voting on the case, [6]first, on whether the accusation brought against the general has been proved, and then, if it has, on whether it is such as to require that the general be deposed. [7]The same provincial should announce the votes; to suffice they must be more than two thirds. In such a case, the election of another general should be taken up immediately, [8]and if it is possible they should not leave the room until the Society has a superior general. [9]If the matter cannot be resolved on that day, it should be concluded on the following or as quickly as possible, in the manner stated in Part VIII [694–710].

[783]   B. [1]*Nevertheless they should keep the matter as secret as possible, even in regard to the other members of the Society, until the truth has become apparent,* [2]*so that if what the four assistants were convinced of proves incorrect the general's name may not be wrongly tarnished.*

[784]   5. [1]If the defects are found to be such that they require not his deposition but his correction *[C]*, four persons should be charged with examining what correction should be given. [2]If their votes split equally and they do not agree, they should add one or three more persons in order to determine what is expedient in our Lord.

---

[18] **Clarified by** *CN* 376, §3, 1°; §5.

[19] **Clarified by** *CN* 363. (See note 14 to [778].)

[785]   C. ¹When the faults are found insufficient for the general's deposition, other matters should be taken up so that it may appear that the congregation was called to discuss them, thus covering over the matter of the general. Indeed, as far as possible, this should never be made public. ²Likewise, those aware of the matter, particularly the provincials, should be forewarned when they are summoned, and strongly admonished after the matter has been clarified, not to disclose it to anyone. ³If the decision is made to depose him, they should also treat with the superior general secretly about his voluntarily resigning his office, so that this may be made public and his sin, and deposition because of it, may be concealed.

[786]   6. ¹If the case arises that the superior general becomes unable to govern the Society [D], the matter should be discussed partly in his presence and partly in his absence, ²to discern **whether a vicar ought to be chosen to hold the entire authority of the superior general, though not the title, for the rest of the former general's life; ³and if this decision seems good to more than half, it must be carried out.**²⁰ ⁴But if this does not seem necessary, there should be an investigation as to whether the Society would do well to provide other ministers in addition to those whom the general already has, ⁵so that through his being relieved and aided in this way no deficiency in the government of the Society may be felt. ⁶In this matter too that should be followed which more than half of the participants in the congregation ordain.

⁷If the question happens to be about a dignity ordinarily incompatible with the general's office and if there is not such a command from the sovereign pontiff that its obligation could be under pain of sin, the question should not be brought up for discussion. ⁸For it should be held as certain that the general should not and may not consent to accept it [E].

[787]   D. ¹A general would be totally unable if he has lost the use of reason or is so gravely ill with an incurable infirmity that he cannot attend to the affairs of his office and there is no hope of his being able to do so later. ²Should the infirmity not be such as to preclude hope of his recovery, the general himself without a general congregation could appoint a vicar to perform all the general's functions until he recovers, at which point the authority which had been given the vicar would cease.

[788]   E. ¹From this it is evident that a congregation need not be summoned to decide this where there is no command from the Apostolic See obliging the general or the Society under sin if it is not carried out (as has been stated).

> *Text of the Constitutions resumes on page 392.*

---

²⁰ **Modified by** *CN* 366, §§2–4.

CHAPTER 3

VARIOUS FORMS OF A VICAR OF THE SUPERIOR GENERAL[77]

367   A vicar of a superior general is constituted, either to act in place of the general after the termination of his office (because of death, resignation accepted by a general congregation, or other reasons), until the election of his successor, or to assist the general while he is still living, or even sometimes to be his substitute.[78]

Article 1: A Vicar General after a Superior General's Death or after He Has Been Judged to Be Very Seriously Incapacitated for Governing the Society

368   §1. A vicar general who is to govern the Society after the general's death or after he has been judged to be too seriously incapacitated to govern according to the Constitutions[79] and the Complementary Norms[80] ought to be designated by the general himself. The document by which he is designated is to be signed by the secretary of the Society in the presence of the fathers of the General Curia who have a right in virtue of their office to attend a general congregation and who are actually present. It is to be given for authentication to the two assistants for provident care who are oldest by profession and is to be read by the older of the two.

---

[77] The expression "vicar general" is used here only when a vicar fully substitutes for a superior general, otherwise simply the designation "vicar." The same is true when one speaks generically of a vicar.

[78] See P. VIII, c. 4, no. 1 [687]; P. IX, c. 4, no. 6 [773]; c. 5, no. 6, D [786, 787]; GC 31, d. 41, no. 3.

[79] P. IX, c. 4, no. 6; c. 5, no. 6 [773, 786].

[80] *CN*, no. 366, §3.

§2. If a vicar general has not been designated by the deceased general or by the general judged to be very seriously incapable for governing, one should be elected according to the norm in the Formula of a Congregation for Electing a Temporary Vicar General.[81]

369   §1. The duty of a vicar general after the death of the superior general or after he has been judged to be gravely incapacitated for governing the Society is

1° To convoke a general congregation, to prepare for it, and to preside over it until the election of the general; or in the second case, until a different decision is taken by the general congregation, unless he retains his condition as vicar

2° To take the place of the general in governing the Society[82]

§2. In this governance he has the same power as the general,[83] to be carried out according to what is set down in the rules of his office.

Article 2: A Vicar While the Superior General Is Still Living

370   §1. In the very act of presenting his resignation, the superior general can appoint from among the electors of the congregation a vicar general who will carry out the office after his resignation has been accepted; but if he does not wish to designate anyone, the vicar general will be the oldest by profession of the assistants for provident care.[84]

§2. This vicar general has the same powers as a vicar after the death of a general, until the election of a successor.

371   A perpetual vicar, perhaps at times elected by a general congregation as a coadjutor vicar, can be constituted without right of succession or with right of succession (after the permission of the Holy See has been obtained insofar as it is necessary)

---

[81] *CollDecr* d. 262, §§1–2 (GC 4, d. 43); *CN*, no. 368, §1; see P. VIII, c. 4, no. 1, A [687, 688].

[82] See P. VIII, c. 4, no. 1, A [687, 688]; *Office of Vicar*, no. 1; GC 31, d. 43, no. 1.

[83] *Office of Vicar*, nos. 6, 9.

[84] See *Form. of Gen. Congr.*, no. 88, §1.

with power to be determined by the congregation itself in all details, as in each case it seems good to the congregation.[85]

372 §1. In the case of a long absence or for handling extraordinary business or because of a serious illness that impedes him from carrying out his office, the superior general has the right to substitute for himself a temporary vicar with those powers which will seem good to him.[86]

§2. If the general for whatever cause is completely impeded physically from carrying out his office for a long time or for a time whose duration the majority of the assistants for provident care judge they cannot foresee, and if the general has not appointed a vicar for this eventuality, a vicar general should be constituted as soon as possible according to the norm of the Formula for Electing a Temporary Vicar General; he will govern the Society according to the norm of the Office of a Vicar General for the time that the general remains impeded.

373 The superior general also has the right to appoint a vicar to assist him as often as it may seem to him to be necessary or convenient to do so, with those powers that will seem good to him.[87]

CHAPTER 4

THE ASSISTANTS FOR PROVIDENT CARE AND THE GENERAL'S ADMONITOR

374 §1. The assistants for provident care must remain with the superior general; he is not permitted to send them far away from himself for a long time without necessity or a serious reason. But if he does send them, they are not to offer an excuse but are to obey him. Even more so is it fitting for them to obey if they are sent by the supreme pontiff, although the superior general at his discretion should see whether the supreme pontiff should rather be asked to consent to send someone else.[88]

---

[85] See *Form. of Gen. Congr.*, nos. 92, §3; 94, §1; P. IX, c. 4, no. 6 [773]; c. 5, no. 6 [786].

[86] *CollDecr* d. 262, §3 (GC 30, d. 71; see GC 1, d. 85); see P. IX, c. 5, D [787].

[87] See *CollDecr* d. 262, §4 (GC 31, d. 41, no. 3).

[88] *CollDecr* d. 265, §1 (see GC 1, d. 86); P. IX, c. 5, no. 2, A [779, 780].

§2. Without necessity, neither the superior of the General Curia nor the secretary of the Society should be chosen from among the assistants for provident care.[89]

375   Besides other business expressly mentioned, assistants for provident care have a deliberative vote in all matters in which provincials have a deliberative vote outside the time of a general congregation.[90]

376   §1. Their office, also as general counselors,[91] continues until the election of new assistants for provident care, which takes place in every general congregation. Former assistants can be reelected to the same office.[92]

§2. Assistants for provident care cannot resign from their office either at their own discretion or at that of the general.

§3. But it is the right and the obligation of the general to substitute others for them

1° If they should die

2° If, after consultation with the other assistants for provident care, he judges them unworthy of their office

3° If, after consultation with the other assistants for provident care, he judges that, because of notably impaired strength or for another reason, they are so unequal to their task that it is foreseen that the Society may thereby be in danger of serious harm

4° If for the same or another grave reason they themselves request it of the general, after consultation with the other assistants for provident care

5° If for a long period of time they either must be away or cannot perform their office for reasons of health

§4. In the first four cases of §3 above, a new assistant for provident care is to be appointed; in the fifth case, a substitute for him is to be appointed.

§5. As soon as possible, the general must seek the approval of the assistants for provident care and the provincials, after he has given them appropriate information about the man he

---

[89] *CollDecr* d. 265, §2 (GC 1, d. 89; GC 4, d. 32; see GC 20, d. 5).

[90] *CollDecr* d. 267 (GC 5, d. 16; see dd. 60, 4°, and 65).

[91] GC 34, d. 23, E, III, no. 1.

[92] GC 34, d. 23, E, II, no. 1, 4°.

has chosen. The approval of a majority of the assistants for provident care and the provincials is required for the validity of the appointment. Therefore, until such time as this majority is ascertained, the new assistant for provident care does not have the right to cast a vote on matters in which the Institute gives a deliberative vote to such assistants, nor does he have a right to attend congregations, whether a general congregation, a congregation of procurators, or a congregation to elect a temporary vicar.

§6. A substitute assistant has the same rights, under the same conditions, but for no longer than the assistant for whom he is substituting is absent or, in the judgment of the general, is impeded; neither does a substitute assistant ever, when the regular assistant is present, have a right to a congregation, whether a general one, or a congregation of procurators, or a congregation for electing a temporary vicar.[93]

377 A temporary vicar general who takes office when a general dies or has been judged to be too incapacitated to govern must have four assistants for provident care or their substitutes. Therefore, if any one of them is lacking, a temporary substitute must be designated according to the norm of nos. 7 and 12 of the Office of Vicar General.[94] Such a substitute has the same rights as substitutes appointed by the general and approved by a majority of the assistants for provident care and the provincials, with the exception of the right to a general congregation or a congregation for electing a temporary vicar.[95]

378 §1. Those who must take the oath prescribed for assistants for provident care[96] are the following:

1° Assistants for provident care whom a general congregation elects, in the presence of the congregation itself and immediately after the election.

2° Assistants for provident care and their substitutes whom a general has named, in the presence of those fathers of the general curia who by reason of office have a right to attend a general congregation, but not before a majority of assistants for

---

[93] *CollDecr* d. 269 (GC 30, d. 72; GC 31, d. 44, nos. 3–4; GC 32, d. 15); P. IX, c. 5, no. 3 [781].

[94] *Office of Vicar*, no. 7, as revised by GC 31, d. 43, no. 3.

[95] *CollDecr* d. 270 (GC 20, d. 18).

[96] See P. IX, d. 5, no. 4 [782].

provident care and provincials have approved their nomination. However, if the general should die before they take the oath, then there is no need for them to do so.

§2. The oath is not a necessary condition for assistants for provident care and their substitutes to acquire the rights mentioned in no. 376, §§5–6.[97]

379   §1. The general's admonitor, who can be chosen freely from the assistants for provident care or from other members of the Society, must be professed of the four solemn vows.[98] He should be a man who is a good religious, familiar with God in prayer, advanced in age, of sound and mature judgment, well versed in the Institute and matters of the Society, possessing great zeal for the Institute joined to discretion and prudence, not at all credulous or timid; rather he should be such as would be thought acceptable to the superior general and not apt to betray his office or the good of the Society because of human respect.[99]

§2. What is legislated in no. 376 about the election of assistants for provident care, their duration in office, and the substitution for them should be applied to the admonitor as well;[100] however, if the admonitor is absent for only a brief time, the general himself can substitute another for him.[101]

CHAPTER 5

THE COUNCIL OF THE SUPERIOR GENERAL AND HIS OTHER HELPERS

Article 1: The Council of the Superior General

380   §1. The council of the superior general will be composed of about twelve members.

§2. To the council belong the assistants for provident care, regional assistants, and other general counselors to whom some

---

[97] *CollDecr* d. 271 (GC 6, d. 27, no. 2; GC 19, d. 6); see P. IX, c. 5, no. 4 [782]; *Form. of Gen. Cong.*, no. 137.

[98] *CollDecr* d. 272, §1 (GC 2, d. 22; GC 4, d. 15).

[99] *Form. of Gen. Cong.*, no. 139.

[100] *CollDecr* d. 272, §2 (GC 3, d. 42; GC 4, d. 24; GC 6, d. 27, no. 2; GC 17, d. 8).

[101] *CollDecr* d. 272, §2 (GC 3, d. 42).

sector or aspect of the life of the universal Society is entrusted by the superior general. One and the same person can combine different functions. The secretary of the Society is the secretary of the council, but he is not a general counselor.[102]

§3. During a general congregation, the superior general will appoint at least as many general counselors as are necessary to carry out the functions of the regional assistants. He will choose these counselors from lists prepared in advance by the electors of each assistancy. Each of these lists will contain three names, usually drawn from the membership of the respective assistancies. But outside this process, the general, with a deliberative vote of the assistants for provident care and after hearing the opinions of the other general counselors, can appoint other general counselors, who will be in charge of important areas of the Society's life. Former general counselors can be reappointed by the superior general.[103]

381 §1. It is recommended that the general counselors who are not assistants for provident care remain in office for six to eight years, and that they should not all be replaced at the same time.[104]

§2. Outside the time of a general congregation, when appointing a general counselor to carry on the function of a regional assistant, the superior general will seek from the provincials of the respective assistancy three names of candidates, from which he will make the appointment.[105]

§3. Outside the time of a general congregation, for appointing a general counselor who will not be an assistant for provident care or a regional assistant, the superior general should hear the opinions of the other general counselors and seek the deliberative vote of the assistants for provident care.[106]

382 §1. The council should collaborate organically with the general to determine policy and to make decisions and carry them out. They should not only consider matters proposed to them by the general but should also propose matters to be con-

---

[102] GC 34, d. 23, E, I, nos. 14.

[103] GC 34, d. 23, E, II, no. 1, 1°–2°, 4°.

[104] GC 34, d. 23, E, III, no. 2.

[105] GC 34, d. 23, E, III, no. 3.

[106] GC 34, d. 23, E, III, no. 4.

sidered and promote discernment regarding serious and universal matters.[107]

§2. If Father General sets up a reduced group within the council to deal with administrative matters and current questions that do not require the cooperation of all the counselors, it is recommended that the assistants for provident care should be part of it and that all its members have a certain stability in office, so that they are not changed too often or several changed at the same time.[108]

§3. Major officials and sectorial secretaries will participate in meetings of the general council whenever their particular competence would be helpful, and in enlarged meetings which will be called periodically.[109]

Article 2: Major Officials

383 §1. Besides a secretary of the Society who assists the superior general in carrying on ordinary business,[110] there should also be a general procurator and a general treasurer, appointed by the general.

§2. The general procurator should handle the business of the Society with the Holy See and other affairs entrusted to him by the general, and for the most part he should remain with the general.[111]

§3. It is the task of the general treasurer to care for temporal business pertaining to the universal Society and for those items that the general has committed to his care, even though they are of a more restricted character.[112]

§4. A general postulator can be appointed by the superior general to act in his name in causes of canonization of Servants of God from the Society.[113]

---

[107] GC 32, d. 15, B, no. 3, a.

[108] GC 34, d. 23, E, I, no. 6.

[109] GC 34, d. 23, E, I, no. 5.

[110] See P. IX, c. 6, no. 8, E, 9 [800–802].

[111] See P. IX, c. 6, no. 12 [806].

[112] GC 27, *CollDecr* d. 273; see P. IX, c. 6, no. 12 [806].

[113] See "Norms for Causes of the Saints," Feb. 7, 1983 (*AAS* 75 (1983): 396–97).

Article 3: Expert Counselors and Sectorial Secretaries

384   §1. The superior general should have expert counselors who are necessary for considering major aspects of the life and apostolic activity either of the entire Society or of some principal part of it. These will help him in a special way by their advice in such matters.[114] For the most part they should not remain in this position for more than about eight years.[115]

§2. Some of these expert counselors should generally be designated executive sectorial secretaries and placed in charge of the offices that exist in the Curia for these matters or that it may seem appropriate to establish.

385   In general, care should be taken that the superior general does not lack any type of help which is necessary or useful for fully and expeditiously carrying out his office.[116]

Article 4: Visitors

386   §1. The superior general can send visitors into the provinces on whatever occasion, for whatever length of time, and with whatever authority and jurisdiction seem good to him. However, it is recommended that they do not long remain in office nor enjoy indeterminate authority and jurisdiction.

§2. Upon the death of the general, the office of Visitors continues until either the vicar general, having heard the general counselors, or the new superior general determines otherwise.[117]

SECTION 3

GOVERNANCE OF PROVINCES AND REGIONS (MISSIONS)

CHAPTER 1

ERECTION OF PROVINCES AND REGIONS (MISSIONS) AND ASCRIPTION OR APPLICATION TO THEM

387   §1. The Society is divided into provinces and regions (which can also be called missions).

---

[114] See GC 31, d. 44, no. 7, 3°.

[115] See GC 32, d. 15, no. 3, c.

[116] See P. IX, c. 6, no. 13 [809].

[117] See *CollDecr* d. 274 (GC 31, d. 45, no. 1; d. 43, no. 4).

§2. Regions (missions) are either dependent on some province or immediately subject to the superior general; in the latter case, they are called independent.[118]

388 §1. By universal law and our own law, the general can establish, unite, divide, or suppress provinces and regions (missions), once he has given the matter careful consideration and has discussed it with the general counselors.[119]

§2. A province should not be established if it does not have at least fifty ascribed members and unless there is hope that its territory can exist independently of some other one and carry on apostolic activities proper to the Society.

§3. For the most part, several provinces are not to be established in the same territory, even where a difference in language or nationality exists. Nor as a rule should houses of one province be established in the territory of another province. But the general, after hearing the opinions of the major superiors concerned and under conditions to be approved by him, can permit this in favor of those who are suffering persecution on behalf of Christ or for other serious reasons.[120]

389 §1. Each person belongs to that province to which he was admitted; it is the prerogative of the general alone to transcribe someone definitively into another province.

§2. By mutual consent of the provincials involved, members of one province can be sent to another province or applied to it temporarily.

§3. Those members should be applied to another province who receive as their principal task a stable assignment directed primarily to the good of that province and not their own, whether for a definite or an indefinite time; the application lasts until some other provision is made for them.

§4. Those men are not to be applied to another province who are living in it for reasons of studies, probations, health, or business that is not the responsibility of that province; nor are those who are assigned to a house or a work that is immediately dependent on the general or that has been declared by the gen-

---

[118] See *CollDecr* d. 19, §2; GC 33, d. 3, no. 1, §2.

[119] See *CollDecr* d. 275, §1 (GC 1, d. 108; GC 2, d. 36; GC 4, d. 6); Pius VII, *Sollicitudo omnium ecclesiarum;* CIC 621.

[120] See *CollDecr* d. 275, §2 (GC 31, d. 48, no. 10; see GC 7, d. 21; GC 23, d. 35).

eral a work common to several provinces (provided that they belong to one of those provinces).[121]

390 §1. Those who are staying in another province, even if they are not applied to it and even if they are staying there but a brief time, nonetheless are dependent upon the superiors of this province, particularly as regards religious discipline and the exercise of the ministry; these superiors are to look after them with no less paternal solicitude than they have for their own subjects.

§2. But if they have come for the sake of transacting business and there is no local superior whom they ought to consult insofar as possible, they should utilize the guidance of the provincial of the place.[122]

CHAPTER 2

SUPERIORS OF PROVINCES AND REGIONS (MISSIONS)

391 §1. The duty of major superiors is to foster in the provinces or regions entrusted to them religious life, the training of our men, apostolic ministries, and observance of the Constitutions and our Institute; and with the aid of competent assistants, they are to take care of temporal administration, seeking always in all things the greater service of Christ's Church.[123]

§2. Although their power is communicated by the general and is to be exercised under his direction and in subordination to him,[124] this power, as given to them either by common law or the Society's law in virtue of their office, is ordinary power.[125]

§3. The particular and proper duty of major superiors is to visit the houses and works of their province or region.[126] They ought diligently to aid rectors and local superiors in carrying out

---

[121] *CollDecr* d. 277, §§1–3 (GC 7, d. 60; GC 23, d. 35; GC 28, d. 43; see GC 7, d. 59; GC 9, d. 33; GC 14, d. 23; GC 16, d. 18; GC 18, d. 16; GC 24, d. 13, 3°).

[122] *CollDecr* d. 277, §4 (GC 23, d. 35; see GC 11, d. 32).

[123] See GC 31, d. 46, no. 3; see P. IX, c. 6, no. 6 [797].

[124] See P. VIII, c. 1, no. 4 [662].

[125] GC 31, d. 46, no. 1.

[126] See P. VIII, c. 1, I [670]. (See *Norms of Governance for Provincials,* nos. 60–66 [*ActRSJ* 16:585–88]).

their own function, showing them confidence and sharing broad power with them as the matter may demand.[127]

392   It is a right proper to provincials, but not to any regional (mission) superiors,

1° To give his judgment in case of the resignation of the general, which is treated in no. 362, §2[128]

2° To vote in the election of an assistant for provident care, his substitute, and the admonitor, outside the time of a general congregation, according to the norm of nos. 376, §§3–4; 379, §2[129]

393   According to need, major superiors are to be assisted by helpers; but above all they are to have a socius, appointed by the general, observing what is said in no. 356, §1, about consultors and an admonitor.[130]

394   In general, and with due regard for no. 392, whatever in the Institute is said of provincials is, unless the contrary is clear, to be understood as well of superiors of independent regions (missions); but what is said of superiors of dependent regions (missions) must be understood with whatever restriction was imposed when they were established or else is in the rules.[131]

CHAPTER 3

INTERPROVINCE COOPERATION

395   §1. Today many problems are global in nature and therefore require global solutions. Human society itself tends toward a certain unity. Hence, it is appropriate that our Society, which forms one international apostolic body, should live its universal spirit more profoundly, should effectively coordinate its resources and means and strengthen its structures, either those already established or other more flexible ones which render global and

---

[127] See GC 31, d. 46, no. 3; P. IV, c. 10, nos. 4, 5, B [423–25]; P. VIII, c. 1, no. 4 [662].

[128] GC 31, d. 41, no. 2, §4.

[129] *CollDecr* d. 269, §5 (GC 31, d. 44, no. 3); see P. IV, c. 2, no. 3, A [322, 323]; P. IX, c. 4, no. 1 [773]; c. 5, no. 3 [781].

[130] See P. IX, c. 6, no. 14 [810].

[131] GC 27, *CollDecr* d. 20.

regional cooperation easier, so that it may more efficaciously respond to these problems.[132]

§2. According to the genuine spirit of our vocation,[133] that open and complete cooperation which today is more and more a requisite for apostolic action should be promoted among all the Society's members, whatever their province or region, as well as that spirit of union and charity that boldly rejects every brand of particularism and egoism, even of a collective kind, and reaches out readily and generously to the universal good of the Society in the service of God's Church.[134]

396 Approximately every six years beginning from the last general congregation, the superior general shall convoke a meeting of all provincials, in order to consider the state, the problems, and the initiatives of the universal Society, as well as international and supraprovincial cooperation.[135]

397 §1. Major superiors should turn their attention to the needs of the whole Society. They should look on interprovincial and international activities, houses, and works as part of their duty and responsibility and willingly help them according to the measure and proportion worked out by the superior general for each of the individual provinces or regions.

§2. If they judge that because of their proper talents and the movement of grace, some of their subjects would in a special way advance the good of souls in another province, they ought to be prepared, where it seems appropriate, to allow it according to well-ordered charity; moreover, using norms for the choice of ministries in a supernatural spirit, they should not hesitate to discontinue some established works of their own province that seem less useful, in order to undertake a more fruitful or a more needed ministry elsewhere.[136]

398 §1. To be promoted among our members or institutions enjoying similar or complementary expertise are mutual help and

---

[132] See GC 34, d. 3, nos. 8, 23; d. 5, no. 11; d. 21, nos. 2, 3, 5; GC 32, d. 4, nos. 69, 81.

[133] See P. III, c. 2, G [304]; P. IV, *Pream.* [308]; P. VII, c. 1, no. 1, B [603, 605]; GC 31, d. 48, no. 5; GC 32, d. 2, no. 23; d. 4, nos. 68–69, 81.

[134] GC 31, d. 48, nos. 1–2; see GC 32, d. 2, nos. 16, 23.

[135] GC 34, d. 23, C, no. 4.

[136] *CollDecr* d. [414] (GC 30, d. 49, 2°); see GC 31, d. 46, no. 3; d. 48, no. 1.

intercommunication as well as cooperation, so that more universal problems may be addressed in union with other women and men of goodwill and with organizations pursuing the same objectives.[137]

§2. Recommended are the mutually enriching exchanges between provinces united to one another by some special bond, with thoroughly redefined goals and manners of proceeding, in order to achieve greater solidarity and a more effective matching of resources with needs.[138]

§3. Development of conferences of major superiors of the same region or similar cultures is to be promoted. Among their principal objectives are the following: to foster a sense of universality in the provinces; to facilitate unity, communication, and a common vision among superiors; to point out priorities and coordinate common activities; and to stimulate those superiors to offer mutual assistance in fulfilling their responsibilities for the Society and the Church. The statutes of these conferences are to be approved by the general.[139]

§4. As the conferences become more structured, true and productive interprovincial and supraprovincial cooperation will require the effective leadership of a moderator. His function will be to assist in the development of a common vision for the region and for the whole Society; to guide the efforts of the major superiors toward the discerning of priorities, planning, and decision making; to carry out decisions and implement policies; to oversee common undertakings, projects, and services; and to promote every form of cooperation among members and works of the provinces and regions of the conference.[140]

399   The authority of the moderator and the responsibility of the major superiors of the conference, along with procedures for making decisions, are to be specified in its statutes. The moderator must have the authority needed to call its major superiors to plan and set priorities; and then to call them to carry out the required actions both within the provinces and regionally. The major superiors themselves remain jointly responsible to imple-

---

[137] See GC 34, d. 21, no. 14.

[138] See GC 34, d. 21, no. 15.

[139] See GC 34, d. 21, nos. 16, 18–20; GC 31, d. 48, no. 7.

[140] GC 34, d. 21, nos. 20–21; see also no. 28.

ment actions decided upon and to provide the resources needed to sustain common works.[141]

400   Even where conferences of major superiors have already been established, the general can grant authority to another to deal with interprovincial business that exceeds the power of the conference or its moderator and therefore devolves upon the general himself. In such cases, the major superiors and the moderators themselves are subject to the person thus appointed, who will observe clearly defined norms as he works to resolve either a particular problem or even one that pertains to the common good of a region.[142]

SECTION 4

HOUSES AND WORKS OF THE SOCIETY AND THEIR GOVERNANCE

401   §1. Houses of the Society are of different types:

1° Houses dedicated to apostolic functions, which can have joined to them institutes or apostolic works (pastoral institutes, parishes, retreat houses, reviews, colleges, universities, centers of doctrinal research and/or publication, and the like)

2° Houses for the service of the Society: either for the spiritual formation or studies of our members (our seminaries or houses of probation and formation) or for the care of our elderly and infirm (infirmaries)[143]

§2. The word "house" when used without qualification can designate all of these, unless something else appears from the context.[144]

402   §1. The faculty of erecting any independent houses of the Society or of converting them to other very different uses, with due observance of the law, belongs to the superior general.[145]

---

[141] See GC 34, d. 21, no. 22.

[142] GC 31, d. 48, no. 8, 3° a-c.

[143] See GC 32, d. 12, nos. 16–22; *Institute,* passim.

[144] Thus, the word "house" in the Constitutions generally designates "a house dedicated to apostolic functions."

[145] See P. IX, c. 3, no. 17 [762]; CIC 609, §1; CCEO 509, §1.

§2. To him also belongs the faculty to grant to apostolic institutions canonical juridical personality independent of our communities, according to the norm of law.[146]

§3. The faculty of dissolving, alienating, or transferring houses of any type as well as apostolic institutes of the Society belongs to the general, according to the norm of law, after hearing his council and the major superior under whose jurisdiction it is located.[147]

403   The service of authority proper to a local superior refers to the individual members of the community and to the community itself as a whole.[148] He should understand as applying to himself what is said about superiors in general in nos. 349–54.

§2. It is the responsibility of the superior, after he has shared with the individual in his discernment, to see to it that the apostolic work of each is properly integrated into the global mission of the Society. It pertains to him to focus the mission assigned to each by the major superior and to promote the sense of apostolic solidarity of all the members of the community, even of those who may be engaged in very diversified activities.[149] He should foster spiritual discernment in common where the proper dispositions for it exist, according to our way of proceeding in the Society. He should keep the community united in love and obedience.[150]

---

[146] See GC 32, d. 12, no. 20; CIC 1303, §1, 1°; 134, §1.

[147] Approved by Pope John Paul II, Letter of June 10, 1995, from Secretariat of State. By this norm are **modified** the words of the *FI* of Julius III, no. 2, by which the power to alienate and dissolve houses and colleges is given to a general congregation, and in *Const.*, P. VIII, c. 2, no. 2 [680]. **Abolished** are P. IV, c. 2, no. 3, toward the end, A [322, 323]; c. 11, no. 2 [441]; P. IX, c. 3, nos. 5, 17, 18 [743, 762, 763]. **Clarified** are P. IV, c. 2, no. 3, toward the beginning [322]. See CIC 616, §1; CCEO 510.

[148] See P. III, c. 1, no. 23 [284]; c. 2 nos. 2–6 [292–304]; P. VI, c. 1, no. 1 [547]; P. VII, c. 2, no. 1 [618]; P. VIII, d. 1, no. 3, G [659, 667]; P. IV, c. 10, no. 5, B [424, 425].

[149] See GC 32, d. 4 nos. 65, 67; d. 11, no. 29.

[150] See GC 32, d. 11, no. 24; Letter of Father Peter-Hans Kolvenbach, Nov. 5, 1986, "On Apostolic Discernment in Common," no. 41 (*ActRSJ* 19:692–93); GC 32, d. 11, no. 29.

404   §1. As necessity demands, the local superior should be helped by assistants.[151] In addition to a treasurer, he should have a minister to help him in preserving the order of the community, to look after all needs, and to supervise offices that deal with material life.[152]

§2. Insofar as possible there should also be in every house a spiritual director, appointed by the provincial, with due respect for the freedom of each one to go to his own spiritual director.[153]

405   Vice-superiors of dependent houses have the authority that they have received from the major superior or the local superior.

406   §1. If one person alone cannot effectively carry out the governance of both the community and the apostolic institute of the Society associated with it because of their importance or complexity or for other reasons, it is the right of the major superior to establish either a vice-superior (or "superior of the community"), to whom the superior habitually delegates the care of the community and its members, or a "director of the work," whatever may be his title, to whom he habitually delegates responsibility for directing the institute or apostolic work. Such delegated vice-superiors or directors of the work are immediately dependent on the one appointed as the superior, and should give him an account of the office entrusted to him.

§2. When, however, the governance of an apostolic institute, whether proper to the Society or entrusted to its responsibility and conjoined to a community, is independent of the community or for various reasons ought to be independent, a director of the work can be appointed who is immediately dependent on the provincial in carrying out his function, with due observance of any existing civil regulations. This can also be the case when an apostolic work is connected with several communities. Its director depends on the superior of the community to which he belongs in other aspects of his personal religious life.

§3. When there is question of works of greater importance, namely, an educational institution, a center of research and social action, a periodical of great influence, and so on, the major superior should not make changes in governance, as mentioned

---

[151] See P. IX, c. 6, no. 14 [810].

[152] See P. III, c. 1, no. 16 [271]; P. IV, c. 10, no. 7 [431].

[153] See *CollDecr* d. 283 (GC 7, d. 80, no. 19; GC 24, d. 20, no. 2; see GC 18, d. 22; GC 30, d. 40).

in §§1–2, without the general's approval.[154] When he gives such approval, he will also determine the way a director of the work is to be appointed, insofar as this is necessary, in view of the concrete situation.

407   §1. A "director of the work" in institutes proper to the Society or entrusted to its responsibility, or even considered as such in the public mind because he received from it his mission to undertake this work, has the religious-apostolic authority, as defined in his appointment, that enables him to effectively direct our members who work with him and the institute itself to the end proposed, according to its proper Ignatian character.[155]

§2. Even if the local superior (or "vice-superior of the community") does not have the direction of the apostolic institute, he nevertheless retains the responsibility to confirm his brethren in their apostolic mission and to see to it that their religious and community life is such as to enable them to fulfill that mission with God's grace.[156]

§3. There should always exist, strengthened if necessary by appropriate statutes, a close collaboration in their respective functions between the superior (or vice-superior of the community) and the director of the work; even though they have distinct functions to fulfill, they work in one and the same area of responsibility and mission in a way that is complementary and unified. The relation each of them has with the members both of the community and of the work should be clearly defined, as well as the relation of the members with each of them.[157]

§4. A Jesuit community associated with an apostolic work has the role of sharing the basic inspiration of the Society with the entire apostolic community composed of laity and religious; it will share by means of word, witness, and inspiration, through the objectives therein set forth, through values discovered and presented, through the human relations proper to every work of the Society.[158]

---

[154] See "Certain Directives Concerning the Distinction and Mutual Relations between Directors of Works and Superiors," *ActRSJ* 16:1024ff.

[155] See GC 32, d. 11, no. 29; "Certain Directives," no. 5.

[156] GC 32, d. 11, no. 28.

[157] See GC 32, d. 11, no. 29; "Certain Directives," no. 7.

[158] See Address of Father Peter-Hans Kolvenbach, S.J., Georgetown University, June 7, 1989.

408   §1. The general can declare a house to be common to its own province and to another province or provinces, or even committed to the shared responsibility of the conference of major superiors, if this seems appropriate,[159] either because the house serves the needs of all these provinces or because all these provinces must contribute to the maintenance of the house, or for both reasons.[160]

§2. In regard to these houses, the following must be observed, with due regard also for no. 389, §4, about nonapplication of members from other provinces to the province in which the house is located:

1° Unless by decree of the general they are placed under the moderator of the conference of major superiors or someone who enjoys special jurisdiction over them, their governance belongs to the provincial in whose territory they are located. But it is appropriate in matters of greater moment that he should consult the provincials of the other provinces with whom each such house is common.

2° When a common work is under the care of a conference, any division at the level of major superior between apostolic responsibility for the work and *cura personalis* of those assigned to it on a permanent basis should be avoided as much as possible, so as to safeguard the normal conditions necessary for authentic Ignatian government.[161]

3° Established rules and objective criteria are to govern the assignment of personnel from the provinces and regions to common houses. When a major superior is asked to make a particular man available for a common house, he should normally give this request a priority at least equal to the needs of his own province or region.[162]

4° Members who work in a common house, although not applied to that province, are subject to the one on whom, according to the norm of 1°, the house directly depends, as if he were their own major superior. Other provincials can (and must) visit their own subjects living in common houses. If they have any observation to make about the house, they should make it

---

[159] See GC 34, d. 21, nos. 22–24.

[160] See *ActRSJ* 14:356.

[161] GC 34, d. 21, no. 23.

[162] See GC 34, d. 21, no. 24.

CHAPTER 6

¹AIDS TO THE SUPERIOR GENERAL FOR THE PROPER PERFORMANCE OF
HIS FUNCTIONS

[789]   1. ²The function proper to the office of the general is not to preach, hear confessions, and perform other similar ministries (though as a private person he will see what he can do in these ministries when the occupations proper to his office leave him opportunity, but under no other circumstances). ³Instead, his office is to govern the whole body of the Society in such a manner that its well-being and proper functioning may through the divine grace be preserved and increased for the glory of God our Lord [A], by employing his authority as is expedient for that end.

[790]   A. ¹*He will achieve this kind of government primarily by the good reputation and example of his life, by charity and love for the Society in Christ our Lord, and by his constant and heartfelt prayer and Masses to obtain the grace of the aforementioned preservation and growth. ²On his own part he should hold these means in high esteem and have great confidence in our Lord, since these are the most efficacious means of gaining grace from his Divine Majesty, the Source of what is longed for. Especially should the general do this as necessities occur.*

   ³*Next, he will achieve this kind of government by his solicitude to maintain the observance of the Constitutions, by keeping himself frequently informed by the provincials of what is occurring in all the provinces* ⁴*and by writing to the provincials his opinion about the matters which they communicate to him, and by so acting that provision is made where it is proper, either through himself or through the helpers who will be described later.*

[791]   2. ¹Presupposing his qualities of strong spirituality and virtue as treated above in Chapter 2 [725–28], he still has need of good

known to the competent superior. But they are not to grant any faculty, dispensation, or permission to their own subjects in a common house, since this pertains to the provincial to whom the governance of the house directly belongs.[163]

409   The same observations about a common house apply, with the necessary adaptations, to a work or apostolic institute common to several provinces.   ∎

---

[163] See *ActRSJ* 14:356.

helpers for more particular matters. ²For although he himself may sometimes handle them directly, he will still need lower superiors, ³who ought to be selected men, to whom he can give considerable authority and ordinarily refer such particular matters.

⁴Among these lower superiors, his more usual dealings will be with the provincials, just as the provincials' dealing will be with the rectors and local superiors, so that subordination may be the better preserved. ⁵Sometimes, however, for the sake of fuller information about everything and other situations which can come up, the general will deal with the rectors or local superiors and also with individual persons. ⁶He will also endeavor to help them with counsel, reprimand, and correction, if necessary. For it pertains to him to supply for the defects of the lower superiors and, with the divine favor and aid, to bring to perfection what has been imperfect in them.

[792]   3.   ¹It will also be helpful in everything for the general to have close at hand the bulls, briefs, and all the concessions which pertain to the founding and the favors or privileges of the Society, and a summary of all of them; ²and likewise a list of all the houses and colleges of the Society with their revenues; and another of all the persons who are in each province. ³This list should contain not only the professed, the formed coadjutors, and the approved scholastics, but also those who are in probation; and on it their names and qualities should be stated. He should have this list renewed each year, if this seems expedient. ⁴Finally, he should be informed about everything so that he may the better be able to make provision in all things for the glory of God.

[793]   4.   ¹As was stated in a general way in Part VI [591] about the members of the Society not engaging in secular affairs even of a pious character, so the general more than anyone ought to avoid engaging in them or in other, even pious, affairs unrelated to the Society, ²in such a way [B] that he lacks time and energy for what is proper to his office, which requires the whole man and more.

[794]   B.   ¹*This means insofar as he is able to excuse himself.* ²*Ultimately, however, discretion will have to indicate whether personally or through other members of the Society on some occasion he ought to undertake the management of some pious works which do not pertain to the Society,* ³*in consideration of their importance in the service of God our Lord, or of the persons urging them upon him.*

[795]   5.   ¹Furthermore, he ought not to occupy himself much in the execution of the particular ministries pertaining to the Society

which others can do *[C]*, as would be, for example, the care of a particular house in regard to its temporal support and government. 2On the contrary, as is stated above [791], he should have his officials in each place, even where he resides. Thus, even if he does not shift his entire burden onto them, he can certainly receive aid from them and they can lessen his concern for such matters.

[796]   *C.* 1*It is more properly the general's task to lay down the order to be followed, if a suitable one should be lacking, in his place of residence and elsewhere as well. But he ought to delegate the execution, as is stated.*

[797]   6. 1Likewise in each province he should have as provincials men worthy of great confidence, being mindful that the good government of the Society depends in great part upon them and the local superiors. 2When they are men of this type and he shares his labor with them in the things he can and meanwhile takes care to be kept informed of everything more important, he will have more time left to himself to deal with matters of universal import which he alone can handle. 3He will also have greater light to see what should be done in connection with them, his mind not losing a part of its light (as often happens) through over-involvement in particular matters and details which can weigh it down and weaken it for matters of universal scope.

[798]   7. 1The superior general needs helpers, not only for more individual matters, as was stated [791, 795, 797], but also for universal matters proper to his own office, so as to carry them out competently and without strain *[D]*.

2Therefore he requires to have someone to assist him with reminders of the numerous matters he must be solicitous to attend to in his office, someone to assist with advice on ordering them, 3and someone to assist with diligent work and labor in executing them. 4For it is certain that no one man's memory could remember so many things; nor, if he could, could a single mind properly think them through and order them; nor, even if he could do that, would one man's energies suffice to execute them.

[799]   *D.* 1*Since he must carry on business with so many persons and deal with matters which are so various and of such great importance, he would carry an unbearable burden if he did not have the help of others. Even with great distraction of mind and shortening of his life, he could not carry this burden well.* 2*Thus it becomes evident that all those who occupy important posts of government and give satisfaction in them*

should have many aids for their task. ³*Thus too the general needs them to perform his office well, promptly, and without strain.*

[800]   8. ¹In regard to the first point, his solicitude to attend to all affairs, the general ought to have one person who ordinarily accompanies him and should be his memory for everything which he must write and discuss, and finally for all the affairs of his office *[E].* ²This person should take on the general's own person and imagine that he carries on his own shoulders the general's whole burden, except for his authority.

[801]   E. ¹*The function of this person will be to gather from all the letters and reports the substance and the points which must be referred to the superior and which require that a reply should be given or something should be done.* ²*Further, according to the extent of the commission which the general gives him, he can reply to the letters, whether the general must sign them or the secretary himself at the general's mandate.* ³*He will show the letters to the general himself or, at his order, to the assistants or to one of them, or to no one, according to what the material treated and the circumstances of the secretary's person require.*

[802]   9. ¹This person ought to be one who is solicitous and prudent and, if possible, learned; one too who has a pleasant personality and a good manner of dealing with all kinds of persons by word of mouth and by letters. ²Above all he should be one in whom confidence can be placed and one who loves the Society in our Lord, so that the general may be better aided and served by him for the glory of God.

[803]   10. ¹The second aid mentioned was counsel for ordering the affairs of moment which occur. How necessary this aid is to the general can be understood from the multitude of those affairs ²and from the nature of the human intellect, which is unable to turn in so many directions with proper attention or to make proper provision for them.

³Consequently, it seems that there ought to be, in the place where the superior resides, some persons of prominence in learning and all good qualities **who may assist him**²¹ and with special care take charge of attending to the universal affairs of the Society which the general entrusts to them. ⁴This care could be divided among them to enable them to penetrate each matter better. ⁵One, for example, could observe the affairs of the Indies, another those

---

²¹ **Clarified by** *CN* **380, 384–85.** (Besides general counselors there are also other counselors of the superior general.)

of Spain and Portugal, another those of Germany and France, another those of Italy and Sicily, and so on as the Society spreads into more regions. ⁶Each one would offer special prayer and be mindful in his Masses of the region particularly entrusted to him, and he would examine what could be most helpful toward achieving the Society's aims in that region; ⁷he would go over the matter with the others where that seems specially called for, and after further discussion they could lay it before the superior.

⁸Likewise, these persons would deal with what is proposed to them by the general or the secretary of the Society, so that matters may be more fully processed before being presented to the superior [F]. ⁹In general, in considering and settling the problems of doctrine and action which require greater thought, these assistants ought to assist the general and lighten his burdens. ¹⁰Besides this function, and the fact that better provision in many matters can be made through them, they could attend to preaching, lecturing, hearing confessions, and other good and pious works, to the divine glory and the aid of souls.

[804]   F. ¹Moreover, more important matters which need to be written, and instructions for members who are sent to various regions, could be discussed with these persons before being written, and the secretary could indicate their opinions to the superior; the same could be done in matters of doctrine. ²Besides lessening the general's burdens, this would lend greater authority to what he ordains.

[805]   11. ¹The number of these assistants will be four for the present, and they may be those mentioned above [779]. ²Although the matters of importance should be discussed with them, the decision will always belong to the general, after he has heard them.

[806]   12. ¹The third point concerns diligent labor in carrying out or executing what has been ordained for essential concerns of the Society; for example, the expediting or dispatching of matters regarding the houses and colleges, the defense of their interests, and in general all business matters. ²For all these matters it will be very helpful, indeed indispensable, to have **the help of a procurator general of the Society**²² resident in Rome. ³He should a man of prudence, fidelity, skill in dealing with others, and all good qualities. {**However, he should not be a professed father**}²³ {**nor live in**

---

²² **Modified by** *CN* 383, §§2–3. (The office of Procurator, described here, is now also fulfilled by the general treasurer.)

²³ **Abolished by GC 34.** (Today there does not seem to be any reason to prohibit him from being professed.)

the house of the professed Society}[24] *[G]*, but in another of which mention was made in Part IV. [4]He also should have his own helpers and necessary aids for the business which he could not do by himself alone *[H]*.

[807]   G.   [1]*{The procurators should ordinarily not live in the houses of the professed Society but in the house assigned to them}.*[25] [2]*However, when they are not handling litigation or when there is some reason of urgent necessity or convenience, they could live for a time in the houses of the professed.* [3]*This should be left to those who have charge of the others in the houses of the professed Society, in accord with the order or commission they have from the general or with what they know clearly to be his intention.*

[808]   H.   [1]*An alternative is that there should be more procurators, according to the circumstances and urgent necessities in diverse and various regions.*

[809]   13.   [1]It seems, therefore, that the general, provided with those aids, ought to employ the time which his health and energies allow him, [2]partly with God, partly with the aforementioned officials and helpers in conferring now with some and now with others, and partly with himself in reflecting privately and thinking out and deciding what should be done with the help and favor of God our Lord.

[810]   14.   [1]The provincial superiors and the rectors of colleges or the local superiors of houses also ought to have their aids, more or fewer in number according to the necessity and importance of the affairs entrusted to them. [2]In particular they should have persons designated to give counsel, with whom they should consult on the matters of importance which arise. But after these consultors have been heard, the decision should remain with the superiors *[I]*.

[811]   I.   [1]*From what has been said about the general, there may be inferred what applies to provincial and local superiors and to rectors of colleges* [2]*with respect to their qualities, authority, function, and the aids which each one ought to have. This can be made explicit in the rules for each of these particular superiors.*

---

[24] **Abolished.** (Once the distinction between houses has been removed in regard to poverty, there is no basis for this prescription.)

[25] **Abolished:** see preceding note.

PART X

¹HOW THE WHOLE BODY OF THE SOCIETY IS TO BE PRESERVED AND INCREASED IN ITS WELL-BEING

[812] 1. ²The Society was not instituted by human means; and it is not through them that it can be preserved and increased, but through the grace of the omnipotent hand of Christ our God and Lord. ³Therefore in him alone must be placed the hope that he will preserve and carry forward what he deigned to begin for his service and praise and for the aid of souls. ⁴In conformity with this hope, the first and most appropriate means will be the prayers and Masses which ought to be offered for this holy intention, and which should be ordered for this purpose every week, month, and year in all places where the Society resides.

[813] 2. ¹For the preservation and growth not only of the body or exterior of the Society but also of its spirit, and for the attainment of the objective it seeks, which is to aid souls to reach their ultimate and supernatural end, ²the means which unite the human instrument with God and so dispose it that it may be wielded well by his divine hand ³are more effective than those which equip it in relation to human beings. ⁴Such means are, for example, goodness and virtue, and especially charity, and a pure intention of the divine service, and familiarity with God our Lord in spiritual exercises of devotion, ⁵and sincere zeal for souls for the sake of the glory of the one who created and redeemed them and not for any other benefit. ⁶Thus it appears that care should be taken in general that all the members of the Society devote themselves to the solid and perfect virtues and to spiritual pursuits, and attach greater importance to them than to learning and other natural and human gifts. ⁷For these interior gifts are necessary to make those exterior means efficacious for the end which is being sought.

[814] 3. ¹When based upon this foundation, the natural means which equip the human instrument of God our Lord to deal with his fellow human beings will all help toward the preservation and growth of this whole body, ²provided they are acquired and exercised for the divine service alone; employed, indeed, not so that we may put our confidence in them, but so that we may cooperate

PART X
THE PRESERVATION AND INCREASE
OF THE SOCIETY

410 §1. As a sign of gratitude and devotion to the Sacred Heart of Jesus, let that feast be solemnly celebrated; and on that day is to be renewed the consecration by which the Society on January 1, 1872, dedicated and consecrated itself totally and perpetually.

§2. The consecration to the Immaculate Heart of the Blessed Virgin Mary is to be renewed each year on the feast of the Immaculate Heart.[1]

411 The sense of belonging and responsibility that each individual one of Ours has toward the whole Society should be manifested in a knowledge of our spirituality, our history, our saints, our apostolic labors, and our men, especially of those who are suffering difficulties for the sake of Christ; it is to be manifested as well by maintaining Ignatian mobility and flexibility with a view to helping any region of the Society whatsoever.[2]

412 §1. All our members should have at heart a shared concern for attracting new members to the Society, especially by prayer and the example of their lives as individuals and in community.[3]

§2. Therefore, we must do everything possible actively to present the Society in such a way that those whom God calls will know and appreciate who and what we are and what is our distinctive way of proceeding in the following of Christ.[4]

§3. We must also promote vocations as widely as possible, in order to reflect the culture and experience of those we

---

[1] See *CollDecr* d. 286 (GC 23, d. 46 nos. 2–3; GC 29, d. 34).

[2] GC 31, d. 19, no. 6, a; see P. VIII, d. 1, no. 9 [673].

[3] GC 33, d. 1, no. 22.

[4] GC 34, d. 10, no. 2; d. 26.

with the divine grace ³according to the arrangement of the sovereign providence of God our Lord. For he desires to be glorified both through the natural means, which he gives as Creator, and through the supernatural means, which he gives as the Author of grace. ⁴Therefore the human or acquired means ought to be sought with diligence, especially well-grounded and solid learning, and a method of proposing it to the people by means of sermons, lectures, and the art of dealing and conversing with others.

[815] 4. ¹In a similar manner, it will help greatly to maintain the colleges in good condition and discipline if the superintendency over them is exercised by persons who cannot receive any temporal gain, ²such as members of the professed Society, ³which will take care that those who possess the talent for it may receive in the colleges formation in Christian life and learning. For these colleges will be a seedbed for the professed Society and its coadjutors. ⁴Furthermore, if universities over which the Society exercises superintendency are added to the colleges, they too will aid toward the same end, as long as the manner of procedure described in Part IV [440–509] is preserved.

[816] 5. ¹Since poverty is like a bulwark of religious institutes which preserves them in their existence and good order and defends them from many enemies, and since the devil uses corresponding effort to destroy this bulwark in one way or another, ²it will be highly important for the preservation and growth of this whole body that every appearance of avarice should be banished afar, ³through the Society's **abstention from accepting fixed income, or any possessions, or recompense**¹ for preaching, or lecturing, or Masses, or administration of sacraments, or spiritual things, as is stated in Part VI [565], and also through its avoidance of converting the fixed revenue of the colleges to its own utility.

[817] 6. ¹It will also be of the highest importance toward perpetuating the Society's well-being to use great diligence in precluding from it ambition, the mother of all evils in any community or congregation. ²This will be accomplished by closing the door against seeking, directly or indirectly, any dignity or prelacy within the Society, ³in such a way that all the professed should promise to God our Lord never to seek one and to expose anyone whom they observe trying to obtain one; also in such a way that {one who can

---

¹ (See notes 9–10 to [555], 11 and 13 to [557], 14 to [561], 17 to [565]).

seek to serve, including minority cultures, immigrants, and indigenous people.[5]

413 The Society should always show itself bound to its benefactors in charity and gratitude. Superiors should ensure that prayers are offered for them and other appropriate signs of our gratitude are shown them.[6]

414 "In the perfect observance of all the Constitutions and in the particular fulfillment of our Institute," our formed members should excel, setting a good example and spreading the good odor of Christ, keeping before their eyes the serious obligation they have of giving edification especially to our younger members.[7]

415 All by earnest reading and meditation (in particular, at the time of the annual Spiritual Exercises, renewal of vows, monthly recollection, beginning of the year, and so forth) should strive ever to know, esteem, and love better our Constitutions and the special nature of our Institute,[8] which are to be faithfully observed, and which for each and all of us are the one, true, and safe way that surely leads to the perfection to which our Lord calls and invites all sons of the Society.[9]

§2. Major superiors, especially at the time of the annual visitation, should see that this is faithfully observed.

416 Finally, those means that are proposed by our holy father Saint Ignatius in Part X of the Constitutions "for the preservation and development not only of the body or exterior of the Society but also of its spirit, and for the attainment of the objective it seeks, which is to aid souls to reach their ultimate and supernatural end,"[10] are to be observed eagerly and diligently by all, with a truly personal sense of responsibility for its increase and development, for the praise and service of our God and Lord Jesus Christ, and the help of souls.[11]

L. D. S.

---

[5] GC 34, d. 10, no. 4.

[6] See P. IV, c. 1, nos. 1–6 [309–19]; P. VII, d. 4, nos. 3–4 [638, 640].

[7] See *CollDecr* d. [99] (GC 28, d. 22, 5°); see P. VI, c. 1, no. 1 [547]; P. IV, c. 10, no. 5 [424]; P. VI, c. 5 [602]; P. IX, c. 3, no. 8 [746]; P. IX, c. 6, A [790]; P. X, no. 13 [826].

[8] See P. VI, c. 1, no. 1 [547].

[9] See *CollDecr.* d. [97] (GC 28, d. 22, 3°); P. IV, c. 10, F [430]; L [439]; P. X, no. 13 [826].

[10] P. X., no. 2 [813].

[11] See P. X, no. 1 [812].

be proved to have sought such a prelacy becomes ineligible and disqualified for promotion to any prelacy}.²

⁴The professed should similarly promise to God our Lord **not to seek any prelacy or dignity outside the Society and, as far as in them lies, not to consent to being chosen for a similar charge unless they are compelled by an order from the one who can command them under pain of sin.³** ⁵Each one should desire to serve souls in conformity with our profession of humility and lowliness, and to avoid having the Society deprived of the men who are necessary for its purpose.

⁶Each one should further promise to God our Lord that if a prelacy outside the Society is accepted through the aforementioned manner of compulsion, **he will afterwards listen at any time to the counsel of whoever may be general of the Society, or of another whom the general substitutes for himself;⁴** ⁷and that if he judges the counsel he has received to be the better thing, he will carry it out *[A]*. He will do this, not because he, being a prelate, has any member of the Society as a superior, but because he wishes to oblige himself voluntarily before God our Lord to do what he finds to be better for his divine service, ⁸and to be happy to have someone who presents it to him with charity and Christian freedom, to the glory of God our Lord.

[818] *A.* ¹*After observing the pressure which has been exerted in so many ways to bring members of the Society to accept bishoprics, and after resisting in many cases and having been unable to resist accepting the patriarchate and bishopric of Ethiopia,* ²*we conceived this aid for the latter undertaking and for other similar ones when resistance may be impossible.* ³*However, the Society does not oblige itself to take up this measure each time one of its individual members must accept a bishopric, but it remains free either to omit it or to take it up where it is judged to be of great importance for the divine service.* ⁴*This simple vow will be made following the profession along with the other vows which have been mentioned.*

[819] 7. ¹Much aid is given toward perpetuating the well-being of this whole body by what was said in Part I [142–44], Part II [204],

---

² **Abolished by GC 34.** (In the spirit of the recommendation made to the superior general by GC 31 in its d. 53, 2°, just as other penalties imposed by law contained in the Constitutions have been abrogated.)

³ **Clarified by** *CN* **139, §1** (approved by Pope John Paul II, letter of June 10, 1995, from Secretariat of State); **§§2–3.**

⁴ **Clarified by** *CN* **142.**

and Part V [516–23] about not admitting a mob and persons unsuitable for our Institute, even to probation, ²and about dismissals during the time of probation when it is found that some persons do not turn out to be suitable. Much less ought those to be retained who are addicted to vice or are incorrigible. ³But even greater strictness should be shown **in admitting persons among the approved scholastics⁵** and formed coadjutors, and strictness far greater still in regard to admission to profession. ⁴This profession should be made only by persons who are select in spirit and learning, and who after prolonged and extensive activity have become well known through various trials of virtue and abnegation, with edification and satisfaction to all. ⁵This is done so that, even though numbers grow, the spirit may not be diminished or weakened, with those incorporated into the Society being such as has been described.

[820] 8. ¹Since the well-being or illness of the head has its consequences in the whole body, it is supremely important that the election of the superior general be carried out as directed in Part IX [723–35]. ²Next in importance is the choice of the lower superiors in the provinces, colleges, and houses of the Society. For in a general way, the subjects will be what these superiors are.

³It is also highly important that, in addition to that choice, the individual superiors should have much authority over the subjects, and the general over the individual superiors; and, on the other hand, that the Society have much authority in regard to the general, as is explained in Part IX [736, 757, 759, 766–88]. ⁴This arrangement is made so that all may have full power for good and that, if they do poorly, they may be fully in subjection.

⁵It is similarly important that the superiors have suitable helpers, as was said in the same part [798–810], for the good order and execution of the affairs pertaining to their office.

[821] 9. ¹Whatever helps toward the union of the members of this Society among themselves and with their head will also help much toward preserving the well-being of the Society. This is especially the case with the bond of wills, which is the mutual charity and love they have for one another. ²This bond is strengthened by their getting information and news from one another and having much intercommunication, by their following one same doctrine, and by their being uniform in everything as far as possible, ³and above all by the bond of obedience, which unites the individuals with their

---

⁵ (Approved brothers are included with the scholastics; see *CN* 6, §1, 2°.)

superiors, and the local superiors among themselves and with the provincials, and both the local superiors and provincials with the general, in such a way that the subordination of some to others is diligently preserved.

[822]   10. ¹Moderation in spiritual and bodily labors and the middle tenor of the Constitutions, which do not lean toward an extreme of rigor or toward excessive laxity (and thus they can be better observed), will help this whole body to persevere and maintain itself in its well-being.

[823]   11. ¹Toward the same purpose it is helpful in general to strive to retain the goodwill and charity of all, even of those outside the Society, and especially of those whose favorable or unfavorable attitude toward it is of great importance for opening or closing the gate leading to the service of God and the good of souls *[B]*. ²It is also helpful that in the Society there should neither be partiality to one side or another among Christian princes or rulers nor should any be perceived; in its stead there should be a universal love which embraces in our Lord all parties (even though they are adversaries to one another).

[824]   B. ¹*We must chiefly retain the benevolence of the Apostolic See, which the Society must especially serve; ²and then that of the temporal rulers and noble and powerful persons whose favor or disfavor does much toward opening or closing the gate to the service of God and the good of souls. ³Similarly, when an unfavorable attitude is noticed in some persons, especially in persons of importance, prayer ought to be offered for them and the suitable means should be employed to bring them to friendship, or at least to keep them from being hostile. ⁴This is done, not because contradiction and ill-treatment are feared, but so that God our Lord may be more served and glorified in all things through the benevolence of all these persons.*

[825]   12. ¹Help will also be found in a discreet and moderate use of the favors granted by the Apostolic See, by seeking with all sincerity nothing else than the aid of souls. For through this God our Lord will carry forward what he has begun; ²and the fragrance [2 Cor. 2:15] arising from the genuineness of the good works will increase the benevolent desire of others to avail themselves of the Society's aid and to help the Society for the end which it seeks, the glory and service of his Divine Majesty.

[826]   13. ¹It will also be helpful that attention should be devoted to the preservation of the health of the individual members *[C]*, as was stated in Part III [292–306]; ²and finally, that all should apply

themselves to the observance of the Constitutions. For this purpose they must know them, at least those which pertain to each one. **Therefore each one should read or hear them every month.**⁶

[827]   C. ¹*For this purpose it is expedient that attention should be given to having the houses and colleges in healthy locations with pure air and not in those characterized by the opposite.*

A.M.D.G.

---

⁶ **Modified by** *CN* **415.** (All are diligently to read and meditate on the Constitutions.)

INDEX OF TOPICS

Conventions Followed

Numbers cited below always refer to **boldfaced** numbers placed at the beginning of one or more paragraphs in the text of the Constitutions or the Complementary Norms.

Numbers enclosed in **square brackets ([ ])** refer to the **Constitutions** with their respective notes; other numbers refer to the **Complementary Norms**.

• A •

Abdication: *see* **Renunciation of goods**

Ability to possess or acquire: *see* **Temporal goods**

Abnegation:

1. *In general:* a great degree of abnegation is required in the Society [103, 308]; — it is often to be the subject in domestic exhortations [280]

2. *In persons:* let novices strive to make progress in it [289], 49; as also the brothers [117] and the tertians [516]; it is presupposed in scholastics [307] and in those who are to be promoted to the profession [519, 819]; — in proportion to each one's progress in abnegation, superiors can grant appropriate liberty, 354 §3

3. *In things:* abnegation: in obedience [284, 547]; — in applying goods in favor of the Society [258]; — in accepting one's grade [111]; — in matters which pertain to the body [296, 297]; — in humble offices [83]; — in desiring the least desirable things [81]; — abnegation of one's own love in chastity, 144 §3; — abnegation required for

personal and communal spiritual discernment, 223 §4; — abnegation in the exercise of the intellectual apostolate, 293 §2. *See also* **Mortification**

Abortion: — a reason for forbidding admission, in the case of those bringing one about or cooperating in one, 28 §1 2°

Abrogation:

1. *In the Constitutions:* [18, 28, 35, 41, 60, 62, 93, 98, 110, 117, 127, 173, 200, 202, 205, 207, 217, 236, 246, 261, 268, 278, 323, 343, 348, 349, 395, 396, 407, 416, 421, 437, 441, 539, 551, 557, 575, 584, 591, 642, 644, 679, 680, 695, 696, 701, 709, 743, 763, 780, 806, 807, 817], in accord with their respective notes.

2. *Of the Collection of Decrees of GC 27, see CN* Introductory Decree, 5°

Absence:

1. *Of a local superior* from his own house: how substitution for him is to be made, 346

2. *Of a major superior* from his province or region: how substitution for him is to be made, 345 §1

manner in which these are to be accepted, with respect to the promotion to final vows, 120 2°; — of extern students regarding their faults [488]

Admonitor: — what his office is regarding any superior [770, 810, 811]; — in general, how appointed, 356 §1; of the superior general: by whom appointed [770], 379 §1; duration of office, 379 §2; what his grade, his talents, and his task should be, 379 §1; — when and in what manner substitution is to be made for an admonitor, 379 §2

Adults: — also are to be educated, 291

Adversaries of the Society: — we should reconcile them to us [426]; — what account of them should be made in choosing missions [622]; — prayer should be offered for them [824]

Advice: — a certain holy advice is to be given to novices [62]; — secrecy thereof regarding things heard when someone is seeking advice, 235 2°; — superiors and directors of works are to avail themselves frequently of their brethren's advice, and are with grateful heart to receive advice they spontaneously offer, 354. *See also* **Consultors**

Affections:
  1. *Ordinate:* — particularly required in an examiner of candidates [143]; — very much required in superiors [423]; — most especially so in the case of the general [725, 728]; — affective formation of novices, 53, 54 §2; — of all who are in formation, 72 §1; — dominion over to be moderated, 147 §4; — third probation as a school of [516], 125 §1
  2. *Inordinate:* — the extent to which these are to impede admission [179]; — and can be a reason for dismissal [210]; — the way in which they grow warm [582]; — and are a danger to union [657];

— towards creatures, to be put aside [288]; — as also a fleshly love for one's neighbor [54, 61]; — care must be taken against, in the renunciation of goods [55, 256, 258]; — in dismissal [222]; — let superiors be free from [222, 726], 352

Age: — the age required for admission [151, 160, 185, 187], 28 §1 6°; — for the canonical beginning of the novitiate, 24 §3; — for first vows, 116; — for last vows (equivalently), 119; — for one to be named a major superior (equivalently), 344 §1; — of the highest superior [732]. — When it is to be a criterion of precedence: in the case of substituting for a superior, 345 §3; in other cases, *see* **Formulas of congregations**

Agreements: — with parents, regarding temporal goods, entered upon on the occasion of the renunciation of goods, 171 4°, 172 §2

Aid of the neighbor: *see* **Souls**

Aides:
  1. *To the superior general:* — why they are needed [798, 799]; — who and of what sort they are to be [760, 765, 800–802, 806], 383–86; — by whom they are to be appointed [760]; by whose funds their expenses are to be paid, 209
  2. *To the provincial and other superiors:* *see* **Officials**

Alienation of goods: — in general [322–23]; — particular matters regarding alienation of certain houses and colleges [322–23, 420, 441, 680, 743, 762, 763], 390 §3

Alms:
  1. *To be accepted:* — what sort of motive is to be hoped for in those who give them [564, 569, 640]; — where they may be sought, 214; — how they are to be asked for [569]; — alms in the churches [567], — in the colleges [331], — on behalf of houses [149, 557, 560, 564, 569]; — what is to be

Alms *(continued)*
　　said about perpetual alms, in par-
　　ticular [564]; — alms for ordinary
　　expenses, 207; — for Masses [4,
　　565, 640], 184 §1; — for minis-
　　tries [4, 565, 566, 640], 182; —
　　for works outside the Society,
　　185, 186
　　2. *To be sought for the poor:* — in the
　　renunciation of goods [53, 54, 59,
　　254]; — taken from the goods of
　　the Society [774, 776], 210 §3,
　　213 §1. *See also* **Causes, pious;
　　Charitable and Apostolic Fund of
　　the Society (FACSI)**

Ambition: — what an evil it is [720,
　　817]; — to be most carefully
　　rooted out [817]; — care to be
　　taken against every sort of it in
　　the matter of academic degrees
　　[390, 478]. *See also* **Ambitioning**

Ambitioning: — the vows of the sol-
　　emnly professed about not ambi-
　　tioning dignities [817], 134, 138–
　　42; — on reporting those who
　　are ambitioning [695, 817], 141;
　　— what if someone should be
　　convicted of ambitioning [695,
　　817]; — commands and penalties
　　against those who would ambi-
　　tion in elections and in congrega-
　　tions [695, 696, 709, 817]. *See
　　also* **Formulas of congregations**

Analysis, sociocultural and religious: —
　　to be used in the choice of minis-
　　tries, 258, §3; — Ours in forma-
　　tion are to be trained in it, 95;
　　even in the practical details of
　　living, 106, §2

Anger: — mutual, among Ours, is not to
　　be tolerated and is at once to be
　　overcome [275]

Annuities: — by whom they can be im-
　　posed upon the goods of the So-
　　ciety [743]; — personal annuities,
　　how to be applied in the renunci-
　　ation of goods, 171 6°

Anointing of the sick: — is to be given
　　to Ours in good time [595]

Apostate from the faith: — the extent
　　to which these are subject to pro-

hibition of admission [22, 165,
　　167], 28 §1 1°

Apostolate: *see* **Apostolic institute; Dia-
　　log; Ecumenism; Education; Intel-
　　lectual apostolate; Missionary
　　service; Missions given by the
　　Supreme Pontiff; Missions given
　　by superiors of the Society; Mis-
　　sion of the Society; Dialog, (3);
　　Souls; Social apostolate; Social
　　communications (media); Spiri-
　　tual Exercises,**

Apostolic activity: — to be joined with
　　prayer, so that we may be able to
　　find God present in the world,
　　223, 224

Apostolic Delegate: — whether one
　　such can, while in office, be pro-
　　moted to final vows, 129

Apostolic institute: — what it is, 188
　　§2; — its establishment with a
　　juridical personhood of its own
　　independent of the community,
　　402 §2; — what its practice of
　　poverty is to be: *see* **Poverty**

Apostolic See: — the Society is joined
　　to it by a special bond and ought
　　to be at its service [824], 2 §2,
　　259; — all of Ours in all places
　　should be prepared to be obedi-
　　ent to it [618], 259; — its good-
　　will is especially to be preserved
　　[824]; — the manner in which
　　favors are ordinarily to be sought
　　from it [552]; — how favors
　　granted by it are to be used
　　[825]; — certain cases are to be
　　brought to it by superiors, 35 §2;
　　— cases in which subjects can
　　recur to it, 35 §§1–2. *See also*
　　**Canon Law; Indults; Magisterium
　　of the Church; Pontifical law
　　proper to the Society; Privileges
　　of the Society; Roman Pontiff**

Appearance, good: — desirable in all
　　who are to be admitted [151,
　　158]; — in those who are to deal
　　with important people [624]; —
　　in the secretary of the Society
　　[802]; — in the general [731]

Application:

1. *Of Ours to another province:* — when it is to be done and when not, 389, §§3–4; — whose task it is to apply and in what manner, 389 §2

2. *Of temporal goods:* — of one's own, to be made in the renunciation: *see* **Renunciation of goods**; — of those accepted by the Society by reason of a renunciation [258, 259], 173

Appointments:

1. *Of superiors:* — the sort of persons to be chosen and the manner of choosing, the gifts and conditions that are necessary, the consultation to be done before their appointment, when their authority begins, how supply for them is to be made in cases of need, how long they remain in office [421, 490, 757, 759, 778], 340–48

2. *Of officials:* — [428, 760, 770, 781], 358, 393

3. *Of examiners for grade:* — 93 §1

4. *Of the primary examiner of candidates:* — [142]

Approval of certain appointments:

1. *Of superiors* — [421, 490, 740], 331 3°

2. *Of province officials* — 358, §1; — of the master of novices and of the tertian instructor, 346 §2

Arabic language: — the extent to which it is to be taught in the Society's universities [447]

Arbiters: — when these are to be elected to choose a general [707]; — when they should be elected to determine business matters: *see* **Definitors**

Arts: — formation in them is to be encouraged, 95

Assistant for the election of a general: — his election and duties [701, 703, 705, 706, 782]

Assistants:

1. *For provident care:*

A. *Their number:* — there are to be four [779], 364 §1

B. *Their appointment:* — they are to be professed of the four vows [780], 364 §1; — their characteristics [779], 364 §§2–3; — by whom they are ordinarily to be chosen [781], 364 §1; — how they are to be chosen in a general congregation, 364 §1; — how long they are to remain in office, 376 §§1–2; — when, by whom, and in what manner others are to substitute for them [781], 376 §§3–5; — how provision is to be made for them, if they are impeded: *see* **Substitute assistant for provident care**

C. *Their office:* — of exercising provident care over the general in the name of the Society: — in general [767]; — in particular [766–77, 779, 782–86], 365, 366 §§1–2, 380 §2; — where they should live [779, 780], 374 §1; — the extent to which they can be absent or can be engaged in other affairs [779, 780], 374; — the oath to be sworn by them, when it is to be sworn, and in regard to what [782], 378; — by reason of their office they are also general counselors, 364 §3; — it is recommended that if a smaller group is formed within the council, they take part in it, 382 §2

D. *Their prerogatives:* — they have a deliberative vote in the naming of general counselors who are not regional assistants, outside of the process that is proper to a general congregation, 380 §3, 381 §3; — they have a deliberative vote in all matters in which provincials have it outside of a general congregation, 375; — the extent to which they can bring it about that a general congregation is summoned [681, 773, 782–88], 366 §3; — as also a congregation for electing a temporary vicar [773, 786], 366 §3 1°; — they have a right ex officio to attend a general congregation, one for elect-

some are to be chosen to do it
[569]; — on behalf of the colleges
[331]. *See also* **Alms**

Benefactors: — how much we owe
them [309]; — a list of them is to
be kept; — a sharing in the good
works of the Society has been
granted to them [317]; — prayers
and Masses prescribed for them
[309, 310, 315, 316, 638, 640]; —
what is to be sought from God
for them [315, 640]; — how
[these prayers] are to be offered
and how other signs of gratitude
ought to be shown them, 413; —
the extent to which those places
are to be preferred [for the establishment of ministries] where
there are benefactors [622]

Benefices, ecclesiastical: — when and in
what matter they are to be renounced [59], 32 §4; — in whose
favor [59, 256]

Biblical Institute, Pontifical: — entrusted to the Society by the Holy
See, 304 §1

Bishop: — ambitioning and accepting
the episcopal dignity, the matter
of the third simple vow of the
professed [817], 139 §1; — without the permission and approval
of the general no one can accept
such a dignity [756]; — what is to
be done when episcopal appointment is proposed for one of Ours,
139 §3; — the meaning of the
vow of listening to the advice of
the general on the part of one
who has been named a bishop,
142; — whether those who have
been named bishops can be promoted to final vows, 129; — the
vow of denouncing those who
ambition the episcopacy, 141; —
the extent to which the faculty of
receiving vows can be given to a
bishop [513], 115. *See also* **Ordinary, local**

Blessed Virgin Mary: — devotion to her
should be nourished, 234, 276 §2;
— fostered, and spread, ibid.; —

it is a means of great import in
growing in the consecrated love
of chastity, 146 §2; — the extent
to which it should be fostered
among Ours by the use of the
rosary [344, 345]; — regarding
the recitation of the Little Office
of the B.V.M. [342, 343]. *See also*
**Immaculate Heart of Mary; Ro-
sary of the Blessed Virgin Mary**

Board: *see* **Food**

Body:

1. *Care of:* — an excessive care is to
be reprehended, but a moderate
one is to be praised [292]. *See
also* **Refreshment** of the Body;
Health

2. *Form of:* — the extent to which
disfigurement is to be considered
a factor in admission, and the
reason for this [185, 186]. *See also*
Appearance, good

Body, dead: — a model of docility in
regard to obedience [547]

Body of the Society:

1. *The entire Society,* i.e., its head and
all its members — [135, 671],
passim

2. *All who live under obedience to the
superior general,* even those without vows — [511], 6

3. *All who are bound by public vows* —
[219, 510, 511, 542], 6 §1 2°–4°

4. *Those bound by final vows* — [59,
510, 511], 6 §1 3°–4°

5. *Members,* to the extent that these
are contrasted with the head —
[134, 135], passim

6. *External matters of the Society,* to the
extent that these are contrasted
with its spirit — [813]

Books:

1. *In general:* — the extent to which
they are to be allowed for the
private use of Ours [372, 373]; —
specifically, in the colleges of
Ours [372]. *See also* **Library; Publishing books and other scholarly
works**

327 §2; — a suitable separation is recommended in them between the place where one lives and the place where he works and studies, 179 §2; — what should be observed in their construction [827], — to whom care for them belongs [326, 740]

Burial: — when the body of a dead person is to be buried [598, 599]; — how the funeral service should be celebrated [598, 600]

Business:

1. *In general:* — how it should be transacted in a province not one's own, 390

2. *Of the Society:* — matters to be handled by the procurator general [806], 383 §2; — by the treasurer general, 383 §3; — by the treasurer of a house [591]

3. *Political:* — in general, what is to be said about social and political involvements and about the responsibilities to be undertaken by each one in these matters, 249; — what should be fostered by all, 299 §2, 301 §1; — what is forbidden to all without special permission of the general, 301 §§1–2

4. *Secular:* — the extent to which it is prohibited to Ours [591, 592], 238; — particularly to the general [793, 794]; — the extent to which this must be guarded against in admissions [185, 188]. *See also* **Foreign to the Institute**

Business, civil: *see* **Business**

Business, matters of; Business, transacting: — in general, superiors should be experienced in [423]; — especially so the general [729]; — as also the assistants for provident care and the other general counselors, 374 §3, 380 §2; — particularly, the procurator general and the treasurer general [806]. — Unanimity of judgment about business matters is to be sought [273]

Business, the carrying on of: — even

the appearance thereof is to be avoided, 215 §1; — the authority in the Society that is competent to permit commercial activity when it is congruent with an apostolate, 215 §2

• **C** •

Candidates for the Society: *see* **Admission,** (1); **Examen,** (2); **Novitiate,** (2)

Canon Law: — the extent to which Ours are to be trained in it [351, 353]; — the extent to which it should be taught [464, 467]; — as regards that part of it bearing on contentious proceedings [446]; — the extent to which expertise in this science is a title to the solemn profession of three or four vows [519], 121 §1 6°, 121 §2

Capital:

1. *Regarding individuals:* — the extent to which it may be possessed even after first vows, 164 §1; — the extent to which it can be augmented by its profit prior to first vows, 57 §2 2°; — after first vows, 164 §1

2. *Regarding apostolic communities:* — the extent to which surplus moneys and wealth of communities ought not be accumulated, but rather should be distributed, apart from a modest sum set aside for unforeseen expenses, 195, 210

Cardinals of the Society named before final vows: — may not take such vows, 129

Care of souls: *see* **Souls; Parishes**

Castigation: *see* **Correction; Penances**

Catalogs: — It belongs to the general to determine which should be prepared [792], 347

Catechesis; Catechism: *see* **Christian doctrine**

Causes:

1. *Legal:* — the extent to which it is legitimate to defend the goods

to which they are to be practiced by Ours, *FI* no. 1 [623, 650]; — social works, 298, 299 §1

Chastity: — vow of, to be pronounced by all [4, 7, 13, 14, 119, 121, 527, 532, 535, 540]; — with what degree of perfection to be observed [547]; — it is a gratuitous gift of God, 144 §2; — by means of it we consecrate ourselves to God and to his service with a singular love, 144 §1; — what the vow implies as far as renunciation and human and spiritual vitality are concerned, ibid.; — it is essentially apostolic, 144 §2; — it makes us free so that we can be "persons for others," 143 §2; — it provides testimony that God is love, 144 §3; — it associates us with the fruitful suffering of the paschal mystery, 145; — it does not diminish one's personality but rather brings it to fullness, ibid.; — it is to be ceaselessly fostered: by means of familiarity with God, by friendship with Christ, and by the sacraments of penance and the Eucharist, 146 §1; — by means of devotion to the Blessed Virgin Mary, 146 §2; — by means of the union of minds and hearts in community living, 146 §3; — by means of all ways that are suitable for doing so, both natural and supernatural, 147 §1; — by means of moderation in human contacts which our ministry involves, in its various dimensions, 147 §2; — by means of taking account of different sensibilities in different cultures, and by means of keeping appropriate professional boundaries in dealing with our neighbor, 147 §3; — by means of the observance of those ascetical norms which wide experience confirms, 147 §4; — all of our members, and in a special way superiors and spiritual directors, should share in a common

responsibility to provide, in different ways, a mutual assistance to all in overcoming difficulties, 148

Children and the uneducated: — they should be trained with special care in Christian doctrine, *FI* no. 1 [527–28, 535]

Choir: — The Society does not make use of [586]; — reasons for this prohibition [586]. *See also* **Chant; Divine Office**

Christian doctrine: — teaching it is a ministry proper to the Society of Jesus, *FI* no. 1 [113, 528]; — the esteem to be accorded it [528], 272 2°; — why and in what sense mention is made of it in the formulas of the final vows of priests [528]; — it is to be taught by the novices [69]; — and by those who are to be promoted to final vows, 128 5°; — and by new provincials and rectors [437]; — it is to be explained to the novices [80, 277], 48 §1; — and to our students; its importance [394, 395, 483], 279 §2, 286, 288 §1, 289 §5, 291; — it is to be taught in churches and elsewhere [645–47]; — the way in which scholastics are to be prepared for this ministry [410, 411]

Christian Life Communities: — their renewal is to be fostered, 270 3°; — they should be established in our schools, 279 §2; — they are to be fostered with special care as a lay association of Ignatian inspiration, 309 §2

Church:

1. *The Holy Catholic Church:* — to serve it, as the bride of the Lord, is an objective of the Society, *FI* nos. 1–2; — we exercise this mission as servants of the universal mission of Christ in the Church and in the world of today, 4 §1; — the mission of the Society is a participation in the entire mission of the evangelizing Church, 245 §1; 246 7°; — all matters in the

Church *(continued)*

Society have its good in view
[136]; — the Society has been
called by supreme pontiffs to collaborate in its radical renewal,
253 2°; — the Society proposes
always to accommodate its mission to the needs of the Church,
1; — prayers are to be offered for
its needs [638]; — abnegation in
the novitiate, in accord with its
call, 49; — let Ours in formation
make themselves familiar with its
sources of spirituality, 69 §1; —
and let them be formed in a
sense of the Church, 70; — their
desire to serve the Church in
priestly love should be fostered,
74; — studies in the Society are
governed by the laws of the
Church, 83 §1; — through their
studies let Ours be rendered capable of skillfully proclaiming to
men and women the truth, revealed by Christ and entrusted to
the Church, 99 §1; — our professors teach in the Church and in
virtue of a mission received from
it; let them allow themselves to
be governed by its will and understanding, 101; — what is to be
said if a professor departs from
doctrine that is in harmony with
the magisterium of the Church,
104; — the ascetical norms of the
Church, laid down to preserve
chastity, are not to be over-
looked, 147 §4; — by means of
the vow of obedience, the Society
becomes a more apt instrument
of Christ in the Church, 149; —
continued renewal of the spiritual
life by means of the sources provided by the Church, 241; — the
Church, conscious of the new
needs for the promotion of justice, 247 §1; — signs of our service of the Church, 252 §1; — the
Society's tradition of serving the
Church in explaining, proclaiming,
and defending the faith, 259; —

the responsibility for promoting
the life of the Church in the cultures of former mission lands,
263 §1; — the calls of the Church
to ecumenical endeavors, 269 §1;
— the will of the Church regarding residences located among the
more neglected groups of people,
273; — the changed discipline of
the Church regarding parishes
entrusted to religious institutes,
274 §1; — the apostolate of education has been commended in a
special manner in our time by the
Church, 277 §1; — the work of
research is most necessary, so
that we may be of assistance to
the Church, 293 §1; — in our theological efforts and in our pastoral choices, we ought to try to
understand the mind of the hierarchical Church, 295; — the social
doctrine of the Church is to be
explained even in spiritual ministries, 299 §2; — the general is to
keep in mind the universal law of
the Church in making decisions
about the special political activity
of anyone, 301 §2; — the insertion of the laity in the mission of
the Church, 305 §1; — their responsibility for fostering the
Church, 308

2. *Church building(s):* — churches are
to be accepted for the good of
souls [555]; — the extent to
which pious foundations or foundations for Masses are permissible [324, 325, 589, 590]; — collection boxes for alms are not to
be placed in the churches [567];
— the sort of poverty which the
churches are to have [4, 554, 556,
561, 564, 572], 199, 191 §4; —
what vows should be pronounced
in them [525, 527, 531, 532]; —
what sort can be [533]; — in our
churches the word of God is to
be carefully preached [645]; —
the same can be done in other
churches [647]

Colleges:
1. *Of Ours: see* **Houses**
2. *Of externs:* — [322–23, 330, 392, 395–96, 397, 420, 422, 440, 680, 743, 762, 763]. *See particularly* **Education,** (2)
3. *International,* of the Society at Rome: (College of St. Robert Bellarmine, of the Gesù): — 304 §2
4. *Russian:* — 304 §1

Colloquy, spiritual: — often to be held between novices and the master [263], 54 §1; — during the time of formation, with a spiritual director, 66; — after the time of formation, 232; — as a means of making progress in chastity, 147 §4, 148 §2

Commerce: *see* **Business, the carrying on of**

Commissaries: — who they are and what power they have [141, 742, 745, 765]. *See also* **Visitors**

Commission: — provincial and interprovincial regarding formation, 61 §§2–3; — on the choice of ministries, 260

Common good: *see* **Universal good**

Common life (as regards poverty): — how it is to be understood [125], 174; — how it is to be preserved [570], 174–75; — how superiors should assist it, 174 2° and 4°; — the meaning, in the Institute, of the commonality of our way of living in externals, *FI* no. 8 [8, 580], 176–78

Communion, sacramental:
1. *Of Ours:* — in general, how often it is to be received [80, 261, 584]; — by scholastics [342, 343]; — how often in particular cases [98, 200, 530, 531, 540, 697]; — as a general norm to be observed by all, 227 §§1–2, 314 §2; — as a means toward making progress in chastity, 146 §1
2. *Of the faithful:* — how Ours are to be trained for its administration [406]; — when and where it is

permitted to administer it [642, 644]. *See also* **Eucharist; Viaticum, Eucharistic**

Community:
1. *In general:* — its origin, purpose, nature, 311, 314–15, 223 §2; — our primary community is the entire Society, 314 §2, 255 §1; — what a local community is, 314 §2, 315; — by means of the local community, of which every Jesuit ought to constitute an active part, each is inserted into the body of the Society, 317; — each community should have its own superior, 318; — as apostolic, communities ought to be aimed at the service of others and should provide a witness to hospitality, simplicity, and poverty, 323; — a community should provide for its apostolic work and for those persons collaborating in it, a fundamental vision of the Society in that apostolate's regard, 407 §4, 307 §1; — as Ignatian, communities should be capable of faithful and friendly communication and of apostolic spiritual discernment in common, 324; — communities are not a deliberative body, but rather merely a consultative one, 151 §3; — in accord with the mission proper to each community, there should be a program of daily life, to be approved by the major superior, that will include a brief period of daily prayer and somewhat longer times for prayerful discussion, 324 §§2–3, 231; — let communities be fostered that consist of priests, brothers, and scholastics, so as to strengthen the sense of a single vocation and mission, 326; — let the brothers be fully incorporated into community life, 326 §3; — let our communities be open and hospitable toward our own men and those who work with us, 327 §3; — solidarity

among all communities requires allowing in them a certain diversity of age, talent, and works, 329

2. *Community life:* — in general: if the community flourishes, the whole of religious and apostolic life is strengthened, and constitutes a testimony that we are disciples of Christ, 316, 146 §3; — it is nourished by mutual sharing of information, consultation, and delegation on the part of superiors, by mutual collaboration, by an order of life, and by a sense of the universal, 319; — let mutual relationships within it be simple and sincere, 308; — a common style of living, 321, 174–76; — let our manner of community living be such as is proper to men consecrated to God, 322; — and at the same time let it foster relaxation of spirit and friendly conversation among our members, 327 §1; — more particular norms, to the extent that they are needed, should be promulgated by major superiors for a given province or region, with the approval of the general, and should be implemented by them with equal vigor, 330

3. *Community life during formation:*
   A. *In the novitiate:* — 43 §2, 50–51
   B. *After the novitiate:* — the sense of community of each man should be carefully tested and formed during these years, 77 §3; — it should foster a participation in the apostolic body of the Society, 76; — it should be adapted to a given set of circumstances of formation, 77 §1; — greater scope is to be given to spiritual conversation, to participation in the celebration of the Eucharist, and to brief daily common prayer, 77 §2; — dialogue should be fostered between those in formation and superiors, 77 §4; — the number of [a community's] members is to

be regulated in such wise that spiritual and fraternal relationships emerge, and also a paternal form of rule, 78; — if those to be formed live in apostolic communities, these latter should undertake the responsibility for formation, 79, 98 §2, 109 §3

4. *Poverty of communities:* — concerning: common life, 174–75; — the tenor of our common life as regards externals, 176–78; — our buildings, as far as poverty is concerned, 179; — the distinction, as far as poverty is concerned, between communities and apostolic institutes, 188–89; — the poverty of communities that are missioned to pastoral work or other apostolic tasks, 190–95; — a possible exception in cases of need, 191 §4; — promoting communities that wish to follow a stricter practice of poverty among the poor with whom they work, 180, 273. *See also* **Charity,** (3); **Dialog,** (2); **Discernment,** (3); **Poverty; Union of minds and hearts**

Companion: — roommates, in the novitiate [249]; — of those who go out [247, 248]; — of scholastics going to class [249, 250]; — of those going on an assignment [624, 659, 660]; — of the master of novices, 54 §2; — of the superior of a province or region: by whom he is appointed, 393. *See also* **Admonitor; Consultors; Officials**

Competition: — the extent to which it is useful among scholastics [383]

Complementary Norms of the Constitutions of the Society of Jesus: — what they are, what is contained in them, their scope, meaning, and force, Introductory Decree 1°–4°, 5 §§1–2

Compositions, literary: *see* **Exercises in formation**

Concealment of reasons prohibiting admission and of "secondary" im-

it [682–86]

B. *Its power:* — the extent thereof, in general [677–81, 820]; — in particular: — it alone has full legislative power, 333; — it can declare the Formula of the Institute, *Fl* no. 2, 21 §1; — in regard to substantials of the Institute, 21 §§1–3; — in regard to elements of the Constitutions that are not substantials, 21 §4; — in regard to laws passed by a general congregation or ordinances of a superior general, 21 §5; — electing a superior general [677]; — naming a perpetual coadjutor vicar [773, 786], 371; — choosing assistants for provident care [781], 364; — choosing the admonitor, 379; — in regard to dismissing [206]; — regarding the aggregation of some institute of consecrated life to the Society, 333 §2

C. *Its manner of proceeding:* — in the election of a general [694–710]; — in other business matters [711–18]; — if there is question of the general himself [782–87]; — regarding the number and value of votes [686]

D. *Its decrees:* — by whom and how these are to be formed [712–18]; — what is required for their promulgation [718], 12 §3; — what are presumed to be laws, 12 §1; — what are not, 12 §2; — their authority [718]; — their place in the Institute: *see CN* Introductory Decree; — how they are to be interpreted, 17; — or to be changed, 21 §5; — dispensation from them, 19

2. *Congregation of a province:* — where and when it is to be summoned [682, 692, 782]; — by whom to be summoned [692, 755]; — what power it has, 333 §4; — in particular regarding the Institute, 22

3. *Congregation of procurators:* — power to suspend a given decree of a general congregation, but no

legislative power properly so called, 333 §4

4. *Congregation to elect a temporary vicar general:* — when to be summoned [687–88], 366 §3 1°, 372 §2; — what sort of vicar should be chosen [687]

Conscience: — let brother candidates be of good [148]. *See also* **Account of conscience; Examen; Manifestation; Obedience**

Conscience, conflict of: *see* **Obedience,** (3)

Consecration:

1. *Ours:* — by means of the profession of the evangelical counsels: meaning and effects, 143 §1; — by means of the vow of chastity, 144 §1

2. *Of the Society* to the Sacred Heart of Jesus and the Most Pure Heart of the Blessed Virgin Mary, 410

Consensus: — of consultors: *see* **Vote**

Conservation:

1. *Of the Society: see* **Society of Jesus**

2. *Of the Institute: see* **Substantials of the Institute**

Consideration:

1. *Of the Institute:* — of the apostolic letters, etc., is to be made during the time of probation [18, 20, 98, 146, 198, 199]; — prior to final vows [98], 128 6°

2. *Of vows to be pronounced:* [525], 128 6°

3. *Of an office:* — to be undertaken by superiors [811]; — by assistants [803]; — by the general [809]

Constancy: — to be hoped for in those to be admitted [156]; — the extent to which the lack of it or remissness of spirit can be a reason for forbidding admission [181]; — it is particularly necessary in the case of the general [730]

Constancy of soul: — required in candidates [51, 126, 156, 181, 511]; — in the case of those who return to the Society [240]; — in the studies of scholastics [361]; — in the general [728]

Constitutions of the Society of Jesus:

1. *In general:* why they were written [134, 136, 746]; — by whom and by reason of what authority, 10 1°, 11; — their order and divisions [135, 137]; — what sort they are [136, 822]; — by whom they were confirmed, 10 1°; — their autograph and official version, 11 §§2–3; — their place in the Institute, 10 1°; — they are to be known and esteemed by all [826], 415; — they are to be explained to tertians, 126; — the extent to which they are to be read: by novices [18, 98, 198, 199]; by all [826], 415; — the obligatory force they have [602]; — what obligation the general has to see that they are observed [746, 790]; — what similar obligation rectors have [424, 425]; — how they are to be observed by all [547, 602]; — who can change them or establish new ones, *Fl* no. 2, 11 §1, 17; — and in what manner, 21 §§3–4, 23; — who can interpret or declare them, 17; — who can dispense in their regard [425, 746, 747], 19; — in regard to colleges [420]. *See also* **Declarations; Laws, (2)**

2. *Repealed prescriptions of: see* **Abrogation**

3. *Modified prescriptions of: see* **Modifications**

Consultations with our members: — of a few, of more than that, and even of all gathered together, assist in knowing the will of God [211], 354 §§1–2; — for lending greater authority [667, 804]. *See also* **Consultors**

Consultors:

1. *Of the superior general or vicar general: see* **Council of the superior general; Counselors of the superior general**

2. *Of other superiors:* — why they are needed [810], 355 §1; — by whom they are appointed, 356 §1; — the way in which Ours are

to cooperate in their selection, 356 §2; — in general, what sorts of business are to be handled by them [431, 810], 151 §1, 354 §§1–2, 355; — in particular [211, 221]; — cases in which, by way of exception, their consent or advice is required for acting validly, 355 §2, 35 §2, 191 §4, 354, 380 §3, 381 §§2–3; — when the advice of others apart from consultors can be sought, 354 §§1–2; — or should be sought, 382 §3; — how often each year and when they should write official letters to major superiors [504, 507], 359

Contentious forum: — the extent to which Ours may render testimony therein [593], 239

Contracts:

1. *Regarding temporal goods:* — general norms for applying the law: *see* **Administration/administrators of temporal goods;** — by whom they may be entered into [743, 745]; — in the making of these, provincials are not to substitute themselves for local superiors without serious necessity, 218

2. *Contract with bishops:* — is to be entered into when the care of diocesan seminaries is undertaken, 290

Contradictors: *see* **Detractors**

Contributions: — by what superiors, for what purpose, and under what conditions these may be imposed on our communities and apostolic institutes [329], 208, 211–13

Contumaciousness: — a reason for dismissal, even of the professed [208]

Contumely: — the extent to which it should be sought and borne [101, 102]

Convalescents: — a house in the country can be had for their use [561]

Conversation:

1. *Among Ours:* — what sort it should be and what fruitfulness it should

apostolate and the intellectual characteristics of all our ministries are to be fostered, 293 §1, 297; — attention is to be paid to the modern culture of communication, 303 §§1–2

2. *As regards our formation,* which should be directed toward: a cultural dialogue and the addressing of problems of the cultures of our own age, 59 §2; fostering communication among our members from other cultures, for which purpose foreign languages are to be learned, 80, 97; a knowledge of the culture of the region where the apostolate will be exercised, 95; acquiring training in the use of the means of the new culture of communications, 96 §2; cultivating an openness toward the cultures of other nations, 99 §2; a critical reading and prudent use of those authors who exercise a greater influence on contemporary cultures, 105; a manner of life that fosters apostolic formation, 106 §2; acquiring a deep and authentic inculturation as well as the sort of union of minds and hearts in the Society and the sort of universalism that is proper to our vocation, 110

"Culture of death" — the congeries of aggressions that threaten human life from its beginning all the way to natural death, 247 §1

Custody:

1. *Civil:* — visiting those held in prisons, *Fl* no. 1 [650]
2. *Of the senses:* — to be maintained diligently by all [250]; — as a means of safeguarding chastity, 147 §4. *See also* **Senses**

Customs: — which can be introduced, and which cannot, into our life, 322

• *D* •

Dangers: — for guarding subjects against them in solicitude and

love, internal and external knowledge of them is necessary for superiors [92]; — other means leading to the same end [265], 148 §2 1°–2°; — given today's dangers against chastity, the ascetical norms of the Church and the Society should not be neglected, 147 §4

Deacons, permanent: — their ordination must be approved by the general, 124; — to what grade they ought to be promoted, ibid.

Deans of faculties: — how many are to be appointed, and what their office is [501, 502]

Death: — in it, God is to be glorified and our neighbor is to be edified [595]; — care must be taken as to what in it will better express a proper dignity and a solidarity with others, 244 §4. *See* **Deceased**

Debts: — Candidates are to be asked about them [42]; — they are to be paid prior to admission [53]; — doubts about them are to be submitted to the judgment of superiors [38]; — when they are a reason for forbidding admission [185, 188]; — or are a reason for dismissal [217]

Deceased:

1. *Of the Society:* — the care they are to be given prior to burial [598, 599]; — suffrages to be offered for them [598, 599]; — where, how, and by whom their obsequies are to be celebrated [598, 600]; — a death in other places in the Society is to be announced [601]; — what is to be said regarding deceased novices [511]
2. *Of externs: see* **Benefactors; Founders; Friends; Suffrages for the dead**

Deceits of the devil: — the method of being on guard against these is to be taught [260]; — what is accustomed to be involved in their cause [182]

Declamations: — of what sort, by

hibition against women's entering the house [267]

3. *Spiritual and apostolic discernment:* — to be exercised in our mission by means of an obedience that is to be embraced and carried into practice, 150 §2; — whence it springs and what makes it up, ibid.; — it is recommended that it be done in common, when the prerequisites for it are present, as a means of seeking the divine will, 151 §§1–2; — its character as merely consultative, 151 §3; — all of our ministries are to be subjected to it, 256 §2; — it should be used as a method of seeking advice on the part of superiors and directors of works, 354 §§1–2; — different forms of sharing within our communities can contain elements of true spiritual discernment in common, 323, 324; — our (local) community is a community of discernment with superiors, 315; — the roles of superiors in such an exercise, 151 §3, 315, 323, 324, 354

Discipline:

1. *Religious:* — both presupposes and makes men who are mature persons, whether superiors or subjects, 350 §2; — it is to be enforced by superiors in a fashion at once paternal and vigorous, 350 §3

2. *In the colleges:*

   A. *Of Ours:* — its importance [815]

   B. *Of externs:* — how it is to be implemented [395–97, 444, 482, 488, 489]; — what things in particular are not to be allowed [482, 486]

Disciplines:

1. *To be learned by Ours:* — general norms concerning the selection of subject matter [351, 366], 82, 83, 86–89, 94, 95–98, 99–102; — certain things about individual subjects [351, 354, 400, 402–14]; — the method of teaching them,

103; — particular norms about individual persons: in general [354–56]; — in regard to candidates for the priesthood, 81 §2; — in regard to the brothers, 81 §3, 83 §3, 98; — regarding continuing formation, 241, 242 §2, 243. *See also* **Studies of Ours**

2. *To be taught by Ours: see* **Education; Universities**

Discord: — its source is to be considered a plague [664]; — and thus he is to be removed or dismissed [215, 665]; — whence discord arises [273]; — how it is to be guarded against: in admission [657, 819], and in those to be sent into the vineyard of the Lord [624]

Dismissal from the Society:

1. *Its importance* in the preservation of the Society [204, 819]; — it should not be done readily, but rather with great consideration [204]

2. *Those who can be dismissed:* — all [204, 205]; — even the general [774]; — the order in which difficulty in dismissing someone increases [204, 205, 208]; — in dismissing, of whose good should consideration rather be given [212]

3. *Reasons for dismissal:* — they should be very just [120]; — what they are, in general [204]; — in particular, they can be reduced to four principal heads, namely [211–17, 664, 665, 819]; — the extent to which ill health cannot be a cause for dismissal [213], 34; — how the reasons are to be weighed [204, 205, 211, 218–22]; — the extent to which they are to be made known to others [227, 228]

4. *The power of dismissing:* — to whom this ordinarily belongs [119, 120, 206, 736, 738]; — a provincial's power [206–8], 33 §§1–2; — the power of a local superior [206, 208]

Divine Office:

1. *Divine offices in general:* — one's neighbor can be assisted by them [640]
2. *Canonical Hours (Liturgy of the Hours):* — are to be recited privately, FI no. 8 [586]; — in what manner, 228; — the extent to which vespers and tenebrae can be sung [587]
3. *Office of the Dead:* — the manner in which it is to be recited for Ours [598, 600]
4. *Little Office of the Blessed Virgin Mary:* — the extent to which it should be said by the scholastics [342, 343]

Division of a province: *see* **Province**

Doctor: — by whom he is to be chosen, how he is to be obeyed, and concerning what matters he is to be consulted [89, 272, 304, 580]

Doctors, holy: *see* **Theology**

Doctorate: *see* **Degrees**

Doctrine:

1. *In general:* — the need for it and ways of propounding it [307, 814], 81, 82; — its scope and measure [351, 360, 446], 81 §§1–3; — required in scholastic candidates [47, 154, 183]; — in those who are to be ordained, 81 §2, 86–90; — in those professed of four vows [12, 14, 518, 519, 819], 121 §1 6°, 121 §§2–3, 93; — in the rector, and in superiors in general [423]; — in the secretary of the Society [802]; — in the general counselors [803]; — in the general [729, 735]
2. *To be upheld in the Society:* — in general, what it ought to be [47, 358, 464, 672, 814]; — in philosophy and theology [47, 273, 274, 358, 464]; — in social matters, 301 §1; — unanimity is to be guarded [47, 273, 274, 358, 671, 672, 821]; — the sort that is to be given to Ours who are to be formed, 99–100, 105; — how

professors ought to comport themselves in this matter, 101–5; — what should be kept in mind in the process of elaborating and expressing theological views, 295; — and what in the publishing of books or other scholarly works, 296. *See also* **Formation (training); Publishing of books and other scholarly works**

Documents, written: — of the vows of devotion [283, 544, 545]; — of first vows [540], 131 §§1–2; — of last vows [527, 530, 532, 535], 133, 134, 136; — of the renunciation of goods, 170, 172; — regarding temporal goods, 194, 201, 222; — permissions given in the area of poverty, 338 §1; — which superiors should have [792, 811]; — whereby major superiors will be assisted [674, 737], 359–61; — which are to be sent to Rome: *see* **Rome**

Dogmatic theology: — in general, the care with which it should be taught [351, 446]. *See also* **Doctrine; Examinations, scholastic; Theology**

Domiciles of the Society: *see* **Houses of the Society**

Dominion: *see* **Possession**

Donations made to us: — prior to final vows, 164 §1; — after final vows, 171 3°; — at any time, 174 3°; — to the houses [331, 562]. *See also* **Alms**

Donors: *see* **Benefactors**

Doubt: — regarding prohibitions against admission, in general, 29; — regarding cases of homicide or abortion [169], 29; — about the suitability of candidates [193, 195, 196], 26 §2; — about their constancy of will [193, 194]; — about their suitability for first vows [100, 514], 117 §2

Dress: *see* **Clothing**

Duration:

1. *Of probations:* — of first probation [18, 21, 190], 31; — of the novi-

younger members by those who have been promoted to grade, 414; — especially required in those who deal with novices [247], 54 §2; — required among those who are to be promoted to the profession of the four solemn vows [819], 121 §1, 1°; — particularly in a rector, and in superiors in general [433], 350 §1; — most especially in the general [726, 733, 790]

Education:

1. *Christian education of candidates* — is to be examined, 26 §2

2. *Educational apostolate:* — its importance and influence on the contemporary mission of the Society, 277 §§1 and 4; — it can be exercised in different ways, 277 §2; — it should advert to the diversity of cultures and situations, 277 §4; — let it extend itself to those from whom there can be hope of greater progress, 278; — its scope regarding all students, regarding Christian students, regarding other students of whatever kind, 279, §§1–4; — attention is to be paid to the means of social communication, 280; — care should be taken of young people who pursue studies in regions different from their own, 282; — particularly, attention is to be paid to those students in non-Catholic schools, 282; — the same as regards our former students, 283; — adults too are to be educated, 291; — priestly training, a work of greatest importance, 290; — collaboration with the laity in its various aspects is to be fostered, 284. *See also* **Schools, public, of the Society; Seminaries; Universities; Youth**

Efficaciousness of external actions: — the source from which it is to be sought [813]; — apostolic efficaciousness and the witness of

evangelical poverty, 159 §2

Elderly, the: — the extent to which they can live in seminaries of Ours and be supported by the resources thereof, 197; — concerning their houses (i.e., infirmaries) and the "Retirement Fund" for their support, 196 §2, 205 2°; — regarding other means of supporting them, 206; — their apostolic fruitfulness and their special mission of praying for the Church and the Society, 244 §§1 and 3; — all, particularly superiors, are to show them special concern, ibid., §2

Elections: — those particularly that are to be held in congregations [677, 679, 688, 692, 719, 770, 781]. *See* **Formulas of congregations**

Eloquence, sacred: — should be taught to Ours [402], 96 §§1–2. *See also* **Preachers**

Emendation: — the extent to which its lack is a reason for dismissal [210, 819]

Endowments: — required in seminaries for Ours [5, 309, 331, 398]; — how these are to be supplied for, 205 1°; — in colleges of extern students (and universities), 199; — how these are to be supplied for, 210 §2, 211, 212; — how much must be given for someone to be considered a founder [319]; — the sort that cannot be accepted [398]; — "Foundations Fund," 205 3°; — "Apostolic Works Fund," 205 4°

Entrance into the Society: — from what day it is to be counted, 40; — the meaning of the fourth simple vow after the two-year period [121, 541], 131 §2

Epistles: *see* **Letters, writing of**

Error in faith: — candidates are to be questioned about this as found in their ancestors [36]; — indiscrete devotions, a source of errors [182]; — the extent to which it constitutes a reason for forbidding admission [22, 24, 165, 166],

Error *(continued)*
28 §1 1°

Establishment of a house or province: *see* Houses; Province

Eucharist, Holy: — it is the center and the origin of unity in our community, 227 §§1–2, 315, 326 §3; — spiritual experience should be fostered in a formation that is nourished by daily reception of the Eucharist, 65; — it is the most advantageous means toward forming one body wholly dedicated to the mission of Christ in today's world, 227 §1; — sharing in the Eucharist in whatever sort of community, ibid., 326 §3; — daily converse with Christ in visits to the Eucharist should be held in esteem, 227 §2. *See* Communion, sacramental; Mass; Viaticum, Eucharistic

Evangelization: — its integral dimensions, 4 §3; — the evangelization of a culture in our mission, ibid.; — our formation should correspond to the needs of evangelization in today's world, 59 §2; — proclaiming the possibility of evangelical union among humankind, 143 §1; — our prophetic mission of serving the new evangelization, 253 6°; — the mission to evangelize peoples, 263 §1; — the work of evangelizing peoples is to be fostered, 264 §§1–2; — contribution along with the laity in proposals for the new evangelization, 309 §3

Examen of conscience: — its importance and meaning, 229; — how often it is to be made [261, 342, 344], 229; — its length, ibid. *See also* Examination

Examination:

1. *Of candidates:* — its purpose [18, 133, 142, 202], 26 §2; — to what should attention be paid in it [143, 144, 189], 26 §§1–2; — what sort of examination is to be proposed: in general [1–103], 26

§§1–2, 30; — in particular: for scholastics [104–13, 116, 119–27], for brothers [114–15, 117–20], for indifferents [130–33]; — how it is to be carried out [2, 23, 31, 32, 145, 146, 193, 196, 198]; — what will help in its performance, 26 §3; — how supply is to be made for any defects that may occur in it, 31; — in what sort of case the examination is to be repeated [242]. *See also* Examiners of candidates

2. *Of novices:* — to be repeated every six months [18, 98, 146]; — to be made anew prior to first vows [121–27], 117 §1

3. *Of scholastics:* — at the completion of studies [128, 129]; — of those who have not been carefully examined before [202]

Examinations, scholastic: *see* Studies of Ours

Examiners of candidates: — how many there should be [196]; — by whom the primary examiner should be appointed [142]; — the sort of person he should be [142, 143]; — what his task is [2, 23, 34, 142–45]. *See also* Examen, (2)

Example:

1. *Good: see* Edification

2. *Evil: see* Scandal

Excelling: — abundance and excellence of doctrine is to be sought [308], 81 §§1–2; — at least in some one discipline [354]; — the special importance of the intellectual characteristic of all our ministries, 297; — in obedience we all ought to excel [547]

Exchanging (borrowing or lending):

1. *Lending:* — when it is permissible for a house to lend things [257]

2. *Borrowing:* — the extent to which this is prohibited, 165 1°

Execution: — in regard to obedience [284, 424, 547, 550], 152; — in the observance of the Institute: necessarily is to be sought from all [547], 415; — in particular, by those who have been advanced to grade, 414; — it is to be fostered by superiors and officials [424], 350, 354 §4, 415 §2; — personal qualities of the general in regard to execution [730]. *See also* **Correction**

Executor: — what is to be said about this office in secular affairs [591], 238

Exercises in formation: — literary [380]; — philosophical and theological disputations [378–79]; — general and particular exercises in philosophy and theology [390]; — apostolic activities, 108. *See also* **Disputations, scholastic**

Exercises of piety: *see* **Piety, exercises of**

Exhortations, domestic: — how often to be given, and on what topics [280, 291]; — what items should be avoided in them [281]

Expenditures: *see* **Account of income and expenses; Manner of living in external matters; Poverty**

Expenses: *see* **Expenditures**

Expenses, common: — how these are to be provided for, 208; — who are to be supported by these, 209. — *See also* **Poverty**

Experience: — of what sort it should be in the formation process, 65; — participation in the experience of the people to whom we are sent, 99 §2; — on the part of those to be formed, experience of life with the poor: of what sort it should be, 106 §3; — let those to be formed be guided by various experiences in their apostolic formation, 107; — provincials should encourage communities that take part in the experience of the life of the poor, 180; — effort should be made to enrich one's own spirituality by means of the spiritual experiences of other religions; 223 §3; — the experience of our members in formation is to be continued, 242 §1; — our el-

derly and infirm make others participants in the experience they have accumulated in the service of our mission, 244 §1; — a more profound spiritual experience, by means of the Spiritual Exercises, as a condition for carrying out our mission, 246 6°; — dialogue should be fostered regarding the religious experience found amidst diverse religious traditions, 266 §2; — other believers are to be helped so that they may experience the merciful love of God in their lives, 270 §3; — to be commended are the experiences of a special personal "juridical bond" with the Society on the part of certain lay individuals in order that apostolic ends may be achieved, 310; — in fostering vocations the experience and culture of those whom we wish to serve should be reflected, 412 §3

Experiments:

1. *In general:* — for discovering the suitability of candidates [147, 193, 196]

2. *Of novices:* — their scope and meaning, 46 §1; — which are the main ones [64–70]; — the extent to which they can be changed or repeated or to which others can be added [64, 71, 746, 748], 46 §1; — when they are to be performed [71, 127]; — the extent to which reports about them are to be sought [73–79]; — the extent to which they are to be repeated in tertianship [516], 126

Externals: — the Society's manner of life in their regard, *Fl* no. 8 [8, 81, 296, 577–80], 176–78; — what is to be noted regarding exceptions as regards: subjects [292], 174, and superiors [579, 581], 175, 180; — what external characteristics are required in candidates [151, 157–61]; — what external defects impede admission [185, 186, 188]; — what external char-

Externals *(continued)*

acteristics are required in the general [731–34]; — external activities are to be intermingled with mental ones [298, 299]

Externs: — care must be had for their edification [148, 161, 218, 230, 637]; — how we are to deal with them, 147 §§2–3, 322; — how we are to speak with them [349], 147 §3; — what is to be said about receiving visits from them, ibid.; — about extending hospitality to them, 327 §3; — their interventions with superiors are neither to be sought nor tolerated, 156; — what is to be said about administering their goods, 166; — about receiving loans from them or having money on deposit with them [257], 165, 219; — on seeking favors from them, even as regards the supreme pontiff [552]

• *F* •

Factions: — In general, how Ours should behave in regard to them [823]; — what is to be said about taking part in political factions, 301 §2

Faculties:

1. *Apostolic:* — what these presuppose [1]; — who are capable of receiving them in the Society [113, 114, 511]; — by whom in the Society and to what extent they are to be communicated [666, 753]; — how and for what purpose they are to be used [825]; — let the general have a list of them [792]; — by private individuals, in what way they are to be sought [552]. *See also* **Indults; Privileges of the Society**

2. *Regarding discipline:* — granted by superiors: how they are to be granted and to be renewed, 338. *See also* **Dispensation**

Faculties of higher studies: — what these are, in general, and in what order they are to be established

[351, 366, 498, 501], 289 §6; — the extent to which others are to be admitted [452]; — what is to be said about their governance [501, 502]; — the extent to which each one is to make progress in them [351, 357, 460], 88; — what is to be said when Ours pursue studies in faculties that do not belong to the Society, 84

Faith:

1. *The Catholic faith:* — its defense and spread is a goal of the Society, *Fl* no. 1; — the service of faith, which seeks justice, enters into dialogue with other traditions, and evangelizes cultures, is the mission of the Society, 4, 245; — the service of faith and the promotion of justice constitute a certain inseparable whole in our activity and in our life, 4 §2; 223 §2. — Means to this end: — in general, the ministries of the Society, both the traditional (in appropriate fashion adapted to our own times) and the new, as also all forms of our apostolate, 256, 257, 254; — in particular, ecumenical dialogue and cooperation, 268; — education, 279 §§2 and 4; — cooperation with the laity, 306 §3, 309 §1; — cooperation among provinces, 395

2. *The spirit of faith:* — the experience of spiritual formation should be grounded in faith, 65; — its mystical dimension should be strengthened in order to encounter other spiritual traditions, 69 §2; — in obedience [84, 85, 284, 286, 424, 434, 547–52, 618, 627, 661, 765], 150 §1, 152; — in poverty [555], 160; — the community of the Society as a community of faith, 227 §1; — continued formation, as a reflection on one's own apostolate under the light of faith, 242 §1; — in the distribution of ministries [606, 618, 621]; — in infirmities and in the weak-

ening of one's powers [272, 304],
244 §1; — at death [595], 244 §4

3. *The doctrine of faith:* — the doctrine
to be handed on in formation
ought to adhere to the faith handed on to the holy ones and
should make that faith be constantly revivified in the hearts of
humankind, 99 §1; — teachers of
Ours should have a care for building up the faith both of those
who hear them and of all the
faithful, 101; — these same men
should teach distinctly the things
which, as doctrines of faith, are
to be held by all, 103 §1

4. *Defection from the faith:* — the extent to which it constitutes a reason for forbidding admission [22,
24, 165–67], 28 1°; — the same
thing, as regards a recent conversion to the faith, 28 5°

Faithfulness: — is required in provincials [797]; — in assistants for
provident care, 364 §2; — in the
secretary of the Society [802]; —
in the general counselors [803];
— in the procurator general and
the treasurer general [806]

Familiarity with God: *see* **God**

Family: *see* **Relatives**

Farm of the community: — whether it is
legitimate to possess one [561–
63]; — the sort that it should be,
193

Fasting: — what is to be said of voluntarily undertaken fasts [8, 582]

Fathers, holy: — their teaching is to be
much esteemed by professors and
scholastics, 102; — let preachers
devote time to the study of them
[351, 353]

Fault: — in cases of dismissals [210]; —
those dismissed without fault, 37;
— one falsely reporting another
is to be reprehended and punished in proportion to the gravity
of his fault, 235 5°

Favors, apostolic: *see* **Faculties**

Fear: — let it yield place to love in the

observance of the Institute [602],
350 §3; — in obedience [547]; —
the fear of God should be added
to love [288]. — Occasionally
even the fear of superiors is useful [667]; — particularly in corrections [270]; — the degree to
which it should be invoked on the
occasion of dismissals [230]

Females: *see* **Women**

Food: — of what sort it should be in
the Society [81, 296, 580], 174 1°,
178 §§1–2, 321; — a time for it is
to be determined [294]; — common life is to be preserved in its
regard, 174 1°; — how our needs
are to be made known to the superior [292, 293], 174 2°; — it is
to be adapted to the needs of
each one [295], 175 1°, 321; —
what is to be said of the sick
[304], 174 1°; — general dispensations in its regard are to be
made known to superiors, 338
§§1–2

Foreign to the Institute:

1. *Pious works:* — concerning choir
[586]; — concerning sung Masses
[586, 587]; — Masses obligatory
by reason of a foundation [324,
325, 589, 590]; — concerning
parishes [324, 325, 588], but see
274 §1; — on the care and governance of religious women and
similar situations [588], 237

2. *Secular business:* — in general and in
particular [591, 592], 238; — giving testimony [593, 594], 239. —
The extent to which dealings in
public life are to be prohibited: as
far as political parties are concerned, 301, §§1–2; — and as far
as concerns offices that carry with
them the exercise of civil authority or the direction of labor unions, 301 §2

Formation (training):

1. *Of Ours:*

A. *In general:* — the apostolic goal
of the Society as the foundation
of our entire formation, 45 §1, 59

God's will is to be acknowledged in the will of the superior [284, 547, 619], 150 §1; — he, however, should seek it [211, 220, 618, 790], 151 §2, 350 §2, 352, 355 §1; — God's wisdom provides prudence in our actions [414, 711, 746]; — how God's changelessness is to be imitated [116]; — and how we can become more worthy of God's liberality [282, 283]; — trust is to be placed in God [67, 414, 555, 595, 812, 814]; — particularly in time of sickness and loss of physical strength, 244 §1; — union and familiarity with God are to be sought [288, 723, 813], 47, 224 §1, 225 §2, 229, 246 6°; — our community derives its origin from God's will, 314 §1; — the love of God is the chief bond of the Society's union [671]

3. *As pertains to the salvation of our neighbor:* — God has given to each of us the care of his neighbor [115]; — God is to be recognized in one's neighbor as in his image [250]; — the knowledge of God and an authentic awareness of him are to be fostered [307, 446], 254; — the promotion of justice desired by God is the embodiment of God's love and saving mercy, 245 §§1–2; — those means are to be preferred that unite the instrument with God [813], 251; — from God alone is our reward to be expected [4, 82, 478]. *See also* **Grace of God; Jesus Christ our Lord; Providence, divine; Spirit, Holy; Wisdom, divine**

Goods, temporal:

1. *Acquisition:* — in general, 184–87; — prior to final vows, which goods Ours acquire for themselves and which for the Society, 164 §1; — after final vows which goods they acquire for the Society [4, 5, 560, 570, 571, 572]

2. *Possession:* — what is permitted to

Ours prior to final vows [54, 59, 254, 255, 348, 571], 165 §1; — after final vows [4, 5, 326, 330, 331, 398, 554–64, 569, 572], — what is permitted to apostolic communities [4, 5, 326, 330, 331, 398, 554–64, 572], 190–93; — what is permitted to seminaries of Ours and infirmaries, *Fl* no. 8 [308, 326, 327], 196–98; — what is permitted to apostolic institutes, 199–200; — what is permitted to the Society, to provinces, to regions, 203–5

3. *Conservation:* — the spirit in which care for them should be exercised by all [305], 217 §1. *See also* **Administration/administrators of temporal goods**

4. *Distribution:* — of surplus and resources of communities, as also of contributions, 210–12; — among apostolic institutes, 212. *See also* **Poverty**

Goodwill: — of externs toward the Society should be fostered and preserved [593]; — particularly that of the supreme pontiff and of persons of great importance [823, 824]; — in particular, in the situation of recalling missionaries [626]; — even that of those who have been dismissed [225]; — and even of those who are our enemies, and why this is the case [426, 824]

Gospel: — the inculturated proclamation thereof in our mission, 4 §3, 245 §3; — it is the role of the general effectively to inspire our service of the Gospel and its justice, 248; — involvement in social and co-operative activities will make our proclamation of the Gospel more meaningful and its acceptance easier, 249 §1; — let our proclamation of the Gospel be conscious of the religious situation of those to whom it is directed, 263 §1; — the Gospel should be inculturated in the media of social

Gospel *(continued)*
    communication, 303 §2; — let the
    expressions of our poverty form a
    visible testimony to the Gospel,
    161; — let scholastics be trained
    to become skillful preachers of
    the Gospel, 96 §1
Governance of the Society:
    1. *In general:* — regarding the power
    of the Society and regarding its
    subjects [602, 677–81, 687, 736,
    753, 757, 759, 765, 791, 797,
    811, 820]; — the sort that its
    governance should be, 349 §1; —
    on shared obligations of superiors
    [269, 270, 423, 424, 693, 711,
    790, 811], 349–54; — concerning
    the assistance that officials should
    render these [superiors] [760,
    770, 779, 810, 811], 355–58; —
    written documents [676, 679,
    790, 792], 359–61; — on interces-
    sions that hinder governance, 156

    2. *On governance of the universal society:*
    — [677, 687, 688, 736–65], 362–
    86

    3. *On governance of provinces and re-
    gions:* — [662, 663, 668, 670,
    778, 791, 797, 810, 811], 387–94;
    — on cooperation among prov-
    inces, 395–400

    4. *On governance of houses and works:*
    — [424–35, 791, 795], 403–4; —
    concerning the division between
    the governance of the community
    and that of the apostolic work,
    406–7; — on common houses
    and works and their governance,
    408–9. *See also* **Superiors**
Grace at table: — is to follow the re-
    freshment of the body [251]
Grace of God: — in accord with the
    measure of it each should seek to
    achieve the goal of the Society, *FI*
    no. 1; — it is communicated as it
    is needed [686]; — it is obtained:
    by Masses and prayers [711, 790,
    812], by familiarity with God
    [723], by our generosity, particu-
    larly in taking vows [282, 283]; —
    how we should cooperate with it,

in general [814]; — in particular,
    as regards fostering vocations
    [144]. — In proportion to the
    grace received, devotion should
    be sought [277]. *See also* **Unction,
    divine**
Grades:
    1. *In the Society:* — to whom belongs
    the entire matter of assigning
    these, *FI* no. 2 [121, 512, 513,
    522, 523, 541, 736]; — differing
    grades of being united with the
    Society [204, 205, 511]; — indif-
    ference as regards grades [10, 15,
    72, 111, 130]; — one should not
    seek to move from one grade to
    another, though it is permissible
    propose manifest what one is
    thinking [116, 117, 542, 543]. —
    The examination for grade, 93,
    121 §2

    2. *Academic grades (degrees):*

    A. *In regard to our members:* — let
    scholastics for the most part earn
    the licentiate in either philosophy
    or theology, 92; — let those who
    show greater studiousness and
    talent seek higher degrees, ibid.;
    — in relation to being promoted
    to the profession of the four
    vows, 12 §§2–3

    B. *In regard to externs:* — [473, 474,
    476, 478, 479, 480, 493, 498,
    499, 508]

Graduates of our colleges: *see* **Colleges;
    Education; Schools, public, of the
    Society**
Grateful spirit: — toward benefactors,
    413
Gratuity of ministries: — stemming
    from the Institute, *FI* no. 1; — its
    goal and meaning [4, 565], 160,
    181, 182 §1; — the reward that
    the Society looks for [82, 478]; —
    in general, what is forbidden [4,
    398, 478, 565–67, 640, 816]; —
    the nature of a stipend [566], 182
    §2; — no dispensation can validly
    be given regarding the gratuity of
    spiritual ministries, 183; — what
    is to be said about stipends for

Masses, 184; — and for other ministries, 185–86; — let the choice of ministries be made with no desire whatever of gain or temporal advantage, 185. — As regards endowments of colleges or funds for Masses: *see* **Endowments; Foundations, pious, or for Masses**

Greed: — is to be avoided carefully, 215 §1. *See also* **Avarice**

Greek literature, study of: — the need for this [447]; — the extent to which Ours are to be trained in it [351, 367, 381], 86; — the extent to which externs students are [457]. *See also* **Humanities**

Gregorian University: — entrusted to the Society by the Holy See, it is immediately dependent upon the general and should be assisted by all provinces and regions, 304 §1

Guests:

1. *Ours (and externs who work with Ours):* — how they are to be received, 327 §2; — the extent to which those who live in another province are subject to the superiors of the one where they are, 390; — those who are permanently ascribed to another province's community are not to be considered guests, 176

2. *Candidates:* — the extent to which they are to be admitted as guests [140, 194]; — those who have been dismissed from some other place [232]; — those who are engaged in first probation are admitted after the fashion of guests [18, 190]. *See also* **Novitiate**

• *H* •

Harm, serious: — when it is a reason for dismissal [212]; — when it makes obligatory the manifestation of the defects of others, 235 3°

Head:

1. *See* **Illness, mental**

2. The superior general, head of the

Society [666]

Health: — care for it is praiseworthy, for the sake of the service of God [212]; — the same contributes to the preservation of the Society [826]; — what sort of health is required in candidates [151, 159]; — consequently they should be questioned about it [44, 107]; — the extent to which compensation can be made for it through other gifts [162]; — its lack: the manner in which this is to be taken into account in admitting [185], 30; — and the extent to which it is a reason for dismissal [212, 213, 216], 34; — the better it is in the scholastics, the more suited they are [334]; — health required for the profession of the four vows, 121 §1 5°; — the manner in which all should take care of their own [292, 293, 296–303, 822]; — and superiors should care for that of their subjects, in general [303, 304, 827], 244 §2; — and for the health of all, in assigning offices [302, 624]; — and of scholastics [297, 339, 463]; — consideration of it should be had: even in the practice of spiritual matters [582]; — in bodily requirements [296, 579]; — in the profession of poverty, in general, 174 1°; — in carrying out pious corporal works [650]. *See also* **Ill, those who are; Sickness**

Heart open to superiors: — in general [91–97, 263, 424, 551]; — as an element of spiritual and apostolic discernment, 150 §2. *See also* **Account of conscience**

Hebrew language: — its importance [447]; — the extent to which it is to be taught [367, 368, 457]

Heretics: — the extent to which those who have been such can be admitted [22, 165–67], 28 §1 1° and 2°; — what must be said of recent converts, 28 5°

Hermits: — the extent to which they

401 §1 1°; — where they can be built [603]; — what sort of ministries they embrace [603, 636–51], 401 §1 1°; — what obligations are not to be undertaken [324, 325, 588, 589], 237; — what their poverty is to be: see **Poverty**, (3, D)

D. *Houses common to several provinces:* — what these are, 408 §1; — their governance, 408 §2

Humanities, study of: see **Studies of Ours**

Humility:

1. *In persons:* — is to be exercised: by all [83, 101, 102, 250, 265, 282]; — by subjects in regard to superiors [84, 284]; — by novices [66, 68, 98, 297], 49; — by indifferents [130, 132]; — by scholastics [111, 289]; — by brothers [114, 117, 118, 132]; — by tertians [516]; — by spiritual coadjutors [111, 116]; — by the professed [111, 817]; — by the admonitor [770, 811]; — by superiors [423, 659], 349 §1; — by the general [725]

2. *In things:* — in chastity, 147 §1, 4; — in poverty, 157; — in the account of conscience [93]; — in the manifestation of defects [63]; — in reprehensions, 235 5°, 350 §3; — in indifference as regards grades in the Society [111, 130]; — in receiving academic degrees [390]; — in the external manner of life [576, 580]; — in clothing [577, 579]; — in begging [82]; — in sickness [89]; — in dealings with others in the community, 320, 325 §2; — in cooperation with the laity, 306 §2

• *I* •

Ignatius, Saint: — The Formula of the Institute was written by him and his companions under the influence of grace, 20 §1; — he wrote the Constitutions by reason of an apostolic permission granted him, 10 1°; — the supreme importance of his Spiritual Exercises for the Institute, life, and apostolate of the Society, 2 §1, 8; — the foundation was laid by him for all our laws, 23. *See also* **Spiritual Exercises)**

Illegitimates: — the extent to which they are to be questioned in the examination for admission [36]

Ill, those who are:

1. *Ours:* — how they should conduct themselves [89, 272, 303, 304, 595], 244 §1; — special care is to be exercised on their behalf [303, 304], 244 §2; — the extent to which they and the elderly can take recreation in the gardens of the colleges [559]; — and may live in the colleges themselves and be supported from both those colleges' revenues and from the Seminary Fund, 197; — what the poverty of infirmaries should be, 196 §2; — concerning the "Retirement Fund" for their support and that of the elderly, 205 2°; — concerning other ways of providing for such care, 206; — superiors are to give them a mission, 244 §3; — how they are to be prepared for death [595, 596], 244 §4

2. *Externs:* — Works of charity are to be fostered in their regard, *FI* no. 1 [650]

Illness, mental: — a predisposition toward such requires great caution in admissions [29, 175], 30; — cannot be a cause for the dismissal of an unwilling subject after first vows, 34 2°. — What is to be said about delirium [597]

Illness of the body (physical or psychic): — is no less a gift than health [272]; — the extent to which it is a reason for forbidding admission [185, 196]; — and to which it is a reason for dismissal [213, 216], 34; — the extent to which mental illness is to be guarded against in admission [29, 175], 30; — the

tent to which having belonged to one constitutes a reason for forbidding admission, 28 4°; — Ours forbidden to undertake the care of one, govern it, or become involved in its affairs, 237

Institute of the Society:

1. *Juridically:* — what is understood by this term [82, 152, 216, 589, 657, 789], 7; — its parts, 8–14; — its obligatory force [602]; — its application, interpretation, and declaration, 15–17; — dispensation from it [425, 746, 747], 19; — its preservation and renewal [136], 20–23; — its acknowledgement by GC 34, 1, 5

2. *Knowledge and observance:*

   A. *Knowledge:* — is to be attained by all [826], 415; — specifically by novices, 48 §2; — after the novitiate, 69 §1; — by those in tertianship, 126; — it is to be fostered in continuing formation, 241; — it should be encouraged by major superiors, 415 §2

   B. *Observance:* — how this is to be attained by all [547, 602], 415 §1; — particularly by formed members, 414; — by superiors, 350 §1, 352; — by the general [790]; — how it is to be fostered by these [291, 424, 746, 790], 350; — in what spirit it is to be attained [602]. *See also* **Constitutions of the Society of Jesus** (1); **Correction; Execution; Rules**

Instruction before entering upon ministries: — the extent to which it is appropriate, and how it is to be given [612–14, 625, 629, 630, 632]; — it is particularly appropriate for confessors [407]; — the extent to which matters being undertaken by the general should be discussed with the assistants [804]

Instruction on sexuality: — is to be given both positively and prudently during the time of formation, 148 §2 2°. *See also* **Chastity**

Instructions of the generals: — the place they have in the Institute and their force, 13 §3

Instructor of third probation: — by whom and in what manner he is appointed, 358 §2

Instrument: — one working to spread the Gospel as an instrument in the hand of God [638, 813, 814]

Instruments for vain purposes: — the extent to which they are forbidden [266, 268]

Insults: — the extent to which they should be desired and endured [101, 102]

Insurance policies: — how it is permissible for provinces and regions to utilize these to provide for the sick and the elderly, 206; — income from these is permitted to communities, 191 §2

Integration: — of the spiritual and apostolic life, 223 §§1–3; — its scope, conditions, means, results, 223 §§3–4, 224 §§1–2; — formation, as a process of personal integration of various aspects, and into the body of the Society, 66 §1; 106 §1; — in a special manner during tertianship, 125 §2. *See* **Formation (training) of Ours**

Intellect: — what endowments are required in this regard in scholastic candidates [106, 154, 183, 184]; — on the part of the superior general [729, 797, 798, 803]; — lack of such is to be guarded against in the admission of candidates [183]; — men of difficult temperament are not to be admitted [152]. *See also* **Discernment**, (1), (2); **Judgment**

Intellectual apostolate: — its importance for our mission in aiding the Church, 293 §1; — thus the need for undertaking it with courageous and self-denying spirit, 293 §2; — in it theological reflection enjoys primacy of place, faithful to the mind of the hierarchical Church and to the sense of

avoided in admissions [29, 175], 30; — likewise a lack of judgment or a notable obstinacy in one's own judgment [184]; — whence arises the danger of erring [55]

2. *One's own:* — submission thereof is to be exercised: in obedience [284, 547], — in following out spiritual direction [263], — in difficulties of conscience [48], — in accepting (an assigned) grade [111], — in following opinions [47, 274]; — obstinacy in this is harmful to any community [184]; — the extent to which it can be a reason for dismissal [216]. *See also* **Discernment**, (1), (2); **Process, Judicial; Union of minds and hearts,** (3)

Junior scholastics: *see* **Scholastics**

Justice, promotion of: — an absolute requirement of the service of the faith, as a mission of the Society, 4 §1, 245 §2; — both elements constitute one and the same mission of the Society, and consequently can in no way be separated from each other in our life and work; they should inform all of our ministries, which must be examined and evaluated in its light, 4 §2, 223 §§1–2, 245 §3, 256 §§1–2, 271 §1, 274 §1, 277 §1, 288 §3, 299 §2; — it is of necessity connected with the inculturated proclamation of the Gospel and with dialogue with other religious traditions, as integral dimensions of evangelization, 4 §3, 245 §3; — it is counted among the calls issued to the Society by recent supreme pontiffs, 253 5°; — more recent and new requirements of the promotion of justice in the world, 247 §1; — action for justice should be concentrated in the transformation of unjust cultural values, 247 §3; — the desire to foster justice will provide scope for involvement in civic and social activity and will lead each one to assume the responsibilities belonging to each in the social order, 249 §§1–2; — in all our ministries communities are to be established which will cooperate in promoting justice, 249 §3; — in cooperating with the laity the Society should in one or other manner promote justice, ibid., 306 §3; — the special function of social centers and information on public life in the light of the social teaching of the Church, 300, 301 §1; — the responsibility we have, those particularly of us who live in wealthier countries, to form public opinion in favor of the promotion of justice, 250. *See also* **Women**

• K •

Kindliness in governance: — in general, *Fl* no. 6; 337; 354 §3; — in the case of the general (and other superiors) [667]; — is to be joined with sternness: by superiors in general [423], 350 §3; — by the general [727]

Knowledge: *see* **Doctrine**

• L •

Labors: — great labors are required by our Institute [308]; — superiors should be supportive of them [423]; — moderation in them leads to the preservation of the Society [822]; — consequently they are to be moderated: in general and in what manner [298, 299]; — in particular, as regards chastisement of the body [300]; — by scholastics [339]; — by formed religious [582]; — by the general [769]; — the brothers are to be instructed in the novitiate as to the apostolic value of their works for the purposes of the Society, 48 §3; — our poverty should be characterized by the desire for work, 161; — the manner of our life ought not exceed

Labors *(continued)*
that of a family of workers, 178
§1; — the fruit or remuneration
for work is a legitimate source of
material goods for our life and
apostolate, 186. *See* **Oriental
churches**

Labors, domestic: — to the extent possible, all should take part in them,
325 §2

Laity: — cooperation with them in mission: to be esteemed, positively
to be fostered, and to be carried
out in humble, friendly, and simple fashion, 305 §1, 306 §§1–2;
— the meaning of their position,
their vocation, and their apostolate in the Church and the world
must be recognized, 305 §2; —
they should be offered opportunities for formation in Ignatian spirituality and in other aspects of
their life for the fostering of their
mission, 306 §1; — we should
cooperate with them in their
works, according to the criteria
that the Society has for selecting
ministries, with a formation for
this that is appropriate both ini-
tially and on an ongoing basis,
306; — cooperation with them in
the works of the Society, 284,
292, 307; — guided by a clear
mission statement that has been
proposed to them, 307 §1, — and
by offering them the means to
better understand the Ignatian
tradition and spirituality, 307 §2;
— the Ignatian exercises, appropriately adapted, should be made
available to them, 271; — toward
them, justice is to be entirely preserved and a cordial cooperation
and full participation (in the apostolate) is to be offered, taking for
granted their assimilation of Ignatian spirituality and the retention
of the final decision in the Society
where the ultimate responsibility
lies, 307, §§3–4; — given these
conditions they can be directors

of the work in the Society, whom
Jesuits are obliged to obey, safeguarding however the Jesuit character of the work, §§3–4; — an
interconnection is recommended
among so many persons who
share in Ignatian spirituality, so as
to ensure their better formation
and their more effective mission,
309 §3; — experimentation with
a "juridical bond" with certain
individuals, whether they form an
association among themselves or
not, is, in accord with norms
given by the general congregation, to be evaluated at a later
date, 310; — this cooperation
requires of us an appropriate initial and ongoing formation, 306
§4. *See also* **Associations, lay, of
Ignatian inspiration**

Languages:
1. *In general:* — to what purposes
their study is to be directed [351,
367]; — and to whom it is to be
allowed [356, 368]; — in what
order they are to be learned in
higher studies [460]; — the extent to which scholastics are to
be trained in their native tongue,
96 §1; — the extent to which the
language of the region is to be
learned [402]; — the language to
be used in letters written for edification [675]
2. *Classical:* — scholastics are to be
trained in these [351], 86. *See*
**Greek literature; Humanities;
Latin language/Latin literature**
3. *Foreign:* — are to be learned by
scholastics and brothers, 97; —
the same is recommended to
those who have finished formation, 242 §2; — are to be learned
by those who are sent to evangelize peoples, 263 §2

Latin language/Latin literature: — candidates for the priesthood are to
be questioned about their knowledge of it [104]; — the extent to
which Ours are to be trained in

Latin literature [351, 366, 381]; — how much competence is to be acquired, 86; — the extent to which it is to be taught in advanced studies [447, 460, 461, 484]. *See also* **Humanities**

Law of charity, internal: — it is imprinted by the Holy Spirit and is of greater importance than external laws [134, 135]; — let scholastics diligently learn from it, 64 §1

Laws:

1. *Of the Church: see* **Canon Law**

2. *Of the Society:* — the need for them [134]; — their basis, 23; — in what spirit they are to be fulfilled [547, 602], 15, 414, 415; — by whom they are to be interpreted or declared, 16–18; — who can dispense in their regard [425, 746, 747], 19; — who can alter them, 21; — in whose jurisdiction lies the full lawmaking power in the Society, 333 §1

3. *Civil: see* **Civil law**

Leaving the house: — what is to be done [80, 247, 248, 349, 350]

Lecturers: *see* **Teachers/professors**

Lectures:

1. *Sacred:* — a ministry proper to the Society, *FI* no. 1 [402, 645]; — more universal than that of hearing confessions [623]; — how scholastics are to be prepared for this [402, 404]; — how they are to be given [402, 403]; — how often and where [645–47]; — who are to be chosen to give them [624]; — how the people can be drawn toward them [587]; — whether a stipend for them can be allowed [4, 565, 816], 182 §§1–2, 183

2. *Scholastic:* — the extent to which public and private lectures are to be attended [369, 370]; — how they should be heard and repeated by scholastics [374, 375]; — the extent to which, in higher studies, certain ones apart from the ordinary ones are to be held

with more solemnity [458]; — the extent to which obligations to give lectures can be undertaken [325, 442]; — what is to be said about repetitions in higher studies [456, 459]; — what is to be observed by professors in lectures [369, 456, 486], 101, 103, 104; — what is to be said of the critical reading by scholastics of authors who exercise a greater influence on contemporary cultures, 105. *See also* **Studies of Ours**

Legacy: — for whom a legacy is acquired by Ours prior to final vows, 164 §1; — after final vows, *FI* no. 7 [4, 5, 557, 560, 570, 571, 572], 171 2°–3°; — the extent to which the Society is capable of receiving legacies, 171 3°

Legitimacy of birth: — must be declared by a candidate [36]

Letter (of the alphabet), a: — even though begun, to be left unfinished: — at the sound of the bell [435]; — at the voice of obedience [547]

Letters/literature:

1. *In general: see* **Studies of Ours**

2. *In particular:* — formation in literature, 95. *See also* **Humanities; Latin; Greek; Vernacular literature**

3. *Epistles: see* **Letters, writing of**

Letters (epistles), annual: — by whom to be written and in what manner, 359

Letters, apostolic:

1. *In general:* — the place they have in the Institute, 9; — they are to be considered during first probation [18, 98, 198, 199], 31; — likewise in second probation, and how often [18, 98]; — and also prior to final vows [98]; — are to be in the possession of the general along with a sort of summary of them [792]

2. *In particular:* — they are mentioned by name: *Regimini militantis* of Paul III [1]; *Iniunctum Nobis* [1];

the secretary of the Society [802];
— imposes on all a care for its
temporal goods [305]; — in admissions, charity for one should
not injure charity for all [189],
148 §2 3°

3. *For superiors:* — is the soul of obedience [547, 551]; — is exercised
in indifference as regards one's
grade [111]; — in regard to the
account of conscience [93], 155

4. *For subjects:* — in general, *FI* no. 6
[667, 811], 340, 349 §1, 350 §3,
352; — in the general, one of his
most important endowments
[667, 727]; — let it be plain in
the correction of defects [269,
270], 235 1°; — toward the sick
[304], 245 §2; — toward those
who are tempted, 148 §2 1° and
4°

5. *For one's brothers: see* **Charity**

6. *For one's neighbor: see* **Charity**

7. *Of externs for the Society: see* **Goodwill**

8. *For oneself:* — the extent to which
it may harm [671]; — to be the
subject of abnegation in the renunciation of goods [258]

• **M** •

Magisterium of the Church: — its
norms are to be observed in the
doctrine that is to be taught by
Ours, 100; — due reverence
should be shown to it, 101; —
what is to be said if a given professor in his teaching departs
from doctrine that is in accord
with it, 104; — we must collaborate with it in order to discern
the movements of the Spirit in
the "sense of the faithful," 295

Magistrates: *see* **Important persons,
princes**

Magnanimity: — it should shine forth in
the superior general [728]; — in
all superiors, 349 §2; — and in
novices, 51, 52

Magnates: *see* **Important persons, princes**

Manifestation:

1. *Of conscience:* — its meaning and
scope [92]; — to whom it is to be
made [93, 95, 97, 263, 424, 551];
— concerning which matters [92,
263, 551]; — with what fidelity
subsequent direction should be
obeyed [263]. *See also* **Account of
conscience; Conversation, spiritual**

2. *Of the defects of others:* — its purpose and the spirit in which it is
to be given and received [63], 235
1° and 5°; — concerning what
matters, to whom, and in what
manner it is to be made, 235 2°–
4°. — manifestation of ambition
[817, 683]; — the vow about denouncing those ambitioning dignities, 134, 141

Manner of living in external matters: *see*
Externals

Marriage: — as an impediment to admission [28, 40, 41, 173, 174,
217]

Mass (Eucharistic Celebration):

1. *Its importance and meaning in the
personal and communitarian life of
the Society:* — during the time of
the novitiate [277]; — during the
subsequent period of formation,
65, 67 §2, 77 §2, 68; — in the
taking, renewing, and observance
of vows [525–26, 530, 531, 533,
540, 546], 131–32, 146 §1; — in
the lives of those who have been
formed [584], 227 §§1–2; — specifically, in community life, 315,
326 §3; — in the help of souls
[640]; — in governing, preserving,
and increasing the Society [790,
812], 412 §2

2. *Celebrating it or participating in it:* —
with what frequency [80, 342–43,
584], 67 §2, 227 §2; — concerning Masses to be celebrated: by
superiors for subjects [790, 811];
— by assistants for provinces entrusted to their care [803]; — by
subjects for the intention of superiors [631, 692, 693, 711]; — for

his powers when the superior is absent, 346; — what is to be said when the minister of the house is not a priest, ibid., §2

Ministries (whereby the Society fulfills its mission):

1. *In general:* — what is their scope, as regards our principal activities, *Fl* no. 1 [636–54], 263–10; — as regards the carrying out of the Society's mission, 256 §1; — as regards the type of persons to whom they are directed [163], 162; — the preferential option for the poor in them, 163, 176 §2, 278; — by whom they are to be allocated: by the supreme pontiff [603–17], 252–53; — by superiors of the Society [618–32, 666, 749, 752], 255; — complete freedom is to be left to superiors [618, 628], 255; — criteria and norms for choosing ministries: the greater service of God and the universal good is to be sought always and in every case [618, 622, 623]; a great suitability for fulfilling the Society's mission, 256 §2, 257; greater need, an element of gratitude, a greater influence on those who govern others, ill will against the Society [622]; spiritual goods are to be preferred to bodily ones, those things that are better as opposed to those that are less good, things that are more urgent as opposed to those less so, the things that only the Society can do, as opposed to those that can be done by others, things that are more certain as opposed to those that are more risk-filled, the easier as opposed to the more difficult, those that have wider effect as opposed to those that have narrower, those things that are longer lasting than those that are less so [623, 650]; — means to be employed in the selection of ministries: sociocultural analysis of the true state of affairs, taken as

well in their religious and political dimensions, 258 §3; to be taken into account are social conditions as well as pastoral programs belonging to the local hierarchy, the availability of manpower, the assistance to be given to the general for more universal concerns, 258 §2, 259; provincial and/or regional commissions are to be utilized, 260; the evaluation of all our ministries, even those of individuals, by means of apostolic spiritual discernment, in the light of the service that must be provided for our mission, 256 §2, 261 §1; — which of our members are to be chosen for various works [624]; — the extent to which they are to be put under the authority of someone and how they are to be guided [612–14, 629, 630, 632], 261 §2; — with what spirit ministries are to be accepted by subjects, and the extent to which they are to be chosen by those subjects themselves [618, 621], 261 §2; — how they are to be carried out to fulfill our mission more efficaciously, 257; — without offense to externs [593, 823, 824]; — two chief methods of carrying them out [92, 603, 626, 636]: in missions outside of our houses [603–35], and in the houses and colleges [362, 437, 603, 636–52]; — general means on which the effectiveness of our ministries depends: careful thought, pure intention, prayer, and consultation to be employed by superiors [618]; — other means to be used by all [637–40, 813, 814, 824], 223–24, 276 §§1–2, 416. *See also* **Gratuity of ministries**

2. *In particular:* — chief ministries of the Society, *Fl* no. 1 [528, 636–53], 263–310; — regarding a secular professional activity, 262; — ministries that are foreign to us

Ministries *(continued)*
[324, 325, 586–90]; — concerning ministries undertaken during the time of the novitiate [70]; — during the time of studies [289, 362, 365, 400, 437], 107, 108, 110. *See also* **Apostolate**

Mission of the Society: — what it is, *FI* no. 1 [3, 156, 163, 258, 307, 446, 586, 603, 813], 4 §§1–2, 223 §1, 245 §§1–2; — its integral dimensions, 4 §3, 245 §3; — the origin and source of this mission, 2; — the documents in which it is set forth and declared, 3, 4 §1; — the conditions for fulfilling it: continual personal conversion to Jesus Christ in solidarity with the poor and the marginalized in the world; a cultural and spiritual dialogue, wherein we attempt to make women and men of diverse peoples capable of seeing God present in their cultures; a profound respect toward the work that the Spirit performs in human persons; the desire to participate in Christ's ministry of healing and reconciling the world; a closer and broader collaboration with others who are pursuing the same scope of activity; a more profound spiritual experience by means of the Spiritual Exercises; a great solidarity, availability, and actual mobility so as to foster the growth of our cooperative activities; an operative freedom to serve all men and women by aiding them in promoting the same spirit of mission, 246; — consequences of this for the formation of Ours: as regards a new vitality for evangelizing this world, afflicted as it is with atheism and injustice, 59 §2; as regards their preparation for specific missions and ministries, for knowing deeply the persons among whom they live, for establishing a solid and true experience of life with the poor,

106; as regards effectively acquiring a deep and authentic inculturation along with a universal spirit that is proper to our vocation, 110; as regards fostering communication with their peers, both those of the Society and those outside it, so as to foster a universal spirit that is open to diverse cultures, 111; — consequences for our vows in general and for the whole of our lives, 143, 144, 149, 151 §1, 161, 176 §2, 223, 241, 244 §3; — consequences for our community life, 150 §2, 323, 326; — consequences for our ministries: the task of the superior general in stimulating our spirits and the task of all of us in collaborating with him, 248; all our ministries, both traditional ones that have been renewed and new ones as well, are to be directed toward this, 256 §1; all of them are likewise to be examined under this heading by means of spiritual discernment, so that, if need be, they might be replaced by others, 256 §2; means to be used so that our institutions might more efficaciously carry out the mission, 257; the primary means in general, 251; — consequences for our cooperation with the laity in mission, 305–10. *See also* **Cooperation, interprovincial and supraprovincial; Laity**

Mission, personal: — is received from the Society through superiors and is always subject to the Society's review, confirmation, or alteration, 255 §2

Missionary service: — all of Ours can be sent, 263 §1; — the special responsibility of those who have been born in former missionary countries, ibid.; — who are to be sent and what sort of availability they should have toward new cultures, 263 §2; — let provinces regard as their proper work the apostolate of evangelization of the peoples that has been entrusted to them, and let them aid it with men and money, 264 §1, 398 §2; — the work of evangelizing peoples is to be fostered and vocations for that purpose should be encouraged, 264 §2

Missions given by superiors of the Society: *see* **Ministries**

Mobility: — a characteristic note of our vocation [82, 92, 304, 308, 588, 603, 605, 626], 2; — the motive and object of the special vow of obedience to the supreme pontiff, *FI* no. 3 [603, 605]; — it is particularly required for the profession of the four vows, 121 §1 4°; — it is necessary for the fulfillment of the Society's mission, 246 7°–8°, 255 §1; — thus everything that could hinder it is to be avoided [586–89]; — it is a sign of the solidarity of each one toward the entire Society, 411

Moderation to be observed: — in labors [298, 822]; — particularly by the general [769, 779]; in disputations [378, 456]; — by professors in proposing new and personal explanations, 103 §2; — how it is to be understood in the matter of poverty, 177–78; — let there be religious moderation in the honor paid to others [250]. *See also* **Discernment**

Moderator of the conference of major superiors: — his office and authority, 398 §4, 399

Modesty: — is to be had in all matters [250]; — is to be observed in speech, ibid.; — in the refreshment of the body [251]; — in going to public classes [349]; — in its relationship with chastity, 147 §§2–4; — in superiors' manner of dealing with subjects [667]; — it is necessary for a collateral superior in admonishing the superior [661]. *See also* **Rules**

Modifications, partial, in certain prescriptions of the Constitutions, in accord with the mode and manner indicated in the notes attached to each by GC 34: — [71, 82, 98, 122, 141, 164, 165, 168, 171, 175, 176, 183, 187, 198, 208, 261, 273, 309–19, 342, 343, 366–83, 430, 439, 514, 516, 518, 525, 526, 555, 562, 584, 588, 640, 653, 673–75, 679, 682, 683, 688, 695, 699, 703, 707, 712, 715, 718, 755, 773, 781, 786, 806, 826]

Money: — the extent to which it is permitted to have it in one's own or in another's possession [57], 165 §1 2°, 165 §§2–3; — the manner in which money brought by novices is to be preserved [57]; — the extent to which it should be carried with one on missions [574, 625]. *See also* **Deposits; Investment of money**

Moral theology: — the account to be made of it in the examination for hearing confessions, 90. *See also* **Doctrine; Examinations, scholastic**

Mortification: — to be sought by all in general [103]; — in particular, as regards love for oneself, as inimical to union and the universal good [217, 671]; — of carnal love [61]; — of worldly love [101]; — in the practice of chastity, 144 §1, 145, 147 §4; — in the matter of poverty, 157, 178 §§1–2. — In particular: regarding novices [297], 49; — regarding tertians [516]; — regarding those promoted to grade [582], 223 §4; — regarding superiors [423], 352; — regarding the general [726]; — how harmful it is, if it is lacking in many [657]. *See also* **Abnegation; Offices; Penances; Senses**

Music: — the extent to which it is permissible to have musical instruments in the house [266, 268]. *See also* **Instruments**

responsibility to be undertaken, 52; — the living of common life, 50; — a more profound initiation into the mystery of Christ and a fuller knowledge of the sources of spiritual doctrine and of the manner of life of the Society of Jesus are to be fostered [277–79, 250–53, 260, 261, 265, 269–70, 272, 273–75, 282, 286–88], 48 §1; — separation from friends and relatives [60, 244–46], 53; — a trusting and free relationship with the novice master [263], 54 §1; — the usefulness for [the novice] in working with other chosen men [271], 54 §2; — other parts of the training: — what is said about later periods of formation is also to be adapted to novices, 45 §2; — practice in domestic exhortations [28]; — their dress [19, 297]; — items proper: to scholastic novices [80, 279, 280]; — to priests [110]; — to brothers [117, 305]; — the semiannual examination [18, 98, 146]; — from the entire two-year period, what is to be expected of the novices [98]; — vows of devotion [17, 205, 208, 283, 544, 545]; — regarding the writing of letters [60, 197, 244, 246]; — on undertaking studies during the time of the novitiate [290], 56 §1; — the extent to which, prior to the end of the two-year period, novices who are not priests may be educated by them, 55 §2; — who are to be admitted to vows, 117 §1; — what should be said about goods actually possessed and about what is to be done with benefices which may possibly be possessed [57, 200, 54, 254–55, 287, 571], 32, 57; — what is to be said about private vows taken prior to entrance, 58. *See also* **Vows**, (2)

Nullity:

1. *Of admission:* — perhaps because of fraud in concealing canonical im-

pediments, or in concealing reasons forbidding admission or so-called secondary impediments [212–13]

2. *Of dismissal:* — one who is dismissed against his will and without fault on his part or a legitimate reason, is to recover his original status without repeating the novitiate, 37

Nuncio, apostolic: — [176]

Nuns (religious women): — the care and direction of these and of any other women of whatever sort who are gathered together in the fashion of religious is not to be undertaken [558], 237. *See also* **Confessors,** *(B)*

• *O* •

Oath: — to be sworn by the electors of the general [701, 705]; — by the assistants for provident care [782], 378

Obedience:

1. *Common:* — in what true obedience consists [84, 85], 143 §2, 149, 150 §1, 152, 153; — its apostolic value, 143 §§1–2, 149; — its grades: what makes it perfect, what imperfect [550]; — it must be joined with charity [547, 551]; — even on the part of superiors [667], 349 §1; — its value and importance: in general [284, 292, 361, 424, 547]; — in particular, it greatly assists union [659, 821]; — all must pay special attention to it [547]; — who should obey, whom they should obey, and in what order all should obey [662, 663, 821]; — with what degree of perfection [84, 85, 284, 286, 424, 434, 435, 547–52, 659, 765]; — in what spirit: God must be kept before one's eyes and recognized in the superior [84, 284, 286, 342, 424, 547, 551]; — in the spirit of love and not of fear [547]; — in the spirit of dialogue with the superior and of individ-

been given, it should be repaired [824]

Offerings, small: — should not be made to important people [568]. *See* **Gifts**

Offices, domestic (listed in the Constitutions): — in general [114, 148, 149, 364, 365]; — in particular: sacristan [433, 302]; secretary [433]; cook [149, 433]; the custodian of alms [149]; the giver of alms [149]; buyer [149]; gardener [149]; doorkeeper [149, 302, 433]; infirmarian [149, 302]; launderer [149, 306, 433]; barber [306]; — what in particular should be said about so-called "humble offices" [13, 68, 76, 83–87, 111, 114, 118, 132, 282]

Offices, ecclesiastical: — which are considered to be dignities, prohibited by the third simple vow of the solemnly professed, 139 §1; — in such cases the general can dispense, by reason of a faculty received from the Holy See, 139 §2

Offices of the Society: — whose prerogative it is to allocate them, *Fl* no. 1 [749, 752]; — norms to be followed in doing so [149, 302, 428, 429, 432, 749]; — with what degree of indifference they should be awaited [114, 302]; — to what extent superiors should be advised if offices injure health [292]; — not interfering in another's office [428]; — with what spirit those offices are to be undertaken in which there is a greater exercise of charity and humility [282]. *See also* **Officials**

Officials: — who are included in this term [798, 811]; — why they are to be appointed [810, 820]; — and what sort of persons they should be [428, 429]; — how they are to be assisted by rules and in other ways [428, 430]; — the extent to which they are to be obeyed [87, 88, 286, 434]; who are considered to be officials of

provinces, 358 §1, 393; — and officials of houses [148, 149, 302, 305, 306, 431, 433, 591], 358 §2; — by whom they are to be named, 358 §§1–2, 393; — concerning their union with superiors and among themselves [434], 354 §4; — by means of whose resources general officials, visitors, and provincials are supported, 209. *See also* **Assistants, (1)**

Opinions: — the extent to which uniformity in opinion is to be sought among Ours [47, 273, 274, 671, 672]; — particularly among professors [47, 273, 274]; — the manner in which one should propose opinions that are probable, new, or private, 103. *See also* **Doctrine**

Opposition: — is not to be feared [824]; — let the general not lose heart on account of any of it [728]

Order:

1. *In general:* — the principle of all ordering is God and his providence [136, 814]; — in the Constitutions, we proceed in a particular order [136]; — in what manner and for what reason [135, 137]; — as well in describing the qualities of the superior general [724]; — the order of life in the Society [602]; — what is to be said of those who do not tolerate order [657]

2. *In particular matters:* — in the examination of candidates [33]; — in correcting others [270]; — in bodily refreshment and sleep [295]; — the sick are to observe the order prescribed for them by the doctor [304]; — in spiritual exercises [583], 47 §2, 67 §§2–3, 225 §1; — in making use of a confessor [584]; — in sending letters for mutual information back and forth [673, 675], 359; — in the election of the superior general [700]; — in speaking during a general congregation [713]; — officials re-

Order *(continued)*

quired for keeping matters in proper order: for the general [813]; and for all superiors [811, 820]

3. *Between superiors and subjects: see* **Obedience**

4. *Domestic:* — in all communities, domestic order is to be established and preserved, and in what matters [294, 435], 324 §§2–3; — in formation communities, 77 §§1–2; — the extent to which it should be changed [435]; — or to which dispensation should be given from it [295]

5. *Of studies:* — the order of studies in general [353, 366, 460, 461]; — the daily schedule regarding lectures, etc. [375, 453, 456]; — what must be observed in introducing variations into it [454, 455]; — the daily order for vacations [462, 463]; — provincial or regional orders of studies are to be drafted and approved by the general, 83 §§2–3

Orders, sacred: — candidates are to be questioned about this matter [45]; — what sort of period of studies should precede ordination to the priesthood [365], 87, 89; — what sort of learning should be attained, 81 §§1–2, 86, 95, 96; — where these studies can be undertaken, 63, 84; — preparation for celebrating the sacraments and for exercising the various ministries of the priesthood [401], 108 §3; — on the ordination of Ours as permanent deacons, 124

Ordinaries: — which superiors ecclesiastical law considers to be "major superiors," 341 §2, §1 1°–2°

Ordinary, local: — regarding his testimony in the fifth experiment of the novices [77]; — concerning the agreement to be entered into with him, when the care of a diocesan seminary is undertaken, 290; — on following his advice,

judgment, and works when choosing our ministries, 259

Ordination, priestly: — its close connection with the definitive incorporation of scholastics into the Society should be kept seriously in mind, 118

Ordinances of superiors: — in general, their necessity, their obligatory force, and their observance [136, 602], 13 §1; — what of those enacted by a general congregation [718]; — a general's power [765, 796], 334 §1; — that of provincials, 330, 334 §2; — the place they occupy in the Institute, as long as they are in force, 13; — who can authentically declare them, 18; — the extent to which they can or should be changed [136], 21 §4

Oriental churches (whether Catholic or separated): — the apostolic labors found in them are to be greatly esteemed; — their results, 275, 227 §2

Oriental Institute: — the Pontifical Oriental Institute, a work entrusted by the Holy See to the entire Society, 304 §1

Origin from non-Christian ancestors: — the extent to which this is to be investigated in [a candidate's] examination [36], 26 §2; — to be dealt with carefully in the admissions process, 30

Outside the house, living: — for a notable period of time, 328. *See also* **Journeys**

• *P* •

Pagans: — the extent to which past adherence to their sect constitutes a reason to forbid admission, 28 §1 1°; — what should be said of those recently converted therefrom, 28 §1 5°; — whether their works should be studied in the schools [359, 468, 469], 105. — Ours can be sent to them [603, 605, 621]; — the extent to which this can be done where there are no Christians [621, 750]; — prayers should be offered for their conversion [638]

Parents: — the extent to which their needs should be carefully considered in the admissions process [36, 37]; — the extent to which, and the reason why, an inordinate affection towards them should be put off [54, 61]; — separation from them is not to impede acquisition of progress in affective balance and supernatural love, 53. *See also* **Relatives**

Parishes: — the extent to which and the reason why they should be undertaken or relinquished by Ours [324, 325, 588], 274 §1; — the sorts of things that they should be, ibid., §2

Participation in the good works of the Society: — has been granted to our founders and benefactors [317]

Passions: *see* **Affections**

Pastor: — is to be well prepared to fulfill his role, 274 §3

Pastoral training of Ours: — what aspects it ought to embrace [400–414], 108 §§3–4; — the manner in which it is to be conveyed, 108 §§1–2; — special concern is to be had as regards the examination for hearing confessions, 90. *See also* **Formation (training) of Ours,** (1, *D*)

Patience: — should be exercised in bearing injuries [102]; — in ill health [89, 272, 304]; — in death [595]; — let not even a sign of impatience be given [250]

Patrimony: *see* **Capital**

Peace: — internal, should be preserved, and externally manifested [250]; — external, should be maintained with all, and what toward this end is to be sought or avoided [443, 491, 593]; — it should be sought with those who have been dismissed [225]; — it should be maintained in dismissing students [489]; — a collateral superior should be, as it were, an angel of peace [661]; — dissidents are to be recalled to harmony, *FI* no. 1 [650]; — the promotion of peace among peoples is part of the promotion of justice, 247 §1, 253 5°; — the scope of interreligious dialogue, 265 §1

Penalties: — to be imposed on Ours for their defects: *see* **Reconciliation, sacrament of**

Penance, sacrament of: *see* **Reconciliation, sacrament of**

Penances:

1. *For defects of Ours:* — the power and obligation that superiors have to impose them, in general [8, 90, 269, 270, 754]; — in particular [imposing penances upon] superiors themselves for negligent or wasteful administration of temporal goods, 216 §4; — on anyone, for falsely accusing someone else, 235 5°; — for violation of the Institute or negligence in its observance, 350 §3; — for violating the confidentiality of consultations, 357; — or in giving information, 361; — for false reporting, 235 5°; — the extent to which penances should be public [270]; — how penances are to be accepted by subjects [90, 98, 269]; — how, indeed, they are to be sought by them [291]

2. *For the faults of students:* — what sorts of penances there should be, and how they should be inflicted [395, 397, 488, 489]

3. *Corporal, of Ours:* — none are common to all by reason of obligation [8, 580]; — the extent to which they should be undertaken [8, 296, 580]; — with what degree of discernment, and with what permission [8, 9, 263, 300, 582]; — in particular, during the time of studies [340, 431, 362, 363]; — insofar as these are noted in the

are in formation, 106 §§2–3; — ministry with these should be undertaken for a certain time by those who are to be promoted to grade, 128 5°; — any ministry of the Society can and should promote justice by means of direct service to the poor and by means of association and solidarity with them, 249 §3, 256 §2; — in a special manner, social centers and social action, 300 §2; — the poor are to be assisted by the Spiritual Exercises, 271 §1; — vocations to the Society from among them are to be encouraged, 412 §3; — the poor are to be assisted by a sharing of goods [562], 210 §3, 213 §1; — extern students who are poor are to be admitted into our schools [338], 278, 287 §1. *See also* **Alms; Charity, works of; Infirmaries**

Positive sciences: — research in them should be fostered, 293 §1; — the extent to which dogmatic theology should be assisted by them [351, 446, 464], 99 §§1–2; — scholastic theology should precede them [366]; — as also philosophy, 289 §6; — the connection between special studies and philosophy and theology should be understood, 94

Possession: — the extent to which Ours can possess items, after first vows [348, 571], 164 §1; — and after final vows [570, 571]; — and communities of Ours assigned to an apostolate [4, 554–56, 561–64, 572], 190–93, 195; — and seminaries and infirmaries of Ours [5, 326, 331, 398], 196–98; — and apostolic institutes, 199; — and the Society as a whole, a province, a region, 203–5

Possession, private: — even the appearance of this is to be avoided, 165 §3. *See also* **Common life**

"Post-Christian" cultures: — the need for dialogue with them, one

based upon a sharing of life and a common commitment favoring progress, freedom, values, and human experience, 246 2°

Postulates to a general or a province congregation: — how they are to be constructed, 22 §2

Postulator general: — by whom appointed, and the nature of his office, 383 §4

Poverty:

1. *In general:* — its importance [553, 572, 816]; — how greatly it is to be encouraged [287, 553, 816]; — what it consists in, and what sort of thing its foundation is, 157, 158; — its apostolic character, 143, 159, 160, 161; — its forms and the characteristics it has that are consonant with the mentality of our times, 161–62; — the special vow of not altering it [553, 554], 134; — to what this obligates, 137

2. *Of individuals:*

   A. *Novices:* — how they are to be exercised in it [57, 67, 285], 49; — the extent to which they can preserve their own goods [54, 59, 254, 255]; — what is to be said about the administration, use, and usufruct of these, 32, 57

   B. *Scholastics and approved brothers:* — the extent to which they can preserve and acquire their own goods [348, 571], 164 §1; — and can exercise an act of proprietorship over them, 164 §2; — what is commanded them regarding the administration, use, and usufruct of their goods, 57 §2; — when and how they should renounce these, 32 §3, 168 — in which houses they may live [5, 326, 554]. *See also* **Renunciation of goods**

   C. *Solemnly professed and formed coadjutors:* — whether they can possess and acquire their own goods [570–72]; — in which houses they ought to live [557, 560]; — the

which one such can be promoted to grade while he continues in this office, 129

Prelates: — we should pray for them [638, 639]. *See also* **Bishop; Ordinary, local**

Prelatures: *see* **Dignities and prelatures**

Prelections: *see* **Lectures**

Preparation for prayer: — adequate time should be given to it, 225 §3

Pride: — no sign of it is to be given [250]; — how its spirit is to be resisted [83, 101, 103, 265]

Priesthood: — the Society is a body or fraternity of priests, 2 §2; — priesthood is required for the solemn profession of four vows [12], 6 §1 4°; — and for the vows of a spiritual coadjutor [112], 6 §1 3°; — to what extent it is required in the one receiving vows [526], 114 §3; — the close connection between priestly ordination and the definitive incorporation of scholastics into the Society; consequences thereof, 118. *See also* **Ministries; Orders, sacred**

Priests:
1. *Ours:* — how often it is recommended that they celebrate Mass [80, 584], 227 §2; — and in what manner [110, 401, 671]; — how often they should confess [80], 227 §3; — how they are to carry out the Liturgy of the Hours, 228; — to continue studies after theology, 240–43 §1; — how they are to assist in domestic duties and labors [276], 325 §2
2. *Externs:* — the extent to which the Society is to adapt itself to their mode of living in external matters, 177

Printing press: — an example of a commercial activity, necessary for or suitable to the apostolate, and for which permission is necessary, 215 §2

Privileges of the Society: — the manner in which their use is dependent

upon the general [753]; — they should be used with moderation [825]; — even novices can enjoy their benefits [511]; — certain of them are listed by name, 24 §3, 32, 56, 116, 117 §2

Probation:
1. *In general:* — how long it lasts in the Society [16, 437, 539, 540, 544], 117 §2, 119; — what is to be said of the probation of those who return to the Society [239, 240, 242], 38
2. *First and second: see* **Novitiate**
3. *Third: see* **Third probation/ tertianship**

Probity: *see* **Virtue**

Process, judicial: — if ever, apart from a provincial or general congregation, it seems good to begin one, recourse is to be had to the general, 339 §2

Proclaiming: *see* **Preaching; Lectures**

Procurator: *see* **Treasurer**

Procurator general: — his office and characteristics [806], 383 §2; — by whom he is appointed [760], 383 §1; — when he is to be assisted by aides [806, 808]; — where he should reside [806], 383 §2; — what is to be said about his support [329]

Procurators in civil matters: *see* **Business**

Procurators to be sent to Rome from the provinces: — to inform the superior general about a great number of matters [679]. *See also* **Congregations of the Society**

Professed, the:
1. *Of solemn vows:* — in general, 6 §1 3° 4°; — their connection with the Society [205, 511]; — Steps to be followed prior to making the profession [528, 551], 128; — the dismissal of the professed is possible [204, 205]; — at what time, and by whom [208], 33 §3; — the manner thereof, 35 §2
2. *Of four solemn vows:* — they are the principal members of the Society

the first vows [14, 121, 348, 511, 541], 131 §2; — of renouncing goods after the first year of probation [54], 32 §2; — of instructing children and uneducated persons in Christian doctrine, as this is expressed in the final vows of priests [528]

Promotion: — to the grades of the Society [516–37], 118–29, 130, 132, 136; — of justice: *see* Justice, promotion of. *See also* Grades, (1); Vows, (2)

Promulgation of the decrees of a general congregation: — what sort is required, and how this takes place [718], 12 §3

Propriety, religious: — certain prescriptions [251]; — it is the explanation for certain prohibitions [266, 268]; — the reason for external propriety in the garments of scholastics [297]; — care is to be taken for external propriety by the syndic (or minister) [271, 431]

Protectors: — the extent to which they can be allowed in the colleges [314], 292

Providence, divine: — from it the protection and growth of the Society are to be hoped for [134, 812]; — in regard to temporal needs [555]; — it rules us, by means of superiors [304, 547]; — its dispositions require our cooperation; how this is true [134, 814]

Provident care to be exercised toward the general by the society: — its importance [820]; — the matters in which it is to be exercised [766–77]; — the manner of its exercise [778–88], 363–65. *See also* Assistants, (1)

Province: — what the term embraces, 387 §1; — whose prerogative it is to create, divide, and suppress a province, 388 §1; — whether more than one can be established in the same territory, 388 §3; — what is required for a province to be established, 388 §2; — care of

provinces is to be divided among the assistants [803]; — who are to be considered as belonging to a province, 389 §1; — those applied to a province: who can and should be such, and who not, 389 §§2–4; — what should be said about those who reside in another province, 390; — the extent to which each province should have its own novitiate, 39 §1; — by whom it is governed: *see* Provincial; — by whom he is to be assisted in his governance, 393, 356 §1, 358 §1; — concerning the poverty of provinces: *see* Poverty; — concerning seeking alms in other provinces, 214; — ordinances, instructions, or norms proper to individual provinces or assistancies (or regions), 330; — concerning mutual relationships among provinces; concerning mutual assistance, 398 §2. *See also* Cooperation, interprovincial and supraprovincial

Provincial: — who is such, 341 1§ 2°; — he is a major superior, 341 §2; — his is ordinary power, 391 §2; — his office is a prelature, 138

1. *Appointment:* — by whom and how he is appointed [757, 778], 343 2°; — let appropriate consultation precede the appointment, 340 §2; — the importance of choosing a suitable person [797, 820]; — the sort of person he should be [791, 797, 811]; — and how he should be known to the general [764]; — of what grade [he should be], 344 §1; — how long his office lasts [757, 758], 348 §§1–2; — by whom substitution for him is made, should he be impeded or die, 345 §§1–3. *See also* Vice-provincial

2. *His power and office in general:* — fostering religious life, the formation of Ours, apostolic ministries, and the observance of the Institute; having care for the adminis-

amount of surplus funds that each community can retain at the end of a year, 195; — approving the goods that apostolic institutes can have, 199; — establishing what is required so that apostolic institutes belonging to the Society can manifest the character and mark of evangelical poverty, 200 §2; — reviewing the budgetary and actual accounts of income and expenses of apostolic institutes, 201; — imposing contributions on communities for the benefit of common expenses, 208; — establishing norms for the sharing of goods of both communities and apostolic institutes, 210 §1, 212; — being vigilant lest superiors introduce or permit some significant change in the administration of goods, 216 §3; — not substituting himself for local superiors in contracts that are within their competence, 218; — allowing Ours to engage in court cases, under certain conditions, 220; — exempting Ours from obedience [663]

G. *Religious life and discipline, and also community life:* — the power and duty of: adapting the time of prayer for each of those already formed, 225 §2; — allowing the adaptation of the annual Exercises to individuals, 231 §1; — inquiring about the manner in which each undergoes these exercises, ibid., §2; — approving the program or order of community life, 324 §2–3; — conferring upon the elderly and the infirm the mission of praying for the Church and the Society, 244 §3; — publishing particular norms established for a given province or region, to be approved by the general, 330; — in regard to communicating edifying news [673–76]

H. *Ministries:* to see to the choice of ministries in his province, 258 §1.

See also individual **Ministries**

I. *Temporal matters: see* **Administration/administrators of temporal goods; Renunciation of goods;** — regarding the distribution of payments assigned to Ours, 187

J. *Letters, documents, books:* — as regards letters to be written or received by reason of office [674, 790]; — as regards documents whereby he ought to be assisted [674]

K. *Congregations:* — as regards a general congregation [682, 684, 686]; — as regards a provincial congregation [682, 692]

L. *Special advice to be given in the dissolution of houses:* — 402 §3

M. *External governance:* — the appointment of superiors and officials [490, 692, 759], 343 3°, 358, 345 §1, 346 §2; — communication with the general and with local superiors [662, 791, 797]; — applying Ours to another province or sending them into such, 389 §§2–4; — members of other provinces living in his province, 390; — those living apart, 317

Prudence: *see* **Discernment**

Public scholastic acts: — to be presented by scholastics at appropriate times [390]; — in higher studies [473, 474, 476]; — the role of the chancellor in these [493]

Publications, periodical: *see* **Periodicals**

Publishing of books and other scholarly works: — the importance of this ministry, 296; — the extent to which Ours require permission of superiors to publish such works [273, 389, 653]; — by what superiors and under what conditions this is to be granted [273, 389, 653]; — those things are to be observed that have been established by the universal law of the Church or by our own law, 296. *See also* **Writing of books**

Punishment of students: — forbidden to Ours [395, 397, 488]

from him are to be sought [552].
See also **Holy See; Magisterium of the Church; Missions given by the Roman Pontiff; Obedience**

Rome: — ordinarily, the place for holding a general congregation [690]; — and for the residence of the general [668, 669, 690]; — and likewise of the procurator general [806]

Room: — the extent to which novices can enter that of another [249]

Rosary of the Blessed Virgin Mary: — by whom especially it is to be recited, and in what manner [344, 345]

Rubrics: *see* **Ceremonies, sacred**

Rule, fundamental, of the Society: — the Formula of the Institute is considered to be such, 9 §1

Rules:
1. *In general:* — the need for them [136]; — who can dispense in their regard [425, 746, 747], 19 §§1–2; — the extent to which they can or should be changed [136], 21 §4; — the extent to which the rules oblige all [602], 415 §1; — how their observance is to be fostered and encouraged, 15, 360, 364 §4; — how often they are to be read and considered: during the time of probation [18, 198, 199]; — and in other times, 415 §1
2. *Rules approved by a general congregation* and their force: — 10 2°, 12 §1 3°; — the Rules of Modesty: their force, 12 §1 3°
3. *What power the general has over them:* — [765, 796], 334 §1; — what power provincials have over them, 334 §2; — how long rules established by a general perdure, 13 §1
4. *Other rules noted in the Constitutions:* — of houses [80, 198, 199, 585, 654]; — of colleges [395, 396]; — of universities [495–97, 509]; — of superiors [789]; — of offices [428]. *See also* **Constitutions of**

the **Society of Jesus** (1); **Institute of the Society**

• **S** •

Sacraments: — their administration is a ministry proper to the Society, *FI* no. 1 [406, 642]; — the manner of administering them is to be learned [406]; — the extent to which novices who are priests can administer them [70, 110]; — their frequent reception is to be recommended [406]; — and particularly to Ours [584]; — sacraments are aids granted by Christ for the passage from temporal to eternal life [595]. *See also* **Anointing of the sick; Communion, sacramental; Confessors/confessions**

Sacred Action: *see* **Mass (Eucharistic Celebration)**

Sacred Heart of Jesus: — in what spirit the devotion to it, as especially entrusted to the Society, is to be understood, fostered, and propagated by us, 276 §1; — how its feast day should be celebrated, 410 §1

Sacristy: — the extent to which revenues can be had for it [554, 555].

Safety of doctrine: — is very greatly to be cared for [358, 464], 100

Satisfaction: — is required in the case of mutual anger [275]; — what is to be provided by those who return to the Society [236–41]

Scandal: — the extent to which it is a reason for dismissal [212]

Schismatics: — those who have been such: the extent to which they can be admitted to the Society [22, 165, 167], 28 1°; — what is to be said of recent converts, 28 5°

Scholastics: — those included in this term [14, 121], 6 §1 2°; — the goal proposed to them [14]; — the sort of persons to be admitted as such: *see* **Vows**, (2, *B*); — they must of necessity be chosen and tested [657, 658, 819]; — their juridical status [121, 537,

Society [802]; — and in the regional assistants [803]; — for what reason it is to be increased as regards subjects [92]; — what is to be said in its regard concerning the sick [292]; — and in particular with regard to the elderly and the infirm, 244 §2; — regarding fraternal solicitude in the correction of defects, 235, 236

Solidarity: — with the entire Society: how it should be shown, 411–12, 416; — of all the communities within a province or region, and beyond their boundaries, 329; — with all our fellow workers, particularly with the poor, 246 1°, 176 §2; — specifically as regards the time of formation, 106 §§2–3

Solidarity with the Society, personal: — stronger than any other bonds, 255 §2; — should stamp any other commitment, thereby transforming it into a "mission," ibid.

Solidity:
 1. *Of doctrine: see* Doctrine
 2. *Of virtue: see* Virtue

Souls:
 1. *The help of souls in general:* — the goal envisioned by the Society, *FI* no. 1 [3, 156, 258, 307, 308, 446, 603, 813]; — the principle governing the entire training of Ours [307, 308, 351, 360, 400–414], 45 §1, 59 §1, 60, 81 §§1, 3–4; — a goal to be sought by means of good example [637]; — and by desires and prayers [638–40]
 2. *The parochial care of souls: see* Parishes

Soundness of body: *see* Health

Sources of the spirituality of the Church and the Society: — are to be rendered familiar to our members during formation, 69 §1; — from them the spiritual life of all is continually to be nourished and renewed, 241

Speaking:
 1. *In general:* — in what manner and concerning what topics we should speak [250]; — manner of speech of the general [726]
 2. *Among Ours:* — with those who are engaged in first probation [191, 197]; — with novices [247]; — by the novices among themselves [249, 250], 43 §2; — in formation communities, 77 §4; — in each of our communities, 320; — with superiors [423, 547, 551]; — by the sick [272]; — concerning defects in speaking: *see* Correction; Defects. *See also* Silence
 3. *With Externs:* — we should assist our neighbor with holy conversation, in general [648]; — in our ministries [624]; — also by the brothers [115]; — the extent to which scholastics should do this [349]; — what is allowed to novices in this matter [60, 244, 246], 53; — during the time of formation after the novitiate [349], 80, 106 §2, 111; — the manner of speaking, the place for it, and the care to be exercised during it, 147 §3, 322. *See also* Externs, Visits of externs

Speech: *see* Correction of defects

Spending: *see* Expenditures

Spirit, Holy: — to each person he gives a particular grace to carry out his own vocation, *FI* no. 1; — writes the law of charity on our hearts [134]; — gives the gift of discernment [219]; — by means of his unction, teaches the way of acting with one's neighbor [414]; — in sending men on mission, his direction is to be followed [624]; — to be invoked when the general is being elected [697, 698, 701]; — when he supplies for the formula of election in the choice of a general [700]

Spirit of the Society: *see* Society of Jesus

Spiritual direction: — what is to be made known, to whom, and the

Studies of extern students: *see* **Schools, public, of the Society**

Studies of Ours:

1. *Required in candidates:* — the extent to which they are to be asked about previous studies [47, 104–7, 111]; — and a sample of these is to be given [109]

2. *In general, and in regard to all:* — the purpose of studies in the Society [307, 351], 81 §§1 and 4; — what should be their general character, 82; — houses of studies [289, 290, 307, 308]; — what is to be said of institutes in which the academic administration is different from the religious one, 63; — and of where Ours pursue studies in faculties or institutes that do not belong to the Society, 84; — general regulations regarding the order of studies [351, 366], 83, §§1–2; — provincial and regional orders of studies, 83 §§2–3; — impediments are to be removed [362, 364, 365] 98 §2

3. *Of scholastics:* — The Society confirms its own option for their in-depth formation in studies, 81 §2; — their duties [360, 361, 374, 376, 384]; — what else it is appropriate for them to do in the matter of reading and reviewing [381, 385, 388, 389]; — the duties of superiors: as regards deciding or arranging for the scholastics' studies [351–57, 367, 369, 381, 388], 85; — concerning their progress in studies [377, 386, 387, 418, 424]; — the duties of the prefect of studies and of the professors [369, 386, 486, 493], 88, 103, 104, 105; — studies prior to entrance into the Society, or undertaken after that time, 86; — philosophical studies, 87; — theological studies, 89; — a licentiate is for the most part to be attained in these subjects by all, 92; — the examination for hearing confessions, 90; — what is to be said of those who prior to entrance into the Society have completed part of their philosophical or theological studies, 91; — formation in literature, arts, sciences (also social sciences) and the culture of the region where the apostolate will be exercised, 95; — formation in social communication and its media, 96 §§1–2; — concerning learning foreign languages other than one's native tongue, 97; — concerning special studies, 94; — regarding the doctrine to be imparted during their training, 99–102; — books and libraries [372]. *See also* **Examinations; Humanities,** study of; **Intellectual apostolate; Pastoral training of Ours; Philosophy; Scripture, Sacred; Theology**

4. *Of the brothers:* — appropriate theological training should be given them, as also training in their own field, also confirmed by academic degrees, 81 §3, 98 §2; — this training is to be regulated in provincial or regional orders of studies, 83 §3; — certain directives for achieving this effectively, 98 §§1–2

Study, interdisciplinary: — should be fostered in the universities, 289 §6. *See also* **Universities**

Style of writing: — the extent to which this is to be practiced by scholastics [381], 95, 96 §1; — by students in the higher classes [456, 484]

Subjects: — will very nearly be what their superiors are [820]; — they should be entirely dependent upon superiors [206]; — in the matter of poverty, 167; — desiring to be entirely known by them [91, 424, 551], 147 §1, 155 §1, 353; — should have recourse to superiors [662]; — should reverence them, seeing Jesus Christ in them, and love them as fathers [84, 85, 284, 286, 342, 424, 548];

discernment, 226, 323, 403 §2; help in safeguarding chastity, 148 §2 3°; — dialogue with subjects in the matter of assigning a mission, 151; — spiritual exhortation [280]; — arranging the order for community life, 324 §§1–3; — receiving vows, 114 §1; — the time of renewal of vows [347]; — goods of Ours deposited, 165 §3; — common life, 174; — temporal administration, 216 §§2–4, 217, 219, 222; — statements of actual and budgeted revenues and expenses of communities, 194; — relationship with the director of the work when he is distinct from the superior, 406–7; — superiors of dependent houses, 341 §1 3°, 405

Supervision of the temporal goods of the Society: — to whom this pertains [326, 419, 815]; — the one through whom it is ordinarily exercised [327, 420, 421, 743, 744, 759]

Support of Ours: — the source from which it may be drawn in apostolic communities [4, 554–61], 190 §2, 191, 182 §2–186; — in seminaries of Ours and in infirmaries, 196; — the extent to which it can be taken from common revenues, 208; — what is to be said in the case of severe necessity, 207

Surplus money and goods: — of communities, to be distributed annually, with the possibility of retaining a limited amount, to be approved by the provincial, for unforeseen expenses, 195

Suspected of heresy or error in the faith, one who is: — the extent to which he can be admitted [22, 24, 166]

Swearing: *see* **Oath**

• *T* •

Talent: *see* **Intellect**

Talents: — those to be required, in general, in the case of candidates for admission to the Society [147, 163]; — the extent to which compensation for these can be allowed [161, 162, 178]; — talents required in scholastic candidates [153–59, 161]; — in candidates for the brothers [112, 114, 148–52]; — in those who are to be admitted to first vows [308, 334], 117 §1; — to last vows, 119, 120; — talents of all the scholastics, 118; — of the formed coadjutors [112, 522], 123; — of the professed of three solemn vows [519–21]; — of the professed of four solemn vows [12, 516–19, 819], 121; — account is to be taken of them in dismissals [205]

Teachers/professors:

1. *Our men in general:* — by whom they are to be appointed [740, 752]; — the extent to which the provincial's permission is required [371]; — the extent to which the principal ones can be changed [491]; — the extent to which those who have not yet begun theology can teach philosophy [417]; — the sort of persons they should be [446–50]; — how many such [456, 457]; — the extent to which they can be appointed extraordinary professors [458]

2. *Of our men:* — the sorts of persons to be chosen, 62; — their office and responsibilities [369, 381, 403, 455, 456, 481, 486, 487], 62, 70, 112; — the sort of doctrine they should adhere to and impart [47, 272, 274, 358, 464], 99 §1, 100, 102; — how they should teach, 101, 103 §§1–2, 105; — in what manner and in what respects they should be an example for our students in apostolic formation, 112; — how they should cooperate in the process of ongoing formation of Ours, 242 §1; — how they themselves should be

taking on the obligations of colleges or universities [325]; in studies [354, 356, 417, 466, 508]; in the choice of ministries [608, 611, 615, 618, 622–26, 629], 258 §1; in providing our neighbors with the assistance of prayer [638, 639]; in undertaking corporal works of mercy [650]; by the general in his disposition of personnel [739]; and in his removal of superiors [736]; in the provident care the Society exercises toward the general [766, 773, 774, 778]

Universities:

1. *In general:* — their very great importance in providing help to souls [622], 289 §1

2. *Of the Society:* — the purpose for which they are undertaken [307, 440, 815], 289 §1; — whose prerogative it is to undertake them, and under what conditions [441, 442, 762]; — by whom and through whom they are to be governed [490, 741]; — what is to be said of their rules [495–97]; — which faculties should exist in them [498, 501]; — which are the principal faculties [446], 289 §6; — what subjects are to be taught [446–52]; — what is to be said of courses and degrees [471–80]; — their officials [490–509]; — whether academic regalia should be worn [508, 509]; — care should be taken that the particular character of our institutions of higher education should be retained, 289 §2; — in their organizational structure and in their actions, that faith should be fostered which does justice, 289 §3; — by means of appropriate governance and management structures, relationships with similar institutions should be fostered, albeit with our institutions' proper characteristics safeguarded, 289 §4; — they should possess a program for the human formation

and for the pastoral care of their students and for persons working in them or associated with them, 289 §5; — they should foster interdisciplinary study, 289 §6. *See also* **Education; Gregorian University; Schools, public, of the Society**

Unlettered, the: — are to be taught Christian doctrine, *Fl* no. 1 [527–28, 532, 535]. *See also* **Christian doctrine**

Use and usufruct of personal goods: — how disposition is to be made of these from the start of the novitiate and prior to first vows, 57.

Use of goods: — what use is such as to be prohibited by poverty [254, 257, 372, 373]; — as to be required by it, 174 3°–4°, 176 §2, 178 §1

• V •

Vanity: — should be trampled underfoot [297]; — instruments for vain purposes are not to be possessed [266, 268]

Vernacular languages/literature: — the extent to which the common language of the people ought to be learned [402]; — the book of the General Examen as written in the language of the place where it is to be used [146]; — one or other language, apart from one's native tongue, should be learned, so as to foster communication, 97, 242 §2; — the extent to which the vernacular can be used in pronouncing vows, 131 §1, 133. *See also* **Languages**

Viaticum, Eucharistic: — the extent to which it should be administered to Ours [595]

Vicar Apostolic: — is governed by the same law as a prefect apostolic. *See also* **Prefect Apostolic**

Vicar general of the Society:

1. *In general:* — when one must be chosen [687], 368 §1; — when one may be chosen [773, 786,

Visiting: — the sick in hospitals, as a ministry of the Society, *Fl* no. 1 [650]; — those of Ours who are dying, the extent to which this is desirable [596]; — leading personages, the manner in which this is permissible [568]. *See also* **Visits of externs**

Visitations:

1. *Visits to the Blessed Sacrament:* — 227 §2

2. *Visitations of houses and works:* — are to be made yearly by major superiors [670], 391 §3; — the manner of doing this in common houses and common works, 408 §2 1° and 2° and 4°; — on the occasion of such, at the beginning of a superior's term, the general permissions and exemptions of our companions should be renewed, 338 §2; — the extent to which the general can visit his subjects [669]

Visitors: — sent by the general: with what jurisdiction and for what length of time [490, 765], 386 §1; — at the death of a general, how long their office lasts, 386 §2; — how they are to be supported [330], 209

Visits of externs: — the manner in which they should be received [194], 147 §3; — in particular, those of persons of high rank [568]; — whether it is permissible to accept anything for our visits elsewhere [565, 566]

Vocation, priestly, of scholastics: — it is in a special way to be explained and fostered, 48 §§2–3, 74. *See also* **Scholastics**

Vocation, religious: — it comes from God [243]; — whence it is to be discerned [243]; — how sacred it is [30]; — one may and should cooperate with it in others and to foster it [51, 144], 412; — by what means this can be done, ibid., §§1–3; — it should be ex-

amined in candidates [51, 142, 193, 195, 196], 26; — in what way they should perceive it [52, 98, 107]; — he lacks it who does not possess the requisite talents [243]; — the manner in which it is to be pondered during first probation [197], 31; — it should be greatly esteemed by those in formation after the novitiate, 64; — constancy in one's first vocation is necessary [18, 30, 116, 117]; — for this, helps are: pondering certain documents in the novitiate [18], the renewal of vows [346], the renunciation of goods in favor of the poor [54]; — regarding this, those are to be questioned who have completed their studies [128]. — What is to be said of those who provide allurements to inconstancy [215]. *See also* **Stability in vocation**

Vote: — of the assistants for provident care in regard to their office, 378; — their right to vote and that of the provincials in certain business matters [773], 392; — of consultors of whatever sort: for the validity of an action neither their consent nor their advice is required except in instances specifically stated in the law, *Fl* no. 2, 355 §2; — a deliberative vote is required in certain business matters, 191 §4, 375, 376 §6, 380 §3, 381 §3; — for a vote to be sent in writing: when this is allowable [323, 773]; — when this cannot be done [685]. *See also* **Formulas of congregations**

Vows:

1. *Private:*

A. *In general:* — candidates should be asked about private vows they have taken [45]; — those taken prior to admission are suspended as long as the one who made them remains in the Society, 58

B. *Of devotion, made by novices:* — [17, 205, 208, 283, 544–45]

205]. *See also* **Chastity; Obedience; Poverty**

Vows, pronouncement of: — in general, what is required for their validity, 130; — in particular, what is to be said about final vows [526]; — other prescriptions regarding all vows [530, 532, 535, 540, 545], 114 §§2–3, 115; — particular points regarding first vows [537, 540], 113 §1, 114 §1 1°, 116–17, 131; — regarding final vows [525–37], 113 §2, 118–29, 132–36. *See also* **Vows**

• W •

Wealth: the extent to which it is desirable in candidates [161]; — in choosing someone for the office of general [733, 734]

Weapons: — none are to be kept in the house [266]

Will: — only God and his will are the first rule of our vocation [84, 284, 547], 149, 150; — gifts required in this area: in candidates for the brothers [148]; in scholastic candidates [153, 156]; in superiors in general [423, 434], 352, 150 §1, 355 §1; in the superior general [725–28]; — defects in this area that can hinder admission [179–82]. *See also* **Affections; Union of minds and hearts**

Wills: — whether it is allowable to undertake the office of will maker, executor, and also of confidential delegate [591, 592], 238 §§1–2

Wisdom, divine: — from it, holy Father Ignatius hoped for favor in writing the Constitutions [134, 136, 307]; — from it comes the religious vocation [243]; — from it is to be expected the light needed for the business to be conducted by a general congregation [711]. *See also* **Union with God**

Women: — concerning the justice that should be fostered in their regard and concerning their being associated with our ministries and insti-

tutions and their sharing in the decision-making process thereof, 247 §2

Word of God: *see* **Preaching; Lectures**

Words, divisive: — when they can be a reason for dismissal [212, 215, 664, 665]

Work: *see* **Labors**

Work, apostolic: *see* **Apostolic institute**; — the extent to which assistance should be provided to apostolic works that are interprovincial and common, 304, 397 §§1–2, 408 §2 3°, 409

Workers: *see* **Ministries**

World, the:

1. *It is proper to our vocation:* — to go to diverse places and live in whatever part of the world and to be sent wherever the greater service of God and the help of souls can be hoped for [82, 92, 304, 308, 588, 603, 605, 626, 749]; — to this purpose is directed the vow of special obedience to the supreme pontiff regarding missions, *FI* no. 3 [603, 605], 2 §1; — consequently a complete availability, mobility, and universality are necessary, 110, 121 4°, 242 §3, 246 7°, 248, 259, 411; — at the service of which is chastity, 144 §2; — consequently our community is a community for dispersion, 255 §1, 312, 314 §2, 315, 317; — thus also the need for communicating with different cultures of the world and for insertion into them, 99 §2, 106 §2, 110, 111, 246 2°; — and for promoting that perfect and open cooperation among the members of the entire Society, of whatever province or region they may be, 396 §2. *See also* **Cooperation, interprovincial and supraprovincial; Culture(s); Insertion**

2. *God is present in the world:* — exercising the ministry of healing and reconciliation, 246 4°; — thus he is there to be sought and found,

World *(continued)*
223 §§3–4; — the world, in great part afflicted with atheism and injustice and increasingly divided by diverse economic, social, and ethnic systems and by other sources of division and opposition, 59 §2, 223 §3, 246 4°

3. *The world, as distinguished from religious life:* — is to be left behind, trampled underfoot, and renounced [30, 50, 53, 61, 66, 297]; — it is to be despised because of the love for and imitation of Christ [101]; — contempt for it assists in the union of minds and hearts [671]; — customs which smack of the world are not to be introduced, 322.

Writing: — can be a distinct task in the colleges [433]; — how it should be done in the school [376]; — in regard to making a summary of such writing or an index [388, 389]; — a ministry that should be fostered, as being very beneficial and entirely consonant with the Society, 296; — in it, let the norms of the Society and of the Church be preserved, ibid. *See also* **Writing; Writing of books**

Writing of books/writers: — the importance of the office of writer [653], 296; — the extent to which books are to be written for the use of Ours in studies [466]. *See also* **Writing of books; Intellectual apostolate**

Writing: *see* **Publishing of books and other scholarly works**

Writs, apostolic: *see* **Letters, apostolic**

Youth: — its training, the call issued to the Society by more recent pontiffs, 253 3°. *See* also **Education, (2); Schools, public, of the Society; Universities**

Zeal for souls: — because of it the Society intends to renew itself constantly, in accord with its proper character and charism, 1; — the need for it on the part of all the Society's members arises from the very purpose of that Society [3]; — of what sort it should be, and its importance [813]; — it embraces all types of humankind [163]; — it is required in candidates [148, 153, 156]; — it should be fostered in novices, 45 §1, 48 §1; — and in those to be formed after the novitiate [307–8, 361], 59, 66 §1, 71, 76, 81, 99, 106, 108; — it should be cultivated by tertians [516], 125 §2; — it should be fostered by those who have completed formation [582, 618, 622, 636], 223, 241; — as also by the elderly and the ill [595], 244 §1; — specifically by the brothers [114, 115], 48, 108 §§3–4; — it should be fostered and directed by superiors [618–19, 650], 151 §1, 258 §1, 350 §1; — it should be strengthened by the union of minds and hearts, 311, 314 §1, 315, 323, 324, 326; — it should be made even more effective by cooperation among provinces and regions, 395 §§1–2, 397 §§1–2